THE HOLY EUCHARIST AND
CHRISTIAN UNITY

* * * * *

Report of the Forty-Third Annual Meeting
of the
Franciscan Educational Conference
St. Pius the Tenth Seminary, Graymoor,
Garrison, New York
August 6–8, 1962

* * * *

Volume XLIII

* *

Published by
The Franciscan Educational Conference
BELLARMINE COLLEGE
Louisville 5, Kentucky

CUM PERMISSU SUPERIORUM

CONTENTS

Papers

iii

OFFICERS OF THE CONFERENCE

President

REV. ERNEST LATKO, O.F.M.

Vice-President

REV. JUNIPER CUMMINGS, O.F.M.CONV.

Secretary

REV. SEBASTIAN F. MIKLAS, O.F.M.CAP.

Treasurer

REV. IRENAEUS HERSCHER, O.F.M.

Commissioners

REV. VINCENT DIECKMAN, O.F.M.

REV. LEO FERREIRA, T.O.R.

REV. DONALD WIEST, O.F.M.CAP.

REV. THEOPHANE MURPHY, S.A.

VEN. BROTHER ISIDORE, O.S.F.

PROVINCIAL SUPERIORS

Very Rev. Dominic Limacher, O.F.M.
Province of the Sacred Heart, St. Louis, Mo.
Very Rev. Sylvanus Becker, O.F.M.
Province of St. John the Baptist, Cincinnati, O.
Very Rev. Donald J. Hoag, O.F.M.
Province of the Holy Name, New York, N.Y.
Very Rev. Terrence Cronin, O.F.M.
Province of Santa Barbara, Oakland, Calif.
Very Rev. Matthew M. De Benedictis, O.F.M.
Province of the Immaculate Conception, New York, N.Y.
Very Rev. Remigius Steczkowski, O.F.M.
Province of the Assumption of the B.V.M., Pulaski, Wis.
Very Rev. Fulgence Boisvert, O.F.M.
Province of St. Joseph, Montreal, Canada
Very Rev. Sebastian Day, O.F.M.
Province of the Holy Spirit, Melbourne, Australia
Very Rev. Charles Murphy, O.F.M.
Province of St. Anthony, London, England
Very Rev. Celsus O'Briain, O.F.M.
Province of St. Patrick, Dublin, Ireland
Very Rev. Benjamin Perez, O.F.M.
Province of the Holy Gospel, Coyoacan, Mexico
Very Rev. David Retana, O.F.M.
Province of SS. Peter & Paul, Celaya, Gto., Mexico
Very Rev. Philip a Jesu Cueto, O.F.M.
Province of SS. Francis and James, Guadalajara, Mexico
Very Rev. William D'Arcy, O.F.M.Conv.
Province of the Immaculate Conception, Syracuse, N.Y.
Very Rev. George Roskwitalski, O.F.M.Conv.
Province of St. Anthony, Baltimore, Md.
Very Rev. Albert Leis, O.F.M.Conv.
Province of Our Lady of Consolation, Mt. St. Francis, Ind.
Very Rev. Matthias Biedrzycki, O.F.M.Conv.
Province of St. Bonaventure, Lake Forest, Ill.
Very Rev. Maurice Gough, O.F.M.Conv.
Province of Bl. Agnellus of Pisa, Liverpool, England
Very Rev. Giles Staab, O.F.M.Cap.
Province of St. Augustine, Pittsburgh, Pa.
Very Rev. Gerard Hesse, O.F.M.Cap.
Province of St. Joseph, Detroit, Mich.

Very Rev. Ignatius McCormick, O.F.M.Cap.
Province of St. Mary, Providence, R.I.
Very Rev. Marie Antoine de Lauzon, O.F.M.Cap.
Province of the Sacred Heart, Montreal, Canada
Very Rev. Fr. Conrad [of Leap], O.F.M.Cap.
Province of St. Patrick, Dublin, Ireland
Very Rev. Fr. Egbert [of London], O.F.M.Cap.
Province of St. Lawrence, London, England
Very Rev. Adelmo Maestrini, O.F.M.Cap.
Commissariat of the Stigmata of St. Francis, N.Y.C.
Very Rev. Fergus Lawless, O.F.M.Cap
Custody of St. Patrick, Los Angeles, Calif.
Very Rev. Fr. Anselm [of Prague], O.F.M.Cap.
Custody of Central Canada, Blenheim, Ont.
Very Rev. Leo Moran, O.F.M.Cap.
Custody of Puerto Rico
Very Rev. Fr. Claude [of Caprio], O.F.M. Cap.
Custody of Australia
Ven. Brother Bertrand Ryan, O.S.F.
St. Francis College, Brooklyn, N.Y.
Very Rev. Bonaventure Koelzer, S.A.
Franciscan Friars of the Atonement, Garrison, N.Y.
Very Rev. Augustine Cestario, T.O.R.
Province of the Immaculate Conception, Hollidaysbury, Pa.
Very Rev. Kevin Keelan, T.O.R.
Province of the Sacred Heart, Loretto, Pa.
Very Rev. Rafael Nadal, T.O.R.
Commissariat of Im. Conception (Spanish), Temple, Texas
Very Rev. Romildo Hrboka, T.O.R.
Commissiariat of St. Jerome (Dalmatian), Millvale, Pa.

The 43rd Annual Meeting of the Franciscan Educational Conference.
St. Pius X Seminary, Graymoor, Garrison, New York

FOREWORD

Christians in our time feel discomfort before the discrepancy between the ideal of the "one" Church and the very real divisions which exist in the body of Christendom. The individual Christian may pick and choose from among the many and complex solutions to this too human, but fundamentally untenable condition of the Church. He cannot, however, accept it as either inevitable or irremediable. Christ's prayer for unity at the first celebration of the Eucharist is a mandate for Christians to repair the tears in the seamless garment which is the Church.

As will be evident from the following pages, the Order of Friars Minor has from its very beginnings taken an active part in the struggle to patch up old splits and to smooth over, in a spirit of charity, unfortunate misunderstandings. A survey of the Franciscan efforts to bring Christians back into one fold introduces these papers which expound the principles of the modern ecumenical movement, and explore the dogmatic bases of Church unity. The most perfect manifestation of Christian solidarity is the Eucharist: "because the bread is one, we though many, are one body, all of us who partake of the one bread" (I Cor. 10:17).

It was apropos that the 1962 meeting of the Franciscan Educational Conference, at which these papers were presented, was hosted by the Friars of the Atonement. Closely identified with the cause of Church union, they sustain an old Franciscan tradition. To them, and to all who participated in the meeting, the officers of the Conference express their indebtedness.

BERARD L. MARTHALER, O.F.M.Conv.
Editor

FRANCISCAN CONTRIBUTIONS
TO CHRISTIAN UNITY

TITUS CRANNY, S.A.

The scope of this paper is enormous. To deal with Franciscanism and Christian Unity in a single talk is almost impossible. But the challenge is attractive and timely, as we live in an era marked so specially by a longing for Unity by groups outside the one fold of Peter. We will strive to present in summary from the work of St. Francis and his followers in the course of seven centuries as well as showing the efforts, accomplishments, and hopes of the present day. We hope that this synthesis will serve to incite those of us who today wear the wool of the Poverello to realize more deeply our own vocation of Unity and to fulfill it with seraphic ardor and enthusiasm.

This study is not a consideration of the mission apostolate including the evangelization of peoples in pagan lands. It deals rather with the work of winning back to the Church those who have fallen from her, or the descendents of those who experienced this spiritual misfortune.

To some extent this account is a martyrology, for many friars and sisters died for the faith, but the apostolate of unity does not consist only of dying for it. It means confessing Christ, loving the Church, and saving souls through preaching, writing, and other works of the ministry.

St. Francis, of course, is the leader and model of the entire enterprise. Nearly all of his great sons shared in this apostolate in some way. St. Anthony of Padua won thousands back to the Church by preaching. St. Bonaventure was the leading light at the council of reunion at Lyons in 1274; St. Lawrence of Brindisi, the third doctor, was a model of patience and learning and wrote to answer the Lutherans and preached to the Jewish people in Hebrew. John Duns Scotus fled from Paris because he would not agree to the intemperate demands of Philip the Fair against the papacy. He was known as the Hercules of the Papists—*Hercules Papistorum*. St. John

1

Capistran, St. Bernardine of Siena, St. James of the Marches, were pillars of unity as well as great friars. The Sisters, too, fulfilled their mission through St. Clare and her apostolate in the cloister. St. Colette of Corbie was an extraordinary character, involved in securing a true pope for the Chair of Peter in the early fifteenth century.

Down to our day the spirit and mission of Francis of Assisi has burned brightly for the cause of Unity. We can think of the Labors of our own religious founder, Fr. Paul James Francis, S.A. (1863-1940), a modern apostle of Unity. Or we may recall the work of Fr. Leopold of Castelnuovo (1866-1942) who offered his life through Our Lady for the cause of Christian reunion. The spirit is always the same—an all-consuming love for souls and an intense loyalty to the Vicar of Christ on earth.

For the sake of convenience I have divided the paper into four sections: (1) the First Period—St. Francis and his times; (2) the Second Period—from the death of St. Francis in 1226 until the division of 1517; (3) the Third Period—from 1517 to 1910, which marks the beginning of the present ecumenical movement; and (4) the Fourth Period—from 1910 until the present day.

First Period: St. Francis and His Times

The great and gentle Francis was a living image of Christ. He shared the Saviour's longing for souls; he felt the voice of the Good Shepherd in the depth of his being; and he longed to bring men to a knowledge and love of the Son of God. He was not an apostle of Unity in the strict sense, as for example St. Josephat, who died a martyr for reunion (1623), but he caught the spirit and message of Christ to such a degree that he led men to Christ and still continues the holy enterprise through the orders that he founded and the missions that he gave to all who regard him as their spiritual father.

St. Francis enunciated the principles of Christian Unity in his love for God, in zeal for souls, and his devotion to the Church. The hymn for his feast day well expresses this point:

> Franciscus vir catholicus
> Et totus apostolicus
> Ecclesiae generi
> Fidem romanae docuit

Presbyterosque monuit
Prae cunctis reveri.[1]

Archbishop Hilarin Felder has written: "As the Eucharist is the true real and substantial Body of Christ, so the Church of God is the mystical Christ; He is our Head, we His members, and the divinely established authorities of the Church are so many links that bind us to Him and communicate to us His life, His salvation. That is the conception of the Church as expressed by the gospel, by the Pauline epistles, by primitive Christianity, by Catholic teaching. Francis grasped this truth with all the depth of his faith and all the warmth of his heart.[2] In the finest sense of the term Francis was an apostle of Unity.

Our holy Father laid down the premise of his program when he said: "Proclaim peace to all, saying: 'The Lord give thee peace.' But as you proclaim peace with your lips, so have it yet more in your heart. Let no one through you be moved to wrath or scandal, but let all be moved by your gentleness to peace, kindness, and concord. For our vocation is to heal the wounded, to bind up what is broken, and to call back the wandering. Many indeed may seem to be members of the devil who will yet be disciples of Christ."[3]

Francis was God's answer to the problem of disunity and discord among the common men, whether in the Church or in the world, at a time when the forces of disruption were reaching a crisis. In the words of an Anglican author, St. Francis was "an agent for transmitting the divine love to those about him." Another admirer of Francis states that "the aim of all his instructions to his followers was finally that of producing and upholding between them a perfect unity to the end that those who had been drawn by the same spirit and begotten by the same Father might be peacefully nurtured in the bosom of the one mother."[4]

Francis lived at the time of the Fourth Lateran Council of 1215. Some authors such as Fr. Cuthbert, O.F.M. Cap., say that he was

---

[1] Office for feast, Oct. 4.

[2] *Ideals of St. Francis* (New York: Benziger, 1926) 56.

[3] L. Wadding, *Opuscula S Francisci*, (Florence, 1880) 272. This is not given in other compilations of the saint's words, but is surely in accord with his spirit.

[4] *Unitas*, Winter 1959.

present at the meeting. Pope Innocent III ordered western bishops to attend and he invited the Catholic and Orthodox bishops of the East to take part. The Council drew up a profesion of faith, *Firmiter,* against the teaching of the Albigensi and the Waldensi. Surely St. Francis assented to the Canons of the Council as a loyal son of the Church.

When Pope Innocent III convoked the Council, he referred to the Tau as the form of the Lord's Cross. "Those who have practiced mortification and conform their lives to the Crucified One will be marked with the sign. They will obtain mercy." Francis surely heeded the words of the Pope. He even set off to Damietta to conquer the Moslems, not by force but by the gospel of love. All his claims and ideals were symbolized in the Tau. The Pope made of the mysterious talisman a Christian renewal, the Tau which Francis was to make his particular emblem and use as his very signature. This letter—the cross—summed up for Francis the Apostolic ideal, the return to Christ, the conversion to the gospel. In a word it was the expression of God's undying and unifying love. Even during the lifetime of Francis the friars turned to the Oriental Catholics and to the separated Christians. In 1217 the Province of the Holy Land was established and a little later a Russian one which established contact with the Catholics and with those separated from the Holy See. Francis, of course, so consumed with zeal, visited the Holy Land and went to the Sultan of Egypt in 1219 in an effort to win this ruler to the faith of Christ.

Our seraphic Father won many souls back to the Church by his simplicity and apostolic zeal, but most of all by his love. Fr. Paul of Graymoor often said that "there were other Catholics as orthodox as St. Francis of Assisi in the thirteenth century but he excelled them all as the Apostle of Unity because he surpassed all men in the burning charity with which he was daily consumed towards God and towards men."[5]

Fr. Paul considered St. Francis as the special saint of Christian Unity because of his universal popularity and because of his message of peace for all the world. He said that Francis was the "Apostle of Church Unity" who "postponed the Reformation for three hun-

---

[5] *Lamp*, March 1926, p. 66.

dred years." He noted too that wherever the saint traveled, Protestantism never took firm root and there was no serious breach in unity. His example of living the gospel won the people to obey their priests and bishops.

But the message of the Poverello is not just for the past but also for the present when the world is so stirred with a longing for unity, "May we not hope," the Graymoor founder wrote, "that after looking with discernment upon the signs of the times, that it is the purpose of God after seven centuries to accomplish a re-incarnation of the spirit of the Seraphic Patriarch among men and to call forth from the ranks of his disciples and spiritual children those who shall meet the particular needs of this generation, rekindling the fire of divine love on earth and recalling men once more to a realizing sense that the 'kingdom of God is not meat or drink but righteous joy in the Holy Ghost,' teaching them also that the prayer of Our Lord *Ut omnes unum sint* lays upon all Christians a grave responsibility and a sublime obligation."[6]

Then Father Paul wrote of the need of the day—a special outpouring of the spirit of St. Francis.

> What is needed now is a double portion of Francis, the Seraphic Saint of love, to descend upon his children in particular and all Christians at large, as the mantle of Elias fell upon Eliseus, in order that by united prayer and brotherly conferences and cooperation the schisms and heresies of the past thousand years may be swept into oblivion and the unity of the Holy Spirit reign among those who confess Jesus Christ as their King, as on the day of Pentecost when the multitude of believers had but one heart and one soul.[7]

And again he declared: "Surely it is the faith and love of St. Francis that need to be revived among us, if the schisms from the Mystical Body of Christ are to be healed and a vast company of baptized Christians be made to dwell together as brethren who are at unity."[8]

As a youth our Seraphic Father heard the voice of Christ from the crucifix of San Damiano: "Francis, rebuild My Church which

---

[6] *Lamp*, Feb. 1926, p. 26.

[7] *Lamp*, March 1926, p. 66.

[8] *ibid.*, 67.

is falling into ruins." At once he began to sweep and clean the buildings in the area; only later did he understand that our Lord referred to His whole Mystical Body. When Francis sought approval from the Holy Father for his brethren, the pope quickly gave it, for he saw in a dream the mighty basilica of the Lateran held in place by the figure of the Poverello.

Second Period: Death of St. Francis 1226 to 1517

Only a few years after the death of St. Francis in 1226, the disciples were active in the work of reunion. Fr. Paul said: "That the healing of the Greek schism was on the heart of St. Francis there can be no doubt and soon after his death it was one of the foremost objects which his sons in religion tried to accomplish."[9]

Adam of Faversham was deputed by Gregory IX to negotiate with the Patriarch of Constantinople about the possibility of reunion in 1232. Five friars induced the Patriarch, Germanos II, to begin negotiations with the Holy See. The Pope sent two Dominicans and two Franciscans as *aprocrisiarii;* though they were not successful, they had made a beginning. In 1247 Pope Innocent IV again sent two friars to Constantinople, Lawrence of Portugal and Dominic of Aragon. Their peaceful approach improved the relations of the Greeks in Cyprus and won over the Patriarch of Antioch. Then at the request of the Greek emperor, the Pope sent the Franciscan general, John of Parma. This friar remained two years in the East and everywhere was treated with the greatest veneration as an "Angel of Peace." Upon the insistence of the emperor, Michael Palaeologus, Pope Urban IV in 1263 again sent four Franciscans, Simon of Auvergne, Peter of Crest, Peter of Moras and Boniface of Ivree. They were later joined by Gerard of Prato and Rayner of Sienna, and worked so well that the Greek emperor was willing to negotiate for union, but negotiations were halted when the pope died in 1264. Among the four friars was Jerome of Ascoli, later Pope Nicholas IV; he managed affairs so well at the Council of Lyons in 1274 that the union was actually accomplished.

Although friars took part in several councils of the Church, from the first Council of Lyons in 1245 to the Vatican Council of 1870,

---

[9] *Words of Father Paul,* 3:5.

they did much in the councils of reunion, those of Lyons in 1274 and of Florence in 1439. Each assembly was called for the primary cause of bringing back separated Christians to the One Fold.

Unfortunately, the reunion of the Greeks with the Church in 1274 was achieved more for political than religious reasons and it could not last. It was accepted by only a small part of the Greek clergy. The memories of the Latin occupation during the Crusades was fresh in their minds, and the demands of the popes after Gregory X had injured the Greek national feeling. But the work of St. Bonaventure was of lasting value and merit for future plans.

Saint Bonaventure

The Second Council of Lyons in 1274 dealt with and effected the return of the separated brethren of the East, but only for a short while. The Holy See was vacant for three years after the death of Clement IV in 1269 due to delays, intrigues and disagreements. Finally, in 1272, Gregory X ascended the throne as the 184th successor to St. Peter. The happy outcome of the election, we are told, came through the persistent and successful intervention of Bonaventure of Bagnorea, General of the Franciscans. His role in Church affairs became increasingly important.[10]

The new Pope was attentive to the advice of the saintly minister General. He admired the noble qualities of his mind and heart and consulted with him on all important matters of Church government. The Holy Father may have also marvelled how this man was able to keep his Order united in the face of opposing pressures. For seventeen years Bonaventure had been guiding the destinies of the great organization so well that he has been called the "Second Founder" of the Seraphic Order.

The first and greatest concern of Gregory X was the reunion of the separated Christians of the East. The bishops of the Greeks and Slavs were looking to the Apostolic See, though their motives were not the highest. Germanos II, Patriarch of Constantinople, had written to the Father of Christendom some years previously to acknowledge his Primacy over all the Church, East and West. Michael Paleologus, now Emperor Byzantinum, was well disposed towards the reunion.

---

[10] Cf. G. Ortoleva, *S. Bonaventura e il secondo concilio di Lione* (Roma, 1874) C 249 in AF III 333.

But the matter could not rest as simply as that. Two centuries of separation since 1054 had intensified difficulties that could not be easily dismissed. Pope Gregory entrusted to Franciscans all preparatory steps in the summoning of the Council, in which the Patriarchates of Constantinople, Antioch, Alexandria and Jerusalem would once again be represented. He chose five friars as his legates in the East.

One of these Legates, John Paraston, was a Greek himself; he had spent much time in Constantinople and knew well the temperment of the people. Reunion without their consent would be dangerous and impermanent. Assisting him were other friars, Jerome of Ascoli (who became Pope Nicholas IV), Raymond Berengarius, Bongratia, and Bonaventure of Mugello, all released for the task by their Minister General, St. Bonaventure. From Constantinople they were to maintain constant contact with Rome, suggesting methods of dealing with the problems of rites and discipline that were certain to arise as the reunion movement progressed.

The Pope selected Bonaventure himself to determine the agenda of the Council. Though a warm friend of the Franciscan General, Gregory X was motivated solely by concern for the Christian Church. He knew well the learning and sanctity of Bonaventure, and so was willing to risk the storm of criticism that would undoubtedly ensue, from the designation of a Franciscan Friar to outline the work which the bishops of the world would undertake in solemn session.

To emphasize the dignity of this assignment, the Pope raised Bonaventure to the rank of Cardinal. Previously, the saint had refused all posts of dignity offered to him. But this was different. . . . he had no choice. At least one writer intimates that Gregory *forced* him to become a Cardinal. There is a charming story of how the saint was washing dishes at a small Convent near Florence when the papal messengers came with the news of his appointment. He quietly bade them wait until he had finished. Even if it might not be true, the tale harmonizes well with what we know of his humble personality. On June 23rd, 1273, Bonaventure was elevated to the dignity of Cardinal of the Roman Church with the title of Cardinal-Bishop of Albano. By special permission he would retain the government of the Franciscan Order until the following year.

After going to Rome to be created Cardinal, Bonaventure returned for a brief visit to Florence and then set out for Lyons, arriving there in the spring of 1274. The Council was set to open May 7. That Bonaventure's part was no small one is indicated by the words of his secretary: "By command of Our Lord Pope, he conducted the principal affairs of the Council." Another author declares that he "presided at the Council and directed everything to the praise and glory of God; so that having overcome the discords and suppressed the difficulties, he was a source of honor and utility to the Church." In all probability, Bonaventure did not preside over the Council since that was the prerogative of the Supreme Pontiff; rather, he would preside over the private meetings of the groups of bishops and arrange the business to be publicly transacted.

Shortly after the Council opened, word came from the East that the Orthodox were willing to submit to Rome. Immediately Gregory relayed the joyous tidings to the entire assembly and, in honor of the occasion, Bonaventure delivered a discourse on the nature of religious unity. This was on May 18. Five weeks later, June 23, the envoys of the Greek and Slav nations arrived at the Council city where they received a royal welcome. On the feast of the Apostles Peter and Paul (June 29) a Pontifical Mass was sung by the Pope in the presence of the representatives from East and West. After the singing of the Epistle and of the Gospel in both Latin and Greek, Bonaventure, luminary of the conclave, gave a sermon on the momentous event, using for his text: "Arise, Jerusalem, and stand on high; and look towards the East, and behold thy children gathered from the rising to the setting sun, by the word of the Holy One rejoicing in the remembrance of God." (Baruch 5:5) Unfortunately, this sermon is not extant.

After the sermon ended, the Creed was sung in both languages. The phrase *filioque* (and from the Son), about which there was so much discussion, was repeated three times. Bonaventure stood with the Eastern prelates whom he had befriended, while tears of joy streamed down his face. Indeed the Greeks had found in him a staunch and loyal advocate. Impressed by his eloquence, affability, and piety, they gave him the affectionate name of Eutychius or Eutyches. In their eyes, Bonaventure was the most popular figure in the entire assembly. His facile and precise diction, his prudent and moderate counsel, his skill in controversial matters and his wonderful ability in straightening out the most intricate problems, won the minds and hearts of all to him. There is this description which reflects his breadth of character: "Such beauty of soul was matched by exterior comeliness; (he was) of imposing stature and with a certain nobility of bearing. His features were handsome and of a serious expression.... His words were calm and his conversation quiet and gentle.... His disposition was more than admirable. His appearance cannot be described as other than that of an angel sent from Heaven, for in his day, there was no one more beautiful, more holy, or more wise. Such affability and grace shown forth in his countenance that he was not only the object of love but of admiration. Those who once beheld him felt themselves drawn instinctively to admire and venerate him as one especially designed to further the interests of religion."

Part of the profession of faith required of the Greek emperor dealt with the supreme authority of the Holy Father, later used in part for the Vatican Council's definition of papal infallibility in 1870. "This same Holy Roman Church itself has over the whole Catholic Church the supreme and full primacy and sovereign authority; which it humbly and truthfully recalls to mind it received from the Lord Himself with all the fullness of power, through blessed Peter, the chief and head of the Apostles, of whom the Bishop of Rome is the successor. And as before all else that Church is bound to protect the true belief, so it is that whenever disputes arise about faith, they must be decided by the judgment of that Church."

July 8 ushered in the fourth session, when documents from the emperor, the Greek Patriarchs, and the Crown Prince were read as testimony of their allegiance to the Holy Father. The day was a joyful one; now at last a breach of over two hundred years was closed. Bonaventure appeared at this meeting and participated in it. But it was to be his last. Worn out by taxing labors, he became ill the day before and was confined to bed, though he wished to be present if possible. Not many days later, Sister Death came to him in one of the little cells of the Lyons friary. Strengthened by absolution from the Pope and consoled by the Holy Viaticum which he received miraculously, he breathed his last on Sunday, July 14.

The funeral of the organizer and director of the reunion Council was held the next day with the Holy Father presiding. Peter of Tarantaise, a Dominican friend and later Pope Innocent V, gave the eulogy, using as his text: "I grieve for thee, my brother Jonathan."

(2 Kings 1:26) Grief for the holy and learned Franciscan was universal. At the next session of the Council (July 16), Pope Gregory ordered every priest and bishop in the world to celebrate Mass for the repose of Bonaventure's soul.

Thus passed one of the greatest figures in the history of the Franciscan Order. He is an eminent Doctor by reason of his learning and eloquence, but he is equally great for his service in bringing souls to union with Christ and His Church. His work for unity continues after his death. Aptly has Bonaventure been hailed as the Seraphic Doctor—seraphic in his love for Christ, seraphic in his love for souls and seraphic in his labors to bring them to union with God. He was seraphic too in his labors for Unity. The purpose of his life may be taken from his own words: "to live in the unity of the Church through observance of God's law, the cohesiveness of God's peace, and harmony of God's praise." He is the writer and preacher of man's union with Christ and in Christ; he is the defender and champion of unity of the Saviour's spotless spouse, the Catholic Church. Franciscans would do well to invoke him as a heavenly patron in the cause of Christian Unity, especially now when the Church and the world await the opening of the twenty-first General Council.

We know how ill-fated the results were. The schism was renewed only eight years later,[12] due chiefly to the antipathy and lack of understanding shown by bodies both of the East and the West.

Since the union was again disrupted after a few years, negotiations began anew during the 14th century and many friars were sent as representatives of the Holy See. Their efforts were crowned with success only at the Council of Florence in 1439, at which the General of the Order, William of Casale, St. Bernardine of Siena and Albert of Sarteano especially merited praise. Franciscans, especially the vicar general of the Observants, James of Primadizzi, had also cooperated in bringing about the union with the Armenians, which took place at the same time. Also about this time, Eugene IV sent some of the friars, under the leadership of Albert, to the Orient to prepare the way for union with the Copts and Jacobites, which was, however, only partially successful. The friars also labored successfully during the 15th and 16th centuries among the Maronites, who had united with

---

[11] F. Dvornik, *The Ecumenical Councils* (New York: Hawthorne, 1960) 59.

the Roman Church in 1182, but manifold abuses threatened the permanence of the union. The Belgian, Grifo, lived among them for 25 years, and built up a worth native clergy.

During this period of the thirteenth and fourteenth centuries we may mention one of the greatest of all Franciscan teachers; Duns Scotus. He was noted for his allegiance to the Holy See. The Pope, he said, has the fullness of jurisdiction so that all Catholics are bound to obey him as Christ Himself. Those who refuse obedience to the Holy Father sin gravely. "For Duns Scotus the Sovereign Pontiff is the Vicar of Christ, the successor of St. Peter, the head of the whole Church, the supreme hierarch, infallible and indefectible by reason of Christ's words to St. Peter; he bases the stability of the Church upon this truth" (Ephrem Longpré, O.F.M.).

In the fourteenth century there were nine friaries of the Franciscan Order serving as mission centers for work among the Christians of the East in the Byzantine Empire. In the same century, there were fourteen Franciscan friaries among the Ukrainians (1390). Many Franciscans became bishops among the Ukrainians. During the reign of Pope Urban VIII Franciscans formed a society of "pilgrims for Christ" who preached the gospel in the Ukraine, Russia, Wallachia, and Tartary, reaching as far as the Caspian Sea. In the next century, another famous Franciscan, St. John Capistran, was given the spiritual care of the Ukrainians by the King of Poland (1451).

At the beginning of the fourteenth century John of Montecorvino, after his work in Persia and Armenia, various other countries of the near East and India, converted the Great Khan and King George of Tenduc. Fr. John celebrated the Liturgy in the church of the Holy Trinity built by the latter according to the Latin rite but in the vernacular. Perhaps he was moved to do this by his previous experience among the Armenians, but his use of the vernacular played no small part in the conversion of many Nestorians in Tenduc. At his death, there were an estimated 100,000 Christians in the Mongolian Empire.

The Franciscan Vicariate in the Mongolian Kingdom of Ripschak (in present day Russia) lasted for two hundred years, with two custodies: at Krim and Sarai (near Stalingrad). The Armenian metropolitan of Caffa pledged obedience to the Holy See in 1318 through the Franciscan Bishop Jerome. Under Usbek-Khan, the

Church flourished as the Franciscans multiplied their mission stations. In 1392, under Pope Boniface IX, Christians in the region of the Caspian mountains numbered some 10,000. Martin V named Fr. Ambrose Scipio bishop of the Caspian region in 1421, and Pope Eugene IV sent twenty Franciscans there in 1433.

Council of Florence

In 1437, Pope Eugene ordered the Minister General, William of Casale, to come to the Council of Ferrara (Florence) and to bring twelve Magistri of the Order with him. Among them were St. Bernardine of Siena, James of the Marches, St. John Capistran and Albert of Sarteano. Of the six who led the disputation against the Greeks were two Franciscans: Aloysius of Fodi (a Conventual) and Peter Perquerius (an Observant)[12].

St. John Capistran induced the patriarches of Jerusalem, Alexandria, and Antioch to send delegates to the Council and brought with himself ambassadors from the Armenians. Others who took part in this were Bartholomew of Tarro and Albert of Sarteano, both men of learning and masters of the Greek language. They returned from Constantinople and brought the patriarch Joseph, the Emperor Paleologus, and a number of Eastern prelates. Other friars who took part were Francis and Louis of Bologna, James of Primadizzi and St. Bernardine of Siena and St. James of the Marches.

St. John Capistran had some time before regulated affairs in the Oriental province of the friars, and had a share in negotiations with the Armenians. Francis a Rimini of Bologna, a famous preacher, was present at the Council of Florence.

The reunion of the Syrians of Mesopotamia was celebrated in the Lateran on September 30, 1444. Abdala, archbishop of Edessa, was sent by the Patriarch Ignatius to represent the Syrian Church. Franciscans who had labored in this country made the reunion possible. Fr. Anthony of Troia was commissary "to the province of Tartary, Assyria, Persia and Ethiopia as well as to the nations of the Nestorians, Maronites, the Druses, and Syrians."[13] Fr. Giovanni was active

---

[12] L. Wadding, *Annales Minorum*, XXV ed. by Eusebius Fermendzin Quaracchi, 1886. Designated as A.M.

[13] *Bullarium Franciscanum*, Rome 1759-68; 1898-04. Designated as B.F.

in reunion with Lebanon and Syria where the Maronites were already united to the Holy See.

At this council the Franciscans had four bishops, their minister general, a provincial, and eight other friars.[14] Franciscans were entrusted with the defense *De primatu ecclesiae romanae* and *De attributis divinis* and had several meetings among themselves in preparation for the discussions at the council.

James of Primadizzi was prominent in his work with the Armenians. John Capistran had been entrusted with the affairs of the oriental province of the Friars Minor and also shared in negotiations with the Armenians. Other friars served in Greece, Constantinople, Venice, Genoa, and in Greek cities around the Black Sea. The friars also served as the pope's messengers to the Nestorians when Pope Eugenius in 1441 invited them to follow the example of the Greeks, Armenians, and Copts in attaining reunion.

There are many reasons why the Council of Florence was not permanently effective, though its conduct might well serve as a guide for future attempts. Wadding shows how the lack of personal interest and contact was an important factor. "There was lacking too what was of the highest necessity, the briefing and sending of doctors and preachers who ought to have been immediately directed to the Greeks in numbers, to explain to them in person what had been done in the Council, to solve the doubts that might arise, and to refute carefully and learnedly the objections raised against it by that most stubborn man, Mark of Ephesus."[15]

In Europe, the Franciscan Order had their most numerous missions on the Balkan peninsula, though friars were zealous and devoted in many other parts of the continent. If the results here were not proportionate to the great sacrifices or to the many martyrs, the reason lies in the political and religious circumstances of the countries.

The friars seem to have labored first in Albania and Montenegro. They were there by 1240. Many bishops from the Order are mentioned in Antivari during the 13th and 14th centuries; about the middle of the 15th century, Eugene Somma is praised by Nicholas V for his untiring labors. Then the Turks came and devastated the land after

---

[14] Marcellino da Ciuezza, *Storia Universale della Missioni Franciscane* (Roma: Prato 1857-95). Designated as Marcell.

[15] *op. cit.*, A.M. IV 9.

the heroic defense of Skanderbeg; they destroyed all the documents which could have given us more accurate information. The friars who were able to save themselves withdrew to the mountains, and from there took care of the few Catholics.

There is more information concerning the missions to Bosnia.[16] The friars came into the country for the first time under Nicholas IV. They came from the province of Dalmatia after King Stephen's request for missionaries who knew the language. The king himself was baptized, but his fervor did not last long. Bosnia became once more the center of Manichean Sects. The Franciscans continued to work under the leadership of Brother Fabian until they were finally expelled and their churches destroyed. In 1340, however, the general, Gerard, with some friars, again entered the country under the protection of the king of Hungary. By his preaching he won a great part of the nobility to the faith. He also established some convents and sent more friars.

Among these friars was John of Aragon, who distinguished himself by his readiness to dispute with the Manicheans, and Peregrin of Saxony, who became the first provincial vicar and then bishop of Bosnia. Despite the unfavorable economic situation of the friars, Pope Gregory XI insisted in 1372 that the Order send new missionaries. In order to obtain his end more certainly, the Pope even permitted the friars to go to Bosnia without the permission of their superiors, and expressly dispensed them from the opposing precept of the Rule. The efforts of the friars were crowned with greater success towards the end of the century. At least the Pope wrote, in 1402, that they had converted more than 50,000 unbelievers. The number of residences had steadily increased, and this gave a firm basis for the missionary activity which was carried on by the Observants in the 15th century.

Pope Eugene IV praised their constancy when he wrote that they "made themselves a wall for the house of the Lord and for the spread of the orthodox faith." Particularly successful there against the Manicheans were St. James of the Marches, St. Capistran, and Fabian of Bachia. When the Bishop of Bosnia asked for more friars in 1451, he offered as the reason: "It is to be well noted that in places occupied by heretics, the heretics disappear before the Friars as wax before a flame." Then, in 1463, the Turks conquered the land

---

[16] B F VI, 433, 478.

and fearfully devastated it. Many friars were killed. Only after the heroic Franciscan Angelus Zvjedzovic, had obtained an edict of toleration for the Catholics from Mohammed II in 1464, could the friars (the only priests still residing there) carry on the necessary care of souls. This they did, indeed, admidst great struggles and continuous persecution. "They live continually in martyrdom," a chronicler writes.[17]

The mission history of Serbia is similar to that of Bosnia. The southern part of Serbia was formerly called Rascia. Induced by the Queen Mother, Helena, who was a Catholic, Nicholas IV, in 1288, sent some Franciscan missionaries. More friars were sent in 1307 at the request of the king. The labors of these missionaries were brought to nought by the vacillating conduct of the king and by the opposition of the Greek schismatics. In 1354, the Pope sent a new band of friars under the leadership of Bartholomew, the Franciscan bishop of Trau (Tragori) in Dalmatia. But when Bajazit I routed the Serbians in 1389, the missions suffered greatly. Only after Tamerlane's victory over the Turks, in 1402, were the Franciscans again able to build monasteries and churches and continue their missionary efforts. At the Council of Florence, the union of the Serbians with the Roman Church was successfully accomplished. But events soon showed that it was merely an external union, entered into through fear of the Turks. While these continued to make great inroads into the country, the opposition at home from the schismatic clergy also increased. The Franciscans were grievously persecuted and thought of leaving the country. When the vicar general, Mark of Bologna, heard of this proposal, he wrote to the friars: "What is it that induces you to value so little the palm of martyrdom? Is that the spirit of true Christians?" Continuing his exhortation, Mark wrote that the entire Order would be disgraced if they should abandon the field of labor entrusted to them because of fear of death. The friars remained in the country. Conditions improved a little after the defeat of the Turks in 1456. But the Turks soon wiped out that disgrace and completely conquered Serbia in 1502. A long period of suffering now began for the missionaries.

At the second Council of Lyons the Pope had wished to unite

---

[17] Gub. V, 138, 161.

Bulgaria,[18] which had joined with the Greek emperor against the Latins. Innocent IV sent Franciscans as his legates to the princes, "because We believe that they will be more acceptable and useful to you, imitating as they do the lowliness of the Savior." But the result of this mission is not known. Later attempts, undertaken by Nicholas IV, likewise were also not successful. The Bulgarians remained hostile to the Roman Church, and in 1314 even killed the Franciscan, Angelus of Spoleto, when he advocated reunion with the Holy See. Conditions improved only after the king of Hungary had subjugated the country in 1366. Numerous Franciscans now arrived, especially from Bosnia, who were able to announce the glad tidings of the Catholic faith without opposition. These missionaries are supposed to have baptized 200,000 unbelievers within a few months. The laborers, however, were too few. In a letter to the general, the king asked for 2,000 more missionaries immediately. The general favored the request and sent a very large group of friars to Bulgaria, who workd with such success that they were able to establish formal parish life in a comparatively short time. The missionaries then requested the Pope to send secular priests to continue the ordinary care of souls, so that they might be free to labor in other places for the conversion of the unbelievers. Some decades later this prosperous mission was destroyed when Bajazet I conquered Bulgaria in 1393. Five Franciscans suffered martyrdom at that time, more through the malice of the schismatics than of the Turks.

The position the missionaries was not much better in the north: Wallachia, Moldavia, Podolia, and the territory along the northern shore of the Black Sea, inhabited by the Cumani. The "Rutheni seu Russi" had been invited to unite with the Roman Church by John of Plano Carpini. His invitation was accepted only in the region around Kiev, where some princes and bishops consented to the union in 1247. In 1359, we meet a Franciscan bishop in Black Russia, Thomas Nimperquey. About 1370, Nicholas Melsat of Crosna labored in the same territory with about twenty-five friars for the extirpation of pagan abuses and for the conversion of the still numerous unbelievers. These friars were permitted to call thirty other friars to assist them in their work without asking the permission of the higher superiors of the Order. But some secular priests,

---

[18] ibid., 105.

among them the bishop of Lemberg and a priest, John, continually aroused difficulties for the friars and thereby harmed the union with Rome.[19]

In Moldavia, Duke Laczko had received baptism in 1371, together with his people. Several years later, the missionaries in Wallachia received their own bishop, the Franciscan Anthony of Spoleto, who also laboured zealously for the conversion of the pagans. The work was difficult and was carried on at the cost of many sacrifices. Greater advances seem to have been made in the fifteenth century, due to the activity of St. James of the Marches and Fabian of Bachia. Their work was wiped out to a great extent after these regions fell under Turkish domination in 1460. In 1476 alone, 40,000 Christians were dragged away into captivity and slavery by the Mohammedans.

In 1439 Pope Eugene sent Fr. Albert of Sarteano to Egypt as Commissary to hold negotiations with the Jacobite Patriarch of Alexandria, John XI, who then sent legates to the Council of Florence, resulting in the reunion of the Jacobites (Feb. 4, 1442). The Coptic Patriarch of Alexandria, John II, also signed an act of union at the Council of Florence, but it never became effective. A later attempt in 1594 to reunite the Copts was also unsuccessful. But when the Capuchins came to Cairo in 1630, the Coptic Patriarch opened all his churches to the friars, and Bl. Agathangelus won converts even from the monks of St. Anthony's monastery in the Thebaid.

Lithuania was pagan until well into the fourteenth century, although the Franciscans had preached the Cross there in the middle of the thirteenth century. Their work, however, had been hindered by the Teutonic Knights, who, for political reasons, had continued to harass also the converted Lithuanians. The friars' position in the country was precarious for other reasons also; for, about 1325, thirty-six Franciscans were murdered by the idolaters in the neighborhood of Wilna. Conditions improved permanently after the prince Jagello was baptized, taking the name of Wladislaw. He furthered the conversion of his people in every way. The Franciscan, Andreas Vazilo, became the first bishop of the country. In the beginning of the fifteenth century, the Polish Franciscan, John (called the Small),

---

[19] B F VI, 463.

labored there with great success. Towards the end of that century, Bl. Ladislas of Gielniow is mentioned with honor as a missionary in Massovia.

In Prussia, Livonia, and Courland also, the Franciscans, by order of Pope Alexander IV, announced the Gospel. Residences were established in those lands although the persecutions at the hands of the pagan population continued for a long time and caused the martyrdom of several friars.

In 1261, Albert became bishop of Marienwarder and founder of the city of Riesenburg. The Teutonic Knights inexplicably caused difficulties for the friars also in these regions, even destroying churches and convents, so that the Pope was forced repeatedly to interfere. The Franciscan archbishop of Riga was obliged to bring charges of this nature against the Knights as late as 1318. After the beginning of the fifteenth century, conditions became more settled, and the friars were able to form a separate custody of four convents. But these were destroyed by the Reformation 100 years later.[21]

The mission in Lapland, which was staffed by friars from Norway and Sweden, towards the end of the fifteenth century, suffered the same fate at the hands of the Reformers.

Other countries of Europe were won for the Catholic Church long before the thirteenth century, excepting southern Spain, which was under Moslem rule, and in part also Corsica, where half-pagan sects found refuge and savage customs darkened the Christian life. After the ex-general, Parenti, had begun a mission there, other friars arrived during the fourteenth century, to continue the work under the leadership of Mundinus of Bologna. The Observants, especially Bl. Anthony of Stronconio, also labored in that country in the fifteenth century.

The kingdom of Valencia, under Moorish domination until 1238, was the scene of the missionary labors of John of Perugia begun in 1231 and Peter of Sassoferato, but they were soon martyred at Teruel.

Berard had already preached, together with his companions, in the country around Granada, and there, in 1397, the open profession of the Christian faith won the martyr's crown for the friars John of

---

[20] Marcell. V, 234.
[21] Marcell. V, 368.

Cetina and Peter of Dueñas. Only after Granada has been conquered in 1492 could there be any thought of a fruitful mission activity there. Cardinal Ximenes certainly did a great deal for the conversion of this kingdom, though his methods cannot be entirely approved.

Prominent at this period of Franciscan Unity was the famous Poor Clare, St. Colette of Corbie. She was a kind of combination of St. Catherine of Siena, St. Joan of Arc, and St. Teresa of Avila. Many felt the power of her personality and the magnetism of her holiness. There was a mysterious fusion of gentleness and strength in her personality, rendered perhaps more striking by the austere pallor of her countenance. Her power was felt by the members of Religious Orders, who sought her spiritual advice and followed it. It was felt by the Avignon Pope Benedict XIII, who constituted her in 1406 as a reformer of the Poor Clares and granted her permission to direct, through his confessor, those Friars Minor who wished to follow the Reform. It was felt by the Minister General of the Observance at Avignon, who gave her authority as Vicar over the friars who adhered to the reform. It was felt, too, by St. John Capistran, who, as legate of Pope Eugenius IV, for the purpose of reuniting to the Observance the other minor reforms, was unable to move her from her allegiance to the Conventuals. And later it was the saint himself, the future conqueror of the Turks, who as Apostolic Nuncio and General Visitor of the Order was entrusted with the mission of officially confirming the privileges already granted to those who accepted her reforms. It was felt, finally, by Amadeus VIII of Savoy, when, owing to his insisting on accepting the tiara of anti-Pope, he beheld rise up against him the woman who had been his friend, and his faithful and protected subjects in the convents of Orbe and Vevey.[22]

The work of social redemption accomplished by the Poor Clares would have passed unnoticed in the world if from time to time some striking incident had not attracted attention to it. The activities of St. Colette, who in the age of St. Joan of Arc labored untiringly to heal the spiritual wounds in the soul of France, provides an instance of one of these episodes. "Sans cesse en route comme aiguille diligente à travers la France dechirée—Colette en recoud par dessous les morceaux avec la charité" so writes Paul Claudel about her. She

---

[22] Cf. B F VIII, 342, 345, 347.

also exercised a great influence over Jacques de Bourbon, a strange personality. A direct descendent of St. Louis of France, he fought unsuccessfully against the Turks in Bulgaria, against the English on the coast of the Channel, and the Armagnacs in France. His last adventure was to marry that criminal princess, Queen Joanna II of Naples. As might have been foreseen, the married life of the Neapolitan princess was so scandalous that after two months he abandoned her. He returned to his estates in France, retaining, however, the title of King of Naples. It was then that he met Mother Colette. At once he felt the fascination of her saintly personality and followed her to Vevey, placing at her disposal everything he possessed. Two of his daughters became Colettines, one of his sons entered the Observants.

On the death of Joanna II he took the habit himself from the hands of Pére Henri de la Baume, the spiritual director of St. Colette, in the Franciscan church at Besancon. From behind the grille of the choir his two daughters and St. Colette were watching and praying. In the small monastery near St. Colette's convent the King, who had become a Franciscan, dug in the garden, helped in the kitchen, dusted and cleaned the furniture like a poor lay brother. Of his past splendor he had kept only a spoon and an olive-wood bowl engraved with his coat of arms on a silver plate. When his last hour drew near he asked to be carried into the church of the Poor Clares and laid down barefoot on a straw mattress in the Chapel of the Blessed Sacrament. His daughters and St. Colette watched over him. "Quelle obligation," exclaimed the dying King, "n'si-je pas à la Sainte qui m'a converti et qui prie pour moi! Oh qu'il est doux de mourir comme je meurs!" This is how Paul Claudel has revisualised the scene.

St. Colette should be remembered for her role in getting the true pope after the Council of Constance. She worked with St. Vincent Ferrer in defense of the Church and in devotion to the Papacy. She is a model for the Poor Clares and all Franciscan sisters in the apostolate of prayer, sacrifice, and apostolic fervor for the cause of Unity.[23]

Third Period: 1517-1910

The sixteenth century ushered in the Protestant revolt, under which

---

[23] B F VII, 352, 358, 377.

the Church reeled but did not collapse. Thousands died for the faith
and in defense of the Papacy. They won heaven with a martyr's
crown. And while we are saddened by such swift and general loss to
the Church, we are also aware that perhaps in no century were there
more saints of diversified holiness as in this one, to serve as living
proof that Christ was with and in His Church. This third period
begins with the defection of Martin Luther in 1517, a year that
coincides with the official division of the First Order of Saint Francis.[24]

Martin Luther honored the Franciscans with an intense personal
hatred. He disliked especially the writings of John Duns Scotus.
Luther confused the counsels with the precepts of the Gospels and he
accused their Founder of having limited to only a small number of
people what should be a law for all, namely the strict observance of
all the Gospel counsels. When the first printed edition of the *'Liber
conformitatum'* of Bartolomeo de Pisa was published in 1410, his
friend, Erasmus Alber, wrote an artrocious libel on the Franciscans:
*Der barfüsser Monck Eulenspiegel und Alcaran mit einer Vorrede
Marthini Luther.* This blasphemous book, which ran in a few years
into three editions, had an alternative Latin title, *Alcoranum Nudipedum,* and was simply a sectarian and satirical parody of the *Liber
conformitatum'* of Bartolomeo de Pisa was published in 1510, his
translation, made by Conrad Badius, *L'Alcoran des Cordeliers,* made it
popular all over Europe. It was from the *Alcoranum nudipedum* that
Protestants, Rationalists, Encyclopaedists and the whole current of
anti-Catholic criticism, from Rabelais to Voltaire, derived their most
unfavourable notions concerning the Franciscans which gained cred-
ence.[25]

Just as the friars had been amongst the earliest to signify their
disapproval of certain clumsy preachers of indulgences who harmed
their own cause, so too they were amongst the first to denounce
Luther. The inrushing wave of heresy scarcely touched them: the
number of apostates from their ranks was small in comparison with
thousands who remained faithful and hundreds of friars who died

---

[24] H. Holzapfel, *History of the Franciscan Order* (Teutopolis, Ill., 1948)
275.
[25] Cf. A. Gemelli, *Franciscan Message to the World* (London: Burns
Oates, 1935) p. 116.

martyrs' deaths. As in the thirteenth century, they remained faithful to Rome; humble in outlook they remained immune in the sixteenth century, thanks to their guiding principle of love, to that spirit of criticism which lies at the root of every rebellion. They exercised their critical faculties on themselves, rather than on their doctrines. Divided amongst themselves over the question of poverty, they were united in face of a common enemy who attacked the Church and the Pope.

The division of the Order into three branches involved a distribution of labor which became a source of strength.

The Conventual friars were men of learning and classical scholars. They worked in university centers, preached in the most important pulpits, spoke before the courts of kings, published apologetical works, and jealously took care of the great basilicas which revealed to the people and to lovers of art and architecture something of the entrancing beauty of Franciscan idealism. The Observants, following the example of St. Bernardine of Siena, cultivated a simple, popular style of preaching based directly on Sacred Scripture. The Capuchins came down from their hermitages into the market-places and preached on "vices and virtues, and damnation and eternal glory," adopting a slightly apocalyptic tone which, added to their rugged appearance, similar to that of the fathers of the desert, made a great impression on the masses of the people. All three branches together constituted an army of no mean strength.

In 1520, the General of the Order, Francis Licheto, ordered every monastery to prepare special preachers to combat Lutheranism; the Chapter General held at Carpi (1521) ordained that special prayers be recited with a view to stiffening the resistance. Prayers were ordered in particular to the Mother of God, the destroyer of all heresies; hence at the end of every canonical hour was to be added: *Gaude et laetare Virgo Mario quia cunctas haereses sola intermisti in universo mundo*, with the versicle *Dignare me laudare te*, and the prayers *Gratiam tuam* and *Ecclesiam tuam*. Resistance was enjoined even to the extent of facing martyrdom: *Ut divini verbi gladio usque ad sanguinem resistantur*. These prayers were often fulfilled literally. From 1520 to 1620, more than 500 friars died for the Faith.

The general of the Observants commanded that the writings of Luther should be burned and that preachers should be appointed to combat the heresy. Many friars and sisters died for the faith. Many priests defended the faith with constancy and heroism so that it is wrong to look upon the times as a period of wholesale apostasy.

The friars in Germany tried to check the ravages of heresy. After the Council of Trent, the defence of the faith was made considerably easier because doubt and hesitation about matters of doctrine were ended. There were great men who stemmed the tide such as Conrad Kling of Erfurt, Matthew Teufel, Bernardine Gebron in West Prussia. John Wild was the best German pulpit orator of the sixteenth century. Mayence remained a Catholic city due to him.[26]

The German friars, living in the center of Lutheranism, sensed sooner than anyone else the need of learning, in order to withstand effectively the onslaughts of the enemy. Aware that Protestants spared no pains to attract scholars with money, John Wild pointed out that the Catholics should remember that the wisest use to which money could be put was that of encouraging study and students. Herborn deplored the low cultural level of many friars who took greater care of the monastery larder than of the library.

In the meantime those whose weapons were already burnished, fought by word of mouth and with the pen; in their tactics they were guided by that sense of actuality which is a distinguishing Franciscan trait. An Alsatian Conventual who died in 1530, John Pauly, a preacher and an able writer, attacked the Protestants with a satirical book *Schimpf und Ernst,* published in 1519, which quickly achieved great popularity, as did the *Narrenschiff* of Brant. With the weapon of ridicule they prevented hundreds of apostasies. Another Alsatian Conventual, Thomas Murner, who had been nominated Poet Laurate by the Emperor Maximilian, made use of his artistic talents and ripe scholarship as a means of stemming Protestant propaganda. At Bale, where he taught law, he was a tower of strength against the Zwinglians, and he became a danger to the English heretics when Henry VIII called him to his kingdom to confute them. He wrote a poem in the form of a dialogue, in which the two speakers were himself and Luther, entitled: *Vom Grossen Luterischen Narren.* In polemics the Franciscans used the weapon of ridicule, but they were careful always to avoid being insolent, for they always looked forward to the possibility of re-

---

[26] H. Holzapfel, *op. cit.*

conciliation. On the other hand, Augustine Alvedt, an Observant who entered into disputation at the Academy of Leipzig with Luther and Erasmus, was labelled by his adversaries with the most bestial epithets, of which the least offensive were: ox and donkey. He replied, however, with great gentleness and self-control, because, as he said: "a Catholic preacher should always aim at one thing only: edification."

In dealing with heretics the Franciscans were the first to employ, instead of direct methods of confutation, those modes of persuasion which the Church heretofore had made use of rather when dealing with schismatics. One of those who used these methods much in harmony with the spirit of St. Francis, was John Wild. This warm-hearted Observant preached for the space of some fifteen years in the cathedral of Mayence, with a vivacity which recalled that of St. Bernardine of Siena and a sweetness which foreshadowed that of St. Francis de Sales. When Albert of Brunswick in 1552 besieged and captured Mayence, he alone of all the priests of the city remained at his post. The soldiers of the victorious army dragged him out of his pulpit, but he made no resistance. Albert of Brunswick attempted to make him discard his Franciscan habit. 'My Lord,' he replied, 'I have worn this dress now for over thirty years. It has never done me any harm, so why should I leave it off now?'

Fr. Augustino Gemelli has written of this period and the friars: "Not to destroy, but to build up; not to abandon scenes of difficulty, but to attempt to improve conditions; not to be terrified by the appearance of heresy, but to believe that, as God has permitted it, He will bring good out of evil—as, for instance, the awakening of drowsy pastors of souls: these were the principles on which John Wild and his brethren acted. When brought into contact with the flame of love, heresy began to lose something of its venom.[27]

An Italian, Padre Luca Baglioni, in his *Arte del predicare* wrote a chapter on 'How to preach to-day against heretics so that they may turn from their errors.' Padre Luca, with acute psychological insight and Franciscan charity, recommended preachers to pray in the first place 'for the conversion of heretics, so that they may be led at least to doubt their falsehoods, since doubting is the first step towards knowing.' Instead of this, many preachers, so he complained, either began to enter into arguments with heretics, or insulted them outright

---

[27] *op. cit.*, p. 123.

from the pulpit. By their disputations they gained esteem of heretics, as being good logicians, or philosophers, but did not convince them; by insulting them they only kept them away from their sermons. In conclusion, no one was converted. Father Baglioni learned this truth from personal experience. After being fired at with a blunderbuss by a heretic whom he had insulted, he learned to walk along a better road and jotted down the following pieces of advice for the benefit of his brethren, who were still beginners in the art of preaching:

> I laid aside for good and all any idea of disputing in public against heretics, in particular against those of their leaders who are still alive. I avoided mentioning either their names, or their writings, in such a way as to convey almost the impression that I knew nothing about them and had never even heard of them. I pretended not to notice even the presence of heretics when they came to listen to my sermons. I dwelt at length only on those parts of their beliefs which are true and held by all Catholics too. I confuted their opinions and pointed out their mistakes, without ever mentioning any of their leaders by name; I endeavored when arguing with them always to be charitable and humble, showing them how truly sorry for them I was, and how anxious and ready I was to help them even at the cost of laying down my life, if needs be, for them. By these and similar means, little by little, I found them coming one after another to ask my counsel and advice. . . . Even men of great weight among them God has granted me in this way to guide towards the path of truth.

This method was adopted, too, by the Spanish Friar Minor, Diego de Estelle, and in general by all those Franciscans who helped to save from Protestantism the Latin nations of Southern Europe, Bavaria, Bohemia and Austria.

It required all the inherent optimism of the Franciscan character not to be crushed by persecution. In the Low Countries the Protestant uprising developed into a national war against the Hapsburgs, and the Geux were incited to sack the Catholic monasteries and convents. In 1572 at Gorcum the Geux swooped down like a band of sea pirates on the coast and hanged a Dominican, an Augustinian, three secular priests and eleven Observants. Amongst the latter were St. Nicholas Pick—who though subjected several times to torture, manfully encouraged his companions to resist to the bitter end—and Father Willaide—an old man of over ninety, who, while he was being butchered, thanked his tormentors for allowing him to die a martyr. St.

Nicholas declared that "I would rather endure death for the honor of God than swerve even a hair's breadth from the faith."

In England, heresy made martyrs. In 1533, Pope Clement VII decided in favor of the validity of the marriage with Catherine and commanded that the union contracted with Anne Boleyn be dissolved. Thereupon the King ordered that John Forrest, the provincial of the Observants and the confessor of the Queen, should be thrown into prison. On the one hand, he hoped thereby to punish Forrest for his former conduct, and, on the other, to warn the Observants not to follow the course of their superior. But the King reckoned here without his friars. The first man in England to come out publicly and condemn his marriage with Anne Boleyn was an Observant, Peto, the guardian of the Observant convent at Greenwich. In 1533, with unheard of courage in a sermon before the King, he told the monarch of his injustice towards his Queen and roundly censured the clergymen who were salving the conscience of Henry. On the following Sunday, a Canon, also in a sermon in the same church, defended the conduct of the King. In the course of his sermon, this Canon began to inveigh against Peto, who was absent on business of the Order. Elstow, one of the friars, interrupted to defend Peto with such warmth and success, that Henry was force to command both the Canon and friar to be silent. On the following day, the two brave friars were summoned before the King's court. The remark of a judge that the two criminals should be thrown into the Thames drew from Elstow this bantering reply: "The way to heaven is just as short by water as by land."[28]

Now the rupture of the King and the Observants was complete. Peto and Elstow, according to some, were thrown into prison; according to other authors they were exiled. In the spring of 1534, Hugh Rich, guardian of Canterbury, and Richard Risbey, the guardian of Richmond, were hanged, drawn, and quartered. In August of the same year, before the other religious had even been threatened in any way by the government, all the Observants were driven from their convents, and more than 200 imprisoned in London. Not one sacrificed his conscience to gain the favor of the King. The condemnation of the friars was postponed due to the intervention of one of their friends.

---

[28] Cf. Francis Borgia Steck, O.F.M., *Franciscan and Protestant Revolution* (Chicago, 1920) 120.

Finally in 1537, after twenty-two friars had died as victims of the squalor and filth of the prison, some were set free; others were sent to more remote prisons, and some were put to death, namely, Anthony Brorbey (Brookby), Thomas Cort, and Thomas Belchiem. On May 22 of the following year, the heroic septuagenarian, John Forrest, was slowly burned to death, because he had defended the authority of the Church and the supremacy of the Pope.

The ancient Faith was restored, in 1553, upon the accession of Queen Mary. The restoration was made easier by the fact that the majority of the common people of England were at heart still Catholic. The Orders were likewise restored, and first of all the Franciscan Observants, who had been the first to suffer. But Mary died after a reign of only five years. Her half-sister, Elizabeth, re-introduced the system of her father. Now, however, the persecutions were to last longer and were to become more terrible than they had been under her father, Henry. This time the clergy of all ranks proved more loyal than during their previous trial. Regarding the conduct of the Franciscans, we shall only repeat the words of an historian of the Order: *"Nemo fuit ex Minoritis, qui in faciem novae Anglicanae Jezabelis forti animo non restiterit."* Therefore, they were honored with a special decree of banishment from the realm. The exiles went to Belgium, the Netherlands, and France. Some remained in disguise in England, while others returned from time to time to help the poor Catholics as much as they could. Among the numerous missionaries who sealed their ministry with their blood, we may mention: Godfrey Jones (d. 1598), Thomas Bullaker (Friar John Baptist, d. 1642), Henry Heath (Friar Paul of St. Magdalen, d. 1643), Arthur Bell (Friar Francis, d. 1643), John Woodcock (Friar Martin of St. Felix, d. 1646), Walter Coleman (Friar Christopher of St. Clare, d. 1645).

In Scotland, the persecution of the Church began in 1559.[29] The Scottish Observants were highly esteemed and sincerely venerated by the people for their purity of life. Several of their number had distinguished themselves for many years by their opposition to the heretics. Such were Friars John and Patrick and Alexander Arbuchell. Little wonder that the heretics on their side hated the friars heartily. Hence, after the new order was installed, the Observants, about 140 in all, were exiled; only a few, two or three, sold their faith

---

[29] H. Holzapfel, *op. cit.*, p. 393.

for the pleasure of remaining in their native land. The others went to the continent, where they were received by the various provinces. One of them was the learned John de la Henry. In 1586, while provincial of the Cologne province, he transmitted to the General Gonzaga an account of the persecutions of the Scottish Observants. It is unfortunate that the Scottish province, which ended so nobly, has not yet been restored.

The story of the suffering of the Irish Franciscans is much longer.[30] Henry VIII tried to introduce his reforms there, but met very energetic resistance. But with Queen Elizabth began 200 years of terrible persecutions in a systematic attempt to crush an unfortunate people—a shameful blot, which every noble minded Englishman must blush to remember. The constancy of the Irish to the Faith despite their miseries is indeed a miracle. The loyalty of the people to the Faith is due in part at least to the heroism of the Irish bishops and clergy, who despised the manifest dangers to their own lives, in order to help and console their people. The landed Orders, whose estates were soon confiscated by the invaders, withdrew to the Continent. The Franciscan Observants also went to the Continent, where they founded convents to keep alive the traditions, the learning and the literature of their homeland, and where they also trained new recruits return to their native land to take the places of their brethren who had fallen on the field of battle. In this way, the Irish province continually renewed its strength even during the darkest periods of the persecutions. The friars in Ireland itself were concealed by loyal families, with whom they shared the common sorrow and dangers. No wonder that the Irish people, even today, have an especially warm spot in their hearts for the sons of St. Francis, who stood by them in their hour of need, strengthened them with the consolations of our holy religion, and, only too frequently, watered the soil of that wonderful island with their blood. The Irishman, Francis Harold, who lived during the period of the persecutions, could pen this description of his confreres about the year 160. "*Reliquis regni religiosis absque invidia maiori labors, patientis et constantia catholici populi religiosis obsequiis insudant, et cum Paulo Apostolo sciunt abundare et penuriam pati.*" Of the martyrs, which between 1540 and 1707 number more than 100, we shall name only the bishops: Patrick O'Hely

---

[30] *ibid.*, 394.

(d. 1578), Cornelius D'Davany (d. 1612), Boetius Egan (d. 1650).
It is also worthy of note that the English episcopate precisely during
the periods of the bitterest persecutions counted not less than eighteen
sons of St. Francis among its members.

The Reformation in Denmark, more than anywhere else, was the
work of ambitious and selfish princes. The Catholic Church there
was, on the whole, free of grave abuses, and the people were deprived
of their Faith through trickery and fraud. Frederick I at his coro-
nation, in 1524, had sworn solemnly to defend and maintain the
ancient religion, but he did just the opposite. The destruction of
the houses of the religious began in 1528, and, within a short time,
all monasteries and convents had disappeared. The religious debate
of 1530, in which Nicholas Herborn, called in derision Stagefyr,
played such an important part accomplished little. During the persecutions the religious conducted themselves admirably, even though
there was no lack of weaklings and apostates. Lack of information
make us unable to say whether these apostates belonged to the
Conventuals or to the Observants. Many convents, as for instance the
one at Istad, had to be besieged in earnest before the friars would
withdraw. Not frequently the friars were cruelly maltreated, and
they generally considered themselves fortunate, if, after being robbed
of all, they were only thrown out into the street.[31]

The Province of Deciae comprised not only the convents in Denmark, but also those in Sweden and Norway.[32] The Franciscans had
dwelt in those lands since 1222. Great had been their labors for the
conversion of the still pagan peoples, which they found there upon
their arrival. The natives on their side, soon grew to love the friars.
The Observance was introduced into these countries towards the end
of the fifteenth century, and by 1517 it counted twenty-two convents
scattered throughout this province. Much research remains to be
done before the final history of the destruction of this province can
be written. Probably, the friaries in Norway and Sweden were destroyed at about the same time as those in Denmark. The Reformation there could succeed only if fraud and trickery were employed.
Despite the death penalty, placed upon any priest who dared to enter

---

[31] *ibid.*, 396.
[32] Marcell. *op. cit.*, VII, 1, 224.

these countries, Wiggers sent missionaries thither from Holland. Their fate and their labors are alike unknown.

Francis of Santa Clara[33] (Christopher Davenport) was prominent in England in later times. He was desirous of winning his country back to the Faith. He explained the XXXIX articles of the Anglican communion in a Catholic sense in an appendix to his work, *Deus, Natura, Gratia*. He made certain concessions which the Church could not recognize and the holy and learned friar had the humiliation of having his work placed on the index by the Inquisition. "Thus it was possible to go too far even in a good cause; Rome saw what we now see plainly, but what the moving characters in the drama could not see. The nation, instead of being ripe for conversation, was in reality drifting away from the Church, and a Puritan reaction was about to set in, almost as disastrous in its consequences as Henry VIII's schism or Elizabeth's apostasy."[34]

The famous Tract XV of Oxford was published in 1841. It followed the path opened by Santa Clara and later generations of Anglo-Catholics were to occupy the position set forth by this friar and the divines at the Sorbonne.[35]

In France, Calvinism, which developed into a political faction, forced weak-kneed Catholics into apostasy and persecuted, tortured and slew those who remained firm. Yet in every town the Friars Minor strenuously opposed heresy by their preaching and by the example of their Christian lives. Side by side with the great preachers and mighty controversialists who entered into public disputation with the Huguenots—there were so many of them that it will be enough to mention here one name only, that of Pere Jean Barrier de Provins—labored other Franciscans of a more humble type. They were men who understood the workings of the minds of the common people, because they had gained experience both in the pulpit and in the confessional; they were beloved by the people, because they were untiring in sick-visiting, in giving alms to the poverty-stricken and attending to the wants of those in prison; ready and anxious to do all that was required of them, they acted as a spiritual leaven on

---

[33] Jeremiah Dockery, O.F.M., *Christopher Davenport* (London: Burns Oates, 1960), 75.

[34] Steck, *op. cit.*, p. 231.

[35] Dockery, *op. cit.*, 133.

the masses of the common people. Aware of the value of associations and of the strength of unity, they formed Confraternities of Penitents, like those which arose in Paris and at Montpelier, joined by men and women of all classes. They formed fresh Confraternities of the Blessed Sacrament, and infused new life into those already existing, since the consecrated host of redemption and victory was one of the mysteries of faith most fiercely and frequently attacked by the Huguenots.[36]

Toward the close of the sixteenth century the French Capuchins developed with astonishing rapidity. They received an added stimulus from the entry into the Order of Henri de Joyeuse, the companion of Nogaret and the favorite of Henry III; he became Friar Angelo and played a large part in preparing the ground for the abjuration of Henry IV.[37]

In 1575 St. Charles Borromeo, a Franciscan Tertiary and Cardinal Protector of the Friars Minor, sent the Capuchins into the Valtellina to counteract Protestant propaganda there; St. Francis de Sales in 1594 invited them to come into the Chablais, into which the Calvinists were penetrating. Their duties were to preach and to enter into public theological disputations, which lasted sometimes for ten days, or a couple of weeks on end. They tackled the most formidable adversaries, winning notable victories. Cherubin Fournier, the confessor of St. Francis de Sales, reduced many Calvinistic theologians to silence; he was considered a redoubtable opponent even by Theodore Beza. When he died the great bishop of Geneva was moved to tears.[38]

The friars defended the faith not only by dying for it, but by living for it, and by their writings and their eloquence. Preaching to the people they preserved them from the harm of the heresies, and by the power of good example showed them the way of salvation.

Lawrence of Brindisi (1559-1619), who wrote so beautifully of Mary and defended the absolute primacy of Christ, is now the third Franciscan doctor of the Church. He is a special model in the work of Unity because of his great holiness and his apostolate to the Jewish people and Lutherans. He preached to the Jews in Hebrew and wrote

---

[36] Gemelli, *op. cit.*, 135.
[37] Holzapfel, *op. cit.*, 395.
[38] B C IX, 269.

against the Lutherans with the famous work, *Lutheranismi Hypotyposis*. He is a model of learning and holiness for all, and especially for the sons of St. Francis.

Friars in the East

The Franciscan apostolate among the Eastern churches in this outline calls for a flashback to Constantinople, where the Order first appeared on the Eastern scene. In 1550 Father John Zuaze of Medina and Friar John of Troia asked permission of the Capuchin Vicar General, Fr. Bernardine of Asti, to go to the East to preach the gospel to the Turks. Pope Julius III gave them permission to go to Constantinople, which they did by sea from Venice. When they began preaching in Constantinople, they were thrown into prison and beaten, but released at the intervention of some Catholic merchants in the city. Deported from the city by ship to Palestine, they visited the Holy Places and went on to Egypt, where they tried to preach to the Governor and his court in Cario. Again imprisoned, they were sentenced to death and died of starvation in an underground dungeon.

In 1583, five Jesuits arrived in Constantinople to help in the work among the Christians there being carried on by Conventual and Observant Franciscans and Dominican friars, but within five years all but one of the Jesuits died of the plague. Fr. Mancinelli, the sole survivor, was recalled to Italy and the Jesuit mission in Constantinople was abandoned. The Sacred Congregation of Propaganda then approached the Capuchin General, Fr. James of Mercato Saraceno, and asked him to send some friars there. At the General Chapter of 1587, Constantinople formally became one of the Capuchin missions. Frs. Peter of the Cross and Denis of Rome were the first to arrive in the city, followed by St. Joseph of Leonissa and his lay-brother companion Br. Gregory of Leonissa.

The stirring account of the sufferings and zeal of these friars in behalf of the Christians of Constantinople equals that of any modern accounts of heroic priests in Communist concentration camps. The zeal of St. Joseph especially, who became a prisoner among the prisoners of the Quassim-pasha, is a heroic chapter in the history of early Capuchin missionary endeavor on behalf of our suffering Eastern brethren. His success in recalling an apostate Greek archbishop to repentance is noteworthy in this account.

A Greek archbishop had apostatized to Mohammedanism out of weakness, but to return to his faith would have meant death, since conversion from Mohammedanism to Christianity was considered a crime punishable by death. Joseph tried to obtain an interview with the Sultan in order to change this law. He succeeded in entering the Sultan's palace and even in preaching to the Sultan, but this daring act brought a sentence of execution on his head. Joseph was nailed to a cross by a hand and a foot and left to die. A fire was kindled beneath the cross. Saved by a miracle after three days of torture, he then returned to Italy, but not without the archbishop. As Fr. Isidore summed up St. Joseph's successful conclusion of his efforts:

> Since Joseph had not been able to make it safe for the arch-bishop he converted to profess his faith in Constantinople, he took him back to Italy. There he went directly to Rome, told the story of his mission to Pope Sixtus V and presented the arch-bishop to him who embraced him and accepted him once again as his son.

When St. Joseph left Constantinople, the Capuchin mission there was temporarily abandoned, to be resumed again in 1622 during the reign of Pope Gregory XV, by Fr. Pacificus of Paris and two other friars. Later the French king erected a college in the hospice of St. Louis in the Pera for the education of youths. The French Capuchins were forced to abandon the mission in 1791, but were replaced by Italian Capuchins until 1881, when the mission was returned to the Paris Capuchins. The next year, with the approval of the Sacred Congregation of Propaganda, Father Arsenius of Chatel-Montagne, superior of the Capuchin Mission in Constantinople, erected the major seminary for Eastern youths of all rites conducted to this day by Capuchins in Constantinople.

A few years after the death of St. Joseph of Leonissa (1612) the Holy See tried to send French Capuchins into Russia, in 1627 and 1633, but the plans were unsuccessful. On April 5, 1661, however, the Congregation of Propaganda assigned Georgia to the Capuchins which had first been assigned to the Theatines, in 1624, by Pope Urban VIII. While the Theatine Fathers did yeoman work, they were unable to continue for lack of sufficient priests. So the first band of Capuchins entered what is now southern Russia under the leadership of Fr. Bonaventure of Sorrento.

The journey of the pioneer Capuchin missionaries to Russia was a difficult one. The Prefect, Fr. Bonaventure, drowned in a river on the way from Mingrellia to Tiflis (Oct. 4, 1663). Before this another friar had died in Smyrna. A third friar, terrified, returned to Mingrellia, and the others, hearing of the war of the Turks against the Georgians, retired to Persia to await the outcome of the conflict. After the war ended the Capuchins once more set out on their journey and arrived in Tiflis, the Capital of Georgia, in 1663, with Fr. Seraphin of Melicocca as their leader. On their arrival the king gave them two houses as gifts, one of which they used for a chapel, the other as a hospice.

The Congregation of Propaganda named Fr. Seraphin the Prefect of the mission in Georgia and sent other missionaries, so that the mission could be extended, first to Gori and then to Imeritia. Fathers Justin of Leghorn and Bernard of Naples distinguished themselves for their zeal and study, the latter especially by his Georgian dictionary and the translation of several books into Georgian. In 1670 two Capuchin missionaries were drowned on the trip from Rome, in the Black Sea. The Prefect, Fr. Seraphin, died in 1675, and was succeeded by Fr. Joseph of Bogognano. Scarcely had reinforcements arrived in the persons of four more missionaries, than Fr. Joseph also died. Though we lack the details of the story, we can, as our Fr. Cuthbert states, well imagine "their sacrifices and trials which can only be realized by those who have lived in that country."

Yet the sufferings of the Capuchins in Georgia bore fruit. The archives of the Capuchins of Florence show that Fr. Justin of Leghorn converted the King of Georgia, as well as the Orthodox archbishop and a number of his clergy. King George sent Fr. Angelus of Figlione to Pope Innocent XI, and the Pontiff replied, in his letter *Inexplicabili exuberantis laetitiae* (May 14, 1688) and graciously welcoming the king to the fold of the Mother Church and imparting to him his Apostolic Blessing.

Pope Innocent sent a similar letter to Barzins, the prince of Georgia, in 1692, after the latter had quelled a revolt incited by the schmismatics. Fr. Julius of Cremona, who was designated Prefect Apostolic of the mission after the death of Fr. Joseph, was the one who converted Prince Barzins, who proved himself a friend and protector of the Capuchins in their later work for reunion. His magnificent profession of faith to Pope Innocent XI is a shining testimony to the Roman primacy on the part of an Eastern ruler in the seventeenth century.

In the midst of another Armenian uprising a plague broke out and the Capuchins gave themselves to the care of the afflicted as they had done so often in their native Italy. Both the Prefect, Fr. Julius of Cremona, and Fr. Bartholomew of Giugliano died nursing the victims of the epidemic. The illustrious Fr. Justin of Leghorn also died in 1691. With the arrival of new recruits in 1692, a new war against the Capuchins began. In 1697 the Armenian bishop drove the friars out of Tiflis, desecrating their church there. Persecutions like these forced the friars to appeal to Pope Innocent XII and the King of Persia. The Pope also appealed for protection for the Capuchins who had come to Georgia, he stated, "for no earthly honor nor gain... but rather in order to point out in sincerity and humility of heart, by the light of Catholic truth, the right way which leads to God."

At the beginning of the eighteenth century a famous Capuchin of the Manzoni family, Fr. Patrick of Milan, did much for the Capuchin missions in (North) Russia, of which he is considered the founder. Born in Barzio in 1662, he became a Capuchin novice in the province of Venice in 1687 and was sent to the Capuchin mission in Georgia in 1702. Like his glorious patron he spent nearly his entire life in incredible labors for the spread of the true faith. In 1715 he founded the friars church and convent in Astrakhan. But it was for his work in Moscow that he became known as the founder of the Capuchin missions in Russia.

In 1685 the Jesuits established a school and residence in Moscow, only to be expelled four years later. In 1691, however, the Tsar recalled the Jesuits and in 1705 called for the Capuchins, praising them for their "piety, holiness, exemplary life and integrity of morals," and promising to build a church and convent for them in Moscow. The Holy See was overjoyed at the Tsar's invitation, and Pope Clement XI wrote, in 1707, expressing his joy and praying to the Father of Lights for the reunion of Russia to the Holy See and the Catholic Church.

Father Patrick, in order to put his mission in Astrakhan on a firm foundation, went to Moscow to obtain the Tsar's permission. Failing twice to obtain his request, he then asked for permission to leave Russia. Then, in 1719, the Tsar expelled the Jesuits from Russia and gave their houses to the Capuchins, in Petersburg, Moscow, and Astrakhan.

The Tsar wanted missionaries who would be dependent on no great prince and who would be able to speak several different languages. The Swiss Capuchins filled his desires quite capably. The Congregation of Propaganda entrusted Kazan and Astrakhan to the Georgian Capuchin prefecture and Petersburg and Moscow to the Capuchins of Switzerland. The first Swiss Capuchins to be sent to Russia were Frs. Venustius of Freiburg, Casimir of Delmont, Ulrich of Goldach, Theodosius of Buswil, Fidelis of Rorshach, and Roman of Porrentury. They were followed by Frs. Peter Chrysologus of Tergeste and Apollinaris Weber shortly afterwards. Fr Apollinaris became Prefect of the mission in 1724.

Fr. Patrick of Milan, founder of the Capuchin mission in Moscow, returned to his province in 1725, and died there a nonagenarian (despite his twenty-three years of labor in Russia) in 1753. The Swiss Capuchins worked on in Moscow, opening schools, preaching the word of God in German, French, Italian and Russian. Fr. Apollinaris gave an account of their labors to Pope Innocent XIII in a letter dated February 20, 1722 and asked for permission to come to Rome. The Pope readily granted the request, but the Tsar held back. Peter the Great had such a high esteem and affection for Fr. Apollinaris that he refused to give him letters of safe passage out of the country, for fear of losing him!

On December 28, 1725, Peter the Great died, and with him the Capuchins lost a powerful and friendly protector. Though he remained high-handed in his dealings with churchmen, he favored the Capuchins. That same year, Fr. Apollinaris left Russia for Poland, never to return. Yet the Order continued to send Priests to Russia. Fr. Fabian of Lubania was prefect of the mission until 1736 and was succeeded by Fr. Gabriel of Bononia, who died in Moscow in 1738.

In 1748 the Capuchins began working among the Cossacks, and in 1750 a Capuchin house was opened in the Ukraine. Under Fr. Ulrich of Rorshach (1755-1757), Bohemian Capuchins began working in Russia. In fact, the Bohemian province had asked that the Capuchin mission in Russia be entrusted to them, but Pope Benedict XIV declined to change the government of the mission. Fr. Ulrich returned to his province in 1760 and sent a long and detailed account of his mission to the Congregation of Propaganda. From the year 1759 nearly all Capuchin missionaries sent to Russia came from the Bohemian province.

Under Catherine II, the Capuchins were persecuted and expelled from Russia. In 1765, the Capuchin Prefect Father Angelus of Raudnitz refused ecclesiastical burial to an unworthy Frenchman, despite the orders of Catherine that he be buried from the Catholic Church. Fr. Angelus and Fr. Aloysius of Prague were thrown into prison and then expelled from Russia. The Sacred Congregation of Propaganda praised the steadfastness of the Capuchins in this matter of principle despite the threat of punishment and exile.

Under Fr. Amatus of Reichstadt the Capuchin prefecture in Russia was extended southwards to Nisna in the Ukraine at the Persian border and the Caucasian mountains. In 1774, under the Prefect of Fr. Romuald of Bus, the Capuchins opened a house in Saratov. Fr. Romuald was the last Capuchin with the title "Apostolic Prefect of Moscow."

With the extension of the jurisdiction of the Nuncio of Warsaw over all of Russia in 1777, the Capuchin prefect's title was changed to "Superior of the Mission," and Capuchin missionaries in Russia designated as "pastors." One of the most remarkable Capuchins of this period was Fr. Eliseus of Budweis, who was deported to Siberia and died in Tobolsk in 1798 at the age of ninety after a marvelous apostolate among both Catholics and Orthodox over a period of forty years.

In 1802, when Georgia was annexed to Russia the Capuchins reopened their missions in Tiflis and Gori, which had suffered at the hands of the Persians in the previous century. Yet there again they suffered much until, in 1830, the convent and church the friars had built in Tiflis and Gori were again destroyed, this time at the hands of the Russians. With the outbreak of a plague, once again the Capuchins spent themselves in caring for the sick. Frs. Philibert of Fossano, Bonaventure of Asti, Basil of Rovigo, Amideus of Fossano and two lay Brothers all fell victims of their self-sacrificing charity. The Prefect, Fr. Francis Anthony of Padua, also died caring for those stricken by the epidemic. His successor, Fr. Philip of Forano, set to work rebuilding once again the Capuchin convent and church in Tiflis. Reading this account of patience and perseverance in the face of ungrateful hatred, we cannot help admiring these Capuchins. Had we been in their place we would probably have asked with St. Peter, "Lord, how often must I see my brother do me wrong, and still forgive him?" (Matt. 18:21). But theirs was the spirit of St. Lawrence of Brindisi who, in commenting on this passage, said that Christ requires the greatest charity of His followers, a charity which shines like fire. This is a fire which, he comments, cannot be extinguished by the waters of countless injuries.

The Russian government began a policy of strangulation, putting obstacles in the way of any new Capuchin missionaries who wished to enter the country. In 1842 decrees from the Russian government directed against the work of the friars multiplied in wave on wave, but the waves broke ineffectually over their heads. So the Russian government resorted to a tactic still in vogue in Russian purges. Calumniating charges were brought against the Capuchins by a priest willing to play along with the government. Though subsequent investigations proved the friars innocent; the government ordered the Capuchins to break off relations with Rome or be expelled. The reply of the Prefect, Fr. Damian, that the Capuchins could never accede to such a denial of their faith brought their expulsion, despite the protests of the people, on January 1, 1845. So it was, after approximately two centuries, that the Capuchins were exiled from Russia in a manner reminding us of the barbarous expulsion of our missionaries from China at the present time.

In Europe the missions in the care of the Order are parts of the Balkan peninsula and some of the islands which are under Turkish domination. The Capuchins have labored in the vicariate of Philippopolis since 1841; in Crete since the middle of the seventeenth century; and on the Ionian Islands, in particular on Cephalonia, since 1793. Of the most importance was the mission of the Order of Constantinople, begun at the beginning of the seventeenth century. In the beginning, French friars alone were permitted to labor in this mission, as in all the other missions of the Orient. In 1795, Italian friars replaced the French until 1881, when due to pressure applied by the French government, Constantinople was again entrusted to the Parisian province, while the Italian friars were allowed to retain other missions in the Orient. Soon thereafter was begun the Institutum Orientis, which has preserved more of an international character.[39]

Soon after the Capuchins had become established in Constantinople, they began to invade Asia. Smyrna was entered first, then Trebizond, Syria, Mesopotamia and Persia. Tibet was also the scene of successful work from 1707-1741. Here Horatius of Penna in particular distinguished himself by spreading religious publications in the native language. After they had been driven out of Tibet, these friars established missions on its borders in Northern India, where they continued to care for many stations. Due to lack of men and resources, the Order was forced to relinquish its missions around Bombay and Madras during the nineteenth century.[40]

In Africa, the Capuchins cared for the mission of Tunis from 1624 until the end of the nineteenth century, and for the territory along the western coast down to the Congo and Angola from 1640 until the French Revolution. Capuchins also labored in Abyssinia, where the Bls. Agathangelus of Vendome and Cassian of Nantes were martyred in 1638. The mission on the Seychelles Islands in the Indian Ocean, entrusted to Capuchins in 1852, is still cared for by them.[41] Likewise, the Order still labors in southern Abyssinia among the Gallas tribe in the missions which were begun in 1845 by the heroic William Massaja, who died as a Cardinal in 1889. In 1894, the Capuchins accepted the care of the Italian colony of Eritrea.[42]

The labors and the sufferings of the friars laboring in the Balkan peninsula under the last of the Turk defy description.[43] It is due solely to the sacrifices and the heroism of the Franciscans that the Catholic Faith was not entirely torn out of the hearts of the people of Bosnia and Herzegovina;[44] for the friars were the only Catholic priests at work in these countries until very recent times. Upon the

---

[39]B C VII, 236.
[40] Cf. Annal. Cap. XXIV, 106.
[41] E F IV, 178.
[42] B C VII, 223.
[43] H. Holzapfel, *op. cit.*, 512.
[44] Marcell. VII 3, 552. Gub. VI 690. D. Fabianich, *Firmani inediti dei Sultani di Constantinopoli di Conventi Francescani e alle autorita civili di Bosnia e di Erzegovina*, Firenze 1884. P. Bakula, *I martirii nella missione Francescana osservante in Erzegovina*, Roma 1862.

occasion of the restoration of the hierarchy in 1881, State and Church authorities were united in their praise of the sons of St. Francis.[45] "During 500 years of persecution, and at the price of the greatest sacrifices, it has fulfilled its noble mission, meriting thereby the gratitude both of the Church and of the State."[46] Pope Leo XIII, upon the same occasion, stated that we must thank the Franciscans that the Catholics of Slavonia and Dalmatia have greater numbers than the schismatics. This was achieved through the immigration of countless Bosnians, whom the friars had saved for the Faith. In Bulgaria and Rumania, too, the Bosnian friars helped to defend the Catholic Faith, although their efforts were not as successful in these countries as in their native land.[47]

In Albania,[48] also, the friars stood in the breach and successfully held back the onrushing tides of the eastern opponents of western culture and of the Roman Church. The Observants had managed to remain in this country, but were too weak to exert much influence until they were re-enforced by the Italian Reformati during the seventeenth century. Bonaventure of Palazzolo brought the Italian Reformati into Albania in 1634. Since that time, they have developed an extensive mission activity in Serbia, Montenegro and Macedonia. The work among the Catholics in these countries was rendered especially difficult by the many abuses which had crept in among the faithful as a result of the encouragement and the bad example of their Moslem neighbors and rulers. Only too frequently such laxities were but the forerunners of a general apostasy. Nevertheless, whole communities in central and northern Albania have remained loyal to the See of Peter and to the religion of Christ, largely as a result of the labors of the faithful friars.[49] Naturally, such results were not achieved in that section of Europe without martyrs.[50] Thus in 1644, Salvator of Offida and Paul of Mantua paid with their lives for their heroism, as did Ferdinand of Albizzola and James Zampa of Sarnano

---

[45] Histor.—polit. Bl. XCVII (1886) 431.
[46] Acta XXV 49.
[47] Marcell. VII 3, 650. Gub. VI 691. E. Fermendzin, *Acta Bulgariae ecclesiastica, Zagabriae* 1887.
[48] Marcell. VII 3, 552. Gub. VI 393, 690.
[49] Heimbucher II (2nd ed.) 426.
[50] Gub. VI 577.

in 1948. Nor must we ignore these friars who labored for several decades in southern Greece and on the islands of the Aegean Sea.[51]

Fourth Period: 1910 to the Present

In this section of the paper I have begun with the year 1910, since this marks the beginning of the modern ecumenical movement by those religious groups separated from the Catholic Church. 1910 witnessed the meeting of the World Missionary Congress at Edinburgh, the date of origin of various movements which have developed into the World Council of Churches with meetings in Amsterdam in 1948, in Evanston in 1954, and in New Delhi in 1961.

During the past half century the Holy Spirit has been alive in the Church and in those outside the Church, shown by an unparalleled longing for Christian Unity. Catholics have realized more deeply the plight of those who "belong" to Christ and the Church in some way but are not members of the Mystical Body. Our separated brethren have come to realize that division is not a blessing but a grave spiritual misfortune. Of this the Holy Office has written: "At this time in many parts of the world, owing partly to various external events and changes of mental attitude, but, under the inspiring grace of God, due chiefly to the common prayers of the faithful, a desire has awakened and is growing daily in the hearts of many who are separated from the Catholic Church, that a reunion be accomplished among all who believe in Christ the Lord. Assuredly to the children of the true Church this is a source of holy joy in the Lord as well as an inducement to lend their assistance to all who are sincerely seeking the truth, by entreating light and strength for them from God in fervent prayer."[52]

Much too has developed in the Church. Though the charity of St. Pius X was indeed genuine and attractive, it was not as expansive as at the present time under Pope John. Many factors stood in the way of a quick or immediate reconciliation, but surely the present Pope is providentially sent by God to initiate a program of Christian renewal and reunion.

In this section I should like to mention some pertinent facts about

---

[51] Saggio n. 92; *Breve istoria delle missioni Francescane nel Pelopanneso del 1690 a 1714 e nelle isole Ionie del 1716 a 1791.*

[52] Monitum Holy Office 1949, *ASS.* vol. 42.

the Unity effort in the Catholic Church, the development of Eastern rites among Franciscans, and present day efforts to bring about reunion.

Father Paul James Francis, S.A.

Foremost among the apostles and leaders of Christian Reunion is the father founder of our religious community, Fr. Paul James Francis (1863-1940). His life is one grand apology for the papacy and the Church, combined with a supreme longing to bring souls to salvation.[53]

Fr. Paul came into the Church in 1909 with his small band of followers, the Society of the Atonement. He called this event "the greatest thing I ever did." He was then 46 years old. He did much to advance the cause of Unity through the establishment of the Chair of Unity Octave, an annual crusade of prayer for Unity, observed each January 18-25. He was co-founder of the Catholic Near East Welfare Association, now a pontifical organization like the Propagation of the Faith. He received many Anglican clergymen into the Church, aided them financially, and opened wide the limited facilities of his religious home to help anyone who had come to his spiritual home in the Church. Many Orthodox priests found a cordial heart and helping hand in Fr. Paul of Graymoor.

Even as an Anglican he said that his belief in the primacy of the pope was due, under God, to the influence of St. Francis. "Since therefore, our faith in the Holy See was obtained through St. Francis, those of our fellow Anglicans, who shall hereafter obtain like faith with us through the extension of the Reunion Movement, will in reality have derived it from the Patriarch of Assisi and thus can be claimed by him as a part of that innumerable progeny of the Catholic faithful whom he has begotten through the spirit. Thus the millions of Anglicans who some day will enjoy communion with the Apostolic See and through that See with the balance of Catholic Christians, will be able to count themselves the children of that blessed Brother Francis, whom God has made the Abraham of a new covenant and pre-eminently the Saint of Church Unity."[54]

---

[53] D. Gannon, *Father Paul of Graymoor* (New York: Macmillan 1951). T. Cranny, *Father Paul: Apostle of Unity* (Graymoor Press: Peekskill, N.Y., 1955).

[54] *Words of Father Paul* 13:16.

Fr. Paul was a man with a cause; an apostle with a mission. He loved Jesus, Mary, and Francis—and through them he gave himself to the Church. He said that St. Francis was "the saint par excellence of Church Unity." When the Graymoor founder began *The Lamp* in 1903 he declared that he placed the venture "under the special protection and patronage of our Immaculate Lady Mary, Queen of heaven, and her seraphic Knight, St. Francis of Assisi, the saint par excellence of Church Unity."[55] To the Poverello he looked to exert his "apostleship of Unity and to restore the Anglican church to her ancient position of obedience and submission to the Holy See."[56]

Unity was the master passion of Fr. Paul's life. In the first editorial of *The Lamp* he wrote in defense of the papacy: "We would rather go to the block with Sir Thomas More and Bishop Fisher then deny that the Bishop of Rome is the successor of St. Peter and the head of the Catholic Church." Later when threatened with an ecclesiastical trial because of his ideas on Unity, he said: "Here to this quiet spot I came as a witness to a great truth and I am ready for anything—for trial, for martyrdom, if need be. Ostracized by the clergy, insulted by many and often reviled, I believe that some day, perhaps not in mine, all the Christian churches will be united under the guidance of the Bishop of Rome."[57]

Fr. Paul's desire for unity was not confined to individual conversions. His apostolic heart sought the reconciliation of entire groups with the Church. "We do wish to convert not only one Episcopalian, but all Episcopalians. We have always been very ambitious in that regard. It is not merely the individual Episcopalian whom we wish to convert to the Catholic Church, but we desire to see the Episcopal Church as a body return to communion with Rome, as the Society of the Atonement made up of Episcopalians was received corporately into communion with Rome ten years ago. Again, we are not satisfied with working and praying for the homecoming of the Episcopalians to the Father's house; it is *all* the 'other sheep' we long to see converted to Catholicism."[58]

The longing of Fr. Paul was an authentic echo of the seraphic

---

[55] Feb. 1903, 2.
[56] *Words of Father Paul* 7:105.
[57] *New York Herald Tribune*, April 20, 1903, 21.
[58] *Lamp*, Feb. 1926.

heart of Francis of Assisi and of the Sacred Heart of the Divine Redeemer. He believed that his community was providentially chosen by God to serve as a means of reconciliation for many souls. "The Society of the Atonement," he wrote, "possesses as part of its organic self-consciousness that it has been especially raised up by God to asume a sacrificial and mediatorial position in relation to the burning question of the present day (Christian Unity). This Society has found a home for itself in the bosom of Peter and as far as its own members are concerned, the problem of Church Unity is happily solved, but for our brethren's sake, *the other sheep*, we cannot rest. The travail of the Good Shepherd is in our souls. . . ."[59]

In all his efforts for Christian Unity Father Paul repeated and developed a constant theme: devotion of the Mother of God. He was like the Poverello in love for Our Lady. The chapel where he came into the Church has the lovely Franciscan name of the Portiuncula: Our Lady of the Angels. Her glories he loved and preached for years before he came to the Fold of Peter. Once inside the Church that love of Our Lady grew to wonderful proportions. He loved Mary under every title and celebrated her feast days with joy and gratitude. But the title and devotion he loved above all else was that which he and Mother Lurana gave to the Mother of God as Anglicans, and were allowed to keep when they entered the One Fold. That was the name of Our Lady of the Atonement.[60]

It was no accident that Fr. Paul founded the Rosary League of Our Lady of the Atonement in 1901 and kept the feast of Our Lady this same year. He believed with all his soul that Mary would be the way by which vast throngs would return to the fold. More souls would come back to the Church through her love, he said, than were ever lost through the defection of Protestants in the sixteenth century and the split of the orthodox in the ninth and eleventh centuries.

He was fond of saying that Our Lady of the Atonement means At-one-ment or Unity. Mary is the model of Unity because of her own nearness to God. She is the Mother of the Church, of all the redeemed, of the elect of Jesus Christ. No one, said Fr. Paul, more than Mary could appreciate the words of the Apostle: "We joy in

---

[59] *Antidote*, March-April, 1930, p. 235.
[60] T. Cranny, *Graymoor's Name for Mary* (Graymoor Press: Peekskill, N.Y., 1955).

God through our Lord Jesus Christ by whom we have now received the Atonement" (Rom. 5:11 King James version).

And so the image of Our Lady with a red mantle, holding the Christ Child in her arms, has become the Graymoor Madonna in many parts of the world. July 9, is the feast of Our Lady of the Atonement, of the highest liturgical rank, and it is a memorial to the love of the Graymoor founders for the Mother of God as well as a legacy to their spiritual sons and daughters to continue the apostolic work which they began. Under the title of Atonement Our Lady is the patroness of the League of Prayer for Unity, with its 175,000 members of many races and peoples.[61]

Father Leopold of Castelnuovo

Another singular apostle of Christian Unity in our age is the holy Capuchin, Fr. Leopold of Castelnuovo whose cause of beatification was formally signed by the Holy Father on May 5, 1962. Croatian by birth, Fr. Leopold entered the Capuchin order with the idea of dedicating his life to bringing back to the unity of the Church the Orthodox Christians of his own country. His superiors, on account of his weak health and for other reasons, did not allow him to undertake this apostolate. So, he offered everything he did—and renewed that offering often—for that intention.[62]

Leopold was born in 1866 in Lower Croatia and was ordained in 1890. After sixteen years in various positions, he was sent to Padua in 1906 where he spent the next thirty-six years of his life. He longed to work for the return of his people, many of whom were orthodox, to the true faith. This idea was with him and struck him with compelling force even before he was ordained. It was the great ideal of his life, but obedience kept him in the confessional where he gave much comfort and strength to countless souls.

Fr. Leopold felt that God had given him a special mission: 'I make bold to say that I have been called by the grace of God to serve the Divine Shepherd by caring for the Oriental Dissidents. There-

---

[61] League approved by Holy See May 30, 1956.

[62] Material for this sketch of Fr. Leopold is based on pamphlet issued in conjunction with the introduction of his cause. For a fuller biography cf. Pietro da Valdiporro, *Un apostolo del confessionale, il servo di Dio P. Leopoldo da Castelnuovo*, Padua 1949.

fore ... before God, with an oath I bind myself actually with all diligence, as far as human frailty allows, to expand all the aspects of my life for the return of Oriental Dissidents to Catholic Unity." One year before he died, he wrote: "The whole reason of my life must be this divine task, that even I in my small way do something, so that at some time according to the ordering of Divine Wisdom disposing all things mightily and sweetly, the Dissident Orientals may return to Catholic Unity."

To fulfill this divine call the humble Capuchin made this vow: "With a vow I bind myself: As often as I offer the Holy Sacrifice of the Mass, unless I am prevented by justice or piety, all the fruit of the sacred sacrifice shall be for the return of the Oriental Dissidents to Catholic Unity. When, however, justice or piety demand otherwise of me, then having fulfilled justice and piety, all the fruit which shall remain over and above shall be for this same purpose. Thence all the other aspects of my life shall be in union with the same Holy Sacrifice for their return, as above, with all diligence, as far as my human frailty allows. I make the purpose of my life the return of the Oriental Dissidents to Catholic Unity that there may be one flock and one shepherd."

Though he was not able to engage in an active apostolate with these people so close to his heart, he offered himself to God as a victim for their return and by prayer, penance and sacrifice sought to win graces for them—the Greeks, Slavs, and other orthodox groups in Yugoslavia. "I write this before God," he declared, "by the grace which has been given me, I again renew my vows and give myself as a victim for the redemption of my brethren through the bloody sacrifice of Christ, which I can offer to God the Father daily at the holy altar."

Leopold was deeply devoted to St. Francis, to St. Josaphat, St. Ignatius Loyola, and to Our Lady. "I entrust to the motherly care of the Blessed Virgin the erring children of the East.... I believe this to be a dogma of the Catholic faith: that the Most Blessed Virgin Mary is another Eve as we believe that Our Lord is another Adam. For this reason I believe in the maternal providence in the Church of the Blessed Virgin Mary according to the mandate given by her dying son on the cross: Behold thy son, behold thy Mother. Just as the Divine Son always intercedes for us in heaven, so also does she intercede before the Father so that what began at the foot of the Cross may be fulfilled in heaven. The Most Holy Virgin is so turned with love and care towards the human race that she is a Victim because of her love for us. And since this love towards us is drawn from the beatific love of God, she with full happiness intercedes for the salvation of mankind, for just as we have an Advocate Jesus Christ with the Father, so we also have an advocate with the Son who with the Son and before the Son intercedes with the Father for the salvation of men."

There are many other statements of similar content, so many renewals of his love for Jesus and Mary as a victim for the return of the separated Eastern Christians. Already his cause for holiness has been introduced and should the Church raise him to public honor, he would be a grand example for all friars and all of the Catholic clergy by way of prayer and sacrifice to aid in the achievement of Christian Unity.

Capuchin apostolate in the East

The following is a brief summary of the work of the Capuchins among the Catholics of the Eastern rites and among the separated brethren whom they seek to win to the unity of the Church.[63]

In *Istanbul* (Constantinople) there are five priests and three brothers from the Paris province. They conduct a minor and major seminary in the country and have care of a small station. In Greece and Crete 8 Greek friars care for the spiritual needs of about 30,000 faithful of the Latin rite spread over 7 stations. The friars are from the Palermo province.

In Bulgaria (Sophia and Philoppopolis) there are friars from this province dependent upon the Brixen province. In December 1960 Fr. Simeon was consecrated the Vicar Apostolic of Sophia and Philoppopolis by a bishop of the Byzantine rite. *Asmaa* is an apostolic vicariate and provincial custody (called Eritrea) is maintained by the friars of the province of Milan. There are 40 Italian priests and 25 Ethiopian priests. The latter are of the Alexandrine-Ethiopic rite and work among Catholics of their own rites and also among the Orthodox Copts. The number of Ethiopian Capuchins increases year

---

[63] Much of the information regarding the Capuchin Apostolate was supplied by Fr. Hermes Krielkamp, O.F.M.Cap.

by year as their formation is guaranteed by a flouishing minor seminary and by a well-organized novitiate and houses of study.

In Addis Ababa, the Capuchins from Malta take care of the Church of the Holy Saviour, though the main work is to administer to the needs of the faithful of the Latin rite. There are five priests attached to the Church and they have opened another center just recently. They also provide services in the Coptic rite.

Trabzon or Trebisonda in Turkey is a mission *sui juris* staffed by 8 priests and 3 brothers of the Parma province. The Capuchin superior is the *ordinarius loci*. The main object of the mission is to keep alive the faith among the Catholics of Greek and Armenian origin and to increase their number.

Syria and Lebanon was erected as a custody in 1955 from the Lyons province. There are 18 priests, 6 brothers, and 4 clerics who staff 9 houses or centers from which the apostolate, primarily among those of the Latin rite is organized. Indirectly they influence those of the Armenian and Maronite rites.

India. In the archdiocese of Trivandrum, which is of the Syro-Malankara rite, four mission stations are entrusted to the Capuchins. These Capuchins are Indian members of the Provincial Commissariate. The main station was Plackode, but Mukhathala is now being organized as the main center; when on visitation early in 1962 Fr. General blessed the foundation stone for the building in this center. The Fathers—there are two of them, Frs. Cuthbert and Willibrord, work among the Catholics of the Syro-Malankara rite, but also among the Jacobite Christians, many of whom have, through the efforts of the Fathers, returned to the unity of the Church.

Also in *India* the parish of Brahmavar (dioc. of Mangalore) is entrusted to the Capuchins. This parish was founded in 1956 expressly to win over the schismatics living there to the unity of the Church. These schismatics are not of the Eastern rite now, whatever their forefathers may have been in the past; they are of Latin rite. The schism occurred when the Catholics of this place refused to accept the change in 1887 when Pope Leo XIII erected Mangalore as a diocese under the jurisdiction of S. Congr. de Prop. Fide; until then they had been under the Padroado. The three friars there are doing very fine work, and quite a number have returned to the true fold.

There are hopes, so some of the leading Catholics there say, of a mass conversion. The schismatics number some 5,000.

In the province of Holland six or seven Fathers of the Byzantine rite, originally organized many years ago for work among Orthodox christians, were forced by the war and its consequences to return to their own country. There, however, they still work among the immigrants of the rite in Holland and also in Germany. They publish a little magazine, now in its ninth year, called "Pokrof."

The Ethiopian College (Pontifical) in the Vatican City, where students, intended for the diocesan priesthood in the Alexandrine-ethiopic rite diocese, are prepared for higher studies in philosophy, theology and canon law, is under the direction of the Capuchins. The present Rector is from the Dutch Province; the Vice-Rector is an Ethiopian from the Eritrea Custody; and the spiritual director is from the Flandro-Belgian Province. This year there are some twenty students in the College. All religious functions, including grace at meals, are according to their own rite.

Friars Minor Conventual

The Conventual "Province of the Orient," formerly serving Greece, Syria and Turkey, has only three houses remaining: one in Istanbul; one in neighboring Büyükdere; and the third in Syria at Damascus. Because of the laws against proselytising, their activities are largely restricted to Latin Catholics.

Conventual friars belonging to the Byzantine rite continue their work, under increasingly difficult circumstances in Romania (est. 1929) and Bulgaria (est. 1939). In 1940 the Paduan province sent bi-ritual missionaries to Albania. Expelled in 1946, they serve the Albanian refugees in Southern Italy (Diocese of Lungro).[64]

Friars Minor

At present the Friars Minor has two independent custodies of the Oriental rite. One is situated in the United States: Our Lady of Perpetual Help Monastery, New Canaan, Conn.

---

[64] Giov. M. Bastianini, O.F.M.Conv., "Apostolato missionario," in *Rinascita Serafica: I frati min. conv. nell'ultimo cinquantennio* (Rome, 1951) pp. 164-165; 168.

The other unit is the newly founded Custody (1962) of the Holy Family in Egypt; it is of the Coptic rite. The latest statistics are as follows: priests—Latin 18, Coptic 12, Greek 1, Maronite 1, Armenia 1; clerics—Latin 1, Coptic 14; laybrothers—Latin 2, Coptic 4; novices (cleric)—Latin 1, Coptic 6. Thus there are in all 61. Up until this year the unit was a commissariat dependent on the Italian Franciscan Province of Tuscany. The future is very promising. Each of the houses has a school adjoining.

The Custody of the Holy Land, although the Friars are almost all of Latin rite, also has a few Friars of one or the other oriental rite.[65]

Third Order Regular and Friars of the Atonement

The Third Order Regular has a number of priests engaged in work with the Oriental rites in southern Europe; some of their priests enjoy bi-ritual facilities. The Friars of the Atonement have five priests with bi-ritual faculties, one of whom is pastor of a parish in Toledo, Ohio. They maintain an Eastern rite chapel at Graymoor, where the liturgy is occasionally offered for the faithful of Eastern rites who come on pilgrimage. They also publish the English edition of *Unitas,* a quarterly devoted to Christian Unity.

* * * * *

Such is the outline of work for Eastern Rites by the members of the Franciscan family. Though it is only an outline, it reveals the character of the apostolate at the present time. We sincerely believe that much more might and should be done in proportion to the numbers of the friars in various sections of the world. It would not be fair to make a comparison, but it seems that the sons and daughters of Francis should be particularly interested and spiritually talented for this modern apostolate of Christian Unity.

It is of interest that the Poor Clares have opened a new monastery in Lebanon, Our Lady of the Unity. By prayer and sacrifice they seek to draw down God's blessings upon a divided and suffering Christendom. The foundress of the Sisters of the Atonement at Graymoor, Mother Lurana Mary Francis, S.A. (1870-1935) was intensely interested in Christian Unity and communicated this interest to her Sisters.

---

[65] General Curia, Friars Minor,

Much might be done on every level, with the friars in their apostolate, with the sisters in the academies and colleges that they conduct. The Third Order is, I think, an untapped mine of apostolic fervor and Christian renewal for the spiritual regeneration of millions of souls. In a way it seems that Francis speaks to us today, of Christian Unity, with the words that come from his dying lips: "Until now, my brethren, we have done so little—now let us begin."

Conclusion

And so we stand on the threshold of a new era in the Church and in the world. The future is fraught with hope and bright with promise; its fulfillment in some measure depends upon us. The legacy of Francis to his "knights of the roundtable" devolves upon us. The Order of the Poverello has always been noted for its allegiance to the Church and its devotedness to the Pope. In the words of the Most Rev. Augustine Sepinski, O.F.M.: "The work of our apostles who often poured out their blood in fidelity to the one fold of Christ, appears as a conspicuous and proper note of our Franciscan life so that quite aptly a certain writer on matters of our Order began his history of the missions of the friars in this manner: 'I now embark upon a veritable ocean, the tract concerning the glorious and holy labor of the Friars Minor throughout the world, the sufferings and deaths which they bore unto the glory of the Church, for the defence and propagation of the Catholic Church!'"[66]

The voice that summons us to prayer, sacrifice, and action today is that of the Vicar of Christ, Pope John. With words spoken in the accents of the Good Shepherd and from a heart filled with compassion His Holiness openly cherishes the hope that "those who have withdrawn themselves from this Apostolic See may, as we confidently hope, accept the invitation to seek and to acquire that unity for which Jesus Christ prayed so intensely to His heavenly Father."[67]

Then his hope becomes a fatherly invitation. "May we," he asks, "in fond anticipation, address you as sons and brethren? May we hope with a father's love for your return? ... Note, We pray, that when We call you fondly to the unity of the Church, We are not inviting you to a strange house, but to your own, to the abode of your

---

[66] Encyclical letter, December 8, 1959.
[67] Data obtained from General Curia Friars Minor.

forefathers. I am Joseph, your brother. Come, make room for us! We desire nothing else, We pray God for nothing other than your salvation and your eternal happiness. Come! This long desired unity, fostered and fed by brotherly love, will beget great peace."[68]

Although the coming council is not called primarily for Unity, it will have a profound effect upon it. The desire for Unity is the breath of the Holy Father's soul. He seeks it, longs for it, and makes it the very purpose of his pontificate. "We wish humbly, but earnestly," he tells us, "to pursue our duty, moved by the word and example which Jesus Christ, the divine Good Shepherd, has given us in the figure of the field white for the harvest, looking to the extensive missions. And they must be brought to me that there may be one fold and one shepherd."[69]

Finally then, for direction, inspiration, and motivation in our apostolate of Christian Unity we turn to our Seraphic Father. He leads us to Jesus; he shows us the way to Our Lady; he is bound inseparably to the Church and the pope. He is our leader—the *dux minorum;* he is our father—the *pater gregum;* he is our model— the *speculum Christi.* In him lives the authentic mission and voice of the Good Shepherd. To him we turn in our desire to exalt the Church and bring men to eternal life. To paraphrase the words of a great friar of our times we can say:

> For Francis, to know is to love and to love is to do. And so he loves the starry sky, "for it is the throne of God"; he loves the earth "for it is His footstool"; he loves Jerusalem, the Holy Roman Catholic Church, "for it is the city of the great King," and he clings to the King, be He in swaddling clothes or in the sacred host, on the cross, or in a leper's garb. To him it is all perfect order, "sweetness of body and soul" and harmony divine. And thus with the simplicity of a child, with the directness and ardour unsurpassed, with a submission that is at once tender, docile, and literal, St. Francis stands before this age as a living proof of the divinity of our faith, of Mother Church— "a glorious church, not having spot or wrinkle or any such thing."[70]

---

[68] *AAS.* June 29, 1959. vol. 54
[69] *AAS.*
[70] Thomas Plassman, Intr. to the Franciscans—Fr. James, O.F.M.Cap.

And the Little Poor Man whom the whole world honors, stands before us today as the apostle and model of Christian Unity, pointing the way for us as members of the Church, and at the same time longing to aid those whose faltering steps and restless hearts are seeking for the peace and love of Christ in the one fold, governed by the Vicar of His love. May Francis live in us that in this age we may be heralds of the great King, passionately imbued with the apostolate of Christian Unity. And may the sweet and gentle Virgin, Our Lady of the Atonement and Mother of Unity, employ us as emissaries of her Son in this great and glorious enterprise: "That all may be one."

THE ECUMENICAL MOVEMENT: A General Conspectus

ROGER MATZERATH, S.A.

The amount of material on the ecumenical movement over the course of the last fifty years is monumental. In treating of the subject, one meets a serious problem not only of adequate coverage, but also of selection. In order to give the best representation, then, within the limits of time and space, neither scanning too thinly nor concentrating too heavily on a single item, it has been thought wise to divide the presentation, after a short introduction and definition of the subject, into two general parts: first, a brief history of the ecumenical movement which will show the character of the main components of the movement, and, secondly, an examination of the heart of the ecumenical movement, namely, its theology of the church with special emphasis on the doctrine of unity.

Introduction and Definition

Among all the activities with which are separated Christian brethren are deeply involved, few have been so singularly praised by the Holy See as the ecumenical movement. Apart from recognition of its existence as a significant fact in religious history, the Instruction of the Holy Office of 1950 extols the movement in unprecedented terms.[1]

The document speaks about "this excellent work of 'reunion' of all Christians" which has arisen "under the inspiring grace of God." Such a divinely inspired desire "that a reunion be accomplished among all who believe in Christ the Lord" is "a source of holy joy

---

[1] *Instructio. Ad Locorum Ordinarios*: "De motione oecumenica." The Instruction is dated, 20th December, 1949, and printed in the *Acta Apostolica Sedis*, 42 (1950), p. 142-147. The date of the issue of the *AAS* is 31 January, 1950, and therefore either 1949 or 1950 may be used to date the Instruction. Translations in English were printed by the Chair of Unity Octave, n.d. (Graymoor, Garrison, N.Y.) and by the *Tablet* (London) on March 4th, 1950.

in the Lord." It is also an inducement to the children of the true Church to assist their brethren especially by entreating light and strength for them from God in fervent prayer.

The work of 'reunion,' however, "belongs above all to the office and charge of the Church." Catholic bishops, therefore, are to bestow upon it their special attention. They are not only to keep it under observation, but also to foster and guide it prudently, and for this purpose the bishops are to appoint suitable priests who shall give close attention to all that concerns the movement. A whole series of safeguards and rules are set forth to regulate discussions with dissident Christians but the direction of the Holy Office is clear that the ecumenical movement is to be made an object of concern by the "whole Catholic people." The document ends by repeating the request for prayers and urges that all Catholics help those who are outside the Fold by their own good moral conduct and edifying life.[2]

The Instruction of the Holy Office has been followed up by the establishment of the Secretariat for the Promoting of Christian Unity—which many people think will become a permanent Roman office—the sending of official Catholic observers to various ecumenical meetings,[3] and the calling of the Second Vatican Ecumenical

---

[2] The pertinent parts of the text are the following:

Iam vero in pluribus orbis partibus, quum ex variis externis eventibus et animorum mutationibus, tum maxime ex communibus fidelium orationibus, afflante quidem Spiritus Sancti gratia, in multorum animis ab Ecclesia Catholica dissidentium desiderium in dies excrevit ut ad unitatem omnium redeatur, qui in Christum Dominum credunt. Quod profecto filiis Ecclesiae verae est causa sanctae in Domino laetitiae simulque invitamentum ad praestandum omnibus sincere veritatem quaerentibus auxilium, ipsis lucem et fortitudinem effusa prece a Deo solicitando. *ibid.*, p. 142.

Quum praefata "reunio" ad Ecclesiae munus et officium potissimum pertineat, speciali cura Episcopos,...eidem attendere oportet. Ipsi igitur non solum diligenter et efficaciter universae huic actioni invigilare debent, verum etiam prudenter eam promovere et dirigere,...*ibid.*, p. 142.

Quo autem tam praeclarum opus "reunionis" omnium christianorum in una vera fide Ecclesiaque magis in dies evadat insignita pars universae animarum curae, totusque populus catholicus ipsam "reunionem" instantius a Deo imploret,...*ibid.*, p. 146.

[3] Notably the five Catholic priests sent as official observers to the Third Assembly of the World Council of Churches held in New Delhi, India, November 18th to December 5th, 1961.

Council. A number of commentators have pointed out that the Council does not have the religious unity of the Christian world as its immediate aim, but there is no doubt that Pope John XXIII had Christian unity in mind when he announced the Council to the world.[4]

What is this council movement which has made such a dramatic stir in the world? The word "ecumenical"[5] is used so often and in so many contexts that some Protestants have been led to call enthusiasts of the movement "ecumaniacs."[6] Needless to say, some Catholics are also wary and full of warnings about the movement.[7] Nevertheless, a knowledge of the nature, history, and theology of the movement is in line with the thinking of the Holy See; a knowledge,

---

[4] Cf. "Pope John XXIII has frequently made it clear that the impending Council must be an invitation to separated Christians to seek Church unity. He has said that the Council must bring about a strengthening of faith and a renewal of Christian life so that our separated brothers may recognize the Church as their Father's House." Lorenz Jaeger, *The Ecumenical Council, the Church and Christendom*, (London: Geoffrey Chapman, 1961), p. 61.

[5] Dr. Willem Adolf Visser 't Hooft has a study on the history and use of the word, "ecumenical" in *A History of the Ecumenical Movement*, edited by Ruth Rouse and Stephen Charles Neill (Philadelphia: Westminster Press, 1954), p. 735-740. He distinguishes seven meanings of the word:
   a) pertaining to or representing the whole (inhabited) earth;
   b) pertaining to or representing the whole of the (Roman) Empire;
   c) pertaining to or representing the whole of the Church;
   d) that which has universal ecclesiastical validity;
   e) pertaining to the world-wide missionary outreach of the Church;
   f) pertaining to the relations between and unity of two or more Churches (or of Christians of various confessions);
   g) that quality or attitude which expresses the consciousness of and desire for Christian unity (p. 735).

[6] Cf. Gerald Kennedy, "The Church and Unity," *The Christian Century*, Vol. 78, No. 6 (Feb. 8, 1961), p. 170.

[7] Cf. the advice given Fr. Bernard Leeming, S.J., before the writing of his book: "You will do no good. The Catholic faithful have no need to know about the opinions of non-Catholics: let them say their prayers and lead a holy life. This is their best contribution towards Christian unity. Nor will you do any good with non-Catholics. . . . Better leave the whole matter alone." *The Churches and the Church* (Westminster, Md.: Newman Press, 1960), p. viii.

moreover, made necessary by the importance of the movement as one of the foremost influences of our age.

The ecumenical movement may be broadly and simply defined as the efforts to unite all Christians in one Church. A more precise definition is not easy to give. Nor is it wise. The ecumenical movement, as a current human activity, implies change, fluidity, growth. What is true of it at one time may not be so at another.[8] Moreover, authors stress different aspects as they view the movement from the *terminus a quo* or the *terminus ad quem*.[9] Nevertheles, the brief definition given does indicate the essential notes of the movement: world endeavor; Christendom; ecclesiological unity.

Some would inject into the definition, as an essential part, the mission of the church. Dr. Visser't Hooft, for example, says that the widely accepted use of the term today is: "that which concerns the unity and the world-wide mission of the Church of Jesus Christ."[10]

No one can deny that an essential *function* of the church is its mission to the world, but is it an essential note of its nature or being? Norman Goodall, an English Congregationalist, in his book on *The Ecumenical Movement,* says that the original source of the ecumenical movement lies in the Christian Faith itself; "... that spiritual power which draws men together in Christ and then sends them out of his name to claim the whole *oikoumene* for him."[11] We concede that the drawing together may be similar to the sending out but we deny that it is an equal process. A change takes place in the act of union in Christ which makes the mission afterwards a consequence and not a constituitive part of unifying action. What men are drawn to is a fully constituted church which gives them the mission to preach in Christ's name. For this reason we prefer not

---

[8] Cf. the address of Dr. Y. T. Brilioth at the Lund Conference of 1952: "Looking back, I seem to discern several stages in the history of our movement. The first stage ... was characterized by a certain minimizing of the differences....During the second stage the real depth of our differences became gradually more and more apparent." Quoted by Fr. Bernard Leeming, S.J., *op. cit.,* p. 63.

[9] Cf. the various definitions given according to different viewpoints in *Catholic Ecumenism,* Edward Hanahoe, S.A. (Washington, D.C.: Catholic University dissertation, 1953), p. 46.

[10] *History of the Ecumenical Movement,* p. 735.

[11] (London: Oxford University Press, 1961), p. 4.

to include the element of mission in the definition of the ecumenical movement. Nevertheless, whether the finding of ecclesiastical unity or the manifesting of this unity is stressed, the ecumenical movement clearly deals with the unity of Christendom.[12] As a working definition, therefore, the one given is, even under various aspects, suitable for present purposes.

I. History

In order to see the ecumenical movement in proper perspective, it is necessary to review briefly the history of the movement. Before proceeding to this task, however, two clarifications are in order.

The ecumenical movement is the effort to unite all Christians in one church. In this sense it is entirely possible to include the Catholic Church as a participant in the ecumenical movement. In fact, as the Instruction of 1950 already quoted affirms with precision, "The work of 'reunion' belongs above all to the office and charge of the Church."[13]

It must be admitted, of course, that the Church views 'reunion' as the inclusion of all men within its own one fold. Such a concept does not as yet find acceptance with Protestants and Orthodox ecumenists. Yet, on the basis of a search for unity, the claim and effort of the Catholic Church is wholly within the purpose and goal of the ecumenical movement.

Moreover, even from a standpoint of ecumenical conversation, the Catholic Church has a place in the ecumenical movement. It is sometimes thought that the office of the Church is to teach and the duty of all those outside the Church is to listen and to accept. As much as this view may appeal to some who view separated Christians strictly as *non*-Catholics, it does not seem to be the viewpoint of the Holy See. As Fr. Gregory Baum, O.S.A. says in his study of the papal documents, *That They May Be One,*

---

[12] Cf. Prof. Henri D'Espine, "...the restoration of Christian unity remains one of the essential objectives, perhaps the essential objective, of the ecumenical movement." *Report of the Central Committee, St. Andrews, Scotland* (Geneva: W.C.C., n.d.), p. 112.

At the bottom the question involves the nature of unity and the nature of the church. As many definitions, therefore, may be formulated as there are views of unity and church.

[13] *AAS*, 42 (1950), p. 143.

We believe, however, that in spite of the unique claims of
the Catholic Church, the view of Christian unity presented in
the papal documents renders a dialogue not only possible, but
necessary. In the writings of the modern popes, dissident
Christianity is never considered as a mission field where the
task of the Church is simply to preach. . . . While the popes
decry anything that looks like dogmatic compromise or even
tends to make Catholic truth appear relative, they do not want
to discourage that contact with dissident thought which is
essential for shaping the Catholic ecumenical witness.[14]

The Catholic Church has a place in the ecumenical movement, and,
from the point of view of the Instruction of 1950, a place by right.
Nevertheless, as a modern historical event, the ecumenical movement
is a product mainly of Protestant and partly of Orthodox effort. It is
as such that we must deal with it in this study.

The second clarification that should be made at this point is that
the ecumenical movement is indeed a movement and not to be confined to any single organization. Many individuals, groups, bodies,
churches, and organizations may contribute to it. None of these can
speak exclusively for the movement.

On the other hand, throughout its history certain individuals and
particular organizations have been outstanding for their contribution
to the formation and progress of the ecumenical movement. Today,
the best representative, the clearest voice, and the guiding inspiration of the movement is the World Council of Churches. It is on this
organization, therefore, that attention must be centered to learn
more about the ecumenical movement. Three elements may be distinguished in the Council's historical development.

a. Missionary Efforts

The beginnings of both the ecumenical movement and the World
Council of Churches lie properly with the activities of missionaries
and mission movements.[15] This should not be surprising. Missionaries laboring in foreign mission fields were the first to feel the
effects of Christian disunity. The duplication of efforts, the rivalry
of churches, the lack of impact on native peoples because of denomina-

---

[14] *Op. cit.*, (Westminster, Md.: Newman Press, 1958), p. viii.
[15] Cf. *History of the Ecumenical Movement*, p. 353 ff.

tionalism, all led missionaries and mission churches to enter into discussions and agreements with each other. Ecumenical considerations were not their prime aim. But joint planning across denominational lines on matters of education, famine relief, and Bible translation; common agreements over territory assignments; and successful mission conferences naturally led many missionaries to become more and more eager for Christian union and less and less happy over Christian disunity.

Three streams gradually swelled the tide of missionary cooperation from the middle of the nineteenth century onwards. Field conferences arising out of mutual problems on the missions have already been mentioned. Often these began on the local level and then grew into national and regional meetings. Such conferences were held, for example, in China, Japan, Africa, and India.

Student movements also helped to lay the groundwork for later ecumenical action by building up interest and undertaking activities for the missions. Among the leading organizations in this area were the Y.M.C.A., the Y.W.C.A., and the World Student Christian Federation. By their united efforts they paved the way for an understanding of Christian effort across denominational boundaries. As one author expresses it, "... the Student Christian Movement has helped generations of students, of every nationality, to understand and experience a quality of Christian discipleship which has given them a profound awareness of an *oikoumene* in Christ."[16]

A third source of ecumenical foundations based on missionary work were the conferences held "at home" in the countries sending forth missionaries. Problems on the mission fields were reflected in the concern of mission societies and mission boards who financed, staffed, and directed mission activities. Here again mutual discussion, planning, and agreements slowly paved the way for ecumenical considerations. Particularly was this true of the six Anglo-American Conferences held between 1854 and 1900 on mission problems.

The last of these international conferences, convened in New York in 1900, led almost naturally and easily into what is now marked by all historians as the modern beginning of the ecumenical movement, the World Missionary Conference, held in Edinburgh, Scotland from June 14 to 23, 1910.

---

[16] *Op. cit.*, p. 8.

Under the dynamic chairmanship of John R. Mott, an American Methodist layman, and with the able assistance of J. H. Oldham as general secretary, 1200 official delegates from 159 missionary societies gathered for the significant meeting. Most of the delegates were from English speaking countries but 170 came from 41 continental missionary societies and 17 delegates came from India, Burma, China, Japan, and Korea—although the Far Eastern participants represented Western missionary societies.

Preparatory work for the Missionary Conference was intense. Commissions diligently drew up material on eight basic topics which formed the core of the actual conference deliberations. The delegates were themselves surprised and delighted at the cooperation and helpfulness exhibited by all, and strongly felt that what had been begun so well should not be allowed to cease with the end of the meeting. A motion for a continuation committee was carried unanimously.

The World Missionary Conference of 1910 had far reaching consequences:

1. It called together on an unprecedented scale from all over the world missionary representatives who met, discussed, and agreed upon many phases of missionary cooperation.

2. It generated a desire, based on the favorable experiences of the Conference, for continued international and interdenominational Christian cooperation and in this way set the scene for subsequent ecumenical conferences.

---

[17] 1. Carrying the Gospel to the world
    2. The Native Church and its Workers
    3. Education in Relation to the Christianization of National Life
    4. The Missionary Message in Relation to Non-Christian Religions
    5. The Preparation of Missionaries
    6. The Home Base of Missions
    7. Relation of Missions to Governments
    8. Co-operation and Promotion of Unity
Cf. Willian Richey Hogg, *Ecumenical Foundations* (New York: Harper, 1951), p. 108.

[18] The International Missionary Council was officially begun in 1921 at a meeting held at Lake Mohonk, New York. Since that time meetings of the Council have been held at Jerusalem in 1928; Tambaram, India, in 1938; Whitby, Ontario, in 1947; Willingen, Germany, in 1952; and Ghana, Africa, in 1957-1958. In November, 1961, the International Missionary Council merged with the World Council of Churches at the Third Assembly of the W.C.C. held in New Delhi, India.

3. It brought the so-called younger churches into the community of older churches and prepared men from both groups for international leadership.

4. It stimulated the kind of theological reflection as well as practical enthusiasm which resulted in organizations directly responsible for the ecumenical movement and the World Council of Churches.

5. The continuation committee resulted, after World War I, in the International Missionary Council.

b. *Faith and Order*

Bishop Charles H. Brent, an American Protestant Episcopalian who attended the World Missionary Conference in his capacity at that time as Bishop of the Philippine Islands, was very enthusiastic about the spirit of his fellow missionaries at Edinburgh. In October, 1910, Bishop Brent communicated this enthusiasm to a large group of American Protestant Episcopalians. He spoke, on the day before the General Convention of the Episcopal Church convened at Cincinnati, to a mass meeting of both Houses of the Convention, delegates of the Women's Auxiliary, and many visitors. The Bishop declared his conviction that the time had come to discuss denominational differences frankly at a world conference on questions of doctrine ministry, sacraments, and church government.[19] His listeners agreed with him and therefore the General Convention officially approved a resolution:

> That a Joint Commission be appointed to bring about a Conference for the consideration of questions touching Faith and Order, and that all Christian Communions throughout the world which confess Our Lord Jesus Christ as God and Saviour be asked to unite with us in arranging for and conducting such a Conference.[20]

A joint commission, consisting of seven bishops, seven presbyters, and seven laymen, was duly appointed and they began their arduous

---

[19] Questions of doctrine are grouped under the heading of "Faith," and matters of the ministry, sacraments, government, and structure of the church are called by the designation, "Order."

[20] *Documents on Christian Unity*, edited by G. K. A. Bell (A selection from the first and second series, 1920-1930, London: Oxford University Press, 1955), p. 12.

task of bringing about the world conference on Faith and Order. World War I held up negotiations, but in August, 1920, a preliminary meeting attended by delegates from 40 nations and representing 70 churches was held in Geneva, Switzerland. Finally, the first World Conference on Faith and Order met in Lausanne, Switzerland, from August 3 to 21, 1927.

The agenda called for consideration of seven topics on the nature of the church, its message to the world, unity, faith, ministry, and the sacrments. The delegates, numbering 400 from 108 churches, heard representatives from seven or eight denominations expound on each subject of the agenda, after which they discussed the matter both together and in separate sections and finally voted on a final draft to be submitted to the churches. Six reports were accepted without difficulty, but because of some difference of opinion on "The Unity of Christendom and the Place of the Different Churches In It," the last report was referred to a Continuation Committee.[22]

Like the World Missionary Conference in 1910, the first Faith and Order Conference was also a landmark in ecumenical history. It broke the ground for churchmen of the most diverse denominations to meet in conference and discuss doctrine. "Younger men in the middle of the 20th century," comments the *History of the Ecumenical Movement*, "can hardly have any idea of how difficult, even impossible, it was, even a generation earlier, to get their fathers to meet at all, or of what mountains of prejudice, suspicion, and hesitation had to be overcome before the first World Conference became feasible."[23] Not only did the delegates to the Lausanne Conference meet and discuss doctrine, but they paved the way to further ecumenical

---

[21] The seven topics were:
1. The call to unity
2. The Church's message to the world: the Gospel
3. The nature of the Church
4. The Church's common confession of faith
5. The Church's ministry
6. The Sacraments
7. The Unity of Christendom and the relation thereto of existing Churches.

Cf. *Faith and Order* (Proceedings of the World Conference), edited by H. N. Bate (London: Student Christian Movement, 1927).

[22] Cf. *History of the Ecumenical Movement,* p. 425.

[23] p. 438.

conversations in which prejudices were broken, disagreements as well as agreements discovered, and attention focused on key matters pertaining to the church, its nature, its work, and above all, its unity.

Secondly, the Faith and Order Conference brought forward with incisive clarity the conviction that division was wrong and that unity was absolutely necessary in the light of the will of Christ.

Some insight was also gained into the reasons for disunity. It was seen that non-theological factors—social, economic, racial—were, in some cases, behind the divisions that had taken place in the course of time.

The realization was in addition somewhat curiously forced upon church leaders that divisions in belief do not necessarily coincide with divisions into denominations. "This fluidity," observes one author, "might betoken the dawn of the much wider unity or of a different pattern of schism."[24]

Finally, the World Conference on Faith and Order through its work, its inspiration, and its subsequent meetings—especially those at Edinburgh in 1937 and at Lund, Sweden, in 1952—has become one of the pillars of the ecumenical movement.

c. *Life and Work*

While the negotiations for the first World Conference of Faith and Order were proceeding, another movement, somewhat different in character, was in progress of formation and actually resulted in a world conference before that of Faith and Order.

This movement, ecumenical in nature but with a different slanting than all previous activities, had its immediate beginnings rooted in four sources. The first was the strong sense of responsibility in various Christian churches for world peace, especially before and after World War I, and a dedicated concern for social justice. Such sentiments naturally led church leaders to get Christians everywhere to unite in the cause of peace and justice.

---

[24] *History of the Ecumenical Movement*, p. 441.

[25] Cf. the official reports:

Second World Conference on Faith and Order, Edinburgh 1937, edited by L. Hodgson (London: Student Christian Movement, 1937).

The Third World Conference on Faith and Order, Lund 1952, edited by O. S. Tomkins (London: Student Christian Movement, 1953).

Another reason, and indeed the primary motive behind all activities of the movement, was the conviction that the Gospel must be applied to all realms of human life, and especially to industrial, social, political, and international problems. The implications of the Gospel, across interdenominational lines and on an international scale, for daily life and the work of man gave rise to the name, "Life and Work" which became the official title of the movement.[26]

The movement had its third source in various international meetings carried on from the beginning of the twentieth century and in particular those conferences held from 1917 onward that had as their focal point the application of the Gospel to problems facing the world. Notable among these were the Neutral Church Conference at Uppsala, Sweden in 1817, the Meeting of the International Committee of the World Alliance for Promoting International Friendship Through the Churches held in 1919 at Oud Wessenaar (near the Hague), the Conference on Christian Politics, Economics, and Citizenship in 1924 at Birmingham, England, and the two preparatory conferences before the first world conference of Life and Work, held in Geneva in 1920 and in Halsingborg, Sweden, in 1922.[27]

The fourth, and in some ways the indispensable, source for the Life and Work movement was Nathan Soderblom, Lutheran Archbishop of Uppsala and Primate of Sweden. It was due to his indefatigable labors, deeply Christian zeal, and exceptional organizational abilities that the Life and Work movement came into being.

The first meeting of the Universal Christian Conference on Life and Work met at Stockholm from August 19 to 30, 1925. Six hundred delegates from 37 countries gathered to discuss the program agenda adopted previously at the Halsingborg meeting. Two outstanding

---

[26] *History of the Ecumenical Movement* says that the term dates historically from a Geneva conference held in 1920, p. 539.

[27] *History of the Ecumenical Movement*, p. 509 ff.

[28] 1. The Church's Obligation in view of God's Purpose for the World
   2. The Church and Economical and Industrial Problems
   3. The Church and Social and Moral Problems
   4. The Church and International Relations
   5. The Church and Christian Education
      Communions.

Cf. *Documents on Christian Unity 1920-1924*, edited by G. K. A. Bell (London: Oxford University Press, 1924), p. 377.

characteristics marked the conference: a concentration on Christian ethics as it applied to social, economic, industrial, and political questions, and a corresponding by-passing of doctrinal matters. The thought of the leaders seemed to be that the conference would get bogged down if the delegates brought in their various denominational beliefs. "Doctrine divides, but service unites" was the guiding consideration.[29] Despite differences of belief and practice among the Christian churches (which would not and could not be settled in the near future at least), Life and Work leaders felt that they could proceed on a united basis in the region of moral and social problems.

The first Life and Work Conference, as the first World Missionary Conference of 1910 and the first World Faith and Order Conference, had far reaching significance for the ecumenical movement.

It was, in the first place, a meeting on an international scale of representatives of various denominations including delegates from some Orthodox churches. This was no small accomplishment after the War. "Even in 1925," comments the *History of the Ecumenical Movement*, "all wise people thought it impossible that such a conference could be held."[30]

The Life and Work Conference, moreover, made a distinctive contribution by uniting Christians on an international and inter-denominational scale in the application of Christian principles to moral, social, and political questions of the day. As the message of the Conference stated, the delegates did not attempt to offer precise solutions to problems, but they did appeal to all Christians to accept full responsibility for bringing about God's kingdom on earth. The Conference also invited each Christian, "in entire loyalty to his own Church ... to have a share in that wider fellowship and co-operation of the Christian Churches of which this Conference is a promise and pledge."[31]

Finally, the Continuation Committee of the Conference, which in 1930 was reconstituted as a permanent body under the title of "The

---

[29] The statement is attributed to Dr. Kapler in a letter from Nathan Soderblom and Henry A. Atkinson to Mr. Gardiner. Adopted at Halsingborg, 1922. Cf. *Documents on Christian Unity 1920-1924*, ibid., p. 378.

[30] *Ibid.*, p. 549.

[31] *Documents on Christian Unity 1920-1930*, pp. 269, 270.

Universal Council for Life and Work," assured the contribution of
Life and Work to the ecumenical movement on a fixed basis.

d. *World Council of Churches*

In July, 1937 Life and Work held a second conference, this time
at Oxford, England.[32] One month later a second world meeting of
Faith and Order met in Edinburgh, Scotland. The time schedule of
the two conferences was not accidental. For some time leaders in
both movements had recognized the affinity existing between them.
Particularly was this true of Life and Work. Although by design
Life and Work did not wish to deal with theology, even at the Stockholm 1925 meeting some delegates insisted that practical action without a theological basis is futile. As time went on this truth became
more and more evident. The answer was plain: Life and Work simply
had to join with Faith and Order.

At their respective meetings in 1937 both Life and Work and Faith
and Order, therefore, took action to put into effect a plan by which
the two movements would be integrated into a single new body to be
called a "World Council of Churches."

Various committees, especially the Provisional Committee, were
formed and various conferences, particularly the Utrecht Conference,
took place. Proceedings were made difficult by the disruption
brought about through the Second World War. Finally, however,
on August 23, 1948 at Amsterdam in the presence of 351 official
delegates representing 147 churches and 44 countries, the chairman
of the session, Archbishop Geoffrey Fisher, announced that the resolution on the formation of the World Council of Churches had been
unanimously adopted. The World Council was a reality.[34]

On August 30th the first Assembly of the World Council adopted

---

[32] The official reports of the world conferences on Life and Work are:
The Stockholm Conference 1925, edited by G. K. A. Bell (London:
Oxford University Press, 1926).
The Churches Survey Their Task (London: Geo. Allen & Unwin,
1937).

[33] As of 1962, the number of member churches is 201.

[34] So far three assemblies of the World Council have been convened:
at Amsterdam, 1948; at Evanston, Illinois, 1954; and at New Delhi,
India, 1961.

its constitution. Among the various stipulations, the two that are of concern to this study of the ecumenical movement are the basis and functions of the World Council.

The constitution of 1948 clearly states at the very beginning that: "The World Council of Churches is a fellowship of Churches which accepts our Lord Jesus Christ as God and Saviour."[35] This basis is not intended to be a statement of creed but rather an orientation and starting point for the work which the World Council undertakes. It is also, obviously, a fundamental criterion which must be met by any church which wishes to join the Council.[36]

The functions of the World Council are, according to its constitution:

1. To carry on the work of the two world movements for Faith and Order and for Life and Work.

2. To facilitate common action by the churches.

3. To promote co-operation in study.

4. To promote the growth of ecumenical consciousness in the members of all churches.

5. To establish relations with denominational federations of world-wide scope and with other ecumenical movements.

6. To call world conferences on specific subjects as occasion may require.

7. To support the churches in their task of evangelism.[37]

---

[35] Cf. the official report on *The First Assembly of the World Council of Churches*, edited by W. A. Visser 't Hooft (New York: Harper, 1949), p. 197.

[36] Cf. "Statement on the Purposes and Function of the Basis" (adopted by the Second Assembly of the World Council of Churches), *The Evanston Report* edited by W. A. Visser 't Hooft (New York: Harper, 1955), p. 306.

The Third Assembly of the World Council in 1961 adopted the following revision of the Basis:

"The World Council of Churches is a fellowship of churches which confess the Lord Jesus Christ as God and Saviour according to the Scriptures and therefore seek to fulfill together their common calling to the glory of the one God, Father, Son, and Holy Spirit."

[37] Official Report on the First Assembly, p. 197, 198.

Cf.: A Report on Programme and Finance from the Central Committee to the Third Assembly contains this general summary of the task of the W.C.C.: "The task of the W.C.C. is to serve the churches in the fulfill-

These functions speak for themselves; they are an indication both of the nature and of the work of the World Council. We may, however, express them in a synopsized form as the functions of the component parts of the World Council, namely of Faith and Order with its emphasis on unity, of Life and Work with its work of service, and, since 1961 when the International Missionary Council was integrated into the World Council at the Third Assembly, of witness to the world through missionary activity and evangelism.[38]

Many more facets of the World Council might be commented upon. What has been given above is simply a brief sketch. Nothing more was intended. It is hoped, however, that the main thrusts of the ecumenical movement have been indicated. They have been placed in the background setting of history to give a better understanding of the depth and complexities of the movement. It remains now to put this picture in still further perspective by an examination of the theology, or more properly, ecclesiology, of the World Council of Churches (W.C.C.), with special attention to its thought on unity.

II. Theology of the World Council of Churches

Such a mountain of written material has been accumulated over the past half-century of the ecumenical movement that it is not an easy task to find a suitable starting point to a study of W.C.C. theology. A solid beginning may be made, however, with the statement received by the Central Committee of the World Council of Churches at Toronto in 1950 on "The Church, the Churches and the World Council of Churches" or, as the sub-title described the report, "The Ecclesiological Significance of the World Council of Churches."[39] This

---

ment of their common God-given calling in the whole world." The report goes on to explain that the W.C.C. exists to serve the churches; it does not legislate for them. The W.C.C. performs tasks which belong to the churches speaking together; it helps the churches see their task as part "of the task of the Church in the whole world, that is to bring the Gospel to all men and healing to all nations." *Evanston to New Delhi* (Geneva: World Council of Churches, 1961), p. 218.

[38] Cf. "The three themes of Unity, Witness, and Service are in the last resort not three, but one." *New Delhi Speaks*, edited by W. A. Visser 't Hooft (New York: Association Press, 1962), p. 28.

[39] The text is printed in the *Ecumenical Review*, vol. III, no. 1, (October, 1950), p. 47-53.

document has not received any official sanction, such as the constitution of the Council has, but it has been so widely praised and referred to that it is in fact, as Professor Henri D'Espine declared at the 1960 meeting of the Central Committee, considered "... to be its (W.C.C.) ecclesiological charter."[40]

The Toronto Statement begins with an introduction setting forth the reason why a declaration is necessary and explaining the limitations within which the statement must be couched. "The World Council," it affirms "represents a new and unprecedented approach of the problem of inter-Church relationships." (II) The nature and purpose of the Council can, therefore, be easily misunderstood and this difficulty necessitates a specifying of its role both in regard to its member churches and "to the Church." The problem, however, is to formulate the ecclesiological implications of the W.C.C. "in which so many different conceptions of the Church are represented, without using the categories or language of one particular conception of the Church." (II) The Central Committee attempts to solve this problem by clarifying first what the World Council is not and then by stating positively the theological assumptions underlying the W.C.C.

"The World Council of Churches is not and must never become a Super-Church." (III, I) This initial declaration of the Toronto Statement attempts to combat what has been a persistent misunderstanding about the W.C.C. The Council is not a super-church; it is not the world church; it is not the *Una Sancta.* Each member church retains the constitutional right to accept or reject declarations or actions of the Council. The only authority that the Council wields is, in the words of William Temple quoted by the Statement, the weight it carries "by its own wisdom."[41]

Some comments are offered by Fr. Bernard Leeeming, S.J., in *The Churches and the Church,* p. 179 ff.

[40] *Minutes and Reports of the Thirteenth Meeting of the Central Committee,* St. Andrews, Scotland, August 16-24, 1960 (Geneva: World Council of Churches, n.d.), Appendix V, p. 117.

[41] The objection apparently shows that the W.C.C. acts much like a world church. Could it lead to the unity desired by the ecumenical movement? Samuel McCrea Cavert, writing on "The Goal of the Ecumenical Movement" in his book, *On the Road to Christian Unity* (New York: Harper, 1961), says: "The Christian world community is best conceived in terms not of administrative authority or control imposed from the center but of a closely knit fellowship of national or regional bodies, all

"The purpose of the World Council of Churches is not to negotiate unions between Churches, which can only be done by the Churches themselves acting on their own initiative, but to bring the Churches into living contact with each other and to promote the study and discussion of the issues of Church unity" (III, 2).

This declaration underlines the function of the W.C.C. to serve its member churches and not to make decisions for them. At the same time the Central Committee indicates what has been the tremendous accomplishment of the Council, namely, that it has brought numerous churches into contact with each other to discuss doctrine, worship, works of charity, and above all, the central problem of unity. No matter how much the W.C.C. may be criticized from many points of view, it cannot be denied that it has drawn many denominations out of isolation, focused attention on the necessity of unity, and stimulated ecumenical thought and action on a scale far surpassing any other body or movement in modern times. It remains to be seen what effect the Vatican Council will have. Up to this time, however, in that area which the Instruction of 1950 calls 'reunion,' it seems that primacy of concern and effort, if not of right, have been in the hands of the World Council of Churches.

"The World Council cannot and should not be based on any one particular conception of the Church. It does not prejudge the ecclesiological problem" (III, 3).

According to this statement, the W.C.C. is not committed to any particular ecclesiology.[42] It does "bear witness to the necessity of a clear manifestation of the oneness of the Church of Christ" (III, 2), and therefore has made numerous declarations on ecclesiastical

---

of which are in full communion with one another, have a ministry and sacraments common to all, and possess an effective instrument for continuous consultation on policy and strategy, for common planning in the whole range of program, and for such limited operational responsibility as may be committed to it. A strengthened World Council of Churches could be the organ of this world community," p. 161.

[42] Fr. Bernard Leeming, S.J., says that to speak of the "ecclesiological problem" is open to misunderstanding. There is no ecclesiological problem as a matter of where the true church is for the Orthodox or Roman Catholics. Therefore, to allow for this consideration—as he believes the W.C.C. wishes to do in its statement—he suggests that it would be preferable to say, "does not prejudge ecclesiological doctrines." *The Churches and the Church*, footnote to page 185.

unity, but these statements are, so to speak, independent of any particular ecclesiology held by specific denominations.

Such a principle leaves the way open to the admission of the Orthodox into the W.C.C. The Orthodox can reject and frequently have rejected the declarations of the Council and they feel free to uphold their own view of the church. Although W.C.C. ecumenical leaders do not accept any particular church as having the fullness of truth, yet theoretically they must also allow the Orthodox claims full hearing and respect.

"Membership in the World Council of Churches does not imply that a Church treats its own conception of the Church as merely relative" (III, 4).

This statement, together with the preceding and following declarations, present all sides of the same reality. The W.C.C., as an organ of the ecumenical movement, does not have any particular ecclesiology; the member churches in belonging to the W.C.C. do not have to give up their own ecclesiologies. Orthodox churches, for example, do not imply, by their membership, that therefore they are giving up their concept about the uniqueness of the church. At the same time, as the Central Committee explains, the principle enunciated is not the expression of latitudinarianism. The W.C.C. is not saying that all views of the church and of unity are equally true. It is simply declaring that it must not espouse any denominational cause; nor need any confession give up its own cause in joining the Council.

"Membership in the World Council does not imply the acceptance of a specific doctrine concerning the nature of Church unity" (III, 5).

Here again, the Toronto Statement goes on to emphasize that the Council stands for Church unity" (III, 5). That much is clear and certain. But the Council does not stand for any particular theory about unity and therefore the Central Committee declares that what *Mystici corporis* says about the error of holding invisible unity to be only unity of the church simply does not apply to the World Council. The Council does indeed include churches among its members who hold that the church is essentially invisible, as it also includes those who believe that visible unity is essential, but the function of the W.C.C. is to bring these sides into ecumenical conversation and not to champion either side *per se*.

After clarifying what the World Council of Churches is not, the

Toronto Statement next defines the positive assumptions which underlie the Council and the ecclesiological implications for those who are
members of the W.C.C.

*"The member Churches of the Council believe that conversation,
cooperation and common witness of the Churches must be based on
the common recognition that Christ is the Divine Head of the Body"*
(IV, 1).

This declaration is a restatement of the Basis of the W.C.C. as
applied to ecclesiology. Beyond the affirmation of Christ as Head
of the church, however, a new note shows itself here. It is the idea
of an imperative. The explanation, for example, given by the Central
Committee contains this sentence: "The fact of Christ's Headship
over His people compels all those who acknowledge Him to enter into
real and close relationships with each other—even though they differ
in many important points" (IV, 1). In some ways the concept that
the consequence of belief in Christ is mutual conversation, cooperation, and witness re-echoes the often repeated dictum that Christ wills
the unity of Christian confessions. The sense of duty is strong in the
ecumenical movement to respond to the call of Christ. It leads perhaps inevitably both to dismay at disunity and at the same time to an
expression of unity such as is contained in the next theological declaration.

*"The member Churches of the World Council believe on the basis
of the New Testament that the Church of Christ is one"* (IV, 2).

The ecumenical movement discovered soon after some initial
meetings and discussions that Christians had unity by their ad-
herence to Christ, the unity of the people of God, unity in the one
Church of Christ. At the first Assembly of the W.C.C., for example,
the Message declared: "We bless God our Father, and our Lord
Jesus Christ, Who gathers together in one the children of God that
are scattered abroad."[43] The report of Section I on "The Universal
Church in God's Design" states: "God has given to His people in
Jesus Christ a unity which is His creation and not our achievement."
And again, "It is our common concern for that Church which draws
us together, and in that concern we discover our unity in relation to
her Lord and Head."[44] There are differences, serious differences, but

---

[43] Cf. official report, p. 9.
[44] *Ibid.*, p. 51.

nevertheless all are in agreement that they have oneness in Christ even while disunity means that the membership of the people of God is wider than that of individual denominations. This is the conclusion which is drawn specifically in the next statement.

"The member Churches recognize that the membership of the Church of Christ is more inclusive than the membership of their own Church body. They seek, therefore, to enter into living contact with those outside their own ranks who confess the Lordship of Christ" (IV, 3).

In commenting on this principle, the Central Committee states that the Church of Rome recognizes that members exist *"extra muros"* who belong *"aliquo modo"* to the Church. It is true that *Mystici corporis* says that some who are "separated" are unsuspectingly "related to the Mystical Body of the Redeemer in desire and resolution,"[45] but they are not members in the proper sense of the word. The often used and indeed apt expression, "brethren" is a recognition of basic ties among all who are Christians, but neither *Mystici corporis* nor any other Roman document makes these brethren members of the Roman Catholic Church.

The consequence, however, for the W.C.C. and for the ecumenical movement, according to the principle of the Toronto Statement, is that each confession has a positive task to seek fellowship with those Christians outside the particular membership of the denomination in question. This is the imperative of the ecumenical movement.

"The member Churches of the World Council consider the relationship of other Churches to the Holy Catholic Church which the creeds profess as a subject for mutual consideration. Nevertheless, membership does not imply that each Church must regard the other member Churches as Churches in the true and full sense of the word" (IV, 4).

The principle stated in this fourth theological assumption of the W.C.C. forms part of the general framework of the Council's structure. On the one hand the W.C.C. must avoid particularism and on the other must preserve the individual member's freedom to hold fast to its own beliefs while entering into ecumenical contact. At the same time the W.C.C. must, as it were, think for itself on issues

---

[45] America Press Edition, #121 (p. 44).

of paramount importance. No doubt this means walking a tightrope, but nevertheless this policy does allow, for example, the various Orthodox churches to participate in World Council deliberations without the implications that such participation could otherwise have.

The Roman Catholic Church has always felt the adverse implications of collaboration in W.C.C. affairs. Participation would, under ordinary circumstances, indicate by implication that the Catholic Church accepted the other denominations as churches in the full and true sense of the word, an implication patently against its claims. Under the understanding of the above principle, however, it would not be at least theoretically impossible for the Catholic Church to join in ecumenical conversations with the W.C.C. members. *De facto* the Church will not join the W.C.C. as the Instruction of 1950 states clearly,[46] but also *de facto* more and more ecumenical conversations have taken place in recent years. If, within the providence of God, large segments of separated Christendom are to return to unity within the Church, it seems only natural that increasing ecumenical conversation must take place. Apart from a miracle such as happened in the case of St. Paul, a step by step approach through explanation, clarification, dissipation of mutual prejudices, friendliness, courtesy, and charity is, humanly speaking, a necessity.

"The member Churches of the World Council recognize in other Churches elements of the true Church. They consider that this mutual recognition obliges them to enter into a serious conversation with each other in the hope that these elements of truth will lead to the recognition of the full truth and to unity based on the full truth" (IV, 5).

A further assumption seems to underlie the assumption of the *vestigia ecclesiae*. It is that each ecclesiastical body has a part or piece of the truth, but that no single organization has the whole truth. Leaders of the W.C.C. affirm in the strongest terms that the true and real church of Christ exists and exists in a most substantial form. They do not say that the divided churches must *become* the one church. Rather, they insist that the church, the true church, the church of Christ has already been given to men and what they are now striving for is to manifest this church more fully and visibly

---

[46] Cf. "Ecclesia Catholica, etsi congressibus ceterisque conventibus 'oecumenicis' non intervenit, . . ." *AAS*, ibid., p. 142.

to the world. Yet, their very striving points to the assumption that the true church, as it exists, cannot be co-terminus with any existing ecclesiastical body. Catholics, of course, cannot accept this assumption and instead make the distinction: the Catholic Church does have all the essential elements and fullness of and from the institution by Christ of His Church; it does not have the fullness of members nor necessarily all the fullness of emphasis on certain doctrines or practices which it should have.

In a certain sense the claims of the Toronto Statement regarding the church and its unity, in the face of the disunity that exists among the member churches of the W.C.C., is an extraordinary exhibition of boldness. Yet the sincerity, earnestness, and effort shown by ecumenical leaders is undeniable; and undeniable too is that the steps taken by the ecumenical movement towards study, discussion, service, and charity all point in a forward direction. No doubt much more work and study needs yet to be done, especially in the field of doctrinal foundations, but what has been done should be given its due.

The sixth, seventh, and eighth theological assumptions of the Toronto Statement are invitations to the member churches to consult together in order to give as much as possible a unified witness, to help each other in need, to refrain from actions incompatible with brotherly love, and to enter into spiritual relationships with each other in order that "the Body of Christ may be built up."[47] These invitations are practical in nature and, while they may be important ecumenical instruments, do not need further comment as illustrating of the ecclesiological basis of the W.C.C.

---

[47] "The member Churches of the Council are willing to consult together in seeking to learn of the Lord Jesus Christ what witness He would have them to bear to the world in His Name," (IV, 6).

"A further practical implication of common membership in the World Council is that the member Churches should recognize their solidarity with each other, render assistance to each other in case of need, and refrain from such actions as are incompatible with brotherly relationships," (IV, 7).

"The member Churches enter into spiritual relationships through which they seek to learn from each other and to give help to each other in order that the Body of Christ may be built up and that the life of the Churches may be renewed," (IV, 8).

The positions arrived at in the Toronto Statement, however, were advanced in some ways by two subsequent documents on ecclesiology and unity. The first is the speech given by the general secretary of the World Council, Dr. Willem Visser 't Hooft and the other is the address given by Professor Henri D'Espine to the Central Committee Meeting at St. Andrew's, Scotland in 1960.

Dr. Visser 't Hooft spoke on the subject of "Various Meanings of Unity and the Unity Which the World Council of Churches Seeks to Promote."[48] The General Secretary addresses himself to the question of resolving the problem of how the W.C.C. takes its stand on the unity of the church and refuses at the same time to embrace any particular doctrine of unity.

Dr. Visser 't Hooft begins by repeating what the Toronto Statement insisted upon, namely, that the W.C.C. cannot make any *a priori* decision to accept a particular conception of unity held by any single member church. By doing so, the W.C.C. would defeat its own purpose of getting churches to discuss their differences. He goes on to say, however, that the W.C.C. is not therefore held back to the bland affirmation that "unity is a good thing" without expressing its convictions about the characteristics of that unity. *De facto* the W.C.C. has made many statements about church unity which become representative of the ecumenical movement when and as much as they are ratified by the member churches. In any case, however, as the General Secretary points out, no dilemma exists between promoting unity and talking about it in definite terms and at the same time not being partisan to any one concept of unity. The W.C.C. can and must do its share to advance the cause and concept of unity.

The second document which sheds much light on the thinking of the World Council on the objection of unity is contained in a speech delivered to the Faith and Order Meeting in 1960. The World Council in various documents has declared that Christ's church is one and that the unity of His church is God's gift to men. The unity which has been given must, however, be manifested more visibly by removing the disunity which exists. The World Council may and must contribute its part to this work and to the ecumenical movement in general without partisan affiliation. Unity, then, is

---

[48] The speech is printed in *The Ecumenical Review*, vol. VIII, no. 1 (Oct. 1955), p. 18-29.

also a goal, an objective, something to be achieved. But what is the nature of that goal? In other words, what is the precise nature of the unity that is sought?

The Faith and Order Commission in its triennial session in 1960 considered the question: what is the nature of the unity that the ecumenical movement is seeking? The answer given by the Faith and Order Commission, quoted by Professor D'Espine, and since adopted by the section on "Unity" at the New Delhi Assembly of the World Council of Churches in 1961, is, the authors admit, neither perfect nor final, but an attempt to spell out what unity must mean in practice. As such it represents the most advanced thinking of the ecumenical movement to-date on unity.

The statement first sets forth what unity does not mean. Unity, it is declared, does not mean uniformity of organization, rite, or expression. On this point the W.C.C. has been very positive for years. One suspects that the position is more of a protest against what is viewed as the "monolithic power" of the Catholic Church that an impartial doctrinal stand. Nevertheless, it forms a solid part of the concept of unity.

More positive aspects are contained in the following declaration:

> We believe that the unity which is both God's will and his gift to his church is being made visible as all in each place who are baptized into Jesus Christ and confess him as Lord and Saviour are brought by the Holy Spirit into one fully committed fellowship, holding the one apostolic faith, preaching the one Gospel, breaking the one bread, joining in common prayer, and having a corporate life reaching out in witness and service to all and who at the same time are united with the whole Christian fellowship in all places and all ages in such wise that ministry and members are accepted by all, and that all can act and speak together as occasion requires for the tasks to which God calls his people.[49]

A detailed comment on all the points raised by the above description of unity would extend this short study of the ecumenical

---

[49] The official report of the New Delhi Assembly of the W.C.C. has not been published at the time of this writing. The above quotation from the *Christian Century*, vol. 79, no. 2 (Jan. 10, 1962), p. 54.

The text from the St. Andrews meeting may be found in the report of the Conference, *ibid.*, p. 113.

movement beyond reasonable proportions. A brief indication, however, of some salient factors will be useful to summarize those elements, which, in the thinking of W.C.C. leaders, are vital for the unity of the church.[50]

The unity desired is visible and is realized particularly on the local level. The geography of unity begins in the concrete dimensions of the community. In this town or village, on this corner of a big city, on this street there must be only one church. When a Christian looks around in his locality—any locality—he should be able to see only a single church as the local representation of the church of Christ. From this point the unity of the church works outward to regional, national, and international manifestations.

The united church must hold "one apostolic faith." No one really disputes this, but the question is: just what does the apostolic faith consist in? One author, J. Robert Nelson, looks at faith as consisting of two concentric rings. The inner core is the heart of the Gospel teaching which must be accepted and cannot be changed. The outer ring corresponds to theological interpretations of the Gospel teaching which are useful and even necessary but which are mutable. He declares that "the ecumenical problem remains one of agreeing on what is central."[51]

The sacraments of baptism and holy communion must be accepted by all. In particular all Christians must be everywhere admitted to the "breaking of the one bread" and not prevented from communion by denominational barriers. The indication of such a goal shows the difficulty that exists for the ecumenical movement. One of the clearest and most painful manifestations of the disunity of Christians is at "the table of the Lord." If ecclesiological unity is to be achieved, eucharistic unity must first be accomplished.

Finally, all ministers and all Christians must be accepted as such by everyone. Such acceptance goes hand in hand with acceptance of the sacraments as administered by any of the member churches of the W.C.C. and presumably also by those Christian churches who are not members of the W.C.C. When the acceptance of ministry and people is accomplished, it is felt that it will lead to a fully com-

---

[50] J. Robert Nelson's analysis on the report on "Unity" at New Delhi was greatly helpful. Cf. *Christian Century*, Jan. 10, 1962, p. 53-55.

[51] *Ibid.*, p. 54.

mitted fellowship of the people of God who will then live a corporate life of witness and service in unity.

Conclusion

The purpose of this paper was to sketch the main lines of the ecumenical movement. It did so by first considering a brief history of the movement and then by examining the movement's theology of the church. Special attention was paid to the views of the W.C.C. on unity.

The ultimate place and influence of the ecumenical movement will have to be left to the evaluation of history. What can even now be said, however, is that, as an international movement, it reflects a basic need of our times—one that will engage not only the Vatican Council but many generations to come. As such it is entirely right and fitting that it be paid the attention it deserves.

ECCLESIOLOGY AND ECUMENISM

EDWARD F. HANAHOE, S. A.

In every age, under the guidance of the sacred magisterium, the resources of faith and reason have been brought to bear by Catholic scholars upon a multitude of questions raised from various sources, which have had the effect of a deeper and richer knowledge of divine revelation. Through these findings, the pastoral activities of the Church have been rendered more efficient and fruitful. The story is told of St. Thomas that, after accompanying a lay-brother to the public market, he came back to the priory and wrote a treatise on buying and selling. His unaccustomed presence in the midst of mundane enterprises raised many questions in his mind which demanded solution, especially their bearing on the field of justice. So, we might say, those questions contributed to the development of moral theology; they shed light on principles already known and demanded their further clarification and explicitation.

Among the many questions raised in our own times is that of the reunion of Christendom. It is not a new question by any means. Even within the lifetime of the Apostles there were assemblies of baptized persons who had separated themselves from the Church; the epistles of the New Testament bear witness to this fact. But, today, the existence of a world-wide movement towards unity on the part of the separated bodies has challenged the attention of all Catholics according to their various offices, capacities and interests. Books and articles are issuing forth from the presses in increasing numbers. One has the impression of great energy, sparked by much enthusiasm and sympathy.

The term generally applied to this complexus of ideas and activities is "Ecumenism." It would take us too far afield at this time to go into the background of this term.[1] Its use in particular connection with

---

[1] Cf. E. F. Hanahoe, S.A., *Catholic Ecumenism* (Washington: Catholic University, 1953), pp. 45-58.

the quest for unity may be said to be of Protestant origin, but it is also used by Catholics today who are interested in these matters. In a Catholic sense, we might define it as an enterprise which seeks reconciliation of dissidents with the Church.[2] Its theological implications will be discussed later. When we use the term in this paper, we mean *Catholic* Ecumenism unless otherwise disignated.

At times, Ecumenism is conceived of in terms of a pastoral enterprise, and, at other times, in terms of a section of sacred theology. Both phases are distinct but not separate. When we direct our attention to the theological side, it is in view of its pastoral objectives; when we think of the pastoral side, it is within the context of doctrine.

It would appear, however, that this effort has not yet crystallized into a clearly defined form in such a way that it would merit a place as a distinct department of theology. At the present time, it presents a confusing picture of disparate contributions in the way of personal essays, conjectures, information, ideas of procedure, with its own language of special words and phrases. There is no question as to the importance of the matter itself, or the legitimacy of the effort, but many profound issues are involved touching on doctrine and the care of souls. The Holy Office made this observation:

> Certain attempts, that are being designated by diverse names in different countries, have hitherto been made by various persons, either individually or in groups, to effect a reconciliation of dissident Christians with the Catholic Church. Such initiatives, however, do not always rest upon correct principles, although inspired by the best of intentions, and even when sprung from sound principles, they do not avoid besetting particular dangers, as past experience has shown.[3]

---

[2] We defined it as follows: "Catholic Ecumenism, *in its most general sense*, is that divinely commanded and divinely sustained work of the reconciliation of all men with God, through their incorporation into the unity of the Mystical Body of Christ, proceeding from the effective direction of the center, which is the See of Peter, to the limits of the world." "Catholic Ecumenism, *in its special sense*, is that divinely commanded and divinely sustained work of reconciliation, which has for its object the conversion and return of baptized dissidents to the unity of the Mystical Body of Christ, which involves their acceptance of the faith and communion of the See of Peter and the Catholic Church through the world." ibid., pp. 50, 51-2.

[3] *Ecclesia Catholica*: Sacred Congregation of the Holy Office, *Instruc-*

In view of this admonition, it is evident that the subject must be approached with serious care. This is especially true when it comes to the question of the formation of clerics in our seminaries. In any other college, they might study literature, physics, economics, etc., as separate subjects which have no relation with one another apart from contributing to the general culture of the individual student. But in a seminary, all the various branches studied either form one and the same science or derive from it. The seminarian's approach to Ecumenism must be in the light of his other studies and be consistent with them. We all know how the enthusiasm and inexperience of youth can be fascinated by what is novel, especially, if it offers a relief from the beaten track of scientific disciplines and captures the imagination. This zeal and energy should not be repressed, but properly directed by sound principles.

The topic assigned is "Ecclesiology and Ecumenism," and it has been well chosen. For, Ecclesiology lies at the heart of Ecumenism. It is principally through this part of sacred theology that the matter is mediated, even though every other part is involved in some way. As the instrument of subjective redemption, the Church, as a consequence, has the function of uniting all men in Christ.[4] Therefore, in the question of the reunion of Christendom, all the lines of enquiry converge on the Church. Our effort here will be a sort of critique of Ecumenism from the aspect of Ecclesiology. There are five basic lines of enquiry: the question of sources, the question of priority, the question of method, the question of principles, and the question of development.

---

tion on the Ecumenical Movement, December 20, 1949 (Graymoor, N.Y.: Chair of Unity Apostolate, 1952) pp. 2-3.

[4] "As He hung upon the Cross, Christ Jesus not only avenged the justice of the Eternal Father that had been flouted, but He also won for us, His brothers, an unending flow of graces. It was possible for Him personally, immediately to impart these graces to men; but He wished to do so only through a visible Church that would be formed by the union of men, and thus through the Church every man would perform a work of collaboration with Him in dispensing the graces of the Redemption. The Word of God willed to make use of our nature, when in excruciating agony He would redeem mankind; in much the same way throughout the centuries He makes use of the Church that the work begun might endure." Pius XII *The Mystical Body of Christ* (New York: America Press, 1943), p. 12 (#16).

The Question of Sources

What we have in mind here is the primary and immediate sources in the development of a Catholic Ecumenism. Pius XII wrote that the "proximate and universal criterion of truth in matters of faith and morals" is the sacred magisterium of the Church.[5] It is quite true that the documents of the magisterium have not treated of everything there is to say on the subject, but what has been treated is normative of future investigations.[6] The Catholic theologian is not simply left to his own resources of ingenuity, erudition and insight; he is not completely independent as regard matter, method or conclusion. It is precisely this area of Ecclesiology and Ecumenism that the directive function of the magisterium has been given insufficient attention. Pius XII noted:

> What is expounded in Encyclical letters of the Roman Pontiffs concerning the nature and constitution of the Church is deliberately and habitually neglected by some with the idea of giving force to a certain vague notion which they profess to have found in the ancient Fathers, especially the Greeks. . . . It is true that the Popes leave theologians free in those matters which are disputed in various ways by men of very high authority in this field; but history teaches that many matters that formerly were open to discussion, no longer now admit of discussion. . . . But if the Supreme Pontiffs in their official documents purposely pass judgement on a matter up to that time under dispute, it is obvious, according to the mind and will of the same Pontiffs, that the matter cannot be any longer considered a question open to discussion among theologians.[7]

---

[5] *Humani Generis*. Cf. Vincent A. Yzermans ed. *Pope Pius XII and Theological Studies* (St. Meinrad, Ind.: Grail Publications, 1957) pp. 85-6.

[6] A serviceable bibliography in this regard would be: Sylvester Alvarez, S.A., *Documents of the Holy See on Christian Unity* (Graymoor, N.Y.: Chair of Unity Apostolate, 1961).

[7] *Humani Generis*. Cf. Yzermans, *op. cit.*, pp. 86-7. In another place he says: ". . . For, unfortunately, it has happened that certain teachers of the Church care little for conformity with the living teaching authority of the Church, pay little heed to her commonly received doctrine clearly proposed in various ways; and at the same time follow their own bent too much, and regard too highly the intellectual temper of more recent writers, and the standards of other branches of learning, which they declare to be the only ones which conform to sound ideas and the standards

With reference to the matter at hand, the Holy Office Instruction on the Ecumenical Movement states:

> Bishops will not allow recourse to a perilous mode of speaking which engenders false notions and raises deceitful hopes that can never be fulfilled. Such would be, for example, the allegation that what is taught in the Encyclical letters of the Roman Pontiffs about the return of dissidents to the Church, or about the Mystical Body of Christ, need not be so rigorously taken, inasmuch as not all things are of faith, or, what is worse still, in matters of dogma not even the Catholic Church is in possession of the fullness of Christ and hence others are in a position of contributing towards its perfection.[8]

From what has been affirmed and what is warned against in the above statements, it should be evident that the primary operative criterion in the question of Ecumenism is the sacred magisterium. This fact should be deeply impressed on the minds of the clerics in our seminaries.

The Question of Priority

A tension arises in regard to the proper placing of Ecumenism with respect to Ecclesiology and other interests. A great deal depends on this question: Is Ecumenism an independent enterprise free to pursue its own aims? If we say yes, then the end of Ecumenism will be the projection of the sympathies, principles and interests of a given author: "According as a man is, such does the end seem to him."[9] The Holy Office has declared the end of Ecumenism as follows:

> ...(Bishops) should ... prudently foster and guide it unto the twofold end of assisting those, who are in search of the truth and the true Church, and of shielding the faithful from the perils which readily follow in the tread of the movement.[10]

We can see here that the end of Ecumenism pertains to Ecclesiology. Now, St. Thomas says:

---

of scholarship." In: "The Teaching Authority of the Church," 31 May, 1954. *ibid.*, pp. 48-9.

[8] Holy Office *Instruction*, etc., *op. cit.*, p. 4.

[9] Aristotle *Nichomachean Ethics* iii, of Summa Theologica I-II, q. 9, a. 2.

[10] Holy Office *Instruction*, etc., *op. cit.*, p. 3.

The rule of government and order for all things directed to an end must be taken from the end. For, since the end of each thing is its good, a thing is then best disposed when it is fittingly ordered to its end. And so we see among the arts that one functions as the governor and ruler of another because it controls its end. Thus, the art of medicine rules and orders the art of the pharmacist because health, with which medicine is concerned, is the end of all the medications prepared by the pharmacist. A similar situation obtains in the art of ship navigation in relation to ship building. . . .[11]

So, we would say that, since Ecclesiology controls the end of Ecumenism, it thereby determines the principles and measures the legitimacy of theories and procedures that are to be followed in Ecumenism.[12]

Constant awarness of this priority is necessary if error is to be avoided. The ideas and activities of Ecumenism touch also on other fields of interest. If one neglects the normative character of Ecclesiology, there is danger of being submerged in these other areas. For example, Ecumenism touches in Protestant Ecumenism, current philosophies, psychology, sociology, etc. If major consideration is given to what is proper to these other interests in such a way as to dominate the approach to the subject, then the character of the subject will be changed.[13] The proper relation of sacred doctrine to other departments of interest is thus explained by St. Thomas:

This science can, in a sense, depend upon the philosophical sciences, not as though it stood in need of them, but only in order to make its teaching clearer. For it accepts its principles, not from other sciences, but immediately from God, by Revelation.

---

[11] St. Thomas *Summa Contra Gentiles* I, 1, i.

[12] "... Now there are two conditions required for things to be well ordered. First, that they be ordained to their due end, which is the principle of the whole order in matters of action. ... Secondly, that which is done in view of the end should be proportionate to that end. From this it follows that the reason for whatever conduces to the end is taken from the end: thus the reason for the disposition of a saw is taken from cutting, which is its end. ..." *Summa Theologica* I-II, q. 102, a. 1.

[13] For the past century, the Holy See has been greatly preoccupied with this tendency: Vatican I condemned the submitting of dogma to the method of systematic doubt; Pius X condemned the submerging of dogma in Kantianism and evolution; Pius XII censured the restless attempts to squeeze Catholic doctrine into the categories of whatever philosophy happens to be fashionable at the moment.

Therefore, it does not depend upon other sciences as upon the higher, but makes use of them as the lesser, and as hand-maidens.[14]

Take sociology: Since Ecumenism bears upon the relation of the Catholic Church to other religious societies, certain data can be gathered by sociologists which will be of much value in the pastoral enterprises of the Church. As the Church is in this world, the carrying out of its pastoral mission requires taking account of the social realities in which it finds itself and acting accordingly. The Catholic Church itself, since it is composed of human beings, participates somewhat in the characteristics of other societies and its impact on the world can be measured by surveys of opinion. But the Church herself cannot be contained completely within the categories of sociology, for it surpasses all other societies "as grace surpasses nature."[15] The conclusions of the sociologists do not determine its nature, its constitution or its principles. Besides that, there is a basic tension between the Kingdom of God and the spirit of the world that will never be eliminated completely.[16] In some areas of tension, to become acceptable

---

[14] *Summa Theologica* I, q. 1, a. 5, ad 2.

[15] "... The Church, a perfect society of its kind, is not made up of merely moral and juridical elements and principles. It is far superior to all other human societies; it surpasses them as grace surpasses nature, as things immortal are above all those that perish. ... the Church in its entirety is not found within this natural order, any more than the whole of man is encompassed within the organism of our mortal body." Pius XII *The Mystical Body of Christ, op. cit.,* p. 32 (#76).

[16] Leo XIII: "The race of man, after its miserable fall from God, the Creator and Giver of heavenly gifts, "through the envy of the devil,' " separated into two diverse and opposite parts, of which the one steadfastly contends for truth and virtue, the other for those things which are contrary to virtue and truth. The one is the Kingdom of God on earth, namely, the true Church of Jesus Christ, and those who desire from their heart to be united with it, so as to gain salvation, must of necessity serve God with their whole mind and with an entire will. The other is the Kingdom of Satan, in whose possession and control are all whosoever follow the fatal example of their leader and of our first parents, those who refuse to obey the divine and eternal law, and who have many aims of their own in contempt of God, and many aims also against God.... At every period of time each has been in conflict with the other ... although not always with equal ardor and assault." *Humanum Genus* in: *Great Encylical Letters of Leo XIII, op. cit.,* p. 83.

to the world is to become alien from Christ. So, Ecumenism can use the information of sociology, but it cannot become a department of sociology.

The case is similar with psychology. Psychology can aid Ecumenism, if by it is meant that we should take account of people as they are, their attitudes, their present state of knowledge, the avenues which are best calculated to impress them, etc. There is nothing new about this. For example, St. Paul's counsels in his pastoral epistles (e.g. I Tim. 5:1-2). St. Gregory's *Regula Pastoralis* gives advice as to how to deal with people in various ways in accordance with their age, character, background, education, disposition, etc.

The Ecumenist can use psychology as an instrument in the way a teacher uses pedagogy.[17] Remember that the object is to "*assist* those who are searching for the truth and the true Church." Part of the "assistance" involves psychology in the sense we have described. But, psychology cannot contain Ecumenism nor determine its theological contents. The matter communicated is derived from revelation. The acceptance of this communication makes certain demands of human nature which are difficult but not impossible with the help of grace. Of its very nature, the commitment must be freely given; hence, the message will be received differently by different people. The commitment is not the result of pushing the right buttons but of an intelligent and free cooperation with divine grace in responding to a truth externally proposed. Psychology is useful to Ecumenism as a handmaid, but it does not supply the content communicated; to use it as a theological method to arrive at this content itself is to fall into subjectivism. We shall see more of this later.

---

[17] "... as there are two ways of being cured, that is, either through the activity of unaided nature or by nature with the aid of medicine, so also there are two ways of acquiring knowledge. In one way, natural reason by itself reaches knowledge of unknown things, and this is called *discovery*; in the other way, when someone else aids the learner's natural reason, and this is called *learning by instruction*.

In effects which are produced by nature and by art, art operates in the same way and through the same means as nature. For, as nature heals one who is suffering from cold by warming him, so also does a doctor. Hence, art is said to imitate nature. For the teacher leads the pupil to knowledge of things he does not know in the same way that one directs himself through the process of discovering something he does not know." St. Thomas *Quaestiones disputatae de Veritate* q. 11 *De Magistro* art. 1. c.

Of course, the major point of contact is with Protestant Ecumenism. The premises, methods and goals as well as the general *ethos* (ways of thinking and doing things, common outlook) of Protestant Ecumenism do not correspond in every respect with what fits in with Catholic Ecclesiology. There is no doubt but that a Catholic Ecumenist should seek to know and even to understand their point of view and take account of it in his dealings with non-Catholics. From the questions raised by Protestant Ecumenism, he can draw from the resources of Catholic doctrine the appropiate answers which will assist them in finding the truth; he will take account of their difficulties; he will evaluate their conclusions; he will presume that they are sincere and honest in their convictions; he will always be kind even when he may disagree. As Pius XII said: ". . . the hand of friendship should be extended to the erring, but no concessions should be made to erroneous opinions."[16] But it is one thing to understand and another to be completely absorbed into the Protestant outlook, which, at times, would seem to occur. Sometimes one has the impression that the approval or the disapproval of the separated brethren constitutes the supreme norm of value, or of truth, or of its presentation. This preoccupation may lead some to a state of mind thus described by Pope Pius XII:

> . . . But some through enthusiasm for an imprudent "irenicism" seem to consider as an obstacle to fraternal union, things founded on laws and principles given by Christ and likewise on institutions founded by Him, or which are the defense and support of the integrity of the faith, and the removal of which would bring about the union of all, but only to their destruction.[19]

Hence, the Holy Office made this admonition:

> . . . They will also be on their guard, lest, under some false pretense, for instance, by stressing things on which we agree rather than those we disagree, a dangerous indifferentism be fomented, particularly amongst those who are less thoroughly grounded in matters theological and not so well trained in their religious practise. For they must beware, lest, from a spirit of "irenicism," as it is called nowadays, Catholic tenets, be they

---

[18] "Discourse to the General Congregation of the Society of Jesus" 17 Sept., 1946. Cf. Gaston Courtois ed. *The States of Perfection according to the teaching of the Church* (Dublin: M. H. Gill, 1961) #219, p. 94.

[19] *Humani Generis.* Cf. Yzermans, *op. cit.,* pp. 82-3.

dogmas or questions connected therewith, in a process of com-progressive assimilation and approximation among the various professions of faith, are so whittled down and somehow made to conform to heterodox teaching as to jeopardize the purity of Catholic doctrine or obscure its clear and genuine meaning.[20]

These, and other, aberrations would not occur if the order of priority were observed, i.e., if the certain principles of Catholic Ecclesiology were viewed as truths to which non-Catholic inquirers were to be assisted in finding, instead of as obstacles to be obscured or modified to accomodate to their wishes. Ecumenism will never attain its end unless the science which controls its end is allowed to direct it.

The Question of Method

Closely akin to the above is the question of method, i.e., the search for an approach to the subject which is properly theological. In its formative stage, as it is yet, a cleavage in methodology in Ecumenism immediately makes its appearance: There are those who work from the premise that divinely-given visible unity is already a permanent reality to be shared with those who do not have it. To put it another way: the end is *given* and the idea is to *assist* those, who have not yet attained it, to find it. On the other hand, there are those who, while not exactly denying the end, propose to consider it as if it were unknown and envision "unity" as a sort of common goal to be attained by all who are divided from one another; they will not presume to suggest the actual nature of the goal. Indeed, one author goes so far as to say that "the day of the Parousia will be the day of the definitive unity of the Church."[21] The divergence of the two methods is fundamental and their incompatibility increasingly manifests itself in the development each makes in pursuing its objective.[22]

---

[20] Holy Office *Instruction*, etc., *op. cit.*, p. 4.

[21] Pierre Micholon "L'Entendue de L'Église" in: Lambert Beaudoin, etc. *Église et Unité* (Lille: Catholicité, 1948) p. 123.

[22] The matter deserves the closest scrutiny. Several analogies will bring out the difference. If a moral problem is proposed to a priest in his capacity as a confessor, two questions may arise in his mind: what is the relation of this problem to the universal norm of morality? and: how can I make this person feel better? The solution will depend much on the order of questions considered. He can obtain both objectives, but if he tries to solve the problem from the aspect of the second question, the

For a properly theological method, we must follow the order of things as they are, i.e., objectively. The mysteries of faith simply *are*, i.e. they are realities existing at this very moment whether or not anyone chooses to think of them or even knows them; they are not experiences or theories thought up by experts. It is in this sense that they are taught by the Church and in this sense accepted on faith based on the wisdom and the truthfulness of God who has revealed them and they are one and the same for all. In the matter of attaining the reunion of Christendom, the same principle prevails; it is not a question of arriving at an acceptable formula, but rather a question of what has been established by God. We must take our bearings from what *is* and not from a convergence of collective desires and conjectures. Pope Leo XIII wrote:

> It is so evident from the clear and frequent testimonies of Holy Writ that the true Church of Jesus Christ is *one*, that no Christian can dare to deny it. But in judging and determining the nature of this unity many have erred in various ways. Not the foundation of the Church alone, but its whole constitution belongs to the class of things affected by Christ's free choice. We must, consequently investigate not how the Church may possibly be one, but how He, who founded it, willed that it should be one.[23]

It is our conviction that the development of Ecumenism should follow the objective order of things. Now, let us take a look at the alternative method, which I believe should be classed as subjective. (But I will not insist on the term). As a lead to grasping this method, let us take this statement from the declaration of the World Conference on Faith and Order which met at Edinburgh in 1937:

> Our unity is of heart and spirit. We are divided in the out-

---

solution might not correspond with the universal norm, and the person will not really be helped at all. Another analogy: In scholastic philosophy, the order of being has priority over the order of thought and is its rule and measure. We first ask the question: *what is,* and, after that: *what can I know?* To reverse the order is to fall into subjectivism and philosophy becomes just a system of ideas which may or may not correspond to actual reality; indeed, it can never be discovered whether they do or not through the use of this method.

[23] Leo XIII *Satis cognitum, The Unity of the Church* (New York: Paulist Press, 1949), p. 7.

ward forms of our life in Christ, because we understand differently His will for His Church. We believe, however, that a
deeper understanding will lead us towards a united apprehension
of the truth as it is in Jesus.

We humbly acknowledge that our divisions are contrary to
the will of Christ, and we pray God in His mercy to shorten the
days of our separation and to guide us by His Spirit into fulness
of unity.[24]

Certainly, it is not my purpose to criticize this statement adversely.
It represents a state of mind which is admirable, edifying and praiseworthy when expressed by the separated brethren. It betokens a
disposition which should give promise of much fruit.

Now, I raise the question: Would it be a good approach for a Catholic Ecumenist to place himself amid their ranks, as it were, and voice
such sentiments and proceed with their same principles? The point
might seem subtle, but I think it is very important. The idea of assisting the separated Brethren in finding the *end* already established
by God, is replaced by a mutual cooperation in seeking a common goal
which as yet lacks specification. If the goal is actually unknown at
present, as it is to the non-Catholics, it is perfectly legitimate to
search out the sources of revelation and pray for light to obtain it.
The part of the non-Catholic is to seek divinely-given unity; the part
of the Catholic is to seek to share this same divinely-given unity with
his separated brethren; it is not his to seek—he already has it.[25] This

---

[24] Leonard Hodgson ed. *The Second World Conference on Faith and
Order* New York: Macmillan, 1938) p. 275.

[25] Pope John XXIII: "It is beyond doubt that the Divine Redeemer
established His Church and endowed and strengthened it with a strong
mark of unity. Otherwise—to use an absurd expression—if He had not
done so, He would have done something completely transitory and at least
in the future, contradictory to Himself, in much the same way as nearly
all philosophies, which depend on the whim of men's opinion, come into
existence one after another in the course of time, are altered and pass
away. But it is plain to all that this is opposed to the divine teaching
authority of Jesus Christ who is the way, the truth and the life (Jn.
14:6).

"This unity, however, venerable brethren and dear children—which as
we said ought not to be something frail, uncertain and unsteady, but
something solid, firm and safe—if it is lacking in other groups of Christians, it is not lacking in the Catholic Church, as all who carefully examine the question can easily observe. It is a unity which is distingushed

particular method, however, abstracts from the actual existence and nature of this unity and places the Catholic Church in the same position as other religious societies and points forward towards some possible future arrangement which is as yet unknown. Let us take a concrete instance: One Catholic Ecumenist writes:

> Every fervent Christian is attached to his own group, to a determined expression of belief, to a particular conception of the Church, and he is obliged to remain faithful to that confession. . . . . What then is to be done? There are not two ways, there is but one—to unite oneself with the prayer of Christ to lose oneself in it, not turning one's attention to dogmatic divergences but concentrating on the profession of baptismal faith which is at the heart of Christianity. This attitude de-- mands a total renunciation, a plunge into a mystery where much is obscure and which transcends all the ideas that we can present to our Lord in the name of our faith; it is the attitude of a soul open to the one sovereign Will of Christ, saying yes to His prayer for unity.[26]

In fairness to the author, let it be said at once that he does not subscribe to indifferentism, as that is commonly understood. On objective grounds, however, we find much difficulty with this statement. In the first place, all Christians are not, objectively, in the same position with respect to true religious unity; Catholics enjoy membership in the Mystical Body of Christ which perpetually enjoys unity by reason of the presence of the Holy Spirit who is its soul and bond. In the second place, the prayer of Christ "that all may be one" was not an ineffective wish or an admonition, but it was an infallibly

---

and adorned by these three marks: Unity of doctrine, of government, of religious practice.

It is a unity which is clearly visible to the gaze of all so that all can recognize and follow it. It has this nature, we say, by the will of the Divine Founder, so that within it all the sheep may be gathered together into one fold, under the guidance of one shepherd; so that all the children may be invited into the one Father's house, founded on the cornerstone of Peter; and so that as a result of it, efforts may be made to link all peoples by this bond of brotherhood to the one kingdom of God, whose citizens joined harmoniously together heart and soul while on earth, may eventually enjoy happiness in heaven." *Ad Petri Cathedram*, Near the Chair of Peter. (Boston: St. Paul's Editions, 1960) pp. 23-24.

[26] Maurice Villain, *The Life and Work of Abbé Paul Couturier Apostle of Unity.* (Haywards Heath, Sussex: Holy Cross Convent, 1959) p. 7.

efficacious prayer of the Son of God asking for this unity as a perpetual external witness to His own divine mission, "that the world
may believe that thou hast sent me." The visible unity of the Catholic
Church is a perpetual miracle attributable only to the power of God.
When a Catholic pronounces this prayer, it is not with the idea that
this unity be accomplished, but that it be extended to embrace those
who are not presently in it, especially those who are marked with the
seal of baptism, and who are, by no fault of their own, separated from
it.

To digress a moment, let us look at the other statement of the
author on the reason for adopting this procedure: "Every fervent
Christian . . . is obliged to remain faithful to his own confession."
When we speak of an "obligation," what do we mean? A moral bond
founded on an objective relation between a command act and a necessary end. Does there exist an *objective* obligation for Catholics to
adhere to the faith? Obviously, yes. Does there exist a corresponding
objective obligation for a non-Catholic to adhere to his own confession?
Obviously, no—there can be no *objective* obligation to profess error.

I do not think that this phase is difficult to see. But the problem
arises in regard to *subjective* obligation, which is the actual perception
of the relation between a commanded act and a necessary end. As
regards Catholics, Vatican I declared:

> There is no parity between the condition of those who have
> adhered to the Catholic truth by the heavenly gift of faith, and
> of those who, led by human opinions, follow a false religion:
> for those who have received the faith under the magisterium of
> the Church can never have any just cause for changing or doubt-
> ing that faith.[27]

As it pertains to the non-Catholic, we might ask first, in the *abstract*:
Can such a *subjective* obligation exist? Yes. We can conceive of a
subjective obligation to obey an invincibly erroneous conscience, and
we must certainly take it into account. We might even normally
presume it, since only God knows interior matters. We must respect
non-Catholics and abstain from attack and ridicule of their position.
But, is that all there is to it? There still exists an *objective* necessity
for their pertaining to the Church. To break the impasse, another

---

[27] Denziger, 1794. Cf. 1815.

element in the order of Divine Providence has to enter in, which is the external proposition of the whole truth. Their conscientious sincerity and devotion to the will of God prepare them to receive the truth after it has been sufficiently proposed. To withhold the proposal of the whole truth on the ¡grounds of the existence of an erroneous conscience, is to abandon the mission of preaching the Gospel; if the Apostles were of that mind, they would never have left the upper room in Jerusalem.

In the *concrete,* does there exist such a conception of an obligation to adhere blindly to a document drawn up by men some four hundred years ago? Allowing for the exceptions I mentioned, I don't think so. My reasons are: (1) Protestants reject the whole notion of infallibility: "No finite authority is going to determine our belief in a final way."[28] If they hold that, they cannot feel obliged to adhere blindly to a human document. (2) These documents are, in great measure, disregarded. (Ask an Anglican, for example, if he feels obliged to adhere to the Thirty-Nine Articles as objects of belief in *periculo salutis.*) Finally, the very existence of an Ecumenical Movement is a virtual declaration that these "confessions" are insufficient and that they must look outside their own denomination if they are to find the whole truth.

That should dispose of the problem of obligation. To return from our digression, we have stated that the author places the Catholic Church in the same position as non-Catholic religious bodies, as a sort of starting point in the quest for unity. It is an attempt to form an Ecumenism independently of Catholic Ecclesiology and operating within the frame of reference of non-Catholic strivings. We can see this in the following passage:

> The problem of Christian unity is not purely and simply coextensive with the idea of "return," because history is irreversible, and one can never again place oneself at the point of separation; its movement is rather one of maturity from within,

---

[28] "It is in this sense of complete obligation to the Word of God as it compels the faith of the believer that Protestantism stands for freedom of personal judgement and belief. No finite religious authority (church, creed or even scripture) can compel conformity of conviction. Every man's faith must be *his own* faith." Dillengberger-Welch *Protestant Christianity* (New York: Scribners, 1954) p. 287.

from a fundamental unity already possessed, towards full unity. It is a problem of "re-membership" or "re-constitution."[29]

There are three basic approaches to unity among Protestant Ecumenists: (1) The idea that unity did exist at one time in the past, but at present the Church is divided;[30] (2) The idea that unity never existed actually except as an ideal to be striven for;[31] (3) The idea that unity always exists in the invisible Church which persists in and through all denominations.[32] The author sets aside the explicit teaching of the sacred magisterium[33] and sweeps together the basic

---

[29] Villain, *op. cit.,* p. 8.

[30] e.g., "Now, as a matter of history, this purpose was fulfilled in the Church of the first days ... the unity of the Church being something that has once been experienced and afterwards lost, not something that we never experienced at all.... At present, men cannot see the Church because it is not one, and we must never rest until they can see it, because it has become one." Spencer Jones, *England and the Holy See* (London: Longmans, 1902) pp. 54, 83-84. This view would characterize the High-Anglican position.

[31] e.g., "A first prerequisite is the abandonment, once and for all, of the widely held myth of an original 'undivided Church.' History recognizes no such reality ..." Henry van Dusen, *World Christianity* (New York: Abingdon-Cokesbury, 1947), p. 69. Another example: "... It must be further recognized that true and complete Christian unity, while implicit from the beginning, can only be attained as a result of spiritual maturity.... Unity, therefore, in the full sense of it, is the goal rather than the starting point." J. Scott Lidgett, "The Wesleyan Methodist Church" in: James Marchant, ed., *The Reunion of Christendom,* (New York: Henry Holt, 1929) pp. 177-8. Liberal Protestant position.

[32] e.g., "First of all, Church unity should be distinguished from Christian unity or the oneness of believers of Christ.... This one invisible Church, as it is often called, persists in and through all visible Churches and denominations, survives their mutations and destructions, and remains intact even amid their conflicts and schisms. That we are all one in Christ is an admitted fact from which we proceed, and the common ground upon which we stand." C. W. Shields *The United Church of the United States,* (New York: Scribners, 1895) p. 67. Generally the evangelical orientation.

[33] "The unity of Christians cannot be otherwise obtained than by securing the return of the separated to the one true Church of Christ from which they once unhappily withdrew. To the one true Church of Christ, we say, that stands forth before all and that by the will of its Founder will remain forever the same as when He Himself established it for the salvation of all mankind." Pius XI *Mortalium animos, The Promotion*

Protestant orientations, even though they are inconsistent with each other.

We would not presume to say that the author denies Catholic teaching; indeed, it might be unjust to suggest it. But, it seems to me, that an Ecumenical orientated in this wise would not quite square with Ecclesiology, at least the Ecclesiology taught in the documents of the Magisterium. The tension would not exist, if the procedure followed the order of reality instead of the order of conjectural ideas which may or may not correspond with reality. We shall see more of this shortly.

The Question of Principles

We do not have the time or the opportunity to expound the whole of Ecclesiology or to draw up a complete system of Ecumenism.[34] We simply intend to indicate some sensitive areas where Ecclesiology should determine the development of Ecumenism.

The basic principle that Ecumenism should derive from Ecclesiology is the unicity of the Church: There is only one Church of Jesus Christ. Pope Leo XIII said:

> ... by the will of its Founder, it is necessary that this Church should be one in all lands and at all times. To justify the existence of more than one Church, it would be necessary to go outside this world and create a new and unheard-of race of men.[35]

Sometimes, we see the expression "corporate union"[36] or "union of churches" which is not seen as a "return," but a simple "union" of a Protestant body with the Catholic Church. Such a concept would seem to ignore the unicity of the Church: The Catholic Church is

---

of *True Religious Unity*, (Washington: National Catholic Welfare Conference, 1928) pp. 14-15.

[34] We have attempted to draw up the lineaments of an Ecumenism in our dissertation: *Catholic Ecumenism* (Washington: Catholic University, 1953).

[35] Leo XIII *Satis cognitum, op. ct.*, p. 8.

[36] See: Laurentius Klein "Has American Ecumenism a Future?" in: *Catholic World* V. 194, no. 1164 (March 1962) p. 334. Distinguish this from "corporate reunion" which is seen as a return to the Catholic Church, but which merits separate consideration. We have treated of this in our *Catholic Ecumenism op. cit.*, pp. 118-148.

THE Church; the separated bodies are not, strictly speaking, churches in the same sense—they are moral bodies of religious purpose, customarily called churches. Pius XII provides the basis for this distinction:

> ... But if we compare a Mystical Body with a moral body, here again we must notice that the difference between them is not slight, rather it is very considerable and very important. In the moral body, the principle of union is nothing more than the common end, and the common cooperation of all under authority for the attainment of that end; whereas in the Mystical Body, of which we are speaking, this collaboration is supplemented by a distinct internal principle, which exists effectively in the whole and in each of its parts, and whose excellence is such that, of itself, it is vastly superior to whatever bonds of union may be found in a physical or moral body. This is something, as we have said above, not of the natural but of the supernatural order. Essentially, it is something infinite, uncreated: "numerically one and the same, fills and unifies the whole Church.[37]

There is no parity, then, between the Catholic Church and any society of baptized persons separated from her. In the one place, we have the Holy Spirit Himself as the principle of its unity; in the other place, the uniting bond is a common will. As the same Pontiff said in the same document, the Church surpasses all human societies "as grace surpasses nature."

The second principle which Ecclesiology gives to Ecumenism is the fact that this one Church perpetually enjoys a divinely-given constitution and a divinely-given visible unity and it is to perdure in this character until the end of time.[38] No other arrangement is to be expected in regard to the nature and essential constitution of the Church than that which is now in force. Accordingly, if there are any studies to be made with respect to the reunion of Christendom, this one Church is the divinely indicated terminus; there is no other to be

---

[37] Pius XII *Mystici corporis, op. cit.,* pp. 31-32.

[38] See note 25 above. As we are not going to set forth the whole of ecclesiology, we understand here under the heading of divinely given unity the truths integral with it, such as, the papacy, infallibiity, the doctrine of membership in the Church, etc. Withe regard to membership, a useful study is: Boisvert, O.F.M., *Doctrina de Membris Ecclesiae* (Montreal: Éditions Franciscans, 1961).

sought. From the side of the separated brethren, divinely-given unity is seen as an objective to be attained; from the Catholic side, divinely-given unity is seen as a benefit to be shared and extended. The Holy Office has directed:

> The whole and entire body of Catholic doctrine is therefore to be proposed and explained. Nothing embraced in the Catholic truth concerning the nature and means of justification, the constitution of the Church, the Roman Pontiff's primacy of jurisdiction and *the only real union effectuated by a return of the dissidents to the one true Church of Christ* must be passed over in silence or cloaked under ambiguous language.[39]

We have noted that some Catholic authors are sensitive to the word "return," in spite of the constant reiteration of this notion by the sacred magisterium. Upon what basis do we use the word "return"? Simply upon past history? No. We base it on the fact that there is only one Church and the fact that there are baptized persons who spend their lives outside its visible bounds. If they were baptized in infancy, they were made members of the Church. At some subsequent point they lost this membership[40] by separating from its faith or jurisdiction for the most part, without any fault of their own. We regard the Church as their proper home and there still exists a bond with this home rooted in the character of baptism;[41] the movement of re-association in the family life is thereby designated as a return. To hold otherwise is to hold that there are several legitimate Churches

---

[39] Holy Office *Instruction*, etc., *op. cit.*, p. 5. See the Note 33 above.

[40] "Since the Mystical Body of Christ, that is to say, the Church, is, like the physical body, a unity, a compact thing closely joined together, it would be false and foolish to say that Christ's Mystical Body could be composed of separated and scattered members." Pius XI *Mortalium animos op. cit.*, p. 15.

[41] "May this wondrous manifestation of unity, therefore, by which the unity of the Catholic Church stands forth for all to see—may these desires, these prayers, by which she implores from God the same unity for all, move your mind and rouse it in a salutary manner. We say *your*— for we are speaking to those who are separated from the Apostolic See. ... Note, we beg of you, that we lovingly invite you to the unity of the Church, we are inviting you not to the home of a stranger, but to your own house, to the Father's house which belongs to all." John XXIII *Ad Petri Cathedram, Near the Chair of Peter* (Boston: St. Paul Editions, 1960) p. 27.

of Christ, or that the one Church is divided into parts, or that the Church is *per se* invisible, or that the separated brethren are to be equated with pagans: all of which are contrary to the truth.

The third principle which Ecclesiology gives to Ecumenism is the nature of the Catholic Faith as a condition of reconciliation with the Church. For one to be reconciled with the Church, it is necessary that he believe, with a supernatural assent, everything that the Church teaches, and in the sense in which she teaches it, on the authority of the truthfulness of God. Moreover, integral with the Catholic Faith is the acceptance of the Church herself as the infallible teacher. To arrive at this point, there is required the free exercise of intellect and will in cooperation with divine grace on the part of every individual. Faith is, by its nature, intellectual, free and supernatural (when we say that the act of faith is free, we mean, of course, physically, and not morally; a person may be capable of accepting or rejecting the faith, but he is objectively obliged to accept it); these properties are also the conditions of efficacious reconciliation with the Church. By its very nature, it is something personal; no one else can acquire it for him; nor can he obtain it by simple acquiescence in a common majority vote; nor merely because he argees with what is proposed, seeing that it accords with his own ideas; nor can it be imposed on him against his will. Pius XII wrote:

> While we want this unceasing prayer to rise to God from the whole Mystical Body in common, that all the straying sheep may hasten to enter the one fold of Jesus Christ, yet we recognize that this step must come of their own free will; for no one believes unless he wills to believe.... The "faith without which it is impossible to please God" is a wholly free "submission of intellect and will."[42]

Our Lord said: "No man comes to me, unless the Father, who sent me, draw him." The same is true for His Church. Ecumenism, then, must take account of the immutable nature of divine truth as proposed by the Church; it must respect the dignity, intelligence and freedom of every individual; it must never forget the supernatural character of divine faith. Finally, the distribution of grace and the diversity of response will determine the actual fruits it obtains. It

---

[42] Pius XII *Mystici corporis op. cit.*, p. 49.

is regrettable that some Catholic Ecumenists oppose the notion of "conversion" almost as much as they detest the idea of "return" which is its correlative. They seem to set little account by the end which Ecclesiology determines and the mystery of the distribution of grace; both of these are outside of their control. Actually, the end is achieved by every conversion that takes place.

Sometimes, there is talk of "corporate reunion" which is the reconciliation of an entire separated body with the Catholic Church. We have discussed this notion more fully elsewhere.[43] Obviously, all who are ready here and now, i.e. who have the faith and acknowledge the Catholic Church as their proper home, let them come. If they would like to arrange to be received together, there is no objection; after receiving instructions, they may make their profession of faith and be received into the Church. But, in the ordinary dispensations of Divine Providence in the distribution of grace, such events rarely take place, especially if it be a question of large numbers. It would be most imprudent, in my opinion, for one who has now received the gift of divine Catholic faith to postpone his reconciliation until everyone in his denomination was ready. Many of these schemes of corporate reunion serve to keep people out of the Church who might otherwise have entered it. This imprudence will be underlined when one considers the necessity of the Church, to be discussed next.

The final principle which we shall mention here that Ecclesiology gives to Ecumenism is the doctrine of the necessity of the Church for salvation.[44] This doctrine should supply the pastoral dynamism of ecumenical effort. Pius XII was prompted by this concern when he wrote:

> We have committed to the protection and guidance of heaven those who do not belong to the visible organization of the Good Shepherd, we desire nothing more ardently than that they may have life and have it more abundantly.... From a heart overflowing with love we ask each and every one of them to be quick and ready to follow the interior movements of grace, and to look to withdrawing from that state in which they cannot be sure

---

[43] Cf. Hanahoe, *Catholic Ecumenism*, pp. 118-148.

[44] We take as normative the Letter of the Holy Office of 8 August 1949 to Most Reverend Richard Cushing, D.D., Archbishop of Boston, relative to Fr. Leonard Feeney. Cf. *Special Unity Documents* (Graymoor: Chair of Unity Apostolate, 1958) pp. 6-9.

of their salvation. For even though unsuspectingly they may be directed towards the Mystical Body of the Redeemer in desire and resolution, they still remain deprived of so many precious gifts and helps from heaven, which one can enjoy only in the Catholic Church.[45]

If this consideration were more operative in the thinking of some ecumenists, their approach to the subject might be different. Making all due allowance for what the theologians call invincible ignorance and good faith and the possibility of sanctifying grace in the dissidents, they still remain insecure in respect to salvation. If they die with at least an implicit intention of entering the Church, animated by perfect charity, they can be saved even though they are not actual members of the Church. We all know that. But is it the function of Ecumenism to keep them in a state of separation from the Church? The question is not intended as irony but is based on a certain vague impression one receives from some of the ideas which are expressed on the subject. For example: the effort to supply justifying reasons for the original breach;[46] the search for theological reasons for keeping the separated brethren where they are because they may have "vestigia ecclesiae," as if they were objectively sufficient,[47] by suggesting that unity is something other than their return to the Catholic Church (as we have seen), by diverting their minds to schemes of corporate reunion which are either impossible (e.g. coming in on their own terms, especially doctrinal) or which refer to possible acts of some people living in a future generation.[48]

---

[45] Pius XII *Mystici corporis op. cit.*, p. 49.

[46] "They should scrupulously take precautions and firmly insist that, in rehearsing the history of the Reformation or the Reformers, the faults and foibles of Catholics are not overemphasized, whilst the blame and defects of the Reformers are dissimulated; nor that rather accidental circumstances be placed in such a light that the main fact, consisting in defection from the Catholic Faith, is allowed to dwindle from sight and mind." Holy Office *Instruction*, etc., *op. cit.*, pp. 4-5.

[47] Cf. our study: "Vestigia Ecclesiae; their meaning and value" in: E. F. Hanahoe and T. Cranny eds., *One Fold* (Graymoor: Chair of Unity Apostolate, 1959) pp. 272-383; and our: *Ecumenism and Conversions* (Graymoor: Chair of Unity Apostolate, 1960).

[48] In the last century the Holy Office censured an enterprise of this sort; one reason given was: "... because the Society, by holding out a vain expectation of these three communions, each in its integrity, and

Of course, there is such a thing as long range planning. We must take people as they are and not anticipate the movements of divine grace by undue pressure and precipitant action; an intermediate preparation of the groundwork is also conceivable. But that is quite another thing from sustaining an illusion that a personal obligation can be transferred to someone else or to the group of which one is a member.[49] It is also quite true that reconciliation with the Church might involve change of atmosphere and status and will very probably require sacrifices which will be very difficult. But, if it is God who requires it through His illuminating grace, it is a matter between the person thus benefitted and God Himself; each must answer for the grace he receives. But if someone comes along with an attractive alternative in which he can secure the good of unity without this change and sacrifice, another element is added to the scale which makes his decision more difficult and which might even outweigh the call of grace.[50] What service is rendered this soul if the attractive

---

keeping each to its own persuasion, coalescing in one, leads the minds of non-Catholics away from conversion to the faith, and, by the journals it publishes, endeavors to prevent it." *Apostolicae sedi* in: E. F. Hanahoe *Two Early Documents on Reunion* (Graymoor: Chair of Unity Apostolate, 1954) p. 9. Also see: Idem, *Cardinal Newman and Corporate Reunion* (Graymoor: Chair of Unity Apostolate, 1951).

[49] An interesting observation of the Abbot of Downside (B.C. Butler): "Any 'return,' corporate or individual, must involve recognition of the Pope as vicegerent of Christ. Once an individual has reached the point of recognizing this truth, he cannot stay outside Catholic unity, since he would in that case be refusing obedience to Christ in the person of His earthly Vicar. It would therefore appear, if only logic and not psychology is considered, that a movement towards corporate reunion with the Catholic Church is likely to be defeated by its own dialectic. It may be taken to presuppose, among other things, a gradual leavening of the non-Catholic body with the principles of the Catholic Faith. But such a process will mean that first an individual here, then another there, will become conscious of the duty, incumbent on each believer, to eschew schismatical allegiances and adhere to the Catholic fellowship. These individuals might be expected to form the spear-point of further movement in the Catholic direction within the separated body; but precisely when they attain to this point of enlightenment they find themselves faced with the duty of what is unattractively called 'individual submission.'" In the introduction to: John M. Todd, *Catholicism and the Ecumenical Movement* (London: Longmans, 1956) pp. xii-xiii.

[50] It would be useful to include an observation made in a letter of Car-

alternative is merely conjectural and has not the remotest likelihood of ever being realized, or which will involve the decision of someone else which may or may not take place, and possibly in a future generation?

Given a clear knowledge of the end sought by Ecumenism, three major considerations set limits to grandiose schemes: the nature of the Catholic Faith, the necessity of the Church, and the order of the distribution of grace. These are prudential norms for any scheme of reunion. It must be remembered that the function of Ecumenism is to *assist* the separated brethren in their search for the truth and the true Church in order that they may enjoy the benefit of divinely-given unity, which means their return to the Catholic Church. The theories and activities of Ecumenism, consequently, are to be measured according to the clarity of their objective in this respect and the efficacy of the means chosen to obtain the end.

The Question of Development

We have examined the bearing of Ecclesiology on Ecumenism and have seen that the first must control the second because it controls its end. The extrinsic matter with which Ecumenism deals is ever changing, varying, moving, contingent, amid divergent situations, emphases, theory, orientation and procedure. This is to be expected, because it is a movement embodying the various influences of personalities, ideas and external events. Through it all runs one dominant

---

dinal Newman to a promoter of corporate reunion: "You know enough of my feelings on the whole subject that there are some things in it, in which I am afraid to follow you. . . . I mean . . . that the tendency of a portion of your pamphlet is . . . to persuade individual Anglicans to wait out of communion with the Catholic Church, till they can come over with the others in a body. There is such an extreme difficulty in rousing the mind to the real *necessity* of leaving the position into which men have grown up . . . that they will easily avail themselves of any slight excuse— and even a hint from a person so deeply respected as yourself . . . is more than sufficient to turn the scale, when the mind is in suspense . . . they have individual souls, and with what heart can I do anything to induce them to preach to others, if they themselves thereby become castaways. . . ." E. S. Purcell, *Life and Letters of Ambrose Phillips de Lisle* (London: Macmillan, 1900) I, 368. For other texts consult our study: *Cardinal Newman and Corporate Reunion* already cited.

desire—a real religious unity founded on the truth and in accordance with the mind of God.

Catholic Ecumenists enter this rolling sea. But they should not launch forth into the deep without chart, compass and sextant. They must take their bearings from what is necessary, permanent and immutable, if they are to be of any service to the separated brethren. They are to draw from the resources of Catholic theology the answers to the questions posed by this movement and to communicate these answers in such a way as will help the separated brethren to find the truth.[51] The directing of the light of Catholic truth upon the questions raised may serve also to illuminate portions of that truth which are as yet implicit or obscure. Thus, Ecumenism can enrich Ecclesiology by unfolding its implications. If it is to do this efficaciously, two principles are required: stability and consistency.

Stability. It is axiomatic in Catholic theology that the doctrines proposed by the Magisterium must always retain the same sense in which they were defined; moreover, the teaching of the Magisterium extends beyond matters of strictly defined dogma.[52] Pius XII declared:

> ... in the setting out and clarification of questions, in the conduct of discussions, and also in the choice of the mode of presentation, they should prudently adapt their speech to the particular genius and propensity of the times. But no one must disturb or upset what ought not to be changed. There has been too much talk, with too little investigation of a "new theology" which, with everything constantly evolving, must also evolve and be always progressing and never reached finality. If such an opinion were to be accepted, what would become of the unchang-

---

[51] In his (Anglican) essay, "Milman's View of Christianity," Newman made this observation: "What man is amid the brute creation, such is the Church amid the schools of the world; and as Adam gave names to the animals about him, so has the Church from the first looked round upon the earth, noting and visiting the doctrines she found there. . . . And wherever she went, in trouble or in triumph, she was still a living spirit, the mind and voice of the Most High; 'sitting in the midst of the doctors, both hearing them and asking them questions'; claiming to herself what they said rightly, correcting their errors, supplying their defects, completing their beginnings, expanding their surmises, and thus gradually by means of them enlarging the range and refining the sense of her own teaching." John Henry Newman, *Essays Critical and Historical* (London: Pickering, 1871) II, 232.

[52] Denziger 1800, 1683-1684.

ing dogmas of the Catholic Church and of the unity and stability of the faith?[53]

The field of Ecumenism is peculiarly susceptible to a certain restlessness with established teaching which some feel too confining (cf. *Humani generis*) and a passion to change everything that may seem to displease anyone. It is quite true that some things might be more fully or more clearly explained, but every new encyclical or definition fills out and throws more light on these truths. No one that I know of goes so far as to seek actual change in the doctrines themselves, but some manifest their impatience with precision in various ways: they may attack those who seek to follow the guidance of the Magisterium and call them "integralists;" they may proceed as if nothing had been taught on the subject; they may give what has been taught a meaning or an inference different from what was evidently intended.

Consistency. We must proceed from what has been clearly taught and examine every conclusion for its harmony with this teaching. There must be consistency. In other words, what is affirmed in one place must not seem to be denied or ignored in another; all the elements of a question must receive due attention within a complete context; regard must be had to the implications of a statement, whether actually contained in it or can be mistakenly inferred from it.[54] Pius XII directed:

---

[53] Pius XII "Discourse to the General Congregation of the Society of Jesus 17 Sept., 1946" in: Gaston Courtois ed., *The States of Perfection according to the teaching of the Church* (Dublin: M. H. Gill, 1961) p. 94.

[54] Vincent of Lerins wrote sixteen hundred years ago: "But perhaps some will say, Is there to be no progress of religion in the Church of Christ? There is, certainly, and very great. . . .But it must be a *progress* and not a *change*: for when each single thing is improved in itself, that is *progress*; but when a thing is turned out of one thing into another, that is *change*. Let, then, the intelligence, science and wisdom of each and all, of individuals and of the whole Church, in all ages and in all times, increase and flourish in abundance and vigor; but simply in its own proper kind, that is to say, in one and the same doctrine, one and the same sense, one and the same judgement. . . . The Church of Christ, being a vigilant and careful Guardian of the doctrine committed to her, makes no change in these at any time . . . her whole endeavor, her one aim . . . is to bring out into clearness what was once vague and incomplete, to strengthen and secure what is already developed and distinct, to keep

... when new or free questions are discussed, let the principles of Catholic teaching shine always before minds. Whatever sounds completely new in Catholic theology ought to be examined with vigilance and caution; what is certain and sure must be distinguished from what is put forward as conjecture, from what a passing and not always praiseworthy fashion can introduce even into theology and philosophy; the hand of friendship should be extended to the erring, but no concessions should be made to erroneous opinions.[55]

It is important to keep this principle of consistency in mind.[56] Inconsistency between the certain principles of Ecclesiology and the development of Ecumenism can manifest itself in three main directions, which have been indicated by the Sacred Magisterium: (1) As regards the end of Ecumenism one can fall into inconsistency by obscurity, significant silence and ambiguity.[57] (2) As regards the

---

watch and ward over doctrine already established and defined." *Commonitorium* N. 28, 32.

[55] Cf. Courtois, *States of Perfection,* etc., p. 94.

[56] Consistency is a confirmative motive of credibility. For example, Newman, in his novel of a conversion, puts these words into the mouth of his central character, an Anglican youth, Charles Reding: "When a system is consistent, at least it does not condemn itself. Consistency is not truth, but truth is consistency. Now, I am not a fit judge whether or not a certain system is true, but I may be quite a judge whether it is consistent with itself. When an oracle equivocates, it carries with it its own condemnation.... This too has struck me: that either there is no prophet of the truth on earth, or the Church of Rome is that prophet.... The Church of Rome has this *prima facie* mark of a prophet, that, like a prophet in Scripture, it admits no rival, and anathematizes all doctrine counter to its own. There is another thing: a prophet of God is of course at home with his message; he is not helpless and do-nothing in the midst of errors and in the war of opinions. He knows what has been given him to declare, how far it extends; he can act as an umpire; he is equal to emergencies. This again tells in favor of the Church of Rome. As age after age comes she is ever on the alert, questions every newcomer, sounds the note of alarm, hews down strange doctrine, claims and locates and perfects what is new and true. The Church of Rome inspires me with confidence; I feel I can trust her." John Henry Newman, *Loss and Gain,* (London: Longmans, Green, 1891) pp. 224-225.

[57] We have already given some of the official admonitions on this practice, but it will be useful to include here Leo XIII's strictures on what was termed 'Americanism': "... For they contend that it is opportune, in order to work in a more attractive way upon the wills of those who

characterization of the present situation one can be inconsistent through incompleteness and exaggeration: by incompleteness i.e. something true as far as it goes, but unsatisfying and tending to engender erroneous conclusions;[58] by exaggeration i.e. in the case of the Church, through excessive denigration, playing down its unique and divine character and playing up accidental human frailties, omitting necessary qualifications and counterbalancing facts, or, in the case of the separated brethren, by emphasizing the good they have (which is not to be denied) while neglecting to point out its objective insufficiency.[59] (3) As regards the status of the separated brethren and the bodies to which they belong and the consequences of such

---

are not in accord with us, to pass over certain heads of doctrines, as if of lesser moment, or to so soften them that they may not have the same meaning which the Church has invariably held.... Far be it, then, for anyone to diminish or for any reason whatever to pass over anything of this divinely delivered doctrine; whoever would do so, would rather wish to alienate Catholics from the Church than to bring over to the Church those who dissent from it. Let them return; indeed, nothing is nearer to our heart; let all those who are wandering far from the sheepfold of Christ return; but let it not be by any other road than that which Christ has pointed out." Leo XIII, *Testem Benevolentiae, Great Encyclical Letters Leo XIII*, (New York: Benziger, 1903) pp. 442-443.

"You must always see to it that you present the truth in such a way that it can be rightly understood and appreciated. Always use clear and never ambiguous terms. Avoid unnecessary and harmful changes of expression which easily modify the substance of the truth. Such has ever been the practice of the Catholic Church. And it agrees with that saying of St. Paul: "It was Jesus Christ, the Son of God, that I ... preached to you; and that preaching did not hesitate between yes and no; in him all is affirmed with certainty." Pius XII, "Address to Seminarians studying in Rome, June 24, 1939," in: Yzermans, *Pope Pius XII Theological Studies, op. cit.*, p. 72.

[58] e.g., By saying, "Christians are divided—Division is contrary to the will of Christ." The statements are true but incomplete. It should be made clear that the situation was brought about by *separation from* the Church, not *division of* the Church itself; moreover, the majority of Christians (the Catholic Church) are not in a condition contrary to the will of Christ in the matter of unity. (*Suppressio veri et suggestio falsi*).

[59] See our study "Vestigia Ecclesiae" referred to above. To put the matter in another way: the *sensus divisus* and the *sensus compositus* might be confused, e.g., by combining what should be distinguished: e.g., The separated bodies have many holy members, *ergo*, they are legitimate churches.

status, it is in this area that we find the most difficulty. This last point deserves fuller consideration.

One writer correctly notes: "... we should learn to engage in correct and objective *thinking* about separated Christians. This means that our thoughts should correspond to our doctrine and to the situations in which the separated brothers find themselves."[60] He could not have stated it better. Now, in the same article, we find the following description:

> ... Besides these practical reasons against concentrating chiefly on individual conversions, there are also theological reasons. During the four hundred years of separation, Protestants have had their own religious experience and have developed their own spirituality. Because of this heritage, based on so many Christian principles, including faith in Christ as God and Saviour, they have their own liturgy, their own theological methods and their own doctrine. In other words, they have their own religious past, their own Christian tradition. No one can deny that they possess real Christian values as well. ... But Protestants possess more than Christian values. It can be proved by historical-theological research that they have received charisms—special supernatural gifts bestowed by the Holy Spirit on individuals and congregations. ... Now it is clear that converts coming into the Church have to abandon only the charisms that are exercised in a congregation. This, however, may not be an easy task for them. Generally the convert has to make heroic efforts to become acquainted with the religious life of his new Catholic parish. ... Because of these factors, many separated Christians remain outside the Catholic Church, although they may have a certain awareness that the Catholic Church may be their Father's house. ...[61]

(The author of the above lines contends that we should work for a "corporate union.")

If all the author wanted to say in the above passage is the fact that, external to the visible structure of the Catholic Church, there are congregations of baptized persons whose members sincerely lead good lives, who hold many things that are true and good, there would be no difficulty in admitting it. Neither would we find difficulty with the

---

[60] Laurentius Klein "Has American Ecumenism a Future?" *op. cit.,* p. 335.

[61] *ibid.,* p. 333.

notion that Ecumenism should take account of this good and of the difficulties of the human level in securing their reconciliation with the Church, and that their intelligence, good faith and personal wishes should be respected at all times. However, the passage quoted bristles with unspoken and implicit suggestions which might be contrary to his intention, but which enter into the total impression we receive. For one thing, the reference to the theologies, might have been more clear if he added that they vary in doctrine from place to place, from time to time, from person to person, that they possibly embody error in content, or, at least, are incomplete and objectively insufficient, that the norm of understanding revelation is *in actu exercitu* if not *in actu signato* their personal judgment or experience;[62] this could not be otherwise, since they lack the guidance of the sacred Magisterium, which enjoys the special assistance of the Holy Spirit. There is no question at all that, amid all of this, there are many flecks of gold— supernatural truths that were orginally derived from the Catholic Church and it is upon these truths that they really live. But these truths and values should not be considered as obstacles to their reconciliation with the Church. Instead they should be used as means of securing their reconciliation with the Church.[63]

The author further states that these separated bodies have received from the Holy Spirit special charisms both as individuals and congregations. We have no intention of limiting the operations of the Holy Spirit, but certain observations are necessary. The charisms mentioned by St. Paul (I Cor. 12-14) were certain extraordinary gifts, particularly noteworthy and frequent in the early days of the Church. These powers are styled *gratiae gratis datae;* they need not be connected with virtue or grace in the possessor[64] (cf. I Cor. 13, 1-2)

---

[62] See Note 28 above.

[63] See our study "Vestigia Ecclesiae" *op. cit.,* pp. 343-380. Also our pamphlet *Ecumenism and Conversions,* pp. 7-15.

[64] St. Thomas says: "Dicendum est autem quod dicere aliquid in Spiritu Sancto potest intelligi dupliciter. Uno modo in Spiritu Sancto movente, sed non habito. Movet enim Spiritus Sanctus corda aliquorum ad loquendum quos non inhabitat; sicut legitur in Joan. 11, quod Caiphas hoc quod de utilitate mortis Christi praedixerat, a semetipso non dixit, sed per spiritum prophetiae. Balaam etiam multa vera praedixit motus a Spiritu Sancto ... licet eum non haberet. ...Alio modo loquitur aliquis in Spiritu Sancto movente et habito ..." In *Epist. I ad Corinthios* c. 12, Lect. i.

for example, Caiphas and Balaam were divine instruments of prophetic pronouncements; they are given for the benefit of others, especially for the up-building of the Church. Whether or not it is a fact that such powers were given to persons who were not actual members of the Church, I am not in a position to judge here. I can see the possibility of a given minister used by the Holy Spirit, *per modum actus*, as an instrument or occasion for a supernatural benefit to some souls in his congregation, say, moving them to true contrition, whether this would be considered as a charism or not is another question. I would have greater difficulty in conceiving such a charism existing *per modum habitus* and most especially *ex officio*.

As regards collective charisms, the notion is not clear. We cannot conceive of the Holy Spirit working against Himself.[65] In the Catholic Church, He is the principle of its unbreakable unity as a Soul in the Body; this relationship may not be predicated of any other society whatsoever.[66] If the Holy Spirit works in some other way in a separated society, (and we do not deny that He does), we cannot conceive of that influence as legitimatizing the separation from the Church, or the formation of another Church (or Churches) alongside the one He inhabits as its Soul, or of appearing to sanction opinions which are opposed to Catholic teachings, or of retaining souls in a state of separation. Whatever graces He bestows upon persons separated from the Church, it must be in the way of drawing them towards the Church and not of keeping them out of it.

---

[65] St. Augustine observed: "... And therefore all congregations, or rather dispersions, which call themselves Churches of Christ, and are divided and contrary to each other, and hostile to the congregation of unity, which is His true Church, do not belong to His congregation because they seem to bear His name. But they would belong to it if the Holy Spirit, in whom this congregation is bound together, were divided against Himself." Sermon 71.

[66] Pope Leo XIII wrote: "Let it suffice to state that, as Christ is the Head of the Church, so is the Holy Spirit her soul. 'What the soul is in our body, that is the Holy Spirit in Christ's body, the Church.' This being so, no further and fuller 'manifestation and revelation of the Divine Spirit, may be imagined or expected; for that which now takes place in the Church is the most perfect possible, and will last until that day when the Church herself, having passed through her militant career, shall be taken up into the joy of the saints triumphing in heaven." *Divinum illud, On the Holy Spirit* (New York: America Press, n.d.) p. 10.

We repeat that no truth possessed or grace received by the separated brethren can be said to be rightly interpreted if they are seen as obstacles to their reconciliation with the Church. Quite the contrary. Any difficulties there may be in this respect are to be sought on the human level.[67] We readily grant that, in all sincerity, these difficulties might assume such proportions as to preclude completely the consideration of their reconciliation with the Church, by producing what theologians, call "invincible ignorance" or "invincibly erroneous conscience." Or, it might be that the whole Catholic teaching has not yet been sufficiently proposed, or that the approach to the Church is gradual, i.e. they move in accordance with the lights given them by God as their studies advance—if they do this, that is all that may be reasonably expected from them.[68]

We certainly cannot help them by thinking up "theological" reasons for perpetuating their separation. The fact that they are involved in an Ecumenical movement shows their recognition of the insufficiency of their present state and its discordance with the most explicit will of

---

[67] Leo XIII wrote: "If those about to come back to their most loving Mother (not yet fully known, or culpably abandoned) should perceive that their return involves not indeed the shedding of their blood (at which price nevertheless the Church was bought by Jesus Christ) but some lesser trouble and labor, let them clearly understand that this burden has been laid on them not by the will of man but by the will and command of God" *Satis cognitum, op. cit.,* p. 4.

[68] Newman spoke to Anglicans thus: "There is one set of persons in whom every Catholic must feel intense interest, about whom he must feel the gravest apprehensions: viz., those who have some rays of light vouchsafed to them as to their heresy or as to their schism, and who seem to be closing their eyes upon it; or those who have actually gained a clear view of the nothingness of their own communion, and the reality and divinity of the Catholic Church, yet delay to act upon their knowledge. You, my dear brethren, if such are here present, are in a very different state from those around you. You are called by the inscrutable grace of God to the possession of a great benefit, and to refuse the benefit is to lose the grace. You cannot be as the others. . . . They have not yet had the call to inquire, to seek . . . and they will be judged according to what is given to them, not by what is not. But on you the thought has dawned, that possibly Catholicism may be true; you have doubted the safety of your present position . . . dare not to fall short of God's grace, or to lag behind when that grace moves forward. Walk with it, cooperate with it, and I know how it will end . . . " John Henry Newman, *Difficulties of Anglicans,* (London: Longmans, Green, 1897) I, 358-60.

Christ. At a time when the various denominations are investigating each other's traditions with a view to arriving at the whole truth, why should Catholic Ecumenists seek to harden their independence with respect to the Catholic Church when it alone has the full answer to what they are seeking? Perhaps it is the fear of seeming arrogant or appearing to offend. But we are not being arrogant when we simply transmit what we have received and we are not being offensive when we seek to be instrumental in securing for them the very benefit they seek, prompted by the highest charity and love of souls. Actually, clarity, firmness of principle and consistency will be the greatest help in the long run.[69] The Holy Office wrote to a group of Anglicans in 1865:

> ... You will also see that every effort at reconciliation must needs be in vain, except on condition of those principles on which the Church was first founded by Christ, and thenceforward in every succeeding age propagated one and the same throughout the world by the Apostles and their successors.[70]

Conclusion

After looking over what I have written, it might appear that undue emphasis has been laid upon the aberrations which Ecumenism might take with respect to Ecclesiology. I would not want it to be understood, however, that I question the legitimacy of the

---

[69] A discerning Anglican wrote many years ago: "From this point of view, instead of saying that she is hopeless because she will not change me ought rather to say that the fact of Rome's not changing is proved to be an abiding fact and must be reckoned with as such. In other words, instead of saying that our end is to change Rome, we should say that the starting point of our enterprises is the fact that she cannot change.

"In the same way, I should say that the proper function of the Anglican Church and also of the Dissenting bodies is to change and to move, since this is in fact what they have ever done. . . .

"One of her own communion has stated the case for us in a form that appears incontrovertible: 'It is,' he observes, 'a startling paradox but an equally certain truth, that in the very 'obstinacy' of Rome lies all hope of reunion. Without it all hope of reunion would be impossible. Without it, the very elements of unity would be hopelessly destroyed.'" Spencer Jones, *England and the Holy See*, (London: Longmans, Green, 1902) pp. 31-32, 34-35.

[70] Holy Office, *Quod vos*, cf. *Two Early Documents on Reunion, op. cit.*, p. 15.

effort itself or the motives of those who are striving for the reconciliation of the separated brethren with the Church. We simply wish to stress the fact that if there is to be a true development, it must be derived from and be consitent with what is permanent and immutable.

Ecumenism can serve the study of Ecclesiology in many ways. Not the least of these is the note of concreteness which it may give, through requiring consideration of the human elements in addition to the scientific categories. The living Church is the divine instrument for the salvation of souls and souls are not abstractions; we must deal with people as they are; the only danger is the direction of sympathy to the errors instead of to the persons.

Another element Ecumenism contributes is the acknowledgement of the actual good that is present in the separated brethren, the realization that we are not working in a vacuum, as it were, with unregenerate pagans who have nothing at all of divine truth or goodness; the only danger here is the exaggeration of its significance which may tend to engender in them a false sense of security—the Church itself is the means of salvation and they are, as yet, linked with her only by what is called an implicit intention. Due regard must be had to *both* aspects: the good itself and its objective insufficiency. Effort must be made to assist them to find the Church through the good they already have and through the external proposition of truths which they do not have and which, in fact, are involved intrinsically with what they already possess.[71]

Finally, Ecumenism impels the consideration of the personal factor in the communication of truth. People are not always logical and penetrating in their judgements; as this particular person is the medium through which one reaches a knowledge of the Church, what that person is will very likely enter into the total impression and eventual evaluation of his message. A long time ago, Aristotle designated what he called *"ethos"* as "the most potent of all the means to persuasion,"[72] and *ethos* is what establishes the personal credibility of the speaker. He says that the elements of *ethos* are: "intelligence, character, and good will."[73] We can see that even in the natural order

---

[71] See our "Vestigia Ecclesia" referred to above.

[72] Aristotle *Rhetoric*, 1-2, 1356a.

[73] *ibid.*, 2, 1, 1378a.

a person renders his message credible by what he *is,* quite as much and even more than by what he *says.* That is why the Holy Office says :

> ... Finally, all must be made conscious of the fact, that for those wandering outside the fold, there is no more efficacious means of preparing the way to embrace the truth and the Church than the faith of the Catholics associated with a good moral conduct and an edifying life.[74]

We have been concerned with the formation of clerics. In my opinion, three basic things should be strongly inculcated: Sound doctrine, prudence and charity. In regard to sound doctrine, we would urge that they derive their ecumenical principles from their standard theology and the documents of the Magisterium instead of from popular authors. The popular authors must be read and evaluated in the light of these documents. Wherever one comes across a gratuitous statement which cannot be identified with the teaching of the Church, it should be examined carefully. This is especially necessary for seminarians, lest attraction for novelty tend to override judgement and the continuity of principles be ignored. Prudence involves a constant awareness of the goal, as we have so frequently mentioned, which is "to assist those, who are in search of the truth and the true Church and to shield the faithful from the perils which readily follow in the tread of the movement," not the least of which is indifferentism. Lastly, charity furnishes the motive and the means—as a motive, which is to help the separated brethren to salvation through participation in the divinely-given unity of the Church; as a means, i.e. by friendliness and patience in all our dealings with them.

---

[74] Holy Office *Instruction,* etc., *op.cit.,* p. 8.

DOGMATIC FOUNDATIONS OF THE UNITY
OF THE CHURCH

SABBAS J. KILIAN, O.F.M.

I. Introduction

His Eminence Augustine Cardinal Bea, S.J., delivering the solemn address at the opening of the academic year at the University of Fribourg, Switzerland, in the Fall of 1961, pointed out to his audience that this twentieth century, so far, has produced four great religious movements: namely, Catholic Action, the liturgical, missionary, and the ecumenical movements. And he added that it seemed to him that at the present time the Holy Spirit is directing the attention not only of Catholics, but also of important circles of separated Christians to the idea of unity.[1]

This is the atmosphere in which we live today. For "there has never been a more ardent effort toward the reintegration of Christians in Catholic unity. There has, perhaps, never been a time when nostalgia for the visible Church was so deep-seated in the heart of Protestantism, or when there was so strong an ambition among

---

[1] "Le siècle où nous vivons connaît quatre grands mouvements religieux: l'*Action catholique*, c'est-à-dire l'apostolat des laïques, qui veut promouvoir dans tous les milieux du peuple chrétien la réalisation d'une vie chrétienne authentique; le *mouvement liturgique*, pui travaille à intérioriser notre vie cultuelle; le *mouvement missionnaire*, qui veut conduire au Christ les nonchrétièns, et le *mouvement oecuménique* qu travaille à réunir tous les baptisés dans *un seul* troupeau sous *un seul* pasteur. A l'heure actuelle, il semble que l'Esprit Saint oriente l'attention, non seulement des catholiques, mais aussi de très larges cercles de chrétiens séparés vers l'idée d'Unité." Aug. Cardinal Bea, "Travail scientifique et enseignement universitaire au service de l'Unité des chrétiens," *Nouvelle Revue Théologique*, LXXXIV (February, 1962), p. 127.—From the same Cardinal see also "The Council and Christian Unity," *Cross Currents*, XII (Spring, 1962), 255-268.

117

Christians to make the fullness of Christian living real in terms of a life of the Church."[2]

Unfortunately, the universal desire for unity, as of now, is far from realization. On the way to union great difficulties remain to be solved. Basic erroneous notions must be clarified or eliminated. And the dogmatic meaning and importance of the unity of the Church must be clearly understood in relation to the fullness of Christian truths.

It is the last of these tasks that we have proposed, though in a small and humble measure, to promote in this study. If we reach the true meaning and glimpse the importance of the unity of the Church by turning to its dogmatic background, we hope to clear up some notions of unity advanced by people who have, in the course of history, identified the dogmatic notion of unity with the juridical structure of the Church.

We are especially thinking of Friedrich Heiler[3] in whose opinion Christianity and the Catholic Church in particular reached the point where the juridical aspects became of primary importance while the intrinsic thought-content, the cult, dogmatic and moral teachings and the soteriological aspects of the Church were given but secondary importance.

This shifting in the consideration of the essential elements of the Church supposedly took place at the end of the twelfth century,[4] a turning point in the history of the Church. Up to that point it was the Spirit of God who guided the Church. Her life was pervaded by the supernatural, her membership oriented to the Almighty.[5] After that time, however, this soteriologically oriented community was turned into a merely human society based on juridical establishments: so much so that the sacred heritage of the old Christian community could hardly be detected in the Church any more.

Heiler and his friends became so imbued with this idea that they carried it to the extreme by professing that this human aspect of

---

[2] Henri De Lubac, S.J., *The Splendour of the Church*. Translated by Michael Mason. New York: Sheed and Ward. 1956. P.10.

[3] Friedrich Heiler, *Der Katholicismus*. Müchen. 1923. P. 276.

[4] Cf. Rudolf Sohm, *Das altkatholische Kirkenreicht und das Dekret Gratians*. Müchen. 1918.

[5] Heiler, *op. cit.*, p. 28.

the Church reached its apex in the Code of Canon Law, the spirit of which is certainly far from that expressed in the writings of the Fathers of the Church.[6] It was their firm conviction that if an ideal Pope ever happened to take over the chair of Peter, his very first act would be to suppress the Code of Canon Law and to restore the Bible to its original exclusive importance.[7]

It is our conviction that this and similar opinions make the path to union very rugged unless everybody involved understands the true nature of the Church and is willing to draw from it the conclusions pertinent to her unity. This is exactly what we intend to do now.

Our task is threefold: i.e., to review the dogmatic aspects of the problem, to discuss those articles of faith which form the basis for the unity of the Church, and to outline the soteriological consequences of this approach to the notion of unity.

II. Definition of Two Basic Terms

To begin this study properly two basic notions of the subject matter, namely, unity and Church, must be correctly defined.

1. *The notion of unity*

The general concept of unity is clearly expressed in the classical formula: "The one is undivided in itself and divided from every other."[1] This formula is entirely negative. It expresses only the negation of division, the exclusion of multiplicity in being: *ens indivisum*. It adds no new reality to it. Consequently, on this universal level of consideration, unity means the same as being. It is one of the transcendentals and convertible with being. "Hence it is that everything guards its unity as it guards its being."[2]

This transcendental unity of being allows us to recognize and to speak of other kinds of unity, that is, of predicamental unities. Nevertheless, while indivision of being forms the basis for trans-

---

[6] *Ibid.*, p. 30.

[7] *Ibid.*

[1] Cf. St. Thomas, *Summa Theologica*, I, q, 11; 30, a. 3; I-II, q. 17, a. 4; see also Louis De Raeymaeker, *The Philosophy of Being*. Translated by Edmund H. Ziegelmeyer, S.J. St. Louis: Be Herder Book Co. 1957. P. 61.

[2] S.T., I, q. 11, a. 1

cendental unity, particular or predicamental unities are based on the indivision of certain sections of being only, and can be called unities only in so far as they are considered in relation to other realities. For this reason they are classified as relative or predicamental unities. They are of two main types: essential and accidental unities. Again, essential unities are subdivided into natural and artificial unities, these latter being realized on moral or juridical entities.

2. *The notion of the Church*

The second notion to be defined is that of the Church. There is no official definition of the Church. Yet, when we analyze the various definitions offered by theologians, the reality of the Church becomes manifest. According to St. Thomas, "the Church, on earth, is the congregation of the faithful."[3] Karl Adam, on the other hand, describes the notion of the Church in this way: "If we ask the Catholic Church herself to tell us, according to her own notion of herself, what constitutes her essential nature and what is the substance of her self-consciousness, she answers us through the mouth of the greatest of her teachers, that the Church is the realization on earth of the Kingdom of God. " 'The Church of today, of the present, is the Kingdom of Christ and the Kingdom of Heaven': such is the empathic assertion of St. Augustine (De civ. Die XX, 9, 1)."[4]

Actually, it is perhaps the definition of St. Robert Bellarmine which is the most tested and the most widely known: "The Church is a society of men united by professing the same faith and by administering the same sacraments under the authority of the legal pastors, particularly the Pope of Rome who is Christ's vicar on earth."[5] Yet, we feel that this definition, while asserting the supernatural character of the Church, appears rather to emphasize the external juridical criteria. My former professor of happy memory, A. Schütz, on the contrary, points exactly to the intrinsic thought-content of the Church, by writing: "The Church is a religious com-

---

[3] S.T., III, q. 8, a. 4; St. Bonaventure, *De Perfectione Statuum*, n. 9.

[4] *The Spirit of Catholicism*. Translated by Dom Justin McCann, O.S.B. New York: The MacMillan Co. 1941. p. 15; see also the definition of the Vatican Council: "Pastor aeternus et episcopus animarum nostrarum, ut salutiferum redemptionis opus perenne redderet, sanctam aedificare Ecclesiam decrevit, in qua velut in domo Dei viventis fideles omnes unius fidei et caritatis vincula continerentur." Denzinger, n. 1821.

[5] "De definitione Ecclesiae," *De Ecclesia militante toto orbe diffusa*, c. 2.

munity whose mission is to carry out, upon the mandate of Christ, the sanctification of man till the very end of time; her members, as the mystical body of Christ, are bound to each other and to God by faith, by the means of salvation and by obedience to legal authority."[6] "The mystical body of Christ,"—this is the most meaningful notion of the Church! As Pius XII worded it: "If we would define and describe this true Church of Jesus Christ—which is the One, Holy, Catholic, Apostolic, Roman Church—we shall find no expression more noble, more sublime, or more divine than the phrase which calls it 'the mystical Body of Jesus Christ.' This title is derived from and is, as it were, the fair flower of the repeated teaching of Sacred Scripture and the Holy Fathers."[7]

Though there is no official definition of the Church, we can note on the basis of the aforementioned definitions that the nature of the Church is as deep and as inexhaustible as is the nature of Our Lord. Each and every one of them is true. Each and every one expresses and reflects the Church to a greater or lesser extent. Yet, all of them together must be taken into consideration if we are to grasp the real meaning and mission of the Church.

3. The state of the question

From what has been said so far we must conclude that the Church, being comprised of one supernatural principle and of a plurality of persons with one common purpose, is an artificial moral entity in the line of essential unities. She has, so to speak, the unity of a living organism in which specialized parts with specialized functions all act for the good of the whole.[8] Consequently, she must be undivided. To guard her being and existence she must guard her unity and indivision. But what is the innermost core of this unity and indivision? The above quoted definitions of the Church have made it clear that there are two constitutive elements in the Church: on the one hand, the visible external element made up by the membership

---

[6] A. Schütz, *Dogmatika*. Budapest. 1937. Vol. II, p. 236; see also A. Schütz, Summarium Theologiae Dogmaticae et Fundamentalis. Budapest. 1936. P. 343.

[7] *Mystici Corporis*. 1943.

[8] Cf. S.T., III, q. 8, aa. 1, 4; see also B. Wuellner, *Dictionary of Scholastic Philosophy*. Milwaukee: The Bruce Publishing Co. 1955. Pp. 127-128.

of the community, the act of incorporation, and the juridical frame-work, hierarchical structure, public profession of faith, visible means of salvation, etc., and on the other hand, the indivisible, intrinsic element, the inner force which animates the community as such and incorporates the individuals into Christ—the mysterious presence of Christ as the head and of the Holy Spirit as the animating principle of the Church; union with both Christ and the Holy Spirit, etc.

These two elements give rise to a double indivision and a double unity for the Church. As a juridical community the Church "is divided from every other" community. She is not only one, she is unique of her kind. As a community animated by a supernatural intrinsic principle she "is undivided in herself." The same centripetal force of the unity of principle draws all her members toward the center of the community: Christ Himself. So much so that in virtue of her intrinsic principle the Church is not only undivided in herself but also indivisible. Consequently, though both extrinsic and in-trinsc unity are inherent in the notion of the Church, the former supposes and is rooted in the latter as in its reason and cause. Ex-trinsic unity can be exposed to danger and can be damaged to a cer-tain extent, intrinsic unity never! Therefore, in order to understand the full meaning of the unity of the Church we must concentrate our attention on the notion of this intrinsic unity.

III. Basic Dogmatic Relationships

The question involved in this inquiry can be worded as follows: What are the fundamental articles of faith regarding the intrinsic unity of the Church? We shall answer this question by investigating three relationships, namely:

1. What is the relationship of the Church through Christ to the Father?
2. What is the relationship of the Church through Christ to the Son?
3. What is the relationship of the Church through Christ to the Holy Spirit?

These three relationships are rooted in the utter dependence of the Church's whole being on Christ. She is His body and His *alter ego* in so far as He continues to live in her, and He in her head. Since the whole theology of Christ has been developed on the basis of these three relationships, we feel that the theology of His mystical body must follow the same course. Besides this general consideration there are also two factual reasons for advancing this approach to the problem: namely, the testimonies of St. Paul and Tertullian in this regard. St. Paul, at the beginning of his Epistle to the Ephesians,[1] clearly expresses this triple relationship of the Church to the Blessed Trinity by ascribing to each Person the action which belongs to Him in the work of our redemption. Tertullian, on the other hand, called the Church the "body of the three Persons" and said that the reason for mentioning the Church at Baptism is that whenever the Blessed Trinity is mentioned, the Church must be mentioned as well, since she is the body of the three Persons.[2] We are convinced, therefore, that the consideration of these relationships will help us to understand the nature of the Church and the necessity of her unity.

1. *What is the relationship of the Church through Christ to the Father?*

By investigating this relationship we intend to discover the deepest metaphysical *ratio*, as it were, of the entity of the Church: that thought-content on which rests her ontological possibility.

A. *The ontological possibility of the Church is rooted in the eternal idea of the Father.*

As the Father's relationship to the Son is grounded in the idea of generation expressed in the Son from all eternity, the Church, too, as the historical expression and representation of the Son incarnate, traces her ontological possibility back to the eternal Idea and decree of the Father.

St. Thomas, speaking of creation, perceived the ontological possibility of each and every created being in the ideas existing in the divine mind: "God is the first exemplar cause of all things. In proof whereof we must consider that if for the production of anything an exemplar is necessary, it is in order that the effect may receive a determinate form. For an artificer produces a determinate form in

---

[1] Eph. 1:1-14

[2] *De Baptismo*, c. VI; P.L. t. I, col. 1315 A; cf. De Oratione, c. II; P.L. t. I, col. 1256-1257; *De Pudicitia*, c. XXI; P. L. t. I, col. 1080 B; see also St. Clement of Alexandria, Paedagogus, lib. I, c. VI; P. G. t. VIII, col. 282 C

matter by reason of the exemplar before him, whether it is the exemplar beheld externally, or the exemplar interiorly conceived in the mind. Now it is manifest that things made by nature receive determinate forms. This determination of forms must be reduced to the divine wisdom as its first principle, for divine wisdom devised the order of the universe, which order consists in the variety of things. And therefore we must say that in the divine wisdom are the types of all things, which types we have called ideas—*i.e.*, exemplar forms existing in the divine mind."[3]

The Church is a being. She has all the characteristics of a true reality. In virtue of her material and formal cause, the visible and invisible elements of her ontological structure, she is a part of history and as such she makes her presence felt in this world. To explain her being and becoming, therefore, we must trace her, too, back to the *rationes aeternae* of the Divine Artificer.

How is this to be understood? Every artist who thinks wisely starts out by making a blueprint. First, he must come up with an idea to be realized, then, in the light of this idea, he must decide on the means and method of realization. Be it a masterpiece or just a simple production by an artisan it is never intended to express an idea of a wholly general, indeterminate nature. It must be precise in its thought-content and very definite in its purpose. For example, the general idea of a house is that it be habitable. Yet, before it can be built, the architect must be supplied with a precise knowledge as to who will live in it or for what other purpose it will be used. Only if he has this information can the architect start drawing up the blueprint in order to build the house with specific purposes. In other words, the general idea must be converted into well detailed, specific information in order to inspire the artist and to enable the contractor to do his job. Otherwise, they would be committed to a purposeless, dull, and montonous undertaking devoid of all value and practicality.

"God, the Creator of the universe, is the greatest Architect. Therefore, before He set in motion the process of creation He had to draw up His divine plans. The general creative intention was not enough. He had to specify the purpose and the kind of His creation...."[4]

This important thesis becomes more evident if considered in the

---

[3] S.T., I, q. 44, a. 3; cf. q. 15, a. 1
[4] A. Horvath, *Krisztus királysága*. Budapest. 1926. P. 165.

light of the notion of objective sanctity. According to the teaching of the Church, every created thing is sacred in so far as, somehow, it participates in the being of God—as it belongs to God and depends on Him in its being and existence. For the notions of belonging and depending imply the act of being so ordained and consecrated by God Himself.

The Church as a creature enjoys this objective sanctity to a greater degree than most other creatures because her ordination and consecration are more specific and more direct. She is not only the determination of an exemplar existing in the divine mind but the *alter ego* of the Son of God Incarnate. Her whole being and existence belongs to and depends on the second Person of the Blessed Trinity. Therefore, in both her ontological thought-content and her eventual becoming the Church is consecrated to the mission of the Son of God. The eternal divine idea of Christ and the eternal divine idea of the Church are one and the same. They belong together. They are inseparable.

The beauty and value of this reflection is fully displayed in the Christocentric approach to the structure of creation. For if it is true that the two divine ideas belong the one to the other and that the eventual realization of the Church is rooted in the eternal divine decree predestining the Son of God to become the Christ of the universe, the Christocentric outlook of creation is, by the same token, an Ecclesiocentric proposition. The Kingdom of Christ means the Kingdom of the Church. And above all, the unique relationship of the Father to the Son must be terminated in the unique relationship of the Father to the Church. Through this analysis of the parallel realities of one God, one Christ, and one Church, then, we have really discovered the ontological foundation of the unity and unicity of the Church.

Let us, therefore, devote ourselves to a consideration of this Christo—Ecclesiocentric structure of creation.

The tone is set by St. Paul, the troubadour of the Firstborn:

"Even as he chose us in him before the foundation of the world, that we should be holy and without blemish in his sight in love. He predestined us to be adopted through Jesus Christ as his sons, according to the purpose of his will, unto the praise of the glory of his grace, with which he has favored us in his beloved son. In him we have redemption through his blood, the remission of sins, according to the riches of his grace."[5] "For in him were created all things in the heavens and on earth, things visible and things invisible, whether Thrones, or Dominations, or Principalities, or Powers. All things have been created through and unto him, and he is before all creatures, and in him all things hold together."[6]

These texts of St. Paul suggest to us that not only creation but also the eternal divine ideas should be looked upon as having one and the same purpose, one and the same center: Christ. This is why the whole history of creation revolves around Him. If we may say so, Christ enters into the picture of creation with God. He co-operates with God in order to make the world the vestige and image of both God and the God-Man. It was, therefore, the intention of God to create and to organize the structure of the world in such a way that it always proclaim the glory of its Creator together with the glory of Christ, the Son of God Incarnate.[7]

B. *Consequences of the Christocentric structure*

It is a well known sociological principle that the more fundamental a relationship is the less it becomes a separating wall between men. It rather unites them.[8] Now, man's relationship to God is the most fundamental of all, for it makes up the entire being and destiny of *mankind*. For it was not only this or that individual man whom the creative act of God ordered to the service of Christ in the Christocentric structure of the world. Mankind as such, the immense society of human beings was the subject matter of that order, in the first instance; and the individual's obligation, in this regard, is but the

---

[5] Eph. 1:4-7

[6] Col. 1:16-17

[7] Cf. Prov. 8:24-31; Ecclus. 24:5; Col. 1:14-18; for the Scotistic idea of the Christocentric world, see Jean-Marie Bissen, O.F.M., "De Primatu Christi Absoluto apud Coloss. I, 13-20. Expositio dogmatica," *Antonianum*, II (1936), pp. 3-26; Jean-Francois Bonnefoy, O.F.M., "A propos de la primauté du Christ," *Verdad y vida*, VIII (1950), pp. 229-35;—, "La place du Christ dans le plan divin de la création," *Mélanges de science religieuse*, IV (1947), pp. 257-84; V (1948), pp. 39-62; Diomede Sacramuzzi, O.F.M., *Duns Scoto Summula*, 1932; A.—D. Sertillanges, O.P., "Religion et universalité," *L'église est une*. Bloud & Gay. 1939; Michael Meilach, O.F.M., *Firstborn Son*. Chicago: Franciscan Herald Press. 1962.

[8] A.—D. Sertillanges, O.P., "Religion et universalité," op.cit. pp. 28-29.

consequence of the collective destiny and responsibility of the community. This twofold aspect of destiny, service and responsibility in the Christocentric structure makes it mandatory that, in order to carry out its basic relational duties expressed in the creative act of God, the community be guided by identical principles in the service of Christ and produce homogeneous forces and patterns of actions to promote the union of its members with Christ. The historical determination and realization of these collective duties toward Christ and the individual is the Church. For "existing as she does by the will of God, the Church is necessary to us—necessary as a means. And more than this. The mystery of the Church is all mystery in little; it is our mystery *par excellence.* It lays hold on the whole of us and surrounds us; for it is in His Church that God looks upon us and loves us, in her that He desires us and we encounter Him, and in her that we cleave to Him and are made blessed."[9]

We do not think that—nor want to give the impression that—on the basis of the preceding considerations, we have found a sure way to prove the necessity of the unity of the Church. We have merely been looking for its ontological thought-content, its inner possibility in the creative act of God. We have found this in the Christocentric structure of the universe: since we have been created for the service and glory of Christ, our whole *raison d'etre* is traced back to, and rooted in, the eternal divine idea of the Incarnation of the Son of God. In virtue of the same creative act of God Christ has determined to carry out the Christocentric orientation of mankind in and through His Church. Therefore, Christ and His Church are inseparable. Their relation is unique, unchangeable and most fundamental.

C. *Articles of faith involved in this relationship.*

It goes without saying that this relationship, being an objective one, is thoroughly supported by certain truths of the Catholic faith: namely,

a. *God is one.* Since His innermost Essence is self-existence, He is *esse per se subsistens.* He is also absolute Intellect and absolute Will in virtue of the identity of His faculties with His Essence. Furthermore, He is pure Act, *Actus Purus*: potentiality, as the sign

---

[9] Henri De Lubac, S.J., *The Splendour of the Church.* Translated by Michael Mason. New York: Sheed and Ward. 1956. Pp. 24-25.

of composition and imperfection, is totally alien to His Being. Due to this fact, the activities of His divine Intellect and Will are the root of all realities: His Intellect designs the exemplar for them by assembling the essential constitutive elements of their essences. His Will puts these exemplars into the existential order, creates and preserves them both as individuals and as parts or members of the whole of mankind and the universe. Consequently, if there are individual or social, collective beings in this world they must constantly bear witness to their *raison d'etre*, the activities of the divine Intellect and Will. The Church is no exception. As a tremendously important moral unit she is a created reality sealed with the oneness of God and the oneness of her relation to Him.

b. *Mankind is one.* We are very much aware of the fact that personality is the apex of the qualities of human nature. The personal being and value of the individual is unsurpassable; therefore in itself it does not depend either on the community or on other individuals. It is constituted directly by its own relationship to God. However, we feel that Father Sertillanges has expressed a great truth by saying that mankind must be one while standing before God and praying to Him.[10] Why? What is the reason for this? If we are not mistaken the reason is a metaphysical necessity: namely, the recognition of the fact that everything depends on God in its being as well as in its mode of being. This dependence is complete and absolute. Metaphysically speaking, it generates a common act of adoration on the part of each rational creature.

Furthermore, the fact that the creation, the fall, and the redemption of mankind each took place through one act seems to underscore the fact that the eternal divine Intellect has also contemplated the individual persons as parts of the whole and that the community of mankind as such has its own direct relationship to God which, in some regard, could become decisive factors for the individual. This means that basically the relationship of the individual to God supposes that of mankind to God and must be in conformity with it. As A. Schütz worded it: "God is one, and the spiritual nature of man is one; therefore, religion, even in the natural order, can be but one;

---

[10] *Op. cit.,* p. 29.

all the more so in the supernatural order."[11] Considered from this basic viewpoint, religion does not tolerate any subjective elements or any contradictory manifestations. It cannot be changed, nor refused. It must be accepted as the adoring recognition and realization of this basic relationship.

c. *Christ is the one final cause of mankind.* Strictly speaking, this is what St. Paul meant by writing to the Colossians, that "He is the image of the invisible God, the firstborn of every creature. For in him were created all things in the heavens and on earth, things visible and invisible...."[12] If he is the image and if we were created in Him and for Him, it can rightly be said with Father Sertillanges, that he is the UNIVERSAL MAN[13] in the sense that He is the goal of each and every man as well as of the whole of mankind. Direct contact with the Christ of history, however, was the privilege of relatively few people. The rest of mankind must seek a union with the Mystical Christ. Where is He to be found? In the Church whose Head and essence He is. And so union with Christ means union with the Church. UNIVERSAL MAN means THE UNIVERSAL CHURCH. Consequently, Christ as the supernatural final cause in the creation of human individuals must be reached in both His historical and His mystical entity. In the first, He must be recognized and accepted as God-Man, the Redeemer of the world; in the second, He must be attained in the Church, the permanent, living organism of His redemptive merits and activities. For the two—Christ and the Church—belong together as two aspects of one and the same relationship to God.

What, then, does the relationship of the Church to the Father mean? It means that one and the same eternal divine forms the root and the ontological thought-content of both the Incarnation and the establishment of the Church. Also, that the same divine idea determines the basic objective of both the human individuals and their community to God. Objectively speaking, therefore, the notion of the unity of the Church is a concomitant to the fundamental notion of religion.

---

[11] *Summarium theologiae dogmaticae et fundamentalis.* Budapest, 1936. P. 364.
[12] Col. 1:15-16
[13] *Op. cit.,* p. 31.

2. *What is the relationship of the Church through Christ to the Son?*

While the relationship of the Church to the Father revealed to us the root and ontological thought-content of the nature and the unity of the Church, her relationship to the Son, in virtue of the Incarnation, will show us the actualization and concrete unity of the Church. In other words, her real existence and concrete unity becomes the realization of that thought-content which we have found in the Divine Creative Act, expressing both the Incarnation and reality of the Church. It was the second Person of the Blessed Trinity who became man in Christ. His personality assumed human nature. Consequently, it is the same Second Person who, in Christ, forms the substance of the Church by continuing His life in her.

If, therefore, we intend to investigate the relationship of the Church to the Son, the problem should actually be worded this way: How is the Mystical Christ realized in the Church? And what is the connection between the Church and the Christ of history?

The content of this problem will, therefore, be reduced to and analyzed in the following elementary aspects:

A. How does the Church depend on Christ a. in her existence; b. in her nature?

B. How is the unity of the Church rooted in Christ a. as a principle; b. as mediator?

A. *The Dependence of the Church on Christ*

a. *How does the Church depend on Christ in her existence?*

In order to answer this question precisely, we must return to the birth of the Church and try to perceive the role of the different causes in her origin. We are especially interested in discovering the efficient, exemplary, formal, material, and final causes of the Church.[14]

aa. In the preceding considerations of this study we have already made it clear that the Church is divine in her origin. Therefore, her efficient cause is God. Nevertheless, a distinction is in order here. In so far as the idea of the Church is concerned, this causality is appropriated to the Father; in relation to her actual existence, however, this causality is appropriated to the Son Incarnate. For in

---

[14] Hermannus Dieckmann, *De Ecclesia,* II, p. 248.

virtue of the definition proper of the efficient cause: an intrinsic principle giving existence.[15] Christ must be looked upon as the immediate Power behind the establishment of the Church. On the ground of both these appropriations the Church fully deserves the title, "*Ecclesia Dei.*"[16] We are also justified in concluding that in virtue of her nature and of her participation in the properties of here efficient cause, she must possess not only indefectibility and sanctity, but also unicity as a fundamental mark of her nature.

That Christ actually founded the Church is a fact so clear in Sacred Scripture that no one can deny it. Furthermore, if we analyze the different elements that entered into her foundation, we will necessarily be led to admit her unity.

The *regnum Dei* announced by God in the Old Testament[17] was realized in the New Testament. Christ Himself, in the very beginning of His public life, spoke of the presence of the Kingdom of God. And He borrowed from the Old Testament not only the term *regnum Dei,* but also the essential elements of that notion. In the Old Testament the real foundation of the kingdom of God was the unique and exclusive covenant between God and the chosen people. The kingdom was looked upon as the community of those who had entered into an alliance with God. This is exactly the notion of the *regnum Dei* applied by Christ to the Church and announced by Him to His first followers: a unique and exclusive new alliance with God, a visible community whose members would be the partakers of the Mysteries of Christ.

Both these communities are the kingdom of God and both have been provided with visible signs of their establishment. However, due to extreme nationalism and other political factors, the *regnum Dei* as announced by Christ had to be dissociated from the erroneous notions advocated by the Jews in their interpretations of the prophecies of the Old Testament. This is why a twofold aspect and consideration was introduced in the notion of the *regnum Dei* in Holy Scripture. The *regnum Dei* of the Old Testament was merely the shadow, the figure, the vestige, in other words, the "*tutor unto*

---

[15] Cf. St. Thomas, *De Veritate*, q. 2, a. 14.
[16] I Tim. 3:15; *ibid.* 3:5.
[17] Cf. I Par. 28:5-7; II Par. 13:8; Dan 2:44.

Christ."[18] It is only in the generic notion of the *regnum Dei* that the Church and synagogue meet. They differ specifically. The first covenant and the synagogue, as the vestige and figure of the Church, had to come to an end with the Incarnation of Christ and with the appearance of the Church.

How did this new *regnum Dei* come about? How was the Church of Christ born? As the doctrine of redemption by Christ and his whole mission as the Saviour was introduced gradually, so was the case with the definition and foundation of the Church. The preparatory work was laid down by the announcement of the new *regnum Dei*. Christ did not want the old leaders and teachers any longer. He chose new ones, the twelve apostles. They became the elite, the governing body of the new community to be born, with the commission to integrate all the followers of Christ into one community by remaining faithful to Him in the teaching of His doctrine: "Who is my mother and who are my brethren?" And stretching forth His hand towards His disciples, He said, "Behold my mother and my brethren! For whoever does the will of my Father in heaven, he is my brother and sister and mother."[19] In opposition to the distorted and wordly notion of the kingdom of God acclaimed by the leaders and teachers of the Jewish people, He announced a new mark for those who would bring to the new community, namely, the fulfillment of the will of the Father. And He did so in virtue of His infallible knowledge that the fulfillment of the Father's will would also bring men to Him and through Him to the Church, since the mission of Christ and the Church is the most perfect realization of the idea and the will of the Father.

What had been expressed by Christ in the above quotation became more concrete in the promise to Peter that he would be the visible head of the Church: "And I say to thee, thou art Peter, and upon this rock I will build my Church, and the gates of hell shall not prevail against it. And I will give thee the keys of the kingdom of heaven."[20] A new community was born, a new rock was chosen in order to construct on it the Church as the *regnum Christi*.

It must also be added that this new community was contemplated

[18] Gal. 3:24.
[19] Matt. 12:48-50.
[20] Matt. 16:18-20.

and founded by Christ as a living organism. Christ first announced it in general terms to Nicodemus: "Amen, amen, I say to thee, unless a man be born again of water and the Spirit, he cannot enter into the kingdom of God."[21] Later on He described the organic character of this community in the parable of the vine-dresser. Every branch in me that bears no fruit, He will take away; and every branch that bears fruit, He will cleanse that it may bear more fruit ... Abide in me and I in you. As the branch cannot bear fruit of itself unless it remain on the vine, so neither can you unless you abide in me."[22] This living organism, with her hierarchical structure, conceived as an instrument for the fulfillment of the Father's will, entered history on the first Pentecost of Christianity as one community of rulers and subjects: "And when the days of Pentecost were drawing to a close, they were all together in one place ... and they were all filled with the Holy Spirit and began to speak in foreign tongues even as the Holy Spirit prompted them to speak."[23]

Therefore, no one can doubt that according to Scripture Christ founded the Church. It is no longer a matter of discussion that He is the efficient cause of the Church. It is Christ who stands behind her. Thanks to His effective power, the Church is a reality.[24]

And so we have completed our investigation into the first aspect of the relationship of the Church to the Son on the basis of causality. It was the Incarnate Son who, as the efficient Cause, fulfilled the eternal divine will by establishing the Church as the new *regnum Dei*.

bb. The exemplary cause is a form conceived in the mind of a free agent that serves as a model for the production of a given effect.[25] From the preceding considerations it is easy to infer that the exemplary cause, according to which the Son Incarnate founded His Church, can be approached from two different points of view. The

---

[21] Jn. 3:5.

[22] Jn. 15:1-2,4.

[23] Acts 2:1-2,4.

[24] Denzinger, *Enchiridion*, 2145.

[25] St. Thomas, *Commentary on the Metaphysics of Aristotle*. Translated by John P. Rowan. Chicago: Henry Regnery Co. 1961. Vol. I, p. 305.

eternal divine decree of the Incarnation already contains the form of the Church conceived by the divine Intellect, and so this divine decree could be considered, to a certain extent, as the exemplar of the Church. However, in this connection, the relation of the divine decree is primarily to the Incarnation and only secondarily to the Church. For the Church as the continuation of the life of the Son Incarnate is rooted in this idea on the condition that the Incarnation will take place. It follows from this, that the immediate exemplar of the Church is Christ Himself, the Incarnate Word, who now as the Christ of history enters into a relation with the Church in order to call His Mystical Body to assure His continuing presence in the current of history. "The exemplary cause of the Church is Jesus Christ, the God-Man, since He unites in His one Person both the divine and human nature, is the Redeemer of the human race, Messiah and King, divine Legate and religious Master. It was in virtue of this theandric exemplar that the Church was founded. For she is a living organism uniting in herself both divine and human, intrinsic and extrinsic elements. She is the great "mystery" of our salvation: she grants and distributes the graces of Christ, the fruits of redemption. She is the messianic kingdom, the depository of Christ's doctrine and the teacher of all nations."[26] In view of this exemplary cause we can understand now St. Paul's encouraging words to the Colossians: "Therefore, as you have received Jesus Christ Our Lord, so walk in him, be rooted in him and built up on him, and strengthened in the faith as you also have learned, rendering thanks abundantly."[27] What St. Paul meant is this: In the life of the Church the exemplary cause must be fulfilled not only in the establishment of the Church, *secundum rationem finis*, in so far as her members are being transformed into the Model of the Church. The Christ of history, therefore, as the immediate exemplary cause of His Mystical Body, impels both the community and the membership to become more and more like Him, the Model of the Church.

cc. A formal cause is the constituent principle that accounts for the specific perfection of a composite being.[28] This means that the quiddity of a composite being always depends on its formal cause.

---

[26] H. Dieckmann, *op. cit.*, p. 248.

[27] Col. 2:6-7.

[28] St. Thomas, *ibid.*

This is why to grasp things in their true nature we have to grasp them in their formal cause. For the intrinsic structure of composite beings always rests on this principle. Very often even their external characteristics are determined by it.

What, then, is the formal cause of the Church? What is that principle in which we can detect her extrinsic and intrinsic unifying powers? In other words, what is the quiddity and what is the extrinsic structure of the Church?

Because the Church is the Mystical Body of Christ, it is evident that Christ Himself must be this constituent principle of the intrinsic and extrinsic perfections of the Church. To be more precise, however, we must make a very important distinction here.

Intrinsically, the Church lives by the merits of Christ. These merits are channeled through faith and the sacraments to those who wish to be united with Christ.[29] The activating principle in this process, however, is the Holy Spirit who as the Spirit of the Church performs these activities: "Now there are varieties of gifts, but the same Spirit; and there are varieties of ministries, but the same Lord.... Now the manifestation of the Spirit is given to everyone for profit."[30]

While the Holy Spirit through the channels of faith and the sacraments establishes this union between Christ and His Church, on the one hand, and between her individual members, on the other, the unity of the extrinsic structure is assured by the communication of the authority and power of Christ to the visible rulers of the Church: "All power in heaven and on earth has been given to me. Go, therefore, and make disciples of all nations, baptizing them in the name of the Father, and of the Son, and of the Holy Spirit, teaching them to observe that I have commanded you; and behold, I am with you all days, even unto the consummation of the world."[31] This shows clearly enough, we hope, how the intrinsic and extrinsic structure of the Church is built on Christ as her formal principle.

dd. A material cause in the constitutive potential principle of a composite being.[32] In virtue of this definition, generally speaking,

---

[29] Matt. 28:20; Mark 16:16.
[30] I Cor. 12:4,11.
[31] Matt. 28:18-20.
[32] St. Thomas, *ibid.*, p. 308.

the material cause of the Church comprises the sum total of those individuals who make up the Church. For the Church is a community embracing many individuals. When Christ sent His apostles to teach all nations, He made it clear that the Church should be a union of many, a community comprising all nations and as many individuals as possible. In speaking of the material cause of the Church, however, we must distinguish two groups of individuals: the first embraces all to whom the appeal has been made and who have the general obligation to enter the Church,[33] and the second embraces the actual membership of the Church. If analyzed, the first classification will reveal the universality and unicity of the Church; the second, the conditions of actual incorporation in the body or in the soul of the Church. We will pass over these aspects at the present, and return to them later when we investigate the true meaning of the traditional axiom: "Outside the Church there is no salvation."

ee. Lastly, we shall determine the final cause of the Church. A final cause is that on account of which something is or is done.[34] It is therefore the goal, purpose, or end in virtue of which a thing is or an action is performed. The proximate goal of the Church is expressed in the mission of the apostles.[35] It contains two great areas of activity: teaching and sanctification. Both of these areas have as their objective the promotion and the preservation of the faith: "Simon, Simon! behold, Satan has desired to have you, that he may sift you as wheat. But I have prayed for thee, that thy faith may not fail; and do thou, when once thou hast turned again, strengthen thy brethren."[36]

The remote goal of the Church not only embraces the teaching and sanctification of her membership on earth but also has as its objective the incorporation of her members of Christ in glory.

The ultimate goal of the Church is beautifully expressed in St. Paul's words: "For he [Christ] must reign, until "he has put all his enemies under his feet." And the last enemy to be destroyed will be death, for "he has put all things under his feet." But when he says all things are subject to him, undoubtedly he is excepted who

---

[33] Cf. Pius XII, *Mystici Corporis.* 1943.
[34] St. Thomas, *ibid.*, p. 307.
[35] Matt. 28:19.
[36] Luke 22:31-32.

has subjected all things to him. And when all things are made to him, then the Son himself will also be made subject to him who subjected all things to him, that God may be all in all."[37] The reign of the Son is continued by the reign of the Church throughout history. In the midst of storms and tempests, she stands firm knowing that she is the *alter ego* of Christ and that her mission and ultimate goal are identical with Christ's. Since He is as man the most sublime creature of the Father, Christ is most faithful in giving glory to the Father— the unique purpose of every creature. So, the Church is the most sublime and unique community for men who seek Christ. Consequently she has been and continues to be throughout history, the most sublime champion of God's glory.

In summary, we can say that every being, simple or composite, individual or collective, must have in its causes a sufficient reason for its existence. On the basis of this truth we have answered the question about the Church's dependence on Christ for her existence by examining the five causes of the Church. And we have concluded that the union of the Church with Christ is most complete and most necessary, for her efficient, exemplary, formal, and final causes are identical with Christ. As such they unify in the one community of the Mystical Body of Christ the material elements of the Church, namely, the individual human beings who are created and ordered by God to become members of Christ.

b. Now we must answer the second part of our basic question: *How does the Church depend on Christ in her nature?*

In explaining the existential dependence of the Church on Christ we had repeatedly to refer to her nature, since the explanation of her causes would have been impossible otherwise. Now we wish to investigate this nature in greater detail by showing its complete dependence on Christ.

Three particular questions must be answered in this regard:

aa. In what sense is Christ the head and principle of the Church and in what sense is the Church the body of Christ?

bb. To what extent does the Church share in the role of the unique mediatorship of Christ?

cc. In what sense is Christ the guarantee for the indefectibility of the Church?

---

[37] I Cor. 15:25-28.

aa. *In what sense is Christ the head and principle of the Church?*

We should bear in mind that Christ desires to incorporate the whole human race into His own life. We exist for Him, we belong to Him and He must provide for us. This truth is stressed in the Church's teaching that Christ redeemed the whole human race OBJECTIVELY, but the SUBJECTIVE redemption of individual souls is not effected automatically: the merits of the objective redemption must be applied and accepted invidually in each case. This means, in other words, that Christ redeemed the human race as a collective unit, and by doing so He offered the human individual the proximate opportunity to obtain his own redemption by applying Christ's redemptive graces to himself. St. Thomas made this twofold truth very clear when speaking of the grace of Christ[38] and the effects of His passion.[39] First of all, he pointed out that grace "is bestowed on Christ's soul as a universal principle for bestowing grace on human nature, according to Eph. 1. 5, 6, *He hath graced us in His beloved Son.*"[40] St. Thomas used the expression "human nature" purposely as a collective term for the whole human race. Later on, in connection with the effects of Christ's passion, he expressed himself more explicitly and more specifically: "Secondly, Christ's passion causes forgiveness of sins by way of redemption. For since He is our head, then, by the passion which He endured from love and obedience, He delivered us as His members from our sins, as by the price of His Passion: in the same way as if a man by the good industry of his hands were to redeem himself from a sin committed with his feet. For, just as the natural body is one, though made up of diverse members, so the whole Church, Christ's mystic body, is reckoned as one person with its head, which is Christ."[41] Then in his reply to the fifth objection, St. Thomas speaks of the application of Christ's passion to the individual: "Christ's Passion is applied to us even through faith, that we may share in its fruits, according to Rom. iii. 25: *Whom God hath porposed to be a propitiation, through faith in His blood.* But the faith through which we are cleansed from sin is not *lifeless faith*, which can exist even with sin,

---

[38] S.T., III., q. 7, a. 11.
[39] *Ibid.,* q. 49.
[40] *Ibid.,* q. 7, a .11.
[41] *Ibid.,* q. 49, a. 1.

but *faith living* through charity: that thus Christ's Passion may be applied to us, not only as to our minds, but also as to our hearts. And even in this way, sins are forgiven through the power of the Passion of Christ."[42] Since the Church is a community formed by many individuals, therefore, Christ reveals Himself as her head and principle in His special relationship to the individual, which is realized through her.

St. Paul put it this way: "And he himself gave some men as apostles, and some as prophets, others again as evangelists, and others as pastors and teachers, in order to perfect the saints for a work of ministry, for building up the body of Christ, until we all attain to the unity of the faith and of the deep knowledge of the Son of God, to perfect manhood, to be mature measure of the fullness of Christ."[43] "Rather are we to practice the truth in love, and so grow up in all things in him who is the head, Christ. For from him the whole body being closely joined and knit together through every joint of the system according to the functioning in due measure of each single part derives its increase to the building up of itself in love."[44] "A husband is head of the wife, just as Christ is head of the Church, being himself savior of the body."[45] "The Church is subject to Christ...."[46] "Christ also loved the Church, and delivered himself up for her, that He might sanctify her, cleansing her in the bath of water, by means of the word: in order that he might present to himself the Church in all her glory...."[47] "He is the head of his body, the Church; he, who is the beginning, the first-born from the dead, that in all things he may have the first place."[48] "Christ is faithful as the Son over his own house. We are that house...."[49]

To express the exact nature of the Church, St. Paul, in the quotations cited above, used the analogy of a living body. In order for the Church to have a vigorous life, she must have a head. It is the function of the head to unite all the various members of the body, to harmonize their activities, and to channel them in such a way that the purpose of the whole be realized. Consequently, the essence of St. Paul's statements can be reduced to this: the Church

---

[42] *Ibid.*, ad 5.
[43] Eph. 4:11-13.
[44] *Ibid.*, 4:15-16.
[45] *Ibid.*, 5:23.

[46] *Ibid.*, 5:24.
[47] *Ibid.*, 5:25-27.
[48] Col. 1:18.
[49] Heb. 3:6.

as a whole can live as an organism only if her members are united by the same head. In short, the same head must be the principle of the individual and corporate life of the community.

The same truth is expressed in the parables of the vine and branches and the bride and bridegroom.[50] The purpose of these parables is identical with that of St. Paul's thought: namely, to prove in concrete fashion that both the Church as a community, and membership in her wholly depend on Christ. In the words of Pius XII: "Christ our Lord brings the Church to live His own supernatural life, by His divine power permeates His whole Body, and nourishes and sustains each of the members according to the place which they occupy in the Body, very much as the vine nourishes and makes fruitful the branches which are joined to it."[51] Therefore, inasmuch as the Church is the continuation of Christ's presence, Christ Himself is her head and principle in order that He may be all in all both for the community and the individual member.

bb. *To what extent does the Church share in the role of the unique mediatorship of Christ?*

"One Lord, one faith, one Baptism, one God and Father of all, who is above all, and throughout all, and in us all. But to each one of us grace was given according to the measure of Christ's bestowal."[52] "He has rescued us from the power of darkness and transformed us into the kingdom of His beloved Son, in whom we have our redemption, the remission of our sins.... For it has pleased God the Father that in Him all His fullness should dwell, and that through him he should reconcile to himself all things, whether on the earth or in the heavens, making peace through the blood of the cross."[53] "So also Christ did not glorify himself with the high priesthood.... For Jesus, in the days of his earthly life, with a loud cry and tears, offered up prayers and supplications to him who was able to save him from death, and was heard because of his reverent submission. And he, Son though he was, learned obedience from the things that he suffered; and when perfected, he became to all who obey him the cause of eternal salvation, called by God a high priest according to

---

[50] Cf. Jn. 15:1-3; Isa 5:4; Jer. 2:21; Matt: 9:15; Apoc. 19:7-8; 21:2
[51] Pius XII, *Mystici Corporis.* 1943.
[52] Eph. 4:5-7.
[53] Col. 1:13, 19-20.

the order of Melchisedech."[54] These and other passages, especially the Epistle to the Hebrews almost in its entirety,[55] are proofs of Christ's mediatorship. Christ is the only mediator between God and the human race. And rightly so, because in virtue of His two natures He shares in both. At the time of the redemption He felt himself bound, as their only teacher and their only priest, to gather together the children of men and return them to the Father.[56] He did even more than this, however: to continue His functions as the only teacher and the only priest of the human race He identified Himself with the apostles and their successors: "All power in heaven and on earth has been given to me. Go, therefore, and make disciples of all nations ... teaching them to observe all that I have commanded you; and behold, I am with you all days, even unto the consummation of the world."[57] "He who hears you, hears me; and he who rejects you, rejects me, and he who rejects me, rejects him who sent me."[58] "He who receives you, receives me, and he who receives me, receives him who sent me."[59]

These texts leave no doubt that Christ identified Himself most perfectly with His Church and her representatives. He gave them His most personal redemptive power when He said to them: "All power in heaven and on earth has been given to me. Go, therefore, and make disciples of all nations. ..." The power is the same, the commission received from the Father is the same, and the faithful are the same. To assure the salutary effects of these common elements of the universal redemption He declared solemnly to them: "Behold, I am with you all days, even unto the consummation of the world." It is as if he said, I am watching over you because it is I who live in you—who teach and sanctify you.—It is this personal redemptive power and its commission that enables the teaching and priestly functions of Christ to be continued in the operations of the Church. Let us now consider them separately.

1. *Teaching function.*—That the teaching function is possessed

---

[54] Heb. 5:5, 7-9.

[55] Cf. 2:14; 3:1, 6; 4:14-16; cc. 7, 8, 9, 10; 13:15; Rom. 5:20; 8:15; Phil 2:6-8; I Tim. 2:5.

[56] Cf. H. Deickmann, *op. cit.*, pp. 209-219.

[57] Matt. 28:18-20.

[58] Luke 10:16.

[59] Matt. 11:40.

and exercised exclusively by the Church follows from the transcendent and supernatural nature of God's knowledge. For anyone else to have that knowledge, it must be communicated by him who is its sole possessor. Christ said in this regard: "All things have been delivered to me by my Father; and no one knows the Son except the Father; nor does anyone know the Father except the Son, and him to whom the Son chooses to reveal him."[60] In order to communicate this knowledge, He undertook to teach His brethren in and through the Church.

Just as Christ, the Prototype of the whole human race in the eternal idea of the Father, fulfills His role as mediator in behalf of humanity, so also revelation, which directly or indirectly always revolves around Christ, contains the divine message spoken to humanity as such. Just as the divine essence is perfect, so too is the divine word. Toward it there is only one attitude: to listen to it, to conserve it, and to fulfill it. In order to listen to the divine word, to conserve and to fulfill it, people must hear it preached. Nor does it suffice that it be proclaimed by the prophet who directly received it from God through the inspiration of the Holy Spirit. It must be announced time and time again in the course of history, because it is the divine word spoken to HUMANITY AS SUCH. This is the duty imposed by Christ on His Church: "Go, therefore, and make disciples of all nations ... and behold, I am with you all days, even unto the consummation of the world." "He who hears you, hears me. . . ." That is why men always listen to the Church. They know that according to Holy Scripture it is Christ who lives in the Church, it is Christ who speaks in the Church, and it is Christ who teaches through the mouth of the Church. She is the only depository of faith. She is the only interpreter and expositor of God's doctrine. She alone was promised the Spirit of truth.[61] For her sake Peter was given the primacy,[62] in order to assure her stability and permanence. Canon Law expresses this thought in this way: "Our Lord Jesus Christ entrusted the deposit of faith to the Church, that under the constant guidance and assistance of the Holy Spirit, she might

---

[60] Matt. 11:27.
[61] Jn. 14:16, 26.
[62] Matt. 16:13-19; Luke 22:31-32.

sacredly guard and faithfully explain this divine revelation."[63] This simply means that the Church is invested with the authority and infallibility of its Founder. And this is why the *Ecclesia docens* has its authority, and why the *Ecclesia discens* must submit to it.

2. *Sacerdotal mission.* Secondly, the Church possesses the sacerdotal mission of Christ. St. Paul explains the fundamental doctrine of Christ's high priesthood in his Epistle to the Hebrews in precisely those chapters where he describes Christ's role as mediator.[64] We find similar refrences in his other epistles, where he speaks of Christ as both priest and victim.[65] In fact, St. Paul is so thorough on this point that we can even gather the essential characteristics of the high priesthood from his epistles. "For every high priest," he writes, "taken from among men is appointed for men in the things pertaining to God, that he may offer gifts and sacrifices for sins."[66] There is no doubt that St. Paul is referring here to the high priesthood of Jesus Christ, for Christ, the God-man, was appointed from among men for men to offer his own life as a gift and sacrifice in order to restore harmony between God and the human race.

St. Thomas, in this connection, taught that man was required to offer sacrifices for these reasons: first, for the remission of sins by which he is turned away from God; secondly, that man be preserved in the state of grace; and thirdly, in order that man's soul be united to God. Then he added: "Now these effects were conferred on us by the humanity of Christ. For, in the first place, our sins were blotted out, according to Rom. iv. 25: *Who was delivered up for our sins.* Secondly, through Him we received the grace of salvation, according to Heb. v. 9: *He became to all that obey Him the cause of eternal salvation.* Thirdly, through Him we have acquired the perfection of glory, according to Heb. x. 19: *We have* [Vulg.,—*Having*] *a confidence in the entering into the Holies* [i.e. the heavenly glory] *through His blood.* Therefore Christ Himself, as man, was not only priest, but also perfect victim, being at the same time victim for sin, victim for a peace-offering, and a holocaust."[67] In other words, Christ,

---

[63]Canon 1322.

[64] Cf. cc. 7, 8, 9, 10

[65] Cf. Phil. 2:6-8; Col. 1:14,22; Eph. 2:3-6; Rom. 8:15; I Tim. 2:5.

[66] Heb. 5:1.

[67] S.T., III. q. 22, a. 2.

priest and victim, by opening up the channels of sanctifying grace, by infusing the supernatural virtues and gifts of the Holy Spirit, made it possible for men to become the adopted sons of God.

This is exactly the mission of the Church established in order to continue Christ's life and work. For "the Church is a religious community to carry out, upon the mandate of Christ, the sanctification of men till the very end of time; her members, as the mystical body of Christ, are bound to each other and to God by faith, by the means of salvation, and by obedience to legal authority."[68] Christ therefore, made the Church the depository of the merits of his redemption. He gave her the power to bind and to loose.[69] He also willed that only through her and in her and with her individual souls obtain salvation and adopted sonship, just as only through Christ and with Christ the human race was given the proximate possibility of redemption. Through His divine command: "Do this in remembrance of me."[70] He authorized His Church, once and for all, to offer sacrifice to God and to administer the sacraments. Since these sacraments, when administered according to the mind of the Church, work *ex opere operato*, they have become the principle means of sanctification and salvation,[71] and the greatest assurance that the Church is an effective instrument in the economy of salvation.

cc. *In what sense is Christ the guarantee for the indefectibility of the Church?*

Positive indefectibility as a characteristic of the Church has two meanings: that unwavering assurance with which the Church announces the truths of faith, and that undiminished energy exhibited by the Church in the turmoil of constant attacks against her very existence. This undiminished energy by which the Church survives is a moral miracle and likewise a motive of credibility. In short, indefectibility means that the Church in her existence and perpetuity is built upon Christ. Negative indefectibility excludes anything that would tend to separate the Church from Christ in her existence, in her deposit of faith, in her role as mediator or in any of the characteristics given her by Christ.

---

[68] A. Schütz, *Dogmatika*. Budapest. 1937. Vol. II, p. 236.
[69] Cf. Matt. 16:19; Jn. 20:22-23.
[70] Luke 22:19.
[71] *Codex Iuris Canonici*, 731.

We have shown previously that Christ shared His own personal redemptive power with the Church in order to enable her to incorporate her members into Himself, to make them adopted sons of His Father, and heirs of the eternal kingdom. Only in virtue of this redemptive power can we understand the words of Christ to Peter: "Thou art Peter, and upon this rock I will build my Church, and the gates of hell shall not prevail against it."[72] Christ's solemn words to His apostles on the eve of His passion likewise establish this truth: "And I will ask the Father and he will give you another Advocate to dwell with you forever, the Spirit of truth whom the world cannot receive, because it neither sees him nor knows him. But you shall know him, because he will dwell with you and be in you."[73] The consoling words of Christ: "And behold, I am with you all days, even unto the consummation of the world"[74] again bring truth out in bold relief. In a similar vein it is because of this power that we can understand St. Paul's words to Timothy: "I write these things to thee ... in order that thou mayest know ...how to conduct thyself in the house of God, which is the Church of the living God, the pillar and mainstay of the truth."[75]

This is another proof that Christ is the power and guarantee of the Church; that He lives in His Church; that He works in her as the one principle of her operation. Everything is centered around Him. All her supernatural relations are rooted in Him. All graces flow from Him. He is the center, the beginning and the end. He is all in all. How could defectibility be found in the Church when Christ is identified with her? Such a view would contradict the words of Christ Himself that the gates of hell would not prevail against His Church.

B. *The unity of the Church and Christ.*

Having established that Christ is the source of the existence and nature of the Church, we now pass on to an investigation of the unity of the Church and Christ. We will treat, first of all of

a. *the unity of the Church rooted in Christ as a principle.*

According to the teaching of St. Thomas, we may define principle

---

[72] Matt. 16:18.

[73] Jn. 14:16-17.

[74] Matt. 28:20.

[75] I Tim. 3:14-15.

in general as "something from which something else either is, becomes, or is known."[76] The nature of a principle, therefore, always involves some kind of procession. This procession can take place either in the order of being or in the order of cognition. Accordingly, we can speak of a real principle or a logical one. A real principle is a being from which another being or modification of being proceeds in some way. A logical principle is a principle of knowledge or a truth from which other truths proceed. Generally speaking we can call a source of knowledge or a source of thought a logical principle.[77]

Applying these considerations to the unity of the Church we may say that Christ is the principle of the Church because she proceeds from Him. As such, He must also be the principle of her unity. In fact, it is in His will that we must find the answers to the questions: Why is it that the Church must be one? Why is it that the Church cannot be but one? However, we have to inquire further to find out whether Christ is a real or only a logical principle of the unity of the Church. In other words, can we conceive of unity as a *res* which would naturally involve some kind of procession from Christ, or should we think of it as a truth—in the ideological order—which would involve a conclusion from another truth?

It is evident that the notion of unity as it pertains to the Church, is not purely a mental construct in the sense that our mind would create this unity but rather, even though it is an ideological being, it has its foundation in reality. In other words, it is not something subjective or an a priori mental structure, but the actual state of affairs outside the mind which forces us to arrive at this concept. For in a concrete reality, each and every characteristic mark or distinguishing feature pertains to reality although it does not have an independent existence. The Church is such a concrete reality in her existence as well in her essential notes. Consequently, if Christ is the real principle of the Church, He is likewise the real principle of her essential marks. Unity is one of them.

Though the notion of unity as applied to the Church is a real objective notion, it may also be viewed as a logical being, as a thought-content, which, as such, can be investigated in the mind. We are

---

[76] Cf. *S.T.*, I, q. 33, a. 1; *De Veritate*, q. 4, a. 2.

[77] Cf. B. Wuellner, S.J., *Dictionary of Scholastic Philosophy.* Milwaukee: The Bruce Publishing Co. 1956. P. 97.

especially thinking here of the constituent elements of the notion of unity and its opposition to the notion of multiplicity. By so doing, we can rightly speak of unity as a logical being even though unity in its concrete reality is the product of a real principle.

In regard to the unity of the Church we are naturally interested in the notion of unity as a real objective concept. Consequently, we view Christ as the great REALITY behind that unity. Our investigation will be based on those facts, parables, and the quotations of Scripture we have already cited or referred to in connection with the symbolism and foundation of the Church.

aa. *The unity of the Church in the Old Testament.*

It was the mission of the Jewish people of the Old Testament that as the chosen people of God they should call into existence the City of God at the time of the Redeemer's coming into this world. PEOPLE OF GOD—CITY OF GOD, these are parallel concepts: the former signifies an already established reality, the latter a yearning yet to be fulfilled. The two notions together gave birth to the Jewish nation's awareness of God's closeness. As there was only one chosen people of God before the coming of the Messiah, so there is only one city of God, one Church of God, after the coming of the Messiah. This is the picture established by the prophets in the chosen people with their metaphors and with the eulogy of the Church to come.[78]

This is the reason why the Church is presented to us in the Old Testament as the kingdom of God which begins to exist with the coming of the Messiah. It is mandatory, therefore, that we find unicity as one of its marks in the biblical description of this new kingdom.

We read in Amos: "In that day I will raise up the tabernacle of David that is fallen; and I will close up the breaches of the walls thereof, and repair what was fallen; and I will rebuild it as in the days of old."[79] "Behold the days come, saith the Lord, when the ploughman shall overtake the reaper; and the treader of grapes him that soweth seed; and the mountains shall drop sweetness, and every hill shall be tilled. And I will bring back the captivity of my people Israel; and they shall build the abandoned cities, and inhabit THEM;

---

[78] Cf. Gen 15:18; Lev. 26:3-13.
[79] Amos 9:11.

and they shall plant vineyards, and drink the wine of them, and shall make gardens, and eat the fruit of them. And I will plant them upon their own land; and I will no more pluck them out of their land which I have given them, saith the Lord thy God."[80]—This text is all the more interesting and all the more valuable in view of the fact that the ninth verse of the same chapter evidently refers to the dispersion of the Jews. Consequently, this description of the happy kingdom cannot be applied to them, but should be taken as that of the Church of Christ the unity and unicity of which are presented to us as the necessary consequences of this description.

The prophet Osee stresses the same truth in the following manner: "And I will espouse thee to me forever: and I will espouse thee to me in justice, and judgement, and thou shalt know that I am the Lord."[81] This act of espousing itself expresses the unity of the Church, for it speaks of the exclusive rights of the bride and bridegroom which involve an unique and exclusive relationship of the one person to the other. But Osee goes still further. In the fourth chapter he touches upon this unity again by comparing the Church to a herd of cattle grazing in a spacious place: "For Israel hath gone astray like a wanton heifer. Now will the Lord feed them, as a lamb in a spacious place."[82]

This notion of unity is also advanced by the prophet when he pictures the conversion of Israel as an act of unification of the already existing herd: "And after this the children of Israel shall return, and shall seek the Lord their God, and David their king; and they shall fear the Lord, and His goodness in the last days."[83]

It must also be added that certain expressions used by the prophet Isaias definitely refer to the unicity of the Church: especially such expressions as supreme judge, lawgiver and king, which implicitly point out the oneness of the Lord's people as a community: "For the Lord is our judge, the Lord is our lawgiver, the Lord is our king, He will save us."[84]

Isaias, by the way, leaves no doubt about the earthly kingdom of

---

[80] Amos 9:13-15.
[81] Osee 3:19-20.
[82] Osee 4:16.
[83] Osee 3:5.
[84] Isa. 33:22.

God being a visible community blessed with perfect unity. His metaphors are unmistakably clear on this point, especially when he compares this kingdom to "his beloved" or to "his vineyard"[85]; when he calls the Lord "father"[87] and "redeemer" of Israel.[88]

Most of all, however, we should keep in mind verses two and three of chapter 2 in which the prophet Isaias treats of the exceptional position of the kingdom by saying: "And in the last days the mountain of the house of the Lord shall be prepared on the top of mountains and it shall be exalted above the hills, and all nations shall flow unto it. And many people shall go, and say: Come and let us go up to the mountain of the Lord, and to the house of the God of Jacob, and he will teach us his ways, and we will walk in his paths, for the law shall come forth from Sion, and the word of the Lord from Jerusalem."[89]

To the unity of this kingdom references are also made by Jeremias and Ezechiel, especially in connection with the description of the alliance concluded between the Lord and His chosen people.[90]

It must also be recalled that the Prophet Malachi is equally expressive in the presentation of the principle of unity in the city of God: the chosen people as one *totum collectivum* in contradistinction to the one God needs but one sacrifice: "For from the rising of the sun even to the going down, my name is great among the Gentiles, and in every place there is sacrifice, and there is offered to my name a clean oblation."[91]

The aforementioned places are, of course, not the only ones found in the Old Testament concerning the unity of the Church. Though we cannot enumerate here all the references of the Old Testament, we should nevertheless like to call attention to some metaphors used repeatedly by the holy writers in order to point out the unity and unicity of the new kingdom of God.

It is our conviction, first of all, that in the promise of the multiplication of the seed of Israel made by the Lord to the patriarchs, the

---

[85] Cf. Isa c. 5.
[86] 40:41.
[87] 63:11.
[88] 44:6.
[89] Isa. 2:2-3.
[90] Jer. 32:40; Ezech. 37:25.
[91] Mal. 1:11.

virtual presence of the Church should already be recognized. For it is a fact that the parable of the stars of the heavens is not applicable to the Jewry of the Old Testament, Israel being one of the smallest nations and well confined to a limited territory. It is nevertheless very applicable to the millions and millions of faithful in the Church, which is unlimited both as to nation and as to territory, in virtue of the fact that all the nations of the world are redeemed and saved by the Son of God through the mediation of the Church.

It must also be noted that the promises of the Lord made to the chosen people are always addressed to them in the second person singular and as such they poignantly bring out an I-Thou relationship in which the addressee must necessarily be only one. This addressee is the Church herself to whom God promised exclusive greatness, blessedness, and universal power: "I will bless them that bless thee, and curse them that curse thee, and in thee shall all the kindred of the earth be blessed."[92] "All these are gathered together; they are come to thee . . . Thou shalt be clothed with all these as an ornament: and as a bride thou shalt put them about thee."[93]

In connection with the promises of the Lord another interesting factor needs clarification. The sacred text always speaks of the multiplication of the seed of Israel, and never of the multiplication of the "thou," the second member of the I-thou relationship. For this I-thou relationship necessarily implies the unicity of the thou, namely, the Church, which as such cannot be multiplied but must be kept intact as a whole, as a *totum collectivum* so that she does not lose her identity. Her individual members, however, to which the words "thy seed" refer can be multiplied, and this is exactly what is meant by the sacred text.

We must arrive at the same conclusion if we analyze such expressions in the Old Testament as "possession," "kingdom," "property," "people" applied by the sacred writers to the new kingdom to be born in such a way that they signified the Church not as part of the kingdom or the people of God, but as equivalent to THE people and THE kingdom of God. In short, the Church was presignified by them as God's personal possession, and the object of His exclusive love: "If therefore you will hear my voice, and keep my convenant you shall

---

[92] Gen. 12:3; 17:4-7; 22:17-18; 26:2-5; 28:13-15.
[93] Isa. 49:18.

be my peculiar possession above all people: for all the earth is mine. And you shall be to me a priestly kingdom, and a holy nation."[94] "And my tabernacle shall be with them, and I will be their God, and they shall be my people."[95] "And I will make with them another convenant that SHALL BE everlasting, to be their God, and they shall be my people..."[96]

Finally, in addition to the aforesaid quotations, we would like to call attention to certain expressions of Isaias and Micheas. Both these prophets further the general notion of unity of the new kingdom by stressing the obligation of accepting and promoting this unity. In the words of Micheas: "I will assemble and gather together all of thee, O Jacob: I will bring together the remnant of Israel, I will put them together as a flock in the fold, as THE sheep in the midst of the sheepcotes. They shall make a tumult by the reason of the multitude of men. For he shall go up that shall open the way before them; they shall divide, and pass through the gate, and shall come in by it, and their king shall pass before them, and the Lord at the head of them."[97]

So great is this obligation for the promotion of the unity of the Church that Isaias threatens with punishment those who fail either to recognize or to serve it: "Arise, be enlightened, O Jerusalem; for thy light is come, and the glory of the Lord is risen upon thee... And the Gentiles shall walk in thy light, and kings in the brightness of thy rising... For the nation and the kingdom that will not serve thee will perish, and the Gentiles shall be wasted with desolation."[98]

These are some of the references of the Old Testament concerning the nature and unity of the Church. Now, what was foretold by the Old Testament became clearly defined and precisely worded by the New in such a way that it is now almost impossible either to deny the unity of the Church or to try to explain it in a merely spiritual or figurative sense.

bb. *THE UNITY OF THE CHURCH IN THE NEW TESTAMENT*

The circumstances of the founding of the Church indicate her unity

---

[94] Ex. 19:5-6.
[95] Ezech. 37:27.
[96] Baruch 2:35.
[97] Mich. 2:12-13.
[98] Isa. 30:1, 3, 12.

and unicity so strikingly that one must look upon it as something deliberately intended by Christ and so belonging to the very nature of the Church. First of all, Christ never spoke of "churches" in the plural; He only spoke of the one Church, His, built on Peter, the visible rock: "Thou art Peter, and upon this rock I will build my church."[99] He did not say "my churches," nor did He make any allusion to a universal but indivisible church which would embrace several branch-churches on an equal footing. Rather, He pointed to Peter, the visible rock, and revealed His intention to build His Church on this visible rock in order to make it unmistakably one and indivisible. The use of the demonstrative pronoun in the pronouncement of our Lord only emphasizes this idea.

Then, He commissioned the apostles as conquerors of the world and sent them to all nations in a very special and unusual way: "All power in heaven and on earth has been given to me. Go, therefore, and make disciples of all nations . . ."[100] He shared His unique personal power with them that they might conquer the whole world for Him. Now, it is only natural that one and the same power of Christ cannot bear contradictory fruits in its effects. All those conquered for Him by that power must belong to one and the same Church.

The same idea had been expressed by Our Lord at an earlier stage of His public life. He called Himself the good shepherd whose purpose is to gather together his dispersed flock: "And other sheep I have that are not of this fold. Them also I must bring, and they shall hear my voice, and there shall be one fold and one shepherd."[101] This idea of "one fold and one shepherd" must have been real to the first Christians for we read of them: "And continuing daily with *one accord* in the temple, and breaking bread in their houses, they took their food with gladness and simplicity of heart."[102] And again: "Now the multitude of the believers were of *one heart and one soul,* and not one of them said that anything he possessed was his own, but they had all things in common."[103]

We can truly say that this first community of Christians was the

---

[99] Matt. 16:18.
[100] Matt. 28:18-19.
[101] Jn. 10:16.
[102] Acts 2:46.
[103] Acts 5:32.

first visible fulfillment of Christ's priestly prayer at the Last Supper:
"Holy Father, keep in Thy name those whom Thou hast given me,
that they may be one even as we are ... Yet not for these only do I
pray, but for those also who through their word are to believe in
me, and all may be one, even as Thou, Father, in me and I in Thee;
that they also may be one in us, that the world may believe that
Thou hast sent me. And the glory that Thou hast given me, I have
given to them, that they may be one, even as we are one: I in them
and Thou in me; that they may be perfected in unity ..."[104]

According to Catholic dogmatic theology the unity of the Father
and the Son is the most perfect possible because it is an essential
unity grounded in the identity of the divine nature. If Christ wanted
His followers to establish and keep a similar unity among themselves,
therefore, this means that He wanted all of them to belong to one
and the same Church blessed with an indivisible unity of principle
and life. What is this principle? Who produces this life?

The New Testament repeatedly refers to Christ as the head of
the Church[105] and to the Church as the body of Christ.[106] Now, to
say that Christ would be head of several bodies would evidently
involve contradiction and an erroneous conclusion on the ground that
in normal conditions only one body belongs to one head. And Paul,
looking at Christ as the most perfect representative of human nature
borrowed His metaphors, without doubt, from the sound side of
human life, and not from occasional aberations which can never
be taken as genuine expressions of true life. If, therefore, he
called Christ the head of the Church, and the Church the body of
Christ he had to refer to them in terms of unity and unicity, meaning
necessarily that Christ the divine head can vivify and nourish but one
Church as His body.

To prove the accuracy of this reasoning we have only to examine
the nature and meaning of some of the metaphors used by Christ
Himself in the description of His Church? How did He visualize her?
How did He depict her life? What kind of symbols did He use to
express her essential marks?

First of all, we would like to mention symbols like "the house of

---

[104] Jn. 17:11, 20, 23.
[105] I Cor. 12:12-27; Eph. 4:15; 5:23; I Tim. 3:15.
[106] Rom. 12:4-5; Col. 1:18.

God"[107] and "the temple of God"[108] Little if any reflection on these symbols is needed to see that the Church of the New Testament emerges as an immense but unique spiritual edifice of the Lord, without parallel in the history of mankind. She remains unbending upon her rock, for the gates of hell shall never prevail against her.

Then we have the symbol of the bride.—According to the teaching of the Bible and the Catholic Church marriage is made up by the indissoluble contract of one man and one woman. Now, in the words of St. Paul[109] Christian marriage is the symbol of the unity of Christ and His Church, of the spouse and the bridegroom, consequently, the mutually exclusive right to each other of the bride and the bridegroom is also the sacred prerogative of Christ and His Church. By the very nature of their union they can neither renounce nor repudiate this unity without renouncing or destroying the very essence of their intimate union.

Christ's third meaningful symbol in regard to the unity of the Church is that of the vine and its branches.[110] The life of the branches is guaranteed by their abiding in the vine; cut off from it, they necessarily perish. In the same way, those who want to survive as members of Christ must abide in His body, the Church: "If anyone does not abide in me, he shall be cast outside as the branch, and wither; and they shall gather them up and cast them into the fire, and they shall burn."[111]

This list of the symbols of the Bible in regard to the unity of the Church is far from being complete. Yet, it gives eminent testimony that the Church must possess unity as one of her essential marks. She is THE house and THE temple of God; she is THE bride of Christ, and she is THE vine of the faithful-branches, therefore, she must be unique in her nature and existence: she can neither be made up of heterogeneous parts nor be treated on an equal footing with other Christian churches. She is THE Church because she is the body of Christ. She is the Church *par excellence* made up of individuals and never of churches as her membership. This is why

---

[107] I Tim. 3:15.
[108] I Cor. 3:17.
[109] Eph. 5:31-32.
[110] Jn. 15:1-6.
[111] Jn. 15:6.

the words of Isaias must be applied to her and to her relationship to other religious communities: "For the nation and the kingdom that will not serve thee, will perish. . ."[112]

This is the state of affairs concerning the unity of the Church as it emerges from the Bible. It is truly there, it is rooted in revelation. And yet, we cannot be satisfied with the discovery of this important fact. This discovery also involves an obligation to work for, and to promote the fulfillment of this revealed truth. This obligation is definitely contained in St. Paul's words: "Until we all attain to the unity of faith and the deep knowledge of the Son of God, to perfect manhood, to the mature measure of the fullness of Christ."[113] And it is also expressed in the words of Christ Himself: "And other sheep I have that are not of this fold. Them also must I bring, and they shall hear my voice, and there shall be one fold and one shepherd."[114]

It is clearly evident by now that the whole logic of this argumentation is shaped by the cardinal truth that the Church is the body of Christ, and the kingdom of God. Consequently, she either exists as such or she does not exist at all.[115] Now, if it is true that the Father's eternal decree of the Incarnation contained the idea of the Church, and if it is equally true that Christ founded the Church as the continuation of His own personal life in order to transmit His redemptive mission and power to individuals, then the universal exclusivity of Christ must contain the universal exclusivity of the Church as well. In St. Paul's words: "I . . . exhort you to walk in a manner worthy of the calling with which you were called, . . . careful to preserve the unity of the Spirit in the bond of peace: one body and one spirit, even as you were called in one hope of your calling; one Lord, one faith, one Baptism; One God and Father of all . . ."[116]

This text of St. Paul, if interpreted correctly, means the following: "There is but one God, one Christ, one Baptism, therefore, there is but one Church." For from God to God there is but one relationship: Christ Himself. And as there is no other way of salvation for the

---

[112] Isa. 60:12.
[113] Eph. 4:13.
[114] Jn. 10:16.
[115] Karl Adam, *op. cit.*, p. 184.
[116] Eph. 4:1-6.

human race but through Christ so there is no other way to Christ but through His Church. Or, since it is impossible to multiply Christ, it is equally impossible to multiply His body. And finally, as it is impossible to divide Christ into parts, so it is impossible to break His Church into fragmentary churches. Since Christ is the head of the Church, it follows that her whole being, her whole existence, her whole undividedness, must be rooted in Him—so much so that even her teaching must come from Christ and must possess the same exclusiveness with which Christ Himself showed the "way, truth, and life" to His followers. "The grace of God in its manifestation is a catholic power, comprehending and grasping all men. So that it cannot manifest itself otherwise than in absolute unity. There can be no contradiction, or dissention, or schism where God is. His truth cannot be otherwise than one truth, one life, one love. And therefore it can be realized in but one form, in a comprehensive fellowship that binds together all men in intimate unity."[117]

This argumentation, therefore, has been offered to the mind by Christ as the principle of the Church—in both of these aspects, moreover: in her becoming and in her existence or being. Now, we can go a step further and consider Christ as the principle of the Church's operation. By doing so we can discover hitherto hidden elements in regard to the unity of the Church. In order to succeed in this point of our study we have to find those activities which were due exclusively to Christ alone and which, if exercised by the Church, must be carried out by her alone and exclusively as well.

b. HOW IS THE UNITY OF THE CHURCH ROOTED IN CHRIST AS MEDIATOR?

Actually, all the activities of Christ had in view His mediatorship and, vice versa, His mediation became the source of, and the springboard for, His activities. "For there is one God, and one Mediator between God and men, himself man, Christ Jesus, who gave himself a ransom for all, bearing witness in his own time."[118] "And this is why he is mediator of a new covenant, that whereas a death has taken place for redemption from the transgressions committed under

---

[117] Karl Adam, *op.cit.*, p. 185.
[118] I Tim. 2:5-6; cf. Eph. 4:7; Heb. 8.25f; 12:24; I Jn. 2:1-2.

the former covenant, they who have been called may receive eternal inheritance according to the promise."[119] The purpose of Christ's coming into this world as Redeemer, therefore, was to reestablish the correct objective order between God and the creature, to assist man in praising the Almighty, and to merit for men sanctifying grace to the measure of His bestowal.

On this threefold ground we can distinguish three activities in Christ as Mediator: namely,

aa. The activities of Christ carried out in virtue of His prophetical office—*munus propheticum*:

bb. the activities of the Great High Priest—*munus sacerdotale;*

cc. the activities of Christ the King—*munus regale*

aa. *The Munus propheticum.* The term 'prophetical office' stands for the wholeness of Christ's teaching. It is not connected with the act of prophesying, in the first instance, but rather with the transmission of truths and the explanation of their content. Thus, in relation to the Church, the prophetical office of Christ embraces all those facts through which Christ either revealed certain knowledge concerning the Church, or in virtue of which He guards the Church as the depository of His truths and preserves her from falling into errors in defining and interpreting those truths.

From what has just been said, one can deduce the following conclusions regarding the unity of the Church. The truths of the Church essentially depend on Christ. Each and every truth has value only in so far as it has been received from Him. Whether this dependence of a revealed truth on Christ is immediate or mediate, its validity always depends on Christ. St. Thomas gives two reasons to explain this fact. In the first place, the object of faith is the First Truth. For faith does not assent to anything, unless it is revealed by God.[120] Secondly, Christ communicated to us what He was commanded by the Father to reveal: "For I have not spoken on my own authority, but he who sent me, the Father, has commanded me what I should say, and what I should declare.... The things, therefore, that I speak, I speak as the Father has bidden me."[121] Christ was the mouthpiece of the Father in communicating the revealed truths

---

[119] Heb. 9:15; cf. Col. 1:15, 18.

[120] *S.T.*, II-II, q. 1, a. 1.

[121] Jn. 12:49-50.

to us. Consequently, the deposit of the Catholic faith as a system of truths is but a body of theses revealing Christ and His different relations. It is Christ, the great Reality, who gives content to and stands behind each and every doctrinal notion, because He is the principle and the light of theology.

It is abundantly clear, therefore, that there is but one guiding principle in theology, Christ Himself; and this one principle cannot produce contradictory effects. As from an acorn only an oak can come, so a principle can produce only its own proper effects. On the one hand, the one Christ guarantees the validity of truths rooted in His own teaching, and on the other hand, the same Christ guarantees the survival of the community whose whole being is based on the acceptance of the same truths.

Besides the content of the truths, we can also invesitgate the manner of their communication. Christ, the most perfect realization of the *munus propheticum,* is the center of all prophetic activity: the prophets preceding Him spoke of Him as the One who was to come; the apostles, doctors, and teachers who came after Him derived their whole teaching from Him. In fact, He commissioned them to do so.[122] Since the Church is the body of Christ, this centrality of Christ's prophetic mission to mankind points to the similar centrality of the Church in the history of Christianity. This parallelism of the two centralities secures the rightful establishment of a whole body of necessary truths in the bosom of the Church, and by the same token excludes even the slightest possibility of contradictory truths or a plurality of contradictory churches.

The *munus propheticum,* therefore, plays a very important unifying role in the conservation of the deposit of faith in the Church. It is at the root of her infallibility in matters of faith and morals. Infallibility is not merely a gift, it is rather a necessary consequence flowing from the fact that Christ is the head of the Church as well as the principle and measure of the truths she has received. Consequently, it is Christ who secures her truths, and it is Christ who, by securing those truths, proclaims the unity and unicity of their depository, the Church.

---

[122] "Sicut omnes prophetae de eo prophetaverunt, ita omnes legati et magistri religiosi, qui post eum veniunt, non sunt nisi missi "apostoli" Christi, Christi annuntiantes doctrinam." H. Dieckmann, *op. cit.,* p. 210.

Here is the mediation of Christ from God to men: mediating the truths of the Eternal Wisdom to the community of which He is the head; and by doing so He has made His Church necessarily one. For the one God, the one Mediator—Jesus Christ—and the one faith necessarily give birth to only one Church. The unity and unicity of the principle of truths creates the real unity of the community which is founded on these same truths.

bb. The *munus sacerdotale*. The mediator mediates not only from God to men, but also upward by bearing aloft man's liturgical praise of God, or the community's sacrifice. This is the *munus sacerdotale* exercised by Christ, and it too offers some considerations in connection with the unifying elements in the Church.

This *munus sacerdotale* must be understood in its universal meaning: Christ is the High Priest of all humanity, of the entire *collectivum*. One and the same sacrifice is always offered by one and the same Christ to one and the same God in the name of one and the same Church. His unique sacrifice on the cross is renewed time and again in the Holy Sacrifice of the Mass in order to pronounce exactly the same result as was accomplished by His death: namely, to reestablish the harmony between God and the human race—or, more succinctly, to restore mankind's most fundamental relationship to God. The Holy Sacrifice of the Church, therefore, must always be looked upon as a renewal and participation in the one and only sacrifice of Christ carried out on the cross—with this difference, that at the death of Our Lord humanity as a whole stood behind the High Priest, whereas the Holy Sacrifice of the Mass is performed by the Church as the executive organ of individual salvation established by Christ Himself. The conclusion, however, is the same in both cases: where there is but one sacrifice and one minister there must be but one community in behalf of which the sacrifice is being offered to God.

As Karl Adam worded it: "There is but one priesthood in the Church, the priesthood of the God-man, who redeemed us by His whole life, but especially by the sacrifice of His death. But because this invisible priesthood of Christ would make use of visible instruments and organs, so that Christ's grace may be ministered to His people in sacramental words and signs, there rightly exists in the Church a visible priesthood. And that visible priesthood has existed from the beginning, though its full significance was not at first mani-

fest to the consciousness of the faithful, nor expressed in a precise
terminology. Whenever the most Holy Eucharist was celebrated and
whenever sins were forgiven, whenever the grace of Christ was imparted under visible forms, then instrumental agents were employed,
and were sometimes called 'presbyteri' or priests, sometimes over-
seers (episcopi)."[123] This is an extremely important truth precisely
from the point of view of the unity of the Church. The *munus
sacerdotale* of Christ is the only legitimate mediation upward, and
if there are human priests in His service their priesthood is essentially rooted in that of Christ, for "the visible priesthood is
nothing else than a visible attestation of the continual living and
working of Christ in the world."[124]

Once again we reached the same conclusion. In connection with the
munus propheticum we discovered the necessity for the unicity of
the Church in Christ considered as the ultimate principle of her truths.
And now, by investigating the *munus sacerdotale*, we have discovered
the necessity for the same unicity in Christ considered as the one
and only High Priest of the Church. Where there is but one priesthood and one sacrifice there can be but one community in order to
fulfill the most sacred wish of the Divine Master.

This unique priesthood, however, can be placed in a still greater
perspective. Not only is it the essential element of the unity of the
priesthood, but it also promotes the unity of the faithful who form
the community. Through the so-called *regale sacerdotium* the faithful
themselves are united to Christ, the High Priest, and participate to
some extent in His priesthood. By doing so—even though unconsciously—they promote Christian maturity in order to understand
and protect the unity of their Church.

What does all this mean? It means that the graces of individual
redemption flow from the mediator to the individual through the

---

[123] Karl Adam, *op. cit.*, pp. 142-143; cf. Karl Adam, *One and Holy*.
Translated by Cecily Hastings. New York: Sheed and Ward. 1951.
Pp. 79, 86-87, 105; Oscar Cullmann, "A Reciprocity of Gifts, "*Perspec-
tives*, VII (January-February, 1962), pp. 14-15. The article originally
appeared in the *Pax Romana Journal*, no. 6, 1961.

[124] Karl Adam, *The Spirit of Catholicism*. P. 143.—"The way to unity
is not from Peter to Christ but *from Christ to Peter*, not from the outer
to the inner but from the inner to the outer." Karl Adam, *One and Holy*.
P. 105.

Church as a *medium*. The Church, being the *alter ego* of Christ, receives all her missions and functions from Him. She is the depository of the treasures and graces of redemption. If, therefore, those graces are necessary for the salvation of the individual then they must be available to each and every one through the community which was founded by Christ as His own representative and dispenser.

Finally, the *munus sacerdotale* as a unifying principle asserts itself in the *ex opere operato* character of the sacraments.—It is the Church which administers the sacraments. Their use is an external sign of belonging to the Church. Nevertheless, through the decree of Christ the sacraments are effective of themselves, for in each and every sacrament one and the same Christ operates by transmitting His graces. This is particularly clear in relation to the three sacraments which impart a character to those who receive them.[125] The sacramental character in fact is the sign that Christ is the center of the life of those who receive those sacraments. In this connection we can rightly quote St. Peter: "You, however, are a chosen race, a royal priesthood, a holy nation, a purchased people; that you may proclaim the perfection of Him who has called you out of darkness into His marvelous light. You who in times past were not a people, but are now the people of God..."[126] The character is given, as it were, in order to seal the community of those who bear it. The community of the "chosen race" which can be called Christ's "holy priesthood," "holy nation," "His purchased people" or simply His Church.

One can now see that the efficacy of the sacraments, the realization of individual salvation in and through the Church, and the unicity of the sacrifice and its minister make it mandatory that the Church,

---

[125] "Character quidem in baptismo et maiore gradu, in confirmatione collatus constituit populum Deo speciali modo sanctum, ad instar fere Israel, qui erat electus et consecratus prae omnibus gentibus. Hinc christianis applicat Petrus verbo olim Israelitis dicta: 'Vos autem genus electum, regale sacerdotium, gens sancta, populus aquisitionis, ut virtutes annuntiatis eius, qui de tenebris vos vocavit in admirabile lumen suum' (I Peter 2:9), quatenus scilicet Christi 'sacredotio configurantue fideles secundum sacramentales characteres, qui nihil aliud sunt, quam quaedam participationes sacerdotil Christi ab ipso Christo derivatae." H. Dieckmann, *op. cit.*, p. 214.

[126] I Peter 2:9-10.

the depository of the *munus sacerdotale* of Christ, be only one.

cc. The *munus regale*. In order to understand the importance of Christ's kingship in regard to the unity of the Church, a clarification of this notion seems to be necessary. What does kingship mean? What are the constitutive elements of this notion?—The history of mankind has produced different types of kingship, but the basic elements of the notion can be reduced to the following criteria:[127] first, a kingship involves the establishment of a monarchic rule. The legislative, judicial, and administrative powers converge in the king's person. He uses those powers in his own name, because he is the personification of his people. For his actions he is responsible but to his own conscience and to God.

Secondly, kingship involves the notion of kingdom (or state). Kingdom has a twofold meaning. It refers to the subjects of the king's powers, on the one hand, and to the land, on the other. If either of these elements is lacking, one can no longer speak of a real kingship.

Thirdly, a title to the kingship is necessary. It can be obtained in one of two ways: by heredity—innate title, or by personal deeds and reputation—acquired title. In either case, the title is always looked upon as the sign of having been chosen by God.

If we turn to Christ now we can say with Pius XI: "To Christ as Man belong the title and power of king in strict reality. For it is only as Man that he may be said to have received from the Father "power and glory and a kingdom" (Dan. 7:13,14), since the Word is consubstantial with the Father and has all things in common with Him, and consequently has supreme and absolute dominion over all created things."[128]

In this text, Pius XI applied to Christ the three criteria of kingship explained above. He mentioned title and power directly, and referred to kingdom by quoting Daniel. It remains to be seen how these three basic elements of the notion of kingship are presented in Holy Scripture in behalf of Christ, and how they throw into relief the notion of the unity of the Church.

Psalm 2 refers to "the decree of the Lord" in virtue of which the nations are given to the Son of the Lord, the appointed King of Sion,

---

[127] Cf. A. Schütz, *Krisztus*. Budapest. 1932. Pp. 190f. Also: Pius XI, *Quas Primas*. 1925.

[128] Quas Primas. 1925.

and the utmost parts of the earth are given Him for His possession.[129] And the psalmist adds: "And now, O ye kings, understand; receive instruction, ye who rule the earth. Serve ye the Lord in fear and rejoice unto Him; with trembling offer homage to him, lest he be angry and you perish from the way, when his wrath is kindled suddenly. Blessed are all who flee to him for safety."[130] Though all the three criteria can be recognized in this text, we feel that it was written by the psalmist in order to reveal the tremendous powers of Christ. The fact that the message of the Lord was addressed to the kings "who rule the earth," and that such expressions as "receive instruction," "serve the Lord," "offer homage," and particularly "flee to him for safety," were used, seem to prove that His powers are absolutely unmatched. What is the title to those powers? Christ has two titles, the decree of the Lord, the eternal predestination by the Father as an innate title, and His life and death as an acquired title. This thought is expressed in psalm 109: "The Lord said to my Lord: "Sit at my right hand, until I make thy enemies thy footstool..." The Lord has sworn and he will not repent: "Thou art a priest forever according to the order of Melchisedech." The Lord is at thy right hand: he will destroy kings in the day of his wrath. He will judge nations..."[131] And what is the kingdom? Besides other references, psalm 44—the wedding song of Christ and His bride, the Church—seems to identify it with the Church. We are especially thinking of two passages of this psalm which establish the Church's universality and exclusiveness respectively. Universality in time and space is referred to in the following promise: "I shall be mindful of thy name unto all generations and generations; therefore the nations shall glorify thee forever."[132] Then, in order to point out the decisive and exclusive nature of the Church as the unique possession of Christ, the Lord says: "Forget thy people and thy Father's house,"[133] "in place of thy fathers there shall be thy sons."[134] The Lord could not ask for greater sacrifice than to forget our own people

---

[129] Vv. 4-9.
[130] Vv. 10-11; cf. psalms 46 and 109.
[131] Vv. 1, 4-6.
[132] V. 18.
[133] V. 11.
[134] V. 17.

and our father's house. Yet, it must be done if they ever become the separating wall between us and the Church of Christ. This is a very definite feature in which, in a tremendous though painful fashion, is reflected the truth that the kingdom of Christ must be one.

Nevertheless, it is perhaps psalm 71 which is the most explicit reference to the unity and unicity of the Church as the kingdom of Christ. "And he shall rule,"—we read—"from sea to sea, and from the river unto the ends of the earth. His enemies shall bow down before him, and his foes shall lick the dust . . . and all the kings of the earth shall adore him, all nations serve him. And in him all the tribes of the earth shall be blessed . . ."[135]

This portrait of the new king and his kingdom became the object of contemplation and rapturous description for Isaias[136] and Daniel.[137] It was finally materialized in the angel's words to Mary: "He shall be great, and shall be called the Son of the Most High; and the Lord God will give him the throne of David his father, and he shall be king over the house of Jacob forever; and of his kingdom there shall be no end."[138]

If we bear all these scriptural references in mind we are bound to admit that the kingdom of Christ is real; it is identified with the Church; it is most universal in time and space; and as such, it is necessarily exclusive in its nature and actual establishment; it is not only one, but also unique.

Let us sum up what we have thus far accomplished by analyzing the second relationship of the Church. First of all, we have explained the relationship of the Church to the Son and we have shown with the help of the five causes how the Church depends on Christ in her existence in so far as her whole life is based on Christ; and how she depends on Christ in her meaning and nature in so far as she is the body of Christ. We have shown, furthermore, that the Church shares in Christ's mediating function—a fact on which her indefectibility is based.

Then, we analyzed the notion of the unity of the Church in the

---

[135] Vv. 8-9, 11, 17.
[136] Isa. 9:6.
[137] Dan. 7:14.
[138] Luke 1:32-33; cf. Apoc. 19:16; Jn. 18:36-37.

light of the Old and New Testaments, and also with the help of human reason we deduced the unity of the Church from Christ as the real principle of the concrete Church and as the Mediator of the human race Who in His *munus propheticum, munus sacerdotale and munus regale* laid down the foundation for the unity of the Church from the viewpoint of doctrine and the mediation of grace. The principal idea, however, has always been the same throughout these investigations: the basic fact that Christ lives in His Church.

3. *What is the relationship of the Church through Christ to the Holy Spirit?*

We read in the encyclical of Pius XII on the Mystical Body of Christ the following passage: "If we examine closely this divine principle of life and power given by Christ, in so far as it is nothing else than the Holy Spirit, the Paraclete who proceeds from the Father and the Son, and who is called in a special way the "Spirit of Christ" or the "Spirit of the Son."[139] For it was by this Breath of grace and truth that the Son made beautiful His soul in the immaculate womb of the Blessed Virgin; this Spirit delights to dwell in the dear soul of our Redeemer as in His most cherished shrine; this Spirit Christ merited for us on the cross by shedding His own blood; this Spirit He bestowed on the Church for the remission of sins, when He breathed on the Apostles;[140] and while Christ alone received this Spirit without measure,[141] to the members of the Mystical Body He is imparted only according to the measure of the giving of Christ, from Christ's own fulness.[142] But after Christ's glorification on the Cross, His Spirit is communicated to the Church in an abundant outpouring, so that she, and her single members may become daily more and more like to our Saviour. It is the Spirit of Christ that has made us adopted sons of God . . ."[143]

This quotation makes it clear that even the third great relationship of the Church is based in her essence and is, so to speak, the fulfillment of the first two relationships. We have found, in fact, that the relationship of the Church to the Father is responsible for her

---

[139] Rom. 8:9; II Cor. 3:17; Gal. 4:6.
[140] Cf. Jn. 20:22.
[141] Cf. Jn. 3:34.
[142] Cf. Eph. 1:8; 4:7.
[143] Cf. Rom. 8:14-17; Gal. 4:6-7.

ontological possibility determined by the eternal divine idea of the Father. We discovered the realization and concretization of this possibility in her relationship to the Son. Now in her relationship to the Holy Spirit we must recognize the efficacious principle of her permanence in such a way that everything she has in virtue of her nature, is realized *hic et nunc* by the Holy Spirit—especially through His gifts and actual grace. In this connection we are particularly thinking of her role as the mystical body of Christ and universal mediator, as well as her indefectibility. Without the assistance of the Holy Spirit the Church could not fulfill these essential roles of her mission. This is why the encyclical says that the Holy Spirit, the Spirit of Christ, is the principle of life and power which constitutes the very source of every gift and created grace. It is exclusively through the interior working of the Holy Spirit that the merits and gifts of Christ, even within the Church, become the possession of both the individual and the community.

If, therefore, we want to investigate the nature of this relationship, we must find those components which are absolutely necessary for the establishment and permanence of Christ's work in the individual and, through the individuals, in the community. Furthermore, we must extend this inquiry to other Christian communities, asking these two questions about them: Is it possible for the communities and for their members to have a relationship to the Holy Spirit? And if so, in what does this relationship consist? The answers to these questions will clarify the different aspects of the unity of the Church which are involved in this third relationship. But to answer these questions correctly, we must first of all explain the teaching of the Scripture concerning the Holy Spirit. In this chapter, then, we will proceed as follows:

A. What does the Bible teach regarding the Holy Spirit?

B. What is the relationship between
    a. the members of the Church and the Holy Spirit;
    b. the Church as a community and the Holy Spirit;
    c. non-Catholic communities and the Holy Spirit;
    d. non-Catholic individuals and the Holy Spirit?

A. *Scripture and the Holy Spirit.*

In this first section we shall focus our attention on the operation of the Holy Spirit, omitting all those scriptural quotations which are not directly connected with the third Person of the Blessed Trinity as an operative principle.

"In the Old Testament the Spirit and Power of God, the Holy Spirit, is presented to us first as the principle of natural life and operation,[144] and then as the distributor of the supernatural gifts [charismata], who descends upon Joseph, the 72 elders, Samson, Gedeon, Saul, and the prophets.[145] Then, in Messionic times, He is presented as the plenitude of all Messianic goods,[146] Who would especially shower His blessings on the Messiah.[147] In the New Testament, too, the Holy Spirit is often described as the plenitude of Messianic goods and as the vivifying principle of the new life given to us by the Reedemer."[148] "When the Advocate has come, whom I will send you from the Father, the Spirit of truth who proceeds from the Father, he will bear witness concerning me."[149] "But I speak the truth to you; it is expedient for you that I depart. For if I do not go, the Advocate will not come to you; but if I go I will send him to you. And when he has come he will convict the world of sin, and of justice, and of judgement."[150] "But when he, the Spirit of truth, has come, he will teach you all the truth. For he will not speak on his own authority, but whatever he will hear he will speak ... He will glorify me, because he will receive of what is mine and will declare it to you."[151]

It was only fitting that even the Apostles, the first dispensers of the mysteries of Christ in the Church, received their commission by receiving the Holy Spirit: "Peace be to you! As the Father has sent me, I also send you. When he had said this, he breathed upon them,

---

[144] Cf. Gen. 1:2; 2:7; 6:3; IV Kgs. 2:16; Isa. 32:15; Ezech. 3:12; 8:3; 11:1-24; 37:8-10; 43:5; Zach. 12:1; Ps. 103:29; Job 12:10; 34:14; II Mach. 7:23; 14:46; Judith 16:17.

[145] Cf. Gen. 41:38 Num. 11:17; Judges 14:6 6:34; I Kgs. 11:6; Isa. 6:8-10; Ezech. 1:7.

[146] Isa. 32:15; 44:1-3; Joel 2:2-8; Zach. 12:10; Ezech. 11:19; 36:26; 37:14; 39:28; cf. Ps. 50:12; 142:10.

[147] Isa. 11:1; 42:1-4; 61:1.

[148] Jn. 4:10; cf. 3:8; 7:38; 20:22; Acts 5:3; 10:19, 44,48; 13:2; 20:28; Rom. 5:5; 8:14-17 I Cor. 2:10; 3:16; 6:11-19; 12:3; II Cor. 3:6; Gal. 4:6; 5:22; Eph. 3:16; II Tim. 1:14; Tit: 1:14.

[149] Jn. 15:26.

[150] Jn. 16:7-8.

[151] Jn. 16:13-14.

and said to them, Receive the Holy Spirit; whose sins you shall forgive, they are forgiven them, and whose sins you shall retain, they are retained."[152]

Now, we must turn to the Acts of the Apostles and the Epistles of St. Paul to discover that the coming of the Holy Spirit must be viewed as an act of witnessing to Christ and that the glorification of Christ is proven to us in the establishment and permanence of the Church.

"Now you have not received a spirit of bondage so as to be again in fear, but you have received a spirit of adoption as sons, by virtue of which we cry, "Abba! Father!" The Spirit himself gives testimony to our spirit that we are sons of God. But if we are sons, we are heirs also; heirs indeed of God and joint heirs with Christ..."[153] "Or do you not know that your members are the temple of the Holy Spirit, who is in you, whom you have from God, and that you are not your own?"[154]

"Wherefore I give you to understand that no one speaking in the Spirit of God says "Anathema" to Jesus. And no one can say "Jesus is Lord," except in the Holy Spirit.

"Now there are varieties of gifts, but the same Spirit; and there are varieties of ministries, but the same Lord; and there are varieties of workings, but the same God, who works all things in all. Now the manifestation of the Spirit is given to everyone for profit. To one through the Spirit is given the utterance of wisdom; and to another the utterance of knowledge, according to the same Spirit; to another faith, in the same Spirit; to another the gift of healing, in the one Spirit; to another the working of miracles; to another prophecy; to another the distinguishing of spirits; to another various kinds of tongues; to another interpretation of tongues. But all these things are the work of one and the same Spirit, who allots to everyone according as he will.

"For as the body is one and has many members, and all the members of the body, many as they are, form one body, so also is it with Christ.

"For in one Spirit we were all baptized into one body, whether Jews or Gentiles, whether slaves or free; and we were all given to

---

[152] Jn. 20:21-23.
[153] Rom. 8:15-17.
[154] I Cor. 6:19.

drink of one Spirit."[155] "For whoever are led by the Spirit of God, they are the sons of God."[156]

In addition to these we find texts in St. Paul's epistles which speak of the Holy Spirit as allotting to everyone according as he will,[157] pleading for us with unutterable groanings,[158] and being grieved because of our sins,[159] etc.

If we view all these references in the framework of the "Gospel of the Holy Spirit"—i.e. the Acts of the Apostles: we obtain a fairly good idea of the operation of the Holy Spirit in the Church. "And when the days of Pentecost were drawing to a close, they were all together in one place. And suddenly there came a sound from heaven, as of a violent wind blowing, and it filled the whole house where they were sitting. And there appeared to them parted tongues as of fire, which settled upon each of them. And they were all filled with the Holy Spirit and began to speak in foreign tongues, even as the Holy Spirit prompted them to speak."[160] "As one unit they received the Holy Spirit; as one unit, controlled and inspired by the Spirit, they break into an outpouring of jubilant praise and thanksgiving to God. It was one Body that spoke, Christ's Body, and it speaks the universal tongues of all mankind . . . on Pentecost, we behold the Spirit flowing from Christ, the Head, to His established members. To the Church, as such, comes the power to fulfill His mission. Pentecost was the Baptism of the Church and Her anointing, correlative with the baptism of Christ. By her baptism she is prepared for Her world ministry; and there is manifested what her gift to the world will be, the Holy Spirit."[161]

This was the beginning of the Church as a community. Then the Holy Spirit revealed His presence in the works of the apostles. For He showed His power in the sermon of Peter,[162] the baptism of the first

---

[155] I Cor. 12:3-13.

[156] Rom. 8:14.

[157] I Cor. 12:11.

[158] Rom. 8:26.

[159] Eph. 4:30.

[160] Acts 2:1-4.

[161] John J. Fernan, S.J., *Theology.*   Vol. III: *The Mystical Christ.* Syracuse, New York: Le Moyne College. 1954. Pp. 6-7.

[162] Acts 2:14-36.

three thousand,[163] the unparalleled charity and the community of goods, of the Church of Jerusalem,[164] the punishment of Ananias and Sapphira,[165] the conversion of Saul,[166] the choosing of Saul and Barnabas for a special commission,[167] the selecting of bishops "to rule the Church of God,"[168] etc.

In the light of these quotations and references one fact stands out very clearly; the Church as a community and her members are in a real relationship to the Holy Spirit. It is our task now to investigate thoroughly this relationship.

B. *Relationships to the Holy Spirit.*

a. *The members of the Church and the Holy Spirit.*

The relationship of individual souls in the Church to the Holy Spirit has a twofold aspect according to the individual's goal, and his means of attaining that goal. For everything that has any influence on the supernatural life of the members of the Church depends on one of these two aspects.

Catholic dogmatic theology very clearly defines the end of man as the achievement of divine sonship. Since this divine sonship means participation in God's own life, it is a totally supernatural end: it is a tending toward the triune Godhead with a claim to participate in His life.

This tending has two integral parts: The first one is an exterior, objective aspect in which we try somehow to grasp God Himself by knowing Him, as it were, with the knowledge of the Son, and by loving Him, as it were, with the love of the Holy Spirit.

The other is an interior element. It represents a transforming, metamorphosing power which makes man similar to God through the mystical process of participation. This process is started by the divine seed of grace. It is precisely the development and growth of this supernatural seed of grace which defines for us the concrete end of the individual. For the divine sonship is realized through the mediation of knowledge and love in so far as a metamorphosis is taking place in the soul: the man of nature is being transformed into a supernatural one through his knowing and loving activities. The supernatural man, the "alter Christus" or divine sonship is,

---

[163] Acts 2:41.
[164] Acts 2:45.
[165] Acts 5:1-11.

[166] Acts 9:1-19.
[167] Acts 13:2.
[168] Acts 20:28.

therefore, the *terminus intrinsecus* of this transformation. Concretely, then, each individual Christian must develop Christ in himself as the image of God; and at the same time, through the very same activities of knowledge and love, he must find God in the deepest sanctuary of His divine existence and life.

This wholly supernatural end makes it mandatory that some kind of supernatural forces be available to man. And such a force is furnished him by the presence of the Holy Spirit within him. If it is true that even Christ's soul was filled with the Holy Spirit,[169] then the same divine presence is an absolute necessity for other men who by themselves are incapable of attaining their supernatural end. For it is in virtue of the Spirit's powers and impetus that men, by transforming their knowing and loving activities, can become capable of achieving supernatural ends. As Merkelbach put it, "the end to which we are ordered consists in our participation in God's life i.e, in seeing and loving God as He sees and loves Himself. This end is absolutely supernatural and therefore, no creature can attain it through the power of his own nature. If man must achieve this by means of his actions, then, some powers or *habitus* must be added to his nature in virtue of which he is elevated above himself, is transplanted to the divine order, and is made capable of eliciting divine operations proportionate to his supernatural end."[170]

Let us look now at the means by which the Holy Spirit enables the individual to attain the divine sonship.

The sanctification of the individual, in a wider perspective, means the application of the merits of redemption to the individual soul. It can be called the fulfillment of Christ's mission to me, taking my personality as the *terminus* of the mission. When it is done, the redemption of Christ becomes the happy procession of the individual: it is the beginning of the divine sonship.

Truly, the work of the Holy Spirit begins only after this first step has been completed. Not that sanctifying grace could be separated from His sanctifying operation; but every operation of the Holy Spirit culminates in securing permanence, and so it is in the life of the individual. Precisely in order to complete and perpetuate the

---

[169] Cf. Luke 1:34; 2:52; 3:22; 4:1; 4:14; 10:21; 11:20; Heb. 9:14.
[170] Cf. B. H. Merkelbach, O.P., *Summa Theologiae Moralis*. Parisiis. 1942. T. I, p. 481. Also: *S.T.*, I-II, q. 109, a. 5.

work of Christ, he also receives with sanctifying grace the super-natural virtues and the gifts of the Holy Spirit. From that very moment he must always be ready to welcome the impulses of the Holy Spirit. The gifts play an especially important role in the life of the soul by making him docile in the hands of the Holy Spirit. While the virtues prepare man for the suggestions of reason, the gifts attune him to the impulses of the Holy Spirit. This fact points to the essential differences between the functions of the virtues and the gifts. In the operation of the virtues man remains the active factor. In the operation of the gifts the Holy Spirit leads and man has but one duty—to follow the divine impulse.

The Holy Spirit, then, with His gifts and actual graces, guards and fortifies the individual's life so that the mission of Christ does not fail in him; so that in the stream of steady growth and flowering, the ideal of the *alter Christus* becomes a reality in him. This is the spiritual "surplus" of the Holy Spirit added to the supernatural life in order to keep it growing. This is that new world in which the light of the Spirit and not the light of reason gives impetus to the actions of the individual. This is that principle which assures the permanence of supernatural life to the extent that the gifts of the Holy Spirit guide man through the labyrinth of human problems ac-cording to the intentions of God. Whereas the supernatural virtues mean only an imperfect participation in the divine nature, since in their operation they have to adapt themselves to the imperfect method of human action, the gifts have no such imperfections thanks to the active impetus of the Holy Spirit.[171] In St. Thomas' words: "The gifts perfect the soul's powers in relation to the Holy Ghost their Mover; whereas the virtues perfect either the reason itself, or the other powers in relation to reason: and it is evident that the more exalted the mover, the more excellent the disposition whereby the thing moved requires to be disposed. Therefore the gifts are more perfect than the virtues."[172]

We have completed our considerations of the individual's relation to the Holy Spirit. Now from these considerations what conclusions can we deduce that will touch on the problem of Church unity?

In virtue of the nature of the divine sonship it is evident that

---

[171] Cf. B. H. Merkelbach, O.P., *op. cit.* p. 496.
[172] *S.T.*, I-II, q. 68, a. 8.

Christ's redemptive mission to the individual soul as a subjective relationship is always the repetition of the one and and only objective redemptive mission of Christ. On this objective element rests the singularity of principle of the divine adoption.

This conclusion is identical with the one reached in our investigation of the Holy Spirit's role in the sanctification of the individual. As for the gifts, the prompting must always come from the Spirit of Christ. Man's attitude is passive. He must accept and not propose. But the Spirit of Christ is essentially the mutual love of the Father and the Son. Even in His gifts and promptings He reveals Himself as such. He communicates what He is. In virtue of this love He holds men together, incites, and prepares them to listen to the divine word and to accept the divine impetus. In other words, He places them on a common ground and on the same road. He makes them members of the same community. And so, through the notions of the divine sonship and the gifts of the Holy Spirit, we necessarily arrive at the notion of the Church as the only society founded by Christ. He founded her for those whom He has called to be adopted sons of God. The Holy Spirit guides her in order that her permanence may be safeguarded until the end of time. And now, these considerations lead us to another important question in connection with the relationship to the Holy Spirit: namely, whether since the Church is made up of a body and a soul, an individual might belong to the soul of the Church without being a member of her body. We will devote more time to this problem later. For the present we must turn to the community of Catholic individuals: the Church herself; and we must find the principle of her permanence in her relationship to the Holy Spirit.

b. *The Church as a community and the Holy Spirit.*

If we want to grasp the real relationship of the Church as a community to the Holy Spirit, we have to return to the society of the first Christians and see how the community was filled with the Spirit of Christ. On Pentecost, we recall, "they were all together in one place." "There is a profound symbolism involved here: our Lord wished to signify to them that the Spirit would be given to them as a body, in their unity with each other. Actually, the Spirit was given, not to isolated individuals, but to a community, the Church. Pentecost dramatizes the fact that the Holy Spirit is the

Soul of the Body of Christ, which is the Church. This fact is of extreme importance for an understanding of the sacramental system of the Church. Because the Holy Spirit was given to the Church, and dwells in her, therefore she cannot communicate Him to her members, and to those who seek membership, through the instrumentality of external rites."[173] And the Church began to communicate the Holy Spirit on the very day of His descent upon them. According to the Acts: "But Peter, standing up with the Eleven, lifted up his voice and spoke out to them ... you will receive the gift of the Holy Spirit. For to you is the promise and to your children and to all who are far off, even to all whom the Lord Our God calls to Himself ... Now they who received his word were baptized, and there were added that day about three thousand souls."[174]

This is how the first community of Christians was born. Its birth and existence possess all the characteristics which we have explained in connection with the relationship of the Church to the Son. In addition to its establishment, however, it needed the descent of the Holy Spirit to become active, efficient, and permanent. For it was only after the infusion of the Holy Spirit in the souls of the first community that the Church could start to manifest her activities: namely, the building of the mystical body of Christ through the concurrence of both the *Ecclesia docens* and the *Ecclesia discens* in the same vivifying principle, the Holy Spirit.

Let us now analyze the vital aspects of this relationship.—First of all, it is the Holy Spirit who secures the most intimate and most complete bond between the *Ecclesia docens* and the *Ecclesia discens*. For, the fact that to become members of Christ's Church men must receive, though in an indirect way, the Holy Spirit, seems to accentuate two things: on the one hand, it becomes plain that to enter the Church one must receive the Holy Spirit; on the other, it underscores the mediative power of the Church in regard to the Holy Spirit. We deliberately use the word *indirect* because we wish to point out the fact that after the descent of the Holy Spirit on the first Pentecost, the Church has always exercised a mediative role in the communication of the Holy Spirit to her individual members. When the Holy Spirit descended upon the apostles directly, He made

---

[173] John J. Fernan, S.J., *op. cit.* p. 7.
[174] Acts 2:14, 38-39, 41.

them and the Church herself through them, His instruments in the economy of grace. Therefore, this mediative role pertains to the Church as a living organism capable of communicating supernatural life.[175]

Furthermore, it is the Holy Spirit who constantly ensures the most complete unity and identity to the Church despite the passing of time and the vastness of space. He does this by protecting and guaranteeing her indefectibility in two ways: namely, by infusing His gifts into the souls of the individual members, and by subjecting the *Ecclesia discens* to the *Ecclesia docens*. By doing so, He eliminates subjectivity in the teaching of the Church, so much so, that if the subjective elements should ever be found in conflict with the objective principles laid down by Christ, they must always be repudiated. This is what Lubac may have had in mind when he said that nobody could believe in the Church unless he received the Holy Spirit. Now, the Holy Spirit descended upon the apostles in order to promote, through them and their successors, the gathering of the faithful into one flock. It is, therefore, the same Spirit Who, in virtue of

---

[175] "Das beständige Sein des göttlichen Geistes unter den Menschen hatte also mit den Aposteln begonnen, die ihn unmittelbar empfingen; es hatte sie die Empfänglichen und im empfangen Tätigen ergriffen und durchdrungen, ein neues Lebensprinzip ihnen mitgeteilt, das, wo Empfänglichkeit für dasselbe vorhanden ist, von ihnen aus sich mitteilen sollte, so dass keiner mehr unmittelbar, wie sie dasselbe erhalten möge, sondern an dem neuen in ihnen gewordenen Leben sich ein gleiches in den Ubrigen erzeuge. Wei das Leben des sinnlichen Menschen nur einmal unmittelbar aus der Hand des Schöpfers kam, und wo nun sinnliches Leben werden soll, es durch die Mitteilung der Lebenskraft eines schon Lebenden bedingt is, so sollte das neue göttliche Leben ein ausströmen aus den schon Belebten, die Erzeugung desselben sollte eine Über-Zeugung sein. Nur wo die Apostel lebten und wirkten, verbreitete sich das neue Leben hin; und wie zu ihrer Zeit räumlich voneinander Entfernte nur durch die von den Gesandten des Herrn ausgehende unmittelbare Lebensmitteilung denselben Geist erhielten; so sollten die der Zeit nach von ihnen Entfernten vermittelst der Glieder, die seiner durch sie teilhafftig wurden, ihn erhalten, so dasse alle Zwischenreihen nur Fortflanzungsstufen bilden, die spätesten Reihen aber, wie die räumlich voneinander entlegensten, von einem und denselben Geiste belebt, eine Gemeinheit darstellen, sich *zu einem gemeinschaftlichen Leben* gestalten, eine Kirche ausmachn sollten." J. A. Möhler, *Die Einheit in der Kirche.* Mainz, 1925. Pp. 10-11.

the same power and in the framework of the same Church, but with the help of diverse pastors, holds together the fold and cares for the flock.[176]

Another vital aspect of this relationship of the Church to the Holy Spirit is found in His continuous assistance in safeguarding the Church's deposit of faith. If it is true that the whole mission of the Church is founded on the continuation and completion of Christ's redemptive work, she needs the assistance of the Holy Spirit. For what revelation really contains must be discovered, defined, and explained in virtue of this assistance. Whether the actual content of revelation is concerned with a truth of faith or a moral law, in its definition and wording the teaching Church needs the assistance of the Holy Spirit. The same is true of the Church's liturgical development in so far as the community must continually be guarded from elements contradictory to its teaching. To this end, the Holy Spirit assists the Christian community in the expression of its faith . In other words, the promptings infused into the souls of Christian individuals through the gifts of the Holy Spirit are provided to the community in the assistance of the same Spirit. It is true that this assistance does not match the active motion of the gifts. It is, however, equally true that without falsifying its real nature this assistance cannot be qualified as completely passive either. It is more correct to say that it does not set things in motion, but it must also be noted that it watches over and guarantees the correct understanding and defining of truths. Could anyone, then, call this assistance completely passive? In the course of history it is the assistance of the Holy Spirit that secures the identity of dogmatic and moral principles, the actual infallibility of the Church, as well as the harmony of her cult with the principles of faith. In short, it is in virtue of the assistance of the Holy Spirit that the Church can fulfill her basic function: namely, to deliver Christ to her members.

Now what pertinent points for the unity of the Church are offered by these considerations?

We repeat once more that we have discovered the ontological possibility of the Church in the eternal divine idea of the incarnation. The Church was set up by Christ, and therefore her unity is rooted

---

[176] Cf. Henri De Lubac, S.J., *Katholizismus als Gemeinschaft.* Köln. 1943. P. 67.

in Him, her principle and mediator. Finally, it is the role of the
Holy Spirit to secure this unity by assuring the Church of her historical identity and permanence.

This third great relationship, therefore, contains and advocates
the notion of unity through the notion of the Holy Spirit's assistance.
For it is one and the same Spirit that breathes in the Church by
guiding the *Ecclesia docens* in the development of her dogmas, moral
laws, and liturgical activities. As Karl Adam puts it: "So the
Church possesses the Spirit of Christ, not as a many of single individuals, nor as a sum of spiritual personalities, but as the compact,
ordered unity of the faithful, as a community that transcends the
individual personalities and expresses itself in a sacred hierarchy.
This organized unity, this community, as germinally given with the
Head, Christ, and depending upon His institution, is a fundamental
datum of Christianity, not a thing created by the voluntary or forced
association of the faithful, not a mere secondary and derivative thing
depending upon the good pleasure of Christians, but a thing which,
in the divine plan of salvation, is in its essence antecedent to any
Christian personality and is to that extent a supernatural thing, a
comprehensive unity, which does not presuppose Christian personalities, but itself creates and produces them.[177] We may add that this
"supra-personal thing" was established by Christ as one visible community. And the one visible community is made a permanent reality
in the endless flow of history by the power and assistance of the
Holy Spirit. Now, since the Church's teaching and power are derived
from the Spirit of Christ, we must conclude that the breath of the
Holy Spirit cannot vivify contradictory communities. His community
must be one, the legitimate continuation of the community of the
first Pentecost. And this is what we call the society of Christ, His
true Church on earth.[178]

One glance at the struggles of the Church against Agnosticism,
Arianism, Protestantism, and Modernism suffice for us to grasp
the truth of Karl Adam's words that "a mere attitude of antagonism
to heresy . . . is not the proper attitude of Catholicism."[179] It is

---

[177] Karl Adam, *op. cit.*, p. 35.
[178] Joseph Ranft, "La tradition vivante. Unité et développement,"
L'Église est une. Bloud & Gay. 1939. P. 119.
[179] Karl Adam, *op. cit.*, p. 172.

forced upon the Church by historical facts. In all truthfulness, the Catholic attitude means self-development, for the Church carries in herself the seeds of eternal vitality and truth: "The strong force which gives it back its inner equipoise is the vital spirit of revelation transmitted in its teaching authority, or, more profoundly, the Holy Spirit living in it. The Holy Spirit gives that secret energy which infuses new life into the weakened parts of the organism and repairs all unnatural dislocations in the Body of Christ."[180] This is why the Church always remains the same. This is why, being totally conscious to her unity and permanence as well as of her unbroken historical identity, she can claim to be the only true Church of Christ. She really has the right to exclusiveness. She possesses the Holy Spirit and as a community she possesses Him exclusively. Bearing in mind this undeniable truth let us now turn to other Christian communities and investigate their relationship to the Holy Spirit.

c. *Non-Catholic communities and the Holy Spirit.*

The solution of this problem is the corollary of the preceding investigations. "In her own eyes the Catholic Church is nothing at all if she be not *the* Church, *the* Body of Christ, *the* Kingdom of God."[181] There is no other alternative. For either the essence of the Church is Christ Himself, or Christ is not her essence at all. If the former is the case—and we have proven it throughout the investigations of the second relationship—there is no doubt that the relationship of the Church must be exclusive. For "there can be no contradiction, or dissention, or schism where God is. His truth cannot be otherwise than one truth, one life, one love. And therefore it can be realized in but one form, in a comprehensive fellowship that binds together all men in intimate unity."[182] This is the actual situation in regard to salvation. Consequently, the Holy Spirit cannot sustain separated communities with His divine assistance. He cannot become the principle and promoter of the articles of faith, moral laws, and liturgical acts which remain alien to Christ and His Church. And so, the teaching church of these communities is not the mediative organ of the Holy Spirit. Due to a lack of immediate descent of the Spirit

---

[180] *Ibid.*, pp. 172-173.
[181] *Ibid.*, p. 184.
[182] *Ibid.*, p. 185.

of Christ upon the teaching Church of these communities, it cannot possess and cannot communicate Him to their individual members. In other words, the separated communities are lacking the unifying principle of the Church in a twofold manner: first, in regard to their *ecclesia docens* in its defining and explaining their articles of faith, their moral laws and their worship. Secondly, in regard to their *ecclesia discens* in its understanding of the same articles and laws and in its worshipping activities. Since this state of affairs seems to be beyond question, we must learn how to live with it. By no means can we avoid facing it, saying that the community as such does not need the unifying principle of the Holy Spirit because He is already present in the Bible and so is already taking care of the life of the Church. No matter how sacred the Bible is, its content and system of truths need explanation, interpretation, and application. This is the duty and mission of the Church, which can be carried out only through the assistance of the Holy Spirit. His work would have fallen short if His inspiration had stopped with the writers of the Holy Bible and had not assured the conservation and understanding of the revealed doctrine.[183] Without the assistance of the Holy Spirit the truth-content of revelation would remain a valueless treasure either untouchable by human beings or exposed to individual misrepresentations and distortions. To guard the identity and organic development of dogmas, moral laws, and cult, it is mandatory that they be written in virtue of the same unifying principle that is present in the *Ecclesia docens* which explains the truth content of the written form, and in the *Ecclesia discens* which accepts and carries out the same truth content. And so, "every separated church which sets itself up against the original Church of Christ stands outside the communion of Christ's grace. It cannot be a mediator of salvation. So far as it is a separated and antagonistic church, it is essentially unfruitful as regards the supernatural life. So that that spiritual unfruitfulness which is predicated in the doctrine is not to be affirmed of the individual non-Catholic, but primarily of non-Catholic communions as such. By that which constitutes their separateness and differentiates them in faith and worship from the Catholic Church, they are able to awaken no supernatural life. Therefore, in so far as they are un-Catholic and anti-Catholic, that is to

---

[183] Cf. J. A. Möhler, *op. cit.*, p. 20.

say in regard to their distinct character, they are not to claim the honourable title of a 'mother' church."[184]

This is the unbending truth in so far as, we repeat, the anti-Catholic character of these communities is concerned. But they are not completely anti-Catholic. As a matter of fact, they have retained quite a few basic theses of the Catholic Church's teaching as well as some of her means of grace. When they stand on these Catholic grounds by remaining faithful to the true teaching of Christ and administering the sacraments in His name they can accomplish genuine supernatural growth and sanctity. Consequently, although these communities, as such, cannot become the mediative organs of the Holy Spirit, they can remain faithful to their Catholic heritage, and to that extent they can witness the sanctification of their members. It remains to see now how it can come about.

d. *Non-Catholic individuals and the Holy Spirit.*

In this regard Karl Adam touched upon the truth by writing: "In so far as they are genuinely Catholic in their faith and worship, it can and will and must happen that there should be, even outside the visible Church, a real growth and progress in union with Christ. So is the promise of Jesus fufilled: "And other sheep I have that are not of this fold."[185] Wherever the gospel of Jesus is faithfully preached, and wherever baptism is conferred with faith in His Holy Name, there His grace can operate. When the disciples would have forbidden a man who had not attached himself to Jesus from casting out devils in His name, Our Lord declared: "Forbid him not. For there is no man that doth a miracle in my name and can soon speak ill of me. He that is not against you is for you."[186]

From these facts we must draw two very important conclusions concerning the relationship of non-Catholic individuals to the Holy Spirit. First of all, it is evident that they can partake of the divine sonship. Provided that they are subjects of invincible error and manifest good faith, Christ's redemptive grace can reach and transform them. Now, if they can become justified, then, they can also receive, together with sanctifying grace, the gifts of the Holy Spirit. Consequently, they can be exposed to His promptings and impulses.

---

[184] Karl Adam, *op. cit.,* p. 189.
[185] Jn. 10:16.
[186] Mark 9:38-39; Karl Adam, *op. cit.,* p. 190.

The Holy Spirit can impel and guide them in order to promote their incorporation into Christ and to further their sanctification. And so, "not merely a Christian life, but a complete and lofty Christian life, a life according to the "full age of Christ," a saintly life, is possible —so Catholics believe—even in definitely non-Catholic communions. It is true that it cannot develop with that luxuriance which is possible in the Church, where is the fulness of Jesus and His Body; and it will never be anti-Catholic in its quality. Yet it will be a genuine saintly life; since, wherever grace is, the noble fruits of grace can ripen."[187]

The second conclusion can be worded in this way. Since the Holy Spirit, as the soul of the Church and the guardian of her unity, moves these individual souls in and through His gifts, these members of the non-Catholic communities belong more to the true Church than to their own communion. Though unconsciously, they still very effectively promote their union with her rather than their own church. And so, if they reach the whole truth of revelation their sincere desire for greater perfection brings them back to the true Catholic community of Christ.

IV. The Teaching of the Fathers of the Church

The key to the understanding of the unity of the Church is the understanding of her true nature. Yet St. Paul called the Church "a great mystery," "magnum mysterium."[1] How, then, can her nature ever be understood by finite human minds? It cannot—if by understanding one means an exhaustive knowledge of her structure as a supernatural perfect society and a comprehension of her supernatural operative principles. A mystery, however, can be approached in an intelligent way because it is revealed by God, the divine Intellect; and the human intellect's natural light, in its sincere and serious effort, is strengthened by the infusion of gratuitous light.[2] Bearing this in mind, we have treated the problem of the nature of the Church in a humble and submissive spirit. On scriptural grounds we have investigated her threefold relationship to the Father, Son, and Holy Spirit, and deduced important conclusions regarding her nature.

---

[187] *Ibid.*, p. 192.
[1] Eph. 5:32.
[2] Cf. *S.T.*, I, q. 12, a. 13, c and ad 1.

In so doing we have been guided by the principle that no Christian would ever deny the reality of the Blessed Trinity or the divinity of Christ. It is our hope that by considering the Church in her relationships to the three Persons of the Blessed Trinity, and by basing our arguments of scriptural texts, we have found the most practicable way of communicating our findings to our separated brethren.

Now, however, we must turn to the Tradition of the Church—for two reasons in particular. First, we would like to show that our approach to the problem is not an innovation. It is found, though in an embryonic form, in the teaching of the Fathers. Secondly, we intend to point out to Heiler and his present day followers[3] that one cannot safeguard the supernatural element in the Church without safeguarding her visible element; namely, her hierarchical structure. This truth, in contrast to Heiler's position, is evident in the teaching of the Fathers. It remains, then, to prove our position.

a. *In relation to the Father.*—We have already referred, at the beginning of this study, to Tertullian's statement that the Church "is the body of the three Persons."[4] Writing on Baptism, he points out that since the pledge to bear witness to the faith—*testatio fidei*—and to solemnly promise salvation—*sponsio salutis*—is taken in the name of the three Persons, "it is necessary that also the Church be mentioned because where the Father, Son, and Holy Spirit are, there is the Church, too, being the body of the three Persons."[5]

In another reference, Tertullian states that the Church properly and principally—*proprie et principaliter*—is the Holy Spirit Himself in whom, due to the unity of the divine nature, the Trinity is present. It is He, then, who gathers the Church's members into one flock.[6]

While these first two texts of Tertullian can only be interpreted in an indirect way of the Father, in his treatise on prayer he mentions

---

[3] Cf. the *INTRODUCTION* of this study.

[4] *De Baptismo*, c. VI; P.L., t. I, col. 1315 A.

[5] "Cum autem sub tribus, et testatio fidei et sponsio salutis pignerentur, necessario adjicitur Ecclesiae mentio, quoniam ubi tres, id est Pater, et Filius, et Spiritus sanctus, ibi Ecclesia, quae trium corpus est." *Ibid.*

[6] "Nam et Ecclesia proprie et principaliter ipse est Spiritus in quo est trinitas unius divinitatis. Pater et Filius et Spiritus sanctus. Illam Ecclesiam congregat, quam Dominus in tribus posuit. Atque ita exinde etiam numerus omnis qui in hanc fidem conspiraverint, Ecclesia ab auctore et consecratore censetur." *De Pudicitia*, c. XXI; P.L., t. I, col. 1080 B.

Him expressly. Speaking of the "Our Father," he says: "And the Church is not overlooked here either. In fact, a mother is recognized both in the son and in the father, since it is through her that they stand in the father and son relationship." One word, therefore, can express our reverence to God and to all those who belong to Him. . . .[7] —These words of Tertullian seem to express two very important facts: first, the divine sonship is extended to men through the perfect cooperation of the Father and the Church. Secondly, they belong together so firmly that the notion of the one involves a reference to the notion of the other. This close relationship, we may add, can be explained through the affinity of Christ's incarnation and the Church's existence in the eternal divine idea of the Father.

St. Clement of Alexandria draws a parallel between the world as the work of the divine will, and the Church as the framework for the salvation of men. Since he introduced this parallel with the observation that "God is never impotent," we can rightly infer that, first, he was thinking of the purposeful and necessary realization of each and every divine *propositum;* second, that the Church, as one of these *proposita,* is as visible and undeniable, in her concrete realization, as the world itself.[8]

St. Epiphanius is perhaps the most explicit in regard to the Church's relationship to the Father. In his *Adversus Haereses* he calls the Church the "truly Christian religion" and adds that the Church has been flourishing for a long time. Her origin goes back to Adam and, even beyond Adam, to all eternity, where she is rooted, together with Christ, in the divine will of the Father, the Son, and the Holy Spirit.[9] We cannot stress this clearcut reference strongly

---

[7] "Ne mater quidem Ecclesia praeteritur, Si quidem in filio et patre mater recognoscitur, de qua constat et patris et filii nomen. Uno igitur genere aut vocabulo et Deum cum suis honoramus, et praecepti meminimus, et oblitos patris denotamus." *De Oratione,* c. II; P.L., t. I, col. 1256-1257.

[8] "Nunquam est enim Deus imbecillus. Quemadmodum enim ejus voluntas est opus, et id mundus nominatur; ita etiam ejus propositum est hominum salus, et ea vocata est Ecclesia. Novit ergo quos vocavit, quos servavit; simul autem vocavit et servavit." *Paedagogus,* lib. I, c. VI; P.G., t. XLII, col. 783 D.

[9] "Superest una, nimirum sancta et catholica Ecclesia, quae vere Christiana religio dicitur; quaeque jam olim et cum Adamo, imo ante Adamum ipsum, adeoque ante omnia saecula cum Christo floruit de Patris ac

enough. The words of St. Epiphanius are so well chosen that there can be no doubt in the reader's mind as to what he really means by them. First, by a regressive gradation, he makes it clear that he means eternity in the absolute sense of the word: *"jam olim et cum Adamo, imo ante Adamum ipsum, adeoque ante omnia saecula. ..."* Then he pointedly says that the will of the Father, the Son, and the Holy Spirit has bound the Church to Christ from all eternity, and that consequently they exist and flourish together: *"ante omnia saecula cum Christo floruit de Patris ac Filii et Spiritus sancti voluntate."*—St. Epiphanius touches on this relationship in another work as well. Speaking if the Blessed Trinity, he emphasizes the trinity of Persons and the unity of the divine nature, adding that the singular unity—*singularis unitas*—of the Father and the Son and the Holy Spirit is expressed in the one substance, one absolute power and one will, on the one hand, and in the one Church, one baptism and one faith, on the other.[10] This parallel between the *una substantia, dominatus unus, una voluntas* and *the una Ecclesia, baptismus unus, una fides* is certainly a very definite expression of St Epiphanius' thought and conviction.

Finally, we would like to call attention to a brief statement of St. John Chrysostom. In his famous 'last sermon' written shortly before he went into exile, he says among other things: "The Church is more lovable to God than the heavens themselves are. He did not assume the substance of the heavens, but He did assume the flesh of the Church: (therefore) the heavens exist for the Church, and not the Church for the heavens."[11]—We have selected this very short reference for two reasons. First, in our opinion, St. John Chrysostom had a very definite notion of the Incarnation of Christ as the commanding idea of creation. Secondly, he clearly perceived the Christo

---

Filii et Spiritus sancti voluntate." *Adversus Haereses*, lib. III, t. II, VI; P.G., t. XLII, col. 783 O.

[10]"Nos igitur Patrem profitemur esse Patrem; Filium, Filium; Spiritum sanctum denique Spiritum esse sanctum: hoc est, Trinitatem in unitatem positam. Singularis quippe Patris ac Filii et Spiritus sancti unitas est, una substantia, dominatus unus, una voluntas: una Ecclesia, *baptismus unus, una fides.*" *Ancoratus*, CXVIII; P.G., t. XLIII, col. 251 A.

[11] "... amabilior enim est Ecclesia Deo, quam coelum ipsum. Coeli corpus non accepit, sed Ecclesiae carnem accepit; *propter Ecclesiam coelum, non propter coelum Ecclesia.*" *Sermo antequam iret in exsilium*, 2; P.G., t. LII, col. 429.

—Ecclesiocentric structure of the created world. So much so, that he did not even establish the complete syllogism of why the Church cannot be for the high heavens. He simply declared, in virtue of the foregoing argument, that the heavens exist for the Church, because, and this is understood, the Church is identical with Christ whose Incarnation is the most lovable reality to the Father.

We feel, therefore, that our conclusions concerning the relationship of the Church to the Father are fully supported by the Fathers of the Church.

b. *In relation to the Son.*—On this point we have more than adequate testimony from the Fathers of the Church. They taught in union, first of all, that the Church was the body of Christ. It is Christ who lives on in the community He founded. He is the head, we are the members. According to St. Clement of Rome, in this body every member counts: even the smallest and most insignificant members are necessary and useful. All the members must breathe together and, in order to conserve the body as a whole, they must subject themselves to the head in unison. This last word, unison, is a very inadequate translation of the following three words of St. Clement: *una subjectione utuntur.*[12] However, it expresses correctly, we think, the idea of the bishop of Rome.—St. Clement of Alexandria, commenting on Eph. 4:13: "until we all attain to the unity of the faith and of the deep knowledge of the Son of God, to perfect manhood, to the mature measure of the fullness of Christ," called Christ the head and only perfect man, *caput et vir, qui solus in justitia perfectus.* We, by comparison, are only infants, but can become perfect by identifying ourselves with the Church whose head is Christ.[13]—Origen, while repeating that the whole Church is the

---

[12] "Exemplo nobis sit corpus nostrum: caput absque pedibus nihil est, sic neque pedes absque capite: minima autem corporis nostri membra, necessaria et utilia sunt toti corpori: tum universa conspirant, et ad conservationem totius corporis una subjectione utuntur." *Epistola I ad Corinthios,* c. XXXVIII; P.G., t. I, col. 283 A; *ibid.,* c. XXXVIII; col. 283 B.

[13] ... haec dicens ad aedificationem corporis Christi, *qui est caput* et *vir,* qui solus in justitia perfectus; nas autem infantes, qui ad inflationem nos sufflant haeresium ventos vitantes, et iis, qui nos aliter docent quam patres, fidem non habentes, tunc perfecti efficimur quando sumus Ecclesia,

body of Christ, adds a new note by calling the *Verbum* the moving and acting principle of the Church as a community as well as of her individual members.[14] And so, the basic truth that the Church is the body of Christ, is a feature of primary importance, pushed to its farthest conclusions in the writings of the Church Fathers. St. Augustine, for example, uses the expression *una quaedam persona*, as it were one person,[15] to express the unity of the head and body of the Church. However, the Fathers never deify the Church! Their attitude in this regard is beautifully expressed in St. Basil's words: "It is not the Church but the head of the Church, Christ, that we adore."[16] No deification, no humanization could, therefore, develop in their teaching. The Fathers of the Church are fully aware of the presence of natural and supernatural, human and divine elements in the Church, and they intend to show both in their writings. It does not really matter whether they refer to the Church as the body of Christ,[17] the structure of a tower,[18] Sion, the mountain of the Lord,

---

capite, Christo scilicet recepto." *Paedagogus*, lib. I, c. V; P.G., t. VIII, col. 271 A.

[14] "...dicimus ex divinis Scripturis totam Dei Ecclesiam esse Christi corpus a Dei Filio animatum, membra autem illius corporis, ut totius, eos esse omnes qui credunt; quoniam, sicut anima vitam et motum impertit corpori, quod a seipso natura moveri vitaliter non potest; ita Verbum totum corpus seu Ecclesiam ad ea quae opus sunt, movens et agens, etiam singula membra eorum qui ad Ecclesiam pertinent, movet, ita ut nihil sine Verbo faciant." *Contra Celsum*, lib. VI, 48; P.G., t. XI, col. 1374 B.

[15] "...unus dicitur Christus caput et corpus suum; ipse dicit cum de conjugio loqueretur: *Erunt duo in carne una: igitur jam non duo, sed suna caro* (Matt. XIX(5,6). Sed forte hoc dicat de quocumque conjugio? Audi apostolum Paulum: *Et erunt duo*, inquit, *in carne una: sacramentum hoc magnum est, ego autem dico in Christo et in Ecclesia* (Eph. V, 31, 32)? Fit ergo tanquam ex duobus una quaedam persona, ex capite et corpore, ex sponso et sponsa." *Enarratio in Psalmum XXX*, 4; P.L., t. XXXVI, col. 232; cf. *Enarratio in Psalmum XXXVI*, 4; ibid., col. 385; *Sermo XCI*, c. VII; P.L., t. XXXVIII, col. 571.

[16] "Ecclesia enim non adoratur, sed caput Ecclesiae Christus." *Homilia in Psalmum XLIV*; P.G., t. XXIX, col. 410 C.

[17] "*Ita et Christus.* Et cum oportuisset dicere, Ita et Ecclesia; hoc enim consequens erat: hoc quidem non dixit, sed illius loco Christum ponit, in altum extollens orationem, et auditorem magis pudore afficiens. Hoc autem vult significare: Ita et Christi corpus, quod est Ecclesia. Sicut enim et corpus et caput unus sunt homo, ita et Ecclesiam et Christum unum esse dixit." St. John Chrysostom, *In Epist. I ad Corinthios*, Ho-

or the holy city,[19] etc., they always try to project into their readers'
or listeners' minds a picture that reflects a perfect combination of
natural and supernatural in the structure and operations of the
Church.

In proof of this we should like to refer, first of all, to St. Gregory
of Nazianzus. In explaining the mystery of the Church by comparing it to a living body, he points out the need for an organic structure,
namely, a presiding, ruling element, and the guided or governed
element. Accordingly, he continues, God has set up the Church in
such a way that some of the members are fed both by word and deed
in order to keep them in line for duty, while others become pastors
and educators in the Church in order to promote her perfection. Due
to their virtues and their familiarity with the things of God, the
pastors and educators are like the soul of the body. But they can
never dispense with the rest of the Church. Both the guided and the
guiding elements are vitally important in the Church: in virtue of
the same spirit they must be brought together, joined and united into
a perfect body worthy of Christ who is the head.[20]

---

milia XXX, 1; P.G., t. XLI, col. 250; cf. *In Epist. ad Ephes.*, c. IV,
Homilia X; P.G., t. LXII, col. 75-76; St. Gregory of Nyssa, *De perfecta
Christiani forma;* P.G., t. XLVI, col. 274.

[18] "Turris quidem quam vides aedificari, ego sum Ecclesia, quae tibi
apparui et modo et prius." Hermas, *Pastor*, lib. 1, Visiones, III, III;
P.G., t. II, col. 901.

[19] "Ecclesiam autem esse corpus Christi, cujus invicem membra sumus,
Apostolus testis est (Eph. I, 23, quae ipsa sit Sion mons Domini, regis
filia, civitas sancta, vivis lapidibus in fundamento prophetarum et Aposto-
lorum aedificata." St. Hilary, *Tractatus in CXXIX Psalmum*, 9; P.L., t.
IX, col 715 B; cf. St. Ambrose, *Enarratio in Psalmum XXXVII*, 9;
P.L., t. XIV, col. 1061 C; St. Jerome, *Dialogus contra Pelagianos*, lib.
I, 16; P.L., t. XXIII. col. 532 C.

[20] "Nam quemadmodum in corpore aliud principatum tenet, ac velut
praesidet, aliud subest et regitur: ad eumdem quoque modum Deus, vel
aequitatis lege, quae meritum cujusque perpendit, vel etiam providentiae,
per quam omnia inter se velut devinxit, hoc in Ecclesiis constituit, ut alii
pascantur et pareant (quibus videlicet id utilius est), ac tum sermone,
tum opere, ad officium dirigantur: alii autem ad *Ecclesiae perfectionem
pastores ac magistri sint*, nimirum qui virtute, conjunctioneque et fami-
liaritate apud Deum, vulgo sublimiores sunt, rationem animae ad corpus,
aut mentis ad animam obtinentes; ut haec duo, hoc est id, quod deficit,
et id quod redundat, inter se, velut in membris, composita et compacta,
spiritusque compage connexa et colligata, unum corpus, omni ex parte

It is evident from the text itself that St. Gregory is thinking of the *Ecclesia docens* and *Ecclesia discens* respectively. But it is equally evident that the *Ecclesia docens* must be accepted as an expression of authority in matters of teaching. This is why the members of the teaching Church are compared to the soul in its relation to the body. It is the soul which vivifies the body, and it is the *Ecclesia docens* which fulfills that function in regard to the rest of the community. On this point we cannot stress strongly enough certain expressions used by St. Gregory of Nazianzus to bring out the importance of cooperation between the teaching and the learning Church. Expressions like *composita et compacta, connexa et colligata*, basically mean exactly the same thing: namely, to be joined and united into one body, to form one whole. Not to deny one or the other, but to have and accept both, to join and unite the two into one organic and living body and, in this way, to make ourselves worthy of being members of Christ Himself.

This element of submission, by the way, is a recurrent theme in the writings of the Fathers of the Church. We find it in St. Clement's of Rome First Epistle to the Corinthians,[21] as well as in St. Ignatius of Antioch. The latter pictures the presbyters of each Christian community as the chords of one and the same harp which blend harmoniously when sounded together with their bishop, the authority of the community. The membership of each church should follow their example in forming one single *chorus*, receiving the gifts *in unitate*, echoing each other in perfect harmony, and singing thanks to the Father in Christ Jesus as one single voice, *voce una*. To share in God's life at all times, then, the members of the Church must live in immaculate unity, *immaculata unitate*.[22] St. Ignatius of Antioch

---

perfectum, atque ipso Christo, qui caput nostrum est, omnino dignum existant." *Oratio* II, III; P.G., t. XXXV, col. 410 BC.

[21] "Vos ergo qui seditionis fundamenta jecistis, *subditi estote* presbyteris, et correptionem suscipite in poenitentiam..." *Epistola I ad Corinthios,*, c. LVII; P.G., t. I, col. 323 B.

[22] "Unde decet vos in episcopi sententiam concurrere, quod et facitis. Nam memorabile vestrum presbyterium, dignum Deo, ita coaptatum est episcopo, ut chordae citharae. Propter hoc in consensu vestro et concordi charitate Jesus Christus canitur. Sed et vos singuli chorus estote, ut consoni per concordiam, melos Dei recipientes in unitate, cantetis voce una per Jesum Christum Patri; quo et vos audiat, et agnoscat ex iis, quae bene operamini, membra esse vos Filii ipsius. Utile itaque est, in immacu-

even says that nobody should perform any functions of the Church in separation from his bishop. For in a local Christian community it is the bishop who represents Christ. Without his authority the multitude could not function as a community, just as the universal Catholic Church could not exist without the presence of Christ in her.[23]

Surprising as it may seem, then, submission to the visible authority of the Church is indeed stressed by the Fathers of the Church as a vital element of her structure and operation—as vital, in fact, as her supernatural element. This is why they usually refer to it in treating of the Church as the body of Christ.[24] St. Ambrose, for example, expresses the conviction of the early Church very forcefully in this way: "Where Peter is, there is the Church; where the Church is, there is no death, but eternal life."[25] It would be difficult indeed, in our opinion, to be more explicit than St. Ambrose in pointing out the importance of the Church's visible element.

The Church Fathers reach the same conclusion, moreover, by examining the Church from the viewpoint of doctrinal unity and uniformity. St. Irenaeus, for example, makes it clear that the Church, throughout the world, assiduously guards and keeps the one, true faith and the identity of truths received from the Lord— so much so, that she can be compared to a house under one rule. In her faith she gives the impression of having but one heart and one

---

lata unitate vos esse, ut et semper participetis Deo." *Epistola ad Ephesios*, c. IV; P.G., t. V, col. 647 B; cf. *Epistola ad Magnesios*, c. VI; ibid. col. 667 B; c. XIII; ibid. col. 671 C; *Epistola ad Philadelphenses*, c. VII; ibid., col. 702 C-703 A.

[23] "Separatim ab episcopo nemo quidquam faciat eorum, quae ad Ecclesiam spectant ... Ubi comparuerit episcopus, ibi et multitudo sit; quemadmodum, ubi fuerit Christus Jesus, ibi catholica est Ecclesia." *Epistola ad Smyrnaeos*, c. VIII; P.G., t. V, col. 714 B; cf. St. Cyprian, *De unitate Ecclesiae*, III; P.L., t. IV, col. 513 A-516 A.

[24] "Omnes enim corpue unum in Christo sumus, singuli autem Christi, atque alii aliorum membra. Alii enim dominantur et praesunt: alii parent ac reguntur. Et quamvis non eadem sit utrorumque actio, siquidem imperare, et imperio regi, non est idem; fiunt tamen utraque unum in unum Christum, ab eodem Spiritu constructa atque compacta." St. Gregory of Nazianzus, *Oratio XXXII*, XI; P.G., t. XXXVI, col. 186 D; cf. St. Jerome, *Epistola LII*; P.L., t. XXII, col 535.

[25] "Ubi ergo Petrus, ibi Ecclesia: ubi Ecclesia, ibi nulla mors, sed vita aeterna." *Enarratio in Psalmum XL*, 30; P.L., t. XIV, col. 1134 B.

soul throughout the world, while in her teaching, tradition, and preaching she speaks as having but one mouth. The fact that different nations speak different languages causes her no difficulty. Her local communities in Germany, Iberia, in the land of the Celts, Egypt, Lybia, in the East or in the center of the world all have one and the same tradition. One could say, in fact, that the preaching of truths in the Church diffuses one and the same light all over the world, just as one and the same sun lights up the entire universe.[26] St. Cyril of Jerusalm has made an observation, on this point, which merits our attention. First, he makes it clear that everything one needs for the knowledge and practice of faith, is given to him in the teaching of the Church. Secondly, he says that this teaching is fortified with all the scriptural references, *ex omnibus Scripturis vallata,* and is presented to the faithful in short, easy sentences to facilitate memorizing them.[27] Because it is the expression of revelation, nothing can destroy this body of truths entrusted to the Church. It is not her own invention, but a gift from God Himself, and therefore invincible and indestructible. In the words of St. Hilary: "It is a characteristic feature of the Church that she triumph when being hurt, that she become understood

---

[26] "Hanc praedicationem cum acceperit, et hanc fidem, quemadmodum *praediximus. Ecclesia, et quidem in universum mundum disseminata, diligenter custodit, quasi unam domum inhabitans: et similiter credit iis, videlicet quasi unam animam habens, et unum cor, et consonanter haec praedicat, et docet, et tradit, quasi unum possidens os. Nam etsi in mundo loquelae dissimiles sunt, sed tamen virtus traditionis una et eadem est. Et neque hae quae in Germania sunt fundatae Ecclesiae aliter credunt, aut aliter tradunt; neque hae quae in Hiberis sunt, neque hae quae in Celtis, neque hae quae in Oriente, neque hae quae in Aegypto, neque hae quae in Lybia, neque hae quae in medio mundi constitutae: sed sicut sol creatura Dei, in universo mundo unus et idem est, sic et lumen, praedicatio veritatis, ubique lucet, et illuminat omnes homines, qui volunt ad cognitionem veritatis venire..." *Contra Haereses,* lib. I, c. X, 2; P.G. t. VII, col. 551 B-554 A.

[27] "Fidem vero in addiscendo atque profitendo, illam solam amplectere et serva, quae nunc tibi ab Ecclesia traditur, ex omnibus Scripturis vallata. Cum enim non omnes possint Scripturas legere, sed alios quidem imperitia, alios vero occupatio quaedam a cognitione impediat: ne anima per ignorantiam intereat, paucis versiculis universum fidei dogma comprehendimus." *Catechesis, V, De fide et symbolo,* XII; P.G., t. XXXIII, col. 519 B-522 A.

while being attacked, and that she draw people to herself while being deserted."[28] What St. Hilary means becomes evident in another passage of the same work. Describing the attitudes of the heretics, he notes that, while all of them are against the Church, they fight each other at the same time and each one claims the victory for himself. Such a victory, however, is really a triumph for the Church; the different factions have nothing in common, and so, fighting each other's opinions and condemning each other's faith, they affirm, in the final analysis, the one true faith of the Church.[29] Anyone who reads these lines with an open mind and a sense of objectivity realizes that this is so in virtue of the indefectibility of the Church. No sect, no heresy possesses this tremendous intrinsic power and assurance for its teaching. It is an exclusive privilege of the Church because it is only she that is built on Christ and can speak in His name. As St. Augustine worded it: "In Christ it is the Church that speaks, and in the Church it is Christ who speaks; the body in the head, on the one hand, and the head in the body, on the other."[30] This doctrinal unity and uniformity, therefore, stresses the conclusion reached by the Fathers of the Church through the distinction of the *Ecclesia docens* and *Ecclesia discens;* namely, that visibility pertains to the nature of the Church, and that the natural and supernatural elements are equally important in her structure and operation.

Yet, there is a third aspect in which the presence of the natural and supernatural elements in the Church's relationship to the Son become evident: namely, the unity and unicity of the Church as a community.

---

[28] "Hoc enim Ecclesiae proprium est, ut tunc vincat, cum laeditur, tunc intelligatur cum arguitur, tunc obtineat cum deseritur." *"De Trinitate,* lib. VII, 4; P.L., t. X, col. 202 B.

[29] "Haeretici igitur omnes contra Ecclesiam veniunt: sed dum haeretici omnes se invicem vincunt, nihil tamen sibi vincunt. Victoria emin eorum, Ecclesiae triumphus ex omnibus est, dum eo haeresis contra alteram pugnat, quod in haeresi altera Ecclesiae fides damnat (nihil enim est, quod haereticis commune est): et inter haec fidem nostram, dum sibi adversantur, affirmant." *Ibid.,* C.

[30] "Loquatur ergo Christus, quia in Christo loquitur Ecclesia, et in Ecclesia loquitur Christus; et corpus in capite, et caput in corpore." *Enarratio in Psalmum XXX,* 4; P.L., t. XXXVI, col. 232.

St. Clement of Rome, for example, strongly rebukes those who try to disrupt the unity of Christ members. He calls such an action "a sedition against our own body"—that body which has been united in virtue of the one God, the one Christ, the grace of the one Spirit who descended upon us, and the one vocation to incorporate in Christ.[31] Visibility is definitely stressed in this notion of unity by Hermas who compares the structure of the one universal Church to that of a tower made up, as it were, of one single stone: *tanquam ex uno lapide aedificata.*[32] St. Ignatius of Antioch, on the other hand, seems to underscore both the natural and the supernatural elements by advising the Ephesians "to remain in Christ in their bodily as well as in their spiritual existence," *carnaliter et spiritualiter.*[33] Then, in reference to the latter, he adds, in another place, that the faithful should receive the Holy Eucharist as the guarantee of the unity of the Church, because there is but one body of Our Lord Jesus Christ, one chalice to express the unity of His blood, one altar, and one bishop.[34] This is the line of thinking which we find again in St. Cyprian. How could anyone—he asks—believe that he still has the faith when he no longer upholds the unity of the Church? And he refers his readers to St. Paul's words to the Ephesians:[35] one body and one Spirit, one hope of your calling, one Lord, one faith,

---

[31] "Nonne nobis unus est Deus, et unus Christus, et unus Spiritus gratiae qui effusus est super nos, et una vocatio in Christo? Cur diducimus et distrahimus membra Christi, et contra proprium corpus seditionem movemus..." *Epistola I ad Corinthios,* c. XLVI; P.G., t. I, col. 303 A.

[32] "Et in hunc modum apparebat structura turris, tanquam ex uno lapide aedificata. Caeteros autem lapides qui afferebantur de terra, quosdam quidem rejiciebant, quosdam vero adaptabant in structuram. Alios excidebant, et projiciebant longe a turri. Alii autem lapides multi circa turrim positi erant; et non utebantur illis ad structuram." *Pastor,* lib. I, Visiones III, II; P.G., t. II, col. 901. t.

[33] "...sed in omni puritate et temperantia maneatis, in Jesu Christo, carnaliter et spiritualiter." *Epistola ad Ephesios,* c. X; P.G., t. V, col. 654 B.

[34] "Studeatis igitur una eucharistia uti; una enim est caro Domini nostri Jesu Christi, et unus calix in unitatem sanguinis ipsius, unum altare, sicut unus episcopus, cum presbyterio et diaconis, conservis meis; ut quod faciatis, secundum Deum faciatis." *Epistola ad Philadephenses,* c. IV; ibid., col. 699 B.

[35] Eph. 4:4-6.

one Baptism, one God.....[36] The series of truths involved in the mystery of the unity of the Church, therefore, is clearly established by St. Cyprian: the one Church is rooted in the one God, was founded by the one Christ, built on the rock of the one Lord as the one *CATHEDRA*, consequently, it is impossible to build another altar or to establish another priesthood beside the only altar and priesthood of the Lord. Those who go against this fundamental thesis, are "adulterous, impious, and sacrilegious" people who violate the divine order in favor of their human furor.[37]

On this point, we should like to add just one more note. St. Clement of Alexandria, writing in the same vein as St. Ignatius and St. Cyprian, but without the vehemence of the latter, makes a very important observation. On the basis of the essence, principle, and excellence of the Church as well as according to the general consensus, it must be admitted that only the ancient Catholic Church possesses the unity of faith.....[38]

---

[36] "Hanc Ecclesiae unitatem qui non tenet, tenere se fidem credit? Qui Ecclesiae renititur et resistit, qui cathedram Petri, super quam fundata est Ecclesia, deserit; in Ecclesia se esse confidit? quando et beatus apostolus Paulus hoc idem doceat et sacramentum unitatis ostendat dicens: *Unum corpus et unus spiritus, una spes vocationis vestrae, unus Dominus, una fides, unum Baptisma, unus Deus* (Eph. IV, 4-6). *De unitate Ecclesiae,* IV; P.L., t. IV, col. 516 A.

[37] "Deus unus est et Christus unus (Eph. IV, 5) et una Ecclesia, et Cathedra una super petram Domini voce fundata. Aliud altare constitui aut sacerdotium novum fieri praeter unum altare et unum sacerdotium non potest. Quisquis alibi collegerit, spargit. Adulterum est, impium est, sacrilegum est quodcumque humano furore instituitur ut dispositio divina violetur. Procul ab hujusmodi hominum contagione discedite, et sermones eorum velut cancer et pestem fugiendo vitate..." *Epistola XL;* P.L., t. IV, col. 345 B.

[38] "Ex iis quae dicta sunt manifestum esse existimo, unam esse veram Ecclesiam, eam quae vere est antiqua, in cujus catalogum referuntur ii qui justi ex proposito. Nam cum unus sit Deus et unus Dominus, propterea id etiam quod est summe venerabile, et ex eo quod sit unicum laudatur, tu quod sit imitatio principii quod est unum. In unius ergo naturae sortem cooptatur Ecclesia quae est una, quam conantur haereses in multos discindere. De essentia ergo et opinione et principio et excellentia, solam esse dicimus, antiquam et catholicam Ecclesiam, in unitatem unius fidei quae est ex propriis testamentis, vel potius ex testamento quod est unum diversis temporibus, in quibus Dei voluntate per unum Dominum congregat eos qui sunt ordinati, quos praedestinavit Deus, cum eos justos

"Essence, principle, excellence," these three words of St. Clement of Alexandria summarize the whole relationship of the Church to the Son. Christ, being her essence and principle, not only exists and mediates in the Church, but He also guarantees her indefectibility, infallibility, and, above all, her unity. The Fathers of the Church recognized and explained all these elements of the relationship. They also recognized and explained the essential note of visibility as well as the necessity for perfect cooperation between the *Ecclesia docens* and the *Ecclesia discens*. By doing so, they proved that one can never exaggerate either the natural or supernatural element in the Church without destroying the very notion of her being.

c. *In relation to the Holy Spirit.*—St. Thomas, discussing the functions of Christ and the Holy Spirit in the structure and life of the Church, wrote the following lines: "The head has a manifest pre-eminence over the other exterior members; but the heart has a certain hidden influence. And hence the Holy Ghost is likened to the heart, since He invisibly quickens and unifies the Church; but Christ is likened to the Head in His visible nature in which man is set over man."[39]—It seems to us that the Fathers of the Church were well aware of these two functions. This is why they developed their teaching on the visible element of the Church in her relation to Christ. And this is especially why they described the role and influence of the Holy Spirit in the way they did.

Hermas, writing about 100 A.D., already refers to the Holy Spirit as the principle whose powers were the key to the entrance into the kingdom of God. Describing the tower of the Church and the virgins supervising the building, he notes that it would be useless to bear the name of the Son of God without wearing the garment of these virgins: to wit, the powers of the Holy Spirit.[40]

---

futuros cognovisset ante mundi constitutionem. Caeterum Ecclesiae quoque eminentia, sicut principium constructionis, est ex unitate, omnia alia superans, et nihil habens sibi simile et aequale." *Stromata*, lib. VII, c. XVII; P.G., t. IX, col. 551 AB.

[39] *S.T.*, III, q. 8, a. 1, ad 3.

[40] "Et dixi: quid est deinde haec turris? Haec, inquit, Ecclesiae est. Et virgines hae, quae sunt, Domine? Et dixit mihi: Hae, inquit, Spiritus Sancti sunt: non aliter enim homo potest in regnum Dei intrare, nisi hae induerint eum veste sua. Etenim nihil proderit tibi accipere nomen Filii Dei, nisi etiam et vestem earum acceperis ab eis. Hae namque virgines, potestates sunt Filii Dei. Ita frustra nomen ejus portabit quis

St. Irenaeus speaks of Him as the Spirit of truth available to the individual in the Church for "where the Church is, there is the Spirit of God; and where the Spirit of God is, there is the Church and all grace." If therefore one does not partake of Him, neither can he be fed by the Church.[41] St. Basil even ascribes the structure and government of the Church—*Ecclesiae ordo et gubernatio*—to the Holy Spirit.[42] He also mentions the gifts in virtue of which the members of the Church can render necessary services to each other in order to complete the body of Christ in the unity of the Spirit.[43] Finally, he remarks that the Holy Spirit is available only in the Church of God for which Christ died and on which the Holy Spirit generously *(large)* descended.[44]

St. Epiphanius sees the unity of the Church in such a prominent light—due to the generosity of Christ and the diffusion of the Holy Spirit—that he regards all other "churches" or religious communities as concubines whether they appeared in the course of history before or after the birth of the one true Church. The testament and inheritance were not entirely foreign to them, it is true; but since they existed outside the Church of God, they could not possess the Holy Spirit as the principle of their community.[45] St. Cyril of Alexandria,[46]

---

nisi etiam potestates ejus portaverit." *Pastor*, lib. III, Similitudines, c. XIII; P.G., t. II, col. 991-992.

[41] "Ubi enim Ecclesia, ibi et Spiritus Dei; et ubi Spiritus Dei, illic Ecclesia, et omnis gratia; Spiritus autem veritas. Quapropter qui non participant eum, neque a mammillis matris nutriuntur in vitam, neque percipiunt de corpore Christi procedentem nitidissumum fontem . . ." *Contra Haereses*, lib. III, c. XXIV, 1; P.G., t. VII, col. 966 C.—Cf. Tertullian, *De Pudicitia*, c. XXI; P.L., t. I, col. 1080 B; St. Clement of Rome, *Epistola I ad Corinthios*, c. XXXVIII; P.G., t. I, col. 283 B.

[42] "Jam vero Ecclesiae ordo et gubernatio nonne palam et citra contradictionem per Spiritum sanctum peragitur?" *Liber de Spiritu Santco*, c. XVI; P.G., t. XXXII, col. 139 D-142 A.

[43] "Sed omnia quidem simul complent corpus Christi in unitate Spiritus; necessariam autem utilitatem sibi invicem reddunt ex donis. Deus enim posuit membra in corpore, unumquodque illorum ut voluit." *Ibid.*, c. XXVI; col. 182 B.

[44] ". . . in sola Dei Ecclesia, pro qua Christus mortuus est, et super quam large Spiritum sanctum effudit . . ." *De Judicio Dei*, prooemium; P.G., t. XXXI, col. 654 B.

[45] "Siquidem Ecclesia ab una fide genita, ac per Spiritum sanctum in lucem edita, una est uni, et una genitrici suae. Tum vero quotcunque post

St. Peter Chrysologus[47], and St. Jerome[48] all stress the quickening and unifying effects of the Holy Spirit's presence. But it is perhaps St. Augustine who found the best way of expressing this truth by saying that when one speaks of unity, multiplicity must also somehow be present. There are many churches and there is only one Church; there are many faithful, but only one bride of Christ. So, many Israelites believed and were filled with the Holy Spirit. When they spread throughout the world and began to preach the truth, the river of God, filled with water, inundated the entire earth.[49]

These are just a few quotations and references from the Fathers of the Church in connection with the role and operation of the Holy Spirit in the Body of Christ. Their testimony is clear and unequivocal: He is the heart of the Church, the center of her operation and the power behind the impulses and promptings accorded to her individual members. Consequently, the Church cannot be pictured as a skeleton, a lifeless *conglomeratum*, or a petrified community. Where the Spirit is, there is life. However, to prove that even the Church Fathers regarded the Church as an immanently active entity, we should quote here just one ancient text. The author is St. Irenaeus. The text is found in his *Adversus Haereses*. Writing about the truth content

---

illam vel ante prodierunt, concubinae nominantur: quae licet a testamento et haereditate non prorsus alienae fuerint, nullam tamen a Verbo dotem obtinuerunt, nec infundentem se Spiritum sanctum in seipsis exceperunt: sed solam cum Verbo in conscientia sua necessitudinem habuerunt." *Adversus Haereses*, lib. III, t. II, VI; P.G., t. XLII, col. 782 D-783 A.

⁴⁶ "Per solam quippe vitam in Christo invenitur, cujus praevius ingressus haberi potest verbum fidei, et cum eo salutare baptisma, familiarem cum Deo conjunctionem in Spiritu efficiens." *Commentarius in Oseam*, LV; P.G., t. LXXI, col. 146 C.

⁴⁷ "Tunc omnes unum, imo unus omnes, quando Dei Spiritus in omnibus vivit unus." Sermo LXXVII; P.L., t. LXI, col 406.

⁴⁸ "Ecclesiam autem Christi, quae habitat bene, et in toto orbe Ecclesias possidet, spiritus unitate conjuncta est..." *Commentariorum in Michaeam*, lib. I, c. I; P.L., t. XXV, col. 1162 C.

⁴⁹ "Si flumina, et unus fluvius; quia propter unitatem multi unum sunt. Multae Ecclesiae, et una Ecclesia; multi fideles, et una sponsa Christi; sic multa flumina, et unus fluvius. Crediderunt multi Israelitae, et impleti sunt Spiritu sancto: inde diffusi sunt per gentes; coeperunt praedicare veritatem, et de fluvio Dei qui impletus est aqua, irrigata est tota terra." *Enarratio* in Psalmum LXV, 14; P.L., t. XXXVI, col. 783.

of the Church's preaching, he notes that the material is constant in every respect, equally enduring, and well documented by the prophets, apostles and all the other disciples of Christ, as he has shown previously. Then he adds that this is the doctrine that we have received from the Church. It is guarded in the Church as in a genuine vessel by the Spirit of God. The same Spirit ever renews the deposit, and by doing so He also rejuvenates the vessel itself.[50]

In our opinion this last text is one of the most important testimonies in all of patristic literature. It shows and proves that the deposit of faith has within itself its own seeds which it can develop in due time according to needs and exigencies. That the Church cannot err in that development, is assured by the assistance of the Holy Spirit. All those who abhor any development in the teaching or the structure of the Church, would do well to bear this passage of St. Irenaeus in mind.

In virtue of the above quoted texts we have already shown the relationship between the Holy Spirit and both the Church as a community and her individual members. It remains, however, to explain the position of the Fathers concerning non-Catholic communities and non-Catholic individuals.

Let us start this part of our inquiry with the non-Catholic communities.

Our first witness is St. Ignatius of Antioch. He begs the faithful for the love of Jesus Christ to accept only Christian food and to abstain from heresy. Then he indicates that spiritual death awaits the faithful outside the true Community of Christ. This conclusion is deduced mostly from the expressions he applies to heresy. The thesis is not worded expressly by St. Ignatius, but words like *"deadly,"* *"to accept death"* can hardly be explained otherwise.[51]

---

[50] "... praedicationem vero Ecclesiae undique constantem, et aequaliter perseverantem, et testimonium habentem a prophetis et ab apostolis, et ab omnibus discipulis, quemadmodum ostendimus per initia, et medietates, et finem, et per universam Dei dispositionem, et eam quae secundum salutem hominis est solitam operationem, quae est in fide nostra; quam perceptam ab Ecclesia custodimus, et quae semper a Spiritu Dei, quasi in vase bono eximium quoddam depositum juvenescens, et juvenescere faciens ipsum vas in quo est." *Contra Haereses,* lib. III, c. XXIV, 1; P.G., t. VII, col. 966 B.

[51] "Obsecro itaque vos, non ego, sed charitas Jesu Christi, solo Chri-

This conclusion is fully supported by another text of St. Ignatius. In the same context he says that heresies are not cultivated by Jesus Christ because they are not of the Father's planting. Then he uses two noteworthy expressions, saying that "if anyone *follows* the originators of schism, he shall not obtain the inheritance of the divine kingdom"; and that "if anyone *espouses* foreign doctrines, he does not agree with the passion" of Our Lord.[52]—These expressions are, no doubt, very strong and very marked. We shall return to them later. At present we only wish to say that in our opinion they are used in relation to heretical communities rather than individuals. Or, if they refer to the latter, they are used in a very qualified sense.— St. Irenaeus, following the same line of thought, further describes the status of the non-Catholic communities by adding two new notes: namely, that the schismatics do not possess the love of God, and that they give preference to personal gains rather than to the consideration of the unity of the Church. Consequently, they *murder* the glorious body of Christ in themselves.[53]

It is however, St. Cyprian who is the most outspoken in connection with non-Catholic communities. We can really say that his writings are permeated with the stern principle: *"Extra Ecclesiam nulla salus."* From his many pronouncements we have chosen the following as a classic example of his convictions and attitude: "If anyone *segregates* himself from the Church, he *joins* an adulterer, and gives up the promises made to the Church. He shall not obtain the merits of Christ... He is an alien, impious person. He is an enemy. For nobody

---

stiano alimento uti, ab aliena autem herba abstinere, quae est haeresis. Isti etiam venenis suis Jesum Christum miscent, loquentes, quae fide sunt indigna; similes iis, qui mortiferum pharmacum cum vino mulso dant, quod qui ignorat, libenter, in voluntate noxia mortem accipit." *Epistola ad Trallianos*, c. VI; P.G., t. V, col. 679 B; cf. *ibid.*, c. VII; col. 679 C.

[52] "Abstinete ab herbis noxiis, quas Jesus Christus non colit, quia non sunt plantatio Patris... Si quis schisma facientem sectatur, regni divini haereditatem non consequitur; si quis ambulat in aliena doctrina, is non assentitur passioni." *Epistola ad Philadelphenses*, c. III; P.G., t. V, col. 699 A.

[53] "Judicabit (Christus) autem et eos, qui schisma operantur, qui sunt inanes non habentes Dei dilectionem, suamque utilitatem considerantes quam unitatem Ecclesiae: et propter modicas et quaslibet causas magnum et gloriosum corpus Christi conscindunt et dividunt, et quantum in ipsis est, interficiunt..." *Contra Haereses*, lib. IV, c. XXXIII, 7; P.G., t. VII, col. 1076 B; cf. *ibid.*, c. XXXIII, 2; col. 1073 B.

can have God for his Father who does not have the Church for his mother ... Whoever does not preserve this unity [of the Church], does not preserve God's laws, does not have faith in the Father and the Son, does not live, and will not have salvation."[54] No wonder a struggle developed concerning the validity of the baptism of the heretics. The fact that the Church made the decision in favor of the validity,[55] however, clearly shows how to interpret St. Cyprian's pronouncements and similar statements from other Fathers of the Church. They must be taken as addressed to separated communities as such, meaning that in so far as they are separated and different from the Church, they cannot become the instruments of the Holy Spirit in promoting the salvation of individual souls. Dividedness, separatedness as such means a new foundation. And in so far as the separated communities breathe the spirit of innovation, they can hardly claim access to the sources and means of salvation of the Catholic Church. Bearing this in mind, we can see that the Fathers of the Church spoke of the heretical or schismatic communities only in so far as they claimed to be different from the Church and to teach a doctrine which would be alien to the deposit of the faith. If they also spoke of individuals, meaning the salvation of individual souls, the context of their pronouncements makes it clear that they were referring to *obdurate* individuals. *For they spoke either of these who personally left the Church to obtain worldly gains or of those who stubbornly remained in separation from the Church. In both cases crime*

---

[54] "Quisquis ad Ecclesia segregatus, adulterae jungitur, a promissis Ecclesiae separatur: nec perveniet ad Christi praemia, qui relinquit Ecclesiam Christi. Alienus est, profanus est, hostis est. Habere jam non potest Deum patrem, qui Ecclesiam non habet matrem. Si potuit evadere quisquam qui extra arcam Noe fuit, et qui extra Ecclesiam foris fuerit evadit ... Qui alibi praeter Ecclesiam colligit, Christi Ecclesiam spargit ... Hanc unitatem qui non tenet, Dei legem non tenet, non tenet Patris et Filii fidem, vitam non tenet et salutem." De unitate Ecclesiae, VI; P.L., t. IV, col. 519-520; cf. the analogy of the *tunica Domini; ibid.,* VII; col. 520 B-521 AB; "Hinc haereses et factae sunt frequenter et fiunt, dum perversa mens non habet pacem, dum perfidia discordans non tenet unitatem." *Ibid.,* X; col. 523 B; "Quidquid a matrice discesserit, seorsum vivere et spirare non poterit, substantiam salutis amittit." *Ibid.,* XXIII; col. 534 B.

[55] Cf. Paul F. Palmer, S.J., *Sources of Christian Theology.* Volume One. Westminster, Maryland: The Newman Press. 1955. Pp. 77-81.

and personal malice are involved. It is only natural that such persons, while they remain in this sinful state, cannot become temples of the Holy Spirit nor members of the living body of Christ. Consequently, unless they repent, they cannot obtain salvation.

To prove our point, in the quotations above we have underlined those words which reflect a personal malice on the part of the individual. But to give further support to this thesis, other texts, too, are available. We shall now try to explain these.

For Hermas, the reasons for being rejected by the Church are *iniquity, deceit,* and *all kinds of evil.* Those who are infected with them can no longer be useful within the structure of the Church; nor can they obtain salvation.[56] Personal malice is also stressed by St. Ignatius of Antioch. This is why we said, above, that his expressions are used in a very qualified sense.[57] The *acts of following and espousing* certainly express steps taken in full knowledge of their consequences. But he made this personal malice especially clear by including a reference to our Lord's passion: "If anyone espouses foreign doctrines, he does not agree with the passion of the Lord." What could he mean by this statement? We are convinced that he meant either the *denial of the divinity of Christ or the denial of redemption.* And we base this conclusion on another text of his where, in a hypothetical fashion, he refers to the purely spiritual creatures of heaven, saying that even the angels, the visible and invisible principalities, would be subjected to judgement if they did not believe in the blood of Christ.[58] For St. Ignatius, therefore, personal malice implies a mortally sinful affront to the body and blood of the Lord, which automatically renders salvation impossible. Tertullian implies personal malice by referring to the intention of *deceiving*[59] on the part

---

[56] "Qui autem recidebantur, et longe projiciebantur a turre, vis scire qui sunt? Volo, inquam, domina. Ii sunt filii iniquitatis, et qui crediderunt in simulatione, et omnis nequitia non discessit ab eis: propter hoc non habent salutem; quoniam non sunt utiles in structura, propter nequitias suas." *Pastor, Visiones,* III, VI; P.G., t. II, col. 903-904.

[57] Cf. the texts of Notes 51 & 52 of this section.

[58] "Nemo erret. Et si coelestes, et gloria angelorum, et principes visibiles et invisibiles non credant in sanguinem Christi, et ipsi judicabuntur." *Epistola ad Smyrnaeos,* c. VI; P.G., t. V, col. 711 C.

[59] "Sed, cum decipiendi gratia praetendunt se adhuc quarere, ut nobis per sollicitudinis injectionem tractatus suos insinuent ... jam illos sic de-

of the enemies of the Church, while St. Cyprian accepts it as a *decision made with the full knowledge of the fact*: "Only those will perish who wanted to perish; only those remain outside the Church who [voluntarily] withdrew from the Church.[60] Personal malice is also presupposed by St. Gregory of Nyssa. It is a basic thesis for Christians that if Christ is the head of the Church, the head and members must be of the same nature. In virtue of this sameness of nature there is a certain necessary connection between the single members and the natural whole of the body. If some one understands this, yet remains outside the Church, he also totally—*omnino*—*separates himself* from the head of the Church.[61]

The whole logic of this personal malice, finally, is beautifully described by St. Augustine. Addressing himself to the heretics and asking them important questions, he sums up their answers by saying: You affirm that you are Christians, are baptized, have faith, are members of the Church, yet you have blemishes and wrinkles in your face. Then, he proceeds to admonish them in this way: "Because you are the blemishes and wrinkles of the Church, how could she be without blemishes and wrinkles at the same time? Unless you want to be identified with the Church which has no blemishes and no wrinkles, you, with your blemishes and wrinkles, cut yourselves off from the rest of the members as well as from the head of the body . . ."[62]

---

bemus refutare, ut sciant nos non Christo, sed sibi negatores esse." *Liber de praescriptionibus*, c. XIV; P.L., t. II, col. 32 B.

[60] "Pereant sibi soli qui perire voluerunt: extra Ecclesiam soli remaneant qui de Ecclesia recesserunt." *Epistola XL;* P.L., t. IV, col. 346 B; cf. *Epistola XXVII;* ibid., col. 306 B; *De unitate Ecclesiae*, III; ibid., col. 512 BC.

[61] "Qui autem Ecclesiae caput Christum esse didicit, illud in primis cogitet, Unam esse capitis et subjecti corporis naturam, et singula membra cum toto naturali quadam necessitudine conjuncta esse, quae partes toti ita conciliat, ut miro consensu inter se conveniant. Ex quo fit ut, si *quid extra corpus est*, id etiam a capite omnino sejunctum sit . . . Nos autem membra sumus, qui in Christi corpus coalescimus." *De Perfecta Christiani Forma;* P.G., t. XLVI, col. 271 D-274 A.

[62] ". . . dicite, inquam, nobis, utrum vos justi estis, an non. Respondent, Justi sumus. Ergo non habetis peccatum? Per omnes dies, per omnes noctes nihil mali facitis, nihil mali dicitis, nihil mali cogitatis? Non audent dicere, Nihil. Sed quid respondent? Nos quidem peccatores sumus; sed de sanctis loquimur, non de nobis. Hoc vos interrogo: Christiani estis? Non dico, Justi estis? Christiani estis? Non audent

And so, we can concude that though the Fathers of the Church did not speak explicitly of the salvation of the individual outside the Church, they did not deny it either. If and when they did seem to deny it, they based their statements and conclusions on personal malice. Our position is in perfect agreement with that of the Fathers. Personal malice and sincere belief in Christ are mutually exclusive; and so, if someone has this sincere belief, we do not think that he could be ever denied the merits of Christ, whom he loves.

V. Consequences of the Threefold Relationship

It remains for us to draw the consequences of these relationships. What can we learn from them in connection with the unity of the Church? What kind of obligations do they force upon us in regard to the same unity?

In order to give the best answers to these questions, we have to take up the consequences one by one. And the very first consequence is concerned with

A. *the essential notes of the unity of the Church*.[1]—We can sum them up as follows: The unity of the Church, by virtue of Christ's decree, necessarily presupposes the visibility of the Church, simply because the Church, through her organization and community character, is the expression and realization of a mystical reality.—Secondly, the mystical character of the Church points to Christ: the Church is the result of the same divine decree which is at the root of Christ's Incarnation. Consequently, the unity of the Church must be *real* to the same great extent that the Incarnation is real.—Thirdly, this divine decree set in motion the process of redemption and divine filiation. Christ consummated His redemptive act by His death on the cross,

---

negare: Christiani, inquiunt, sumus. Dimissa sunt vobis cuncta peccata Dimissa, inquiunt. Quomodo ergo estis peccatores? Sufficient mihi unde vos repellam. Vos christiani estis, baptizati estis, fideles estis, membra Ecclesiae estis, et habetis maculas et rugas? Quomodo ergo est Ecclesia isto tempore sine macula et ruga, cum vos sitis ruga ejus et macula? Aut si non vultis esse Ecclesiam, nisi eam quae sine macula et ruga est, cum rugis vestris et maculis praecidite vos a membris ejus, praecidite vos a corpore ejus. Sed quid adhuc dicam ut se ab Ecclesia segregent, cum hoc jam fecerint? Haeretici enim sunt, jam foris sunt: sum tota munditia sua foris remanserunt. Redite, et audite; audite et credite." *Sermo CLXXXI*, c. III; P.L., t. XXXVIII, col. 980-981.

[1] Cf. Pierre Chaillet, *L'Eglise est une*. Bloud & Gay. 1939. Pp. 127-193

and He established the Church as a mediative organ to transmit the reality of redemption to individuals. Consequently, the notion of the unity of the Church involves a twofold aspect: it means the totality of the objective means of salvation as well as the sum total of the individuals using the means of salvation.[2]—Fourthly, in addition to the objective and subjective unity we can also speak of an historical unity of the Church. For it is the duty of the Church to expound the teaching of Christ and to conserve it in its original purity throughout the succession of time. From this point of view unity means the convergence in the same body of the principles of tradition, of the exclusivity of mission and of the principles of authority. In a word, it means the assurance of identity and permanence throughout the history of mankind.—And finally, the unity of the Church is an entirely positive notion. It is determined in the objective reality of doctrine, cult and organization as well as in the mission of the Church to safeguard that doctrine with the assistance of the Holy Spirit.[3]

All these elements are present in the notion of the unity of the Church. None of them can be ignored without damaging the notion of unity and the nature of the Church. But to uphold and to explain these elements we have to bear in mind the divine decree of the Father, the founding act of Christ, and the presence of the Holy Spirit. These three relationships make up the nature of the Church and determine her ontological and actual, objective and subjective, historical and positive unity.

B. *False notions of the unity of the Church.*—The second important consequence of our investigations is the negative aspect of unity, namely, a clearer view of the defective notions produced throughout the centuries. The Donatists, Pelagians, Catharists, for example, defined the Church as the community of the justified exclusively. The Waldensians and Wycliffians carried this notion so far that they accepted freedom from mortal sin as the true criterion of membership in the Church. These heresies, therefore, denied visibility as an essential element of the Church and thereby reduced the notion of unity to a meaningless and valueless concept.—The Schismatics—the Greek and Russian churches—and the Anglicans, on the other hand, did

---

[2] *Ibid.,* p. 137.
[3] *Ibid.,* p. 138.

not recognize foundation by Christ as the real basis for the authority of the Popes, and so they connected that authority with purely human and historical factors, especially with the Roman Empire. Moreover, by so doing, they disrupted the bonds of real unity and entrusted the fate of their churches to the heads of the various national states. This entrance of civil authorities into the governing body of the church had disastrous effects especially in two directions: first, it suppressed the basic distinction between the teaching and the learning church; secondly, it replaced the supernatural unifying element in the Church with the power of this world. Having so rejected the ontological, actual, objective and subjective unity, they could not even uphold the historical unity of their churches. Sooner or later they broke up into different fragmentary churches, each of them becoming independent of the rest not only in regard to church—politics but also in their articles of faith, moral laws, and liturgical activities.— The Protestant churches lack the correct notion of Church unity mainly for two reasons: they, too, deny visibility as an essential mark of the Church, on the one hand, and do not accept any distinction between objective and subjective unity in the Church, on the other. Since they hold that Christ did not provide His Church with intrinsic and extrinsic unity, she is a multitude of faithful for them rather than an established society. This is why they cannot understand that schisms and heresies do not break up the objective unity of the Church. It is true that due to human factors, mistakes, and abuses large or small groups can detach themselves from the body of the Church, but it is equally true that no group can ever take away from the Church the Father's eternal idea of her, Christ, her head and principle, or the Holy Spirit's presence, power and gifts. And her intrinsic, objective unity is rooted in her relationships to the three Persons of the Blessed Trinity.—It is easy to see now that by leaving out one essential element, real unity is frustrated—even destroyed—in separated communities. Consequently, in their separateness, the vivifying activities of the Holy Spirit as well as His assistance to the permanence of those communities is also terminated. The destruction of the real objective unity of the Church means relinquishing the theocentric character of that unity and replacing it with an heteronomous or autonomous element which can no longer guarantee the divine assistance. This fact explains why the Catholic

Church abhors heresy. Heresy divides and separates by its nature, and so, is basically incapable of promoting unity. The central idea of the heretical communities is no longer the Church as the living body of Christ. It is rather their community in so far as it is an historical product. The Catholic Church's attitude, on the contrary, is totally different: she assumes the duty of convincing and conquering the world. For "Catholicism—regarded in its special character and as contrasted with non-Catholic Christianity—is essentially decision and affirmation, an affirmation of all values wheresoever they may be, in heaven or on earth. All non-Catholic bodies originate, not in unconditional affirmation, but in denial and negation, in subtraction and in subjective selection ... Catholicism insists on the whole God, on the God of creation and judgement ... And it would have the whole Christ, in whom this God was revealed to us, the Christ of the two natures, the God-man, in whom heaven and earth possess their eternal unity ... And it would have the complete community, the *orbis terrarum*, as the medium wherein we grasp this Christ ... Catholism is the positive religion *par excellence*, essentially affirmation without subtraction, and in the full sense essentially thesis. All non- Catholic creeds are essentially anti-thesis, conflict, contradiction, and negation. And since negation is of its very nature sterile, therefore they cannot be creative, productive and original, or at least not in the measure in which Catholicism displayed these qualities throughout the centuries."[4]

C. *The unity of the Church is a motivum credibilitatis.*—Finally, the investigations and considerations of this study lead us to another important consequence, namely, that the unity of the Church must be accepted as a motive of credibility and as such plays a very important role in one's spiritual life. This conclusion is based on the definition of the Vatican Council which among other things explicitly mentions Catholic unity and the invincible stability of the Church as a motive of credibility.[5]

What is credibility? It is a term used in relation to the truths of faith and signifies an external disposition or condition by virtue of which they deserve to be believed. A distinction will make this more clear. Those elements which manifest revelation are called

---

[4] Karl Adam, *op. cit.*, pp. 11-12.
[5] Denzinger, *Enchiridion*, n. 1794.

notes of revelation. Those which discern true revelation from the false are called criteria, and those which render the revealed doctrine worthy of faith are called motives of credibility. It follows from this that credibility is expressed in the judgement elicited in connection with the content of revelation. Strictly speaking, this judgement is brought about in two stages. First, it is expressed in a purely speculative way: the personal attitude of a concrete individual is not taken yet into consideration. The objective grounds of a revealed thesis are presented in an impersonal way. One speaks, then, of evidence of credibility (*evidentia credibilitatis*). In the second stage, however, this judgement is formulated in a very concrete manner and is addressed to the individual. Then, credibility is turned into a necessary act of belief (*credenditas*) which demands that the individual accept the content of revelation. It implies a certain "must" pressing the individual to submit his mind and will to the thesis of revealed doctrine.

Now, where does all this lead in connection with the unity of the Church? Unity as an essential mark of religion is a positive objective criterion. As such, in harmony with other criteria, it testifies with moral certainty on behalf of the divine origin of the religious doctrine. It promotes the rational submission of the human mind in general and concretely urges the compliance of the individual as well. In all truth, the marvelous intrinsic unity and the unshakeable certainty evident in the life and teaching of the Church can never be explained in terms of purely human elements. No such element could be their sufficient reason. Such attributes can be explained only on the basis of a divine intervention, namely, by the Trinitarian relationships of the Church, and especially, by the presence of the Holy Spirit. For the Holy Spirit is her unifying principle. It is indeed the Holy Spirit who continuously upholds and recreates the Church in such a mystical way that her unity is clothed in the garment of permanence. In this fact rests the power and guarantee of the Church as a community as well as the certitude of each of her individual members. For it is this fact which makes the submission of minds and wills relatively easy. Where the power of the Holy Spirit watches over the community, there the individual can obtain the utmost certainty in obtaining the revealed doctrine. Consequently, his submission becomes a real *obsequium rationale,* the most valuable act of a rational creature.

VI. Conclusion

We started this study by asking the question: What is the Church—a mere juridical entity or something deeper and more essential than that? Now we have the answer to that question: The Church is not a mere juridical organization. She is an ORGANISM, the living BODY OF CHRIST! It is in this capacity that she has always been understood and appreciated in Catholic theology. It is in this capacity that she can fulfill her twofold mission, namely, to prolong Christ's life and presence in the community of His disciples in a permanent way and to communicate divine sonship to her individual members. She can do both because her essence and life is Christ Himself. That this objective, sacred element is an essential part of the notion of the Church has been proven by us through the testimony of revelation in general, and through the words of Our Lord in particular. At the same time, we have also proven and from the same sources that the supernatural, mystical element of the Church is realized in her as visible, organized establishment. Consequently, organism and organization, supernatural society and visible hierarchy, mystical life and juridical framework belong the one to the other in the Church, as two vitally important elements of one and the same reality.

The living organism of the Church operates in and through her individual members who promote her cause in virtue of the motions and promptings of the Holy Spirit. The activities of the members are produced in an endless variety, but the Church herself always remains the same—faithful to herself as the body and *alter ego* of Christ—thanks to her vivifying principle, the Holy Spirit.

Finally, this study has shown how any particular truth about the Church, in this case her unity, is implanted within the whole system of truths and how it contributes to the building up of the whole system. As the Church herself, so also the doctrinal principles of her being were transmitted to us by Christ and are continuously protected and guaranteed by the Holy Spirit. Consequently, there is no room for doubts and hesitations concerning her authenticity and mission. She is not a creation of human forces. She is the most magnificent gift of the Blessed Trinity. And so, to understand her nature as well as her fascinating unity we must contemplate her with Christ's eyes in virtue of His timeless words: "I am with you all days, even unto the consummation of the world."[1]

---

[1] Matt. 28:20.

THE CHURCH AND THE EUCHARIST:
An Outline of Eucharistic Ecclesiology in Present Day Orthodoxy

GEORGE ELDAROV, O.F.M.Conv.

The history of the relations between the Eastern Orthodox Churches and the Catholic Church of the West has been seldom free from some sort of controversy about the Holy Eucharist, the Sacrament of love and unity. Leavened or Unleavened Bread, Epiclesis, the use of the Chalice by the laity or its denial to them, Infant Communion—all recall bitter memories of interconfessional strife with rather sparse results, theological or practical.

With this uninspiring prospect in view, it would be far more convenient to refrain from the discussion of another Eucharistic topic, and thus avoid carrying more coals to a well lit fire of controversy. However, the sight of a wholly new field of Eucharistic challenge on the Orthodox side, namely its recent developed Eucharistic ecclesiology, is very tempting. It promises an interesting insight into Orthodoxy, and at the same time seems to offer a few clues to our own theology of the Church. Our acquaintance with it, however limited, can be then truly enlightening.

Despite an express pretense of antiquity, Eucharistic ecclesiology, as a definite attempt to correct or to sustain this or that feature of current ecclesiology, is rather recent. We find a few Eucharistic tenets stressed already by A. S. Khomiakov, and later by several other Russian religious thinkers, like S. Bulgakov, E. N. Trubeckoj and others; but as a full grown system this doctrine is a thing of our days, worked out mainly by N. Afanassev, with the notable supporting contribution of a few other Russian theologians, especially that of G. Florovsky and A. Schmemann.[1]

---

[1] The most comprehensive essay on these authors' doctrine about the Eucharist is that of B. SCHULTZE, S.J., "Eucharistic und Kirche in der russischen Theologie der Gegenwart," *Zeitschrift für katholische Theologie* 77 (1955) 257-300. There are quoted as more or less conscious

Drawing mostly from this last group of authors, I shall propose a short but essential outline of the system, keeping in view particularly the aspects of greater interest to our own doctrine of the Church.[2]

I. Eucharistic Ecclesiology

It is a doctrine, well known in the East as well as in the West, that the Church is the Mystical Body of Christ—"the body of the

---

followers of this Eucharistic trend in ecclesiology: A. S. Khomiakov, E. N. Trubeckoj, G. Florovsky, S. Cetverikov, S. Bulgakov, B. Sove, Cyprian Kern, A. Schmemann and N. Afanassev.

[2] Here is a list of writings where the Eucharistic ecclesiology of these three authors can be more easily seen: the most prolific in this field has been N. AFANASSEV with, "Tajnstva i tajnodejstvija (Sacramenta et sacramentalia)," *Pravoslavnaja Mysl* 8 (1951) 17-34; *Trapeza Gospodnja* (Paris 1952) pp. 93; "L'Apotre Pierre et l'Eglise de Rome," *Theologia* 26 (1955) 466-75, 620-41; "Le Sacrement de l'Assemblée," *Internationale kirchliche Zeitschrift* 4 (1956) 200-13; "La doctrine de la primauté à la lumière de l'esslésiologie," *Istina* (1957, 4) 401-20; *L'Eglise qui préside dans l'amour*, in N. AFANASSEV and others, *La primauté de Pierre dans l'Eglise orthodoxe* (Neuchâtel 1960) 7-64; "*Statio Orbis*," *Irenikon* 35 (1962) 65-75. A. SCHMEMANN deserves great credit for his: "Cerkov i cerkovnoe ustrojstvo," *Le messager de l'Eglise Russe en Europe occidentale* nn. 15 (1948) 2-8, 17 (1949) 11-17, 19 (1949 3-10, 5 (1950) 3-7; "Spor o cerkvi," *ibid.* 2 (1950) 9-17; *O "neo-papizme,"* *ibid.* 5 (1950) 11-18; "Le Patriarche oecuménique et l'Eglise universelle," *Istina* (1954, 1) 30-45; "*Unity*," "*Division*," "*Reunion*" in the Light of Orthodox Ecclesiology," *Theologia* 22 (1951) 242-54; *La notion de la primauté dans l'ecclésiologie orthodoxe*, in N. AFANASSEV and others, *o.c.*, pp. 119-50. Although G. FLOROVSKY cannot be so closely connected with Eucharistic ecclesiology, nevertheless some of this theological positions are often present and easily recognizable in the writings of those more directly involved with this system: "Evcharistija i sobornost'," *Put* 19 (1929) 3-22; *Sobornost. The Catholicity of the Church*, in E. L. MASCALL (editor), *The Church of God* (London 1934) 51-74; *Le Corps du Christ vivant. Une interprétation orthodoxe de l'Eglise* (Neuchâtel 1948) 8-57; *Christ and His Church*, in D. L. BEAUDUIN (offert à), *L'Eglise et les eglises*, II (Chevetogne 1955) 159-70.

Nicholas Afanassev is a professor at the Russian Orthodox Theological Institute of St. Sergius in Paris, while Alexander Schmemann is a professor at the Russian Orthodox Theological Academy of St. Vladimir, New York, where George Florovsky is the Dean. Prof. Schmemann has been invited to the Second Vatican Council as a "guest-observer."

living Christ," as G. Florovsky would say.[3] By necessity then it must have a christological structure:

"...the divine-humanity of Christ (*la divino—humanité du Christ*) constitutes the form of the Church, the ontological law of her structure."[4]

However manifoldly related to God, however grouped in more or less organized religious societies, men cannot attain the condition of *Church* unless they come to possess a most special relationship with Christ by becoming His Body on earth, and this only through a vital, organic union with him.

Often this union is seen more generally as the result of sacramental life among the faithful:

"...the nature of the Church's unity is primarily sacramental, for it is in the sacraments that the fullness of Christ is ever actuated ,and we become participants in it, ever sealing, through the *communicatio in sacris*, our organic unity with one another in Christ's body, and constituting together one Christ."[5]

Eucharistic ecclesiology as such stresses, further, the working of one particular Sacrament that makes the organic union with Christ most true. It is through the Eucharist that the *earthly society* becomes finally Church: this is the thesis of N. Afanassev.[6]

In asserting it, he has in mind a historic Church model, the Christian Church of the first two and a half centuries, from which he draws both inspiration and evidence.[7] But the ultimate theological grounds are to be found in St. Paul, and precisely by comparing the liturgical formula "This is my body," with St. Paul's own concept of the Church as the Body of Christ:

'Now you are the body of Christ, member for member" (I Cor. 12, 27).

---

[3] His basic concept of the Church, in *Le Corps du Christ vivant*. See above n. 1.

[4] A. SCHMEMANN, *Le Patriarche oecuménique...*, p. 33. Cf. G. FLOROVSKY, *Christ and His Church*, pp. 163-5.

[5] A. SCHMEMANN, "Unity"..., p. 246.

[6] Cf. N. AFANASSEV, *Trapeza Gospodnja*, pp. 16-7.

[7] Cf. particularly N. AFANASSEV, "Statio Orbis," p. 67; *L'Eglise qui préside...* pp. 25 ff., 35-61.

As it appears, a link between these two texts must necessarily exist, and the key to it is provided by another text of St. Paul:

> "And the bread that we break, is it not the partaking of the body of the Lord? Because the bread is one, we though many are one body, all of us who partake of the one bread" (I Cor. 10, 16-17).

The implication of these texts seems to be self-apparent: the faithful attain their desired degree of union with Christ and become *Church* by partaking of His Eucharistic Body.[8]

Eucharistic ecclesiology finds the concrete embodiment of this mystical organism in the *local* Church.

The distinctive features of this Church entity are a limited territory and a bishop, and they are both dictated by Eucharistic exigencies. The former flows from the necessity to be part of a Eucharistic assembly. Those who do not take part in a given Eucharistic gathering cannot belong to the particular Church which comes into being through that gathering.[9]

The presence of the bishop is similarly argued as a Eucharistic requirement, both as necessary president of the Eucharist in a given place, and as supreme minister on earth of all sacramental life.[10]

Nothing is clearer to these authors than the ecclesiastical fullness of such a local Church, or—as they also say—its *sobornost* or intensitive catholicity:

> "... each local Church in the unity of the bishop and the people receives the fullness of gifts, is taught the entire Truth and possesses the whole Christ... The Apostolic succession, which is the basis of her catholicity in time, is likewise the basis of

---

[8] Cf. N. AFANASSEV, *L'Eglise qui préside* ..., pp. 26-27.

[9] "Selon l'ecclésiologie alors [first three centuries] en viguer, le signe de l'Eglise locale était l'assemblée eucharistique dans laquelle l'Eglise de Dieu trouvait son expression la plus complète. L'Eglise locale était là où il y avait une assemblée eucharistique. ...

"Dans l'Eglise primitive les limites de l'Eglise locale étaient déterminées par les limites de l'assemblée eucharistique: appartenaient à telle ou telle Eglise ceux qui prenaient part à l'assemblée eucharistique," N. AFANASSEV, *"Statio Orbis,"* pp. 67, 71-2.

[10] "L'assemblée eucharistique et l'évêque sont des notions correlatives. Là où est l'évêque, là est aussi l'assemblée eucharistique; et vice-versa, là où est l'assemblée eucharistique, l'évêque y est aussi," Ib. p. 67.

her catholicity in space: it signifies that each local Church possesses not a portion of the Apostolic gifts, but their fullness, given to her in Christ, which in the last instance is but the fullness of Christ himself, *totus Christus, Caput et Corpus.*"[11]

With this ecclesiastical maturity, go two far-reaching canonical gifts, the autonomy of the local Church and its independence from any other Church entity on earth:

"... the local Church is autonomous and independent, because the Church of God in Christ dwells in her in all her fullness. She is independent, because any power over her, whatever power it be, would be a power over Christ and over His body. She is autonomous, because the Church of God in Christ possesses the fullness of the existence, outside of which nothing else exists, because nothing else can exist outside Christ."[12]

It is clear, from the above-mentioned characteristics, that a local Church cannot fit easily in a *universal* Church, at least as we understand the latter. It cannot be a part of the universal Church, since it has the wholeness of Church-essence. It cannot be a member of the same, since it is already an organic entity of its own, the very Church Body of Christ.

However, according to this line of thought, such incapacity to fit in a universal Church is not the fault of the local Church, but the fault of the doctrine of the Church that has prevailed, both in the West as in the East, since the middle of the third century, when the original apostolic ecclesiology took a wrong turn:

"In a simplified form this conception may be defined as follows: in the Roman theology this organic unity, the Church as an organism, is primarily the Universal Church, that is, the totality of the visible Church on earth, which in the unity of its organization and in its universal structure s the manifestation and the extension of the Mystical body of Christ.... The universal organism of the Church, as a whole, is ontologically

---

[11] A. SCHMEMANN, "Unity"..., pp. 245-6. Cf. also his *Le Patriarch oecuménique*..., pp. 35-6; *La notion de primauté*..., p. 132; G. FLOROVSKY, *Evcharistija*, pp. 13-4; N. AFANASSEV, *L'Eglise qui préside*..., p. 26.

[12] N. AFANASSEV, I. c., p. 28.

anterior to its different parts, and it is only *in* and *through* the 'whole' that the 'parts' are united to the Church."[13]

Eucharistic ecclesiology claims to be far from denying a most real unity among the local Churches that make up the Orthodox world. But instead of applying the categories of *part* and *member* to the local Church and those of *whole* and *organism* to the universal Church, it reserves the latter for the local Church and explains the unity of all the local Churches on a universal level through a new ecclesiological category, that of *identity*. The local Churches throughout the world are tied together by a common bond of fidelity they all must keep towards a single set of essential Church components:

"...the unity of the Churches is just as real as the organic unity of a local Church, which is indeed the unity of the Church, and not merely unity among Churches. The point is not that all these local Churches together constitute a single organism, but that each Church, as church, as sacramental unity, is the same Church, manifested in a given place. This identity is based on the identity in the sacramental structure of every Church, on the Apostolic succession, on the episcopate, on the sacraments. And so, we return to the same organic unity of the church, but in which the churches are not complementary to one another, are not 'parts' or 'members,' each one of them and all together are nothing but one, holy, catholic and apostolic Church."[14]

[13] A. SCHMEMANN, "Unity"...,p. 244. Cf. also *La notion de primauté*..., p. 125-6; *Le Patriarche oecuménique*..., pp. 33-6; N. AFANASEV, *L'Eglise qui préside*..., pp. 12 ff., 61-2. Although Universalistic ecclesiology is more often blamed on the Catholic Church, the Orthodox Church does not always go without censure. Cf. N. AFANASSEV, I. c., p. 10.

[14] A. SCHMEMANN, "Unity"..., pp. 247-8. Cf. *Le Patriarche oecuménique*..., p. 37; La notion de primauté..., pp. 131-2 ff.; N. AFANASSEV, *L'Eglise qui préside*..., p. 29; *L'Apotre Pierre*..., pp. 11-12.

For N. Afanassev this identity is the result of the harmony among the Church and of their mutual acceptance as Orthodox Churches: "Toute la multitude des églises locales forme une union fondée sur l'amour et la concorde... Au point de vue empirique, cela veut dire que chaque église locale accepte et s'approprie ce qui se passe dans d'autres église et que toutes les églises acceptent tout ce qui se passe dans chacune d'entre elles. Cette acceptation, qu'il est admis de désigner par le terme, 'réception' (receptio), est le témoignage d'une églises locale dans laquelle demeure

From all this, the nature of the Orthodox *Oikoumene* is that of a family of identical and autonomous local Churches, or dioceses, each one displaying the same ecclesiastical constituent parts.

It also reveals the Orthodox understanding of, and their approach to, the capital facts of schism and reunion. The falling away of a local Church will appear as the result of a progressive lack of fidelity to the common set of essential Church elements, as the end of a process of voiding itself of "churchliness"; conversely, reunion will not be the absorption of one Church by another Church (as it is charged against Catholic ecumenism), but it will consist in the recovery of Orthodox Church elements on the part of a given separated community, a *growing up in Orthodoxy*, until the stage is reached, where that community appears as bearer of each and every element of Orthodoxy. At the same time it will have become a full-fledged local Church, identical to every other Church within the Orthodox family of Churches.[15]

II. A Catholic Appraisal

Catholic as well as Orthodox critics have found faults with Eucharistic ecclesiology. Traditional Orthodoxy expressed its reservations particularly in a controversy of a few years ago between A. Schmemann and a handful of Russian theologians, notably the Archimandrite Sophronius, the Canonist S. Troicky and Prof. E. Kovalevsky. The more tangible point of dissent was the extent to give to the local Church, which both sides acknowledged as the bearer of all Church power and Church life. Instead of the individual episcopally run local Church corresponding to a diocese or *eparchy*, these other theologians preferred a group of several such local Churches forming together an autocephalous community and thus possessing the desired Church fullness.[16]

---

l'Eglise de Dieu, sur ce qui s'accomplit dans les autres 'eglises, dans lesquelles l'Eglise de Dieu demeure aussi...," N. AFANASSEV, *L'Eglise qui préside...*, p. 31.

[15] Cf. S. BULGAKOV, *The Orthodox Church* (London 1935) pp. 213-18. This approach seems to be very prominent in some places for reunion, as seen in the South India experiment.

[16] Among the writings, critical of the doctrine defended by A. Schmemann, cf. SOFRONIJ, "L'Unité de l'Eglise suivant l'image de la Sainte Trinité," *Messager de l'Exarchat du Patriarche russe en Europe Occi-*

There are also a few Catholic appraisals, either of the system as a whole or of one or another of its tenets.[17] We can easily add a few more points, taking one by one the basic statements of the system as digested above.

The Eucharist productive of the Church. As it stands there is much to be said against this statement. First of all, we know that into the concept and the reality of the Church go many elements which cannot be called strictly eucharistic or even sacramental, such as the unifying power of the faith and of canonical obedience. They must be present even before there can be a Eucharistic gathering! To say the least, these other elements are here neglected, if not explicitly played down.

Secondly, the biblical and historical evidence is definitely scarce and too one-sidedly interpreted. St. Paul does not use only the image of the body when describing the Church of God, but also those of the temple, of the house, of the bride... (II Cor. 6, 16; Eph. 2, 19-20; Heb. 3, 6; I Tim. 3, 15; I Cor. 3, 9; Eph. 5, 22-32). Nor can we forget the image of the Kingdom, the example most generally employed throughout the Gospels. But even accepting the image of the body as a sufficient clue for a deep insight into the nature of the Church, it should not be interpreted within its Eucharistic context only, as St. Paul himself knows also of a more general social and hierarchical context.[18] Similarly, the historical evidence claimed for

---

dentale 2-3 (1950) 33-61; SILUAN, "Obraz edinstva i princip pervenstva v Cerkvi." *ibid.* 21 (1955) 57-75; VL. LOSSKG, *Ecueils ecclésiologiques, ibid.* 1 (1950) 21-8; E. KOVALEVSKY, "Analyse du XXXIV canon apostolique," *ibid.* 2-3 (1950) 67-75; S. TROICKY, "De l'autocéphalie dane l'Eglise," *ibid* 11 (1952) 12-30, 12 (1952) 32-6; Ecclésiologie orthodoxe (De la structure de l'Eglise)," *ibid.* 7-8 (1952) 49-45.

[17] Cf. G. DEJAIFVE, S.J., " 'Sobornost' ou Papauté?" *Nouvelle Revue Théologique* 74 (1952) 355-71, 466-84; C. J. DUMONT, O.P., "Primauté et autocéphalies," *Istina* (1954, 1) 28-30, and footnotes to A. SCHMEMANN, "Le Patriarche oecuménique et l'Eglise orthodoxe," *ibid.* pp. 30-45; B. SCHULTZE, S.J., *Eucharistie und Kirche* (see above n. 1); "Das Problem der kirchlichen Einheit in der Orthodoxie der Gegenwart," *Stimmen der Zeit* 157 (1956) 278-91; G. ELDAROV, O.F.M.Conv., "La posizione subordinata del vescovo nella gerarchia cattolica. Precisazioni a uno spunto recente di due Autori separati," *Miscellanea Francescana* 58 (1958) 512-36.

[18] There is a very rich Catholic literature on the Mystical Body, and it should suffice to mention the classical works by Mersch, Mura, Jurgens-

the unicity of the Eucharistic assembly in each individual local Church during the first two and a half centuries cannot be pushed too far. In the long run it appears more of an exception than a normal condition for the liturgical life of the Church, a life which soon polarized around more than one altar within the same local Church. It came, more than anything else, as a result of the natural growth of the Church.

Finally, the supposed radical switch from the *original* Eucharistic ecclesiology to a wholly different *Universalistic* ecclesiology raises far more ecclesiological problems than it can pretend to solve. Such a change, among other things, could not have happened without also radically affecting the whole structure of the Church and therefore breaking the ground for a completely new Church, no longer the one founded by Christ. Gone then is the doctrine of the indefectibility of the Church of Christ.[19]

And yet, this statement of the Eucharistic ecclesiology can also mean something more acceptable to the doctrine of the Church. There is no doubt that in present day Catholic ecclesiology the relationship between the Eucharist and the Church is more simply perceived than it was several centuries ago. It should suffice to refer to the well known findings of Fr. H. De Lubac, S.J., in his *Corpus Mysticum. L'Eucharistie et l'Eglise au Moyen Age*.[20]—Well after the times of the Fathers of the Church, the ancient theologian saw the Church and the Eucharist as more closely connected than even the Eucharist and the historic body of Christ. Actually he would call the Church the Mystical Body of Christ precisely with regard to the intimate association it had with the Sacramental or *mysterious* presence of Christ in the Eucharist. But in later centuries—namely

---

meier, De Lubac, Tromp, and the impressive production of essays and commentaries following the Encyclical Letter of Pope Pius XII "Mystici Corporis" of June 29, 1943. For a recent essay on St. Paul's understanding of the Mystical Body, cf. B. M. AHERN, C.P., "The Christian's Union with the Body of Christ," *The Catholic Biblical Quarterly* 23 (1961) 199-209.

[19] It must not be forgotten that this ecclesiological *apostasy* is equally shared by the Western and by the Eastern Church, according to our authors, cf. N. AFANASSEV, *L' Eglise qui préside....*, pp. 10, 61-3; A. SCHMEMANN, *La notion de primauté...*, p. 128.

[20] H. DE LUBAC, *Corpus Mysticum. L'Eucharistie et l'Eglise au Moyen Age* (Paris 1949).

after, and because of, the heresy of Berengarius (c. 999-1088)—that connection was almost completely lost sight of. All the better theologians became engrossed in the defence of the identity of the Eucharistic Body of Christ with the "Corpus natum de Maria Virgine. . . ."

A return to Eucharistic categories is, therefore, quite possible to Catholic ecclesiology. To what extent, is another question. It is clear, however, that such a return must never lose sight of what has been rightly expressed in ecclesiology, and particularly of the now better defined role of the teaching and ruling power in the Church, the backbone of post-Tridentine ecclesiology.

The fullness of the local Church. Thus stated, the proposition would empty of any real meaning the universal Church, which claims a fullness of her own. And unwarrantably so. The local Church cannot possibly be the bearer of full ruling and teaching power, otherwise how shall we explain, for example, the undeniable phenomenon of heresy, schism and the falling away of local Churches throughout the long history of the Church?

Nevertheless, there is some room in Catholic ecclesiology for a theory of the fullness of the local Church. If it is true that the local Church is only part of a larger entity, the universal Church, inferior to it and dependent on it, it is also true that the local Church has a fullness of her own, to which nothing can be added and which cannot be a *part* of a superior fullness. It enjoys a sacramental fullness under her bishop, supreme holder on earth of all sacramental power. There is no more of it in Rome than there is in any other diocese of the Catholic world. Along that line the Church is not a monarchic society.

This follows from what we know and hold about the sacrament of Orders, but somehow it has failed to find a right place in our ecclesiology. A chapter on the local Church, side by side in our manuals and catechisms with whatever is properly stressed about the universal Church, would certainly help restore greater balance to current ecclesiology.[21]

----

[21] In our study, quoted above (n. 17), we attempt a further comparison between the sacramental fullness characteristic of the local Church and the jurisdictional fullness (teaching and ruling power) of the universal Church. Cf. G. ELDAROV, "La posizione subordinata del vescovo...," pp. 530 ff.

Ecumenical unity through identity. Compared with what is obtained in the Catholic Church through the threefold bond of faith, jurisdiction and communion, the unity through identity appears to be a very poor quality indeed. Hardly unity at all, it seems more a juxtapostion than union of local Churches.

It is useful, however, to recall that for many an Orthodox this way of looking at the unity of the Orthodox Church on a world-wide or ecumenical basis has a definitely Roman ring. When it was first put forth, Eucharistic ecclesiology was labeled and dismissed from dissenting Orthodox circles as "Orthodox neo-papism."[22] In fact, in the light of Eucharistic ecclesiology, this loosely knit Ecumenical Church must necessarily turn around a center, Rome in the old days, Constantinople today. Though the center is only a local Church, like any other of the Orthodox world, it has a very important ecclesiastical role. As Patriarch Athenagoras of Constantinople put it, stirring a famous controversy:

> "... it is only through her [i.e., the Church of Constantinople], that is, through communion and contact with her, that the local Orthodox Churches are connected to the Body of the Orthodox Church, One, Holy, Catholic and Apostolic...."[23]

Dissent from the center can have far reaching results. It can mean the loss of Orthodox identity, and ultimately the loss of the rank of Church and a lapse into the condition of sub-ecclesiastical community, a sect. All this falls definitely short of the Catholic doctrine of the Primacy, but it is certainly a most welcome step in the right direction. And it is up to the Catholic ecumenist to assist this promising trend till it grows into a full Catholic doctrine of the Center.

---

[22] Cf. A. SCHMEMANN, "O 'neo-papizme,'" *l.c.; Le Patriarche oecuménique...*, pp. 30-1.

[23] Cf. this Encyclical of Patriarch ATHENAGORAS in French translation in *Istina* (1954, 1) 46-47, the quotation p. 47.

THE EUCHARIST, BOND OF UNITY,
IN ST. PAUL

Sylvester Makarewicz, O.F.M.

The various problems which threatened the unity of the Church at Corinth are ultimately solved by St. Paul in the light of the principle that Christians have been called by God "into fellowship *(eis koinōnian)* with his Son, Jesus Christ our Lord" (I Cor 1:9). The key word in this verse is *koinōnia*, a Greek word which can hardly be translated into English. Neither "communion" nor "fellowship" is a completely satisfactory rendition of the Greek. "Communion" is etymologically the nearest but it has been restricted in our usage to the Eucharist. On the other hand, "fellowship" has been so over-worked that it often connotes nothing more than a social club of some nature or another.

The fundamental idea of *koinōnia*, however, is quite clear: it is "to share in something with another." Thus Christians form a "partnership" or a "joint-ownership" in which they share with one another not only their material goods but also the Gospel (1 Cor 9:23), faith (Phlm 6), suffering (Phil 3.10) and consolation (2 Cor 1:7), the Holy Spirit (2 Cor 13:13) and future glory (I Pt. 5:1). These things are shared in common, however, always with reference to the Christian's vital relationship to Christ. The emphasis falls not on social unity among Christians but on their union with Christ. The faithful have been called by God into "fellowship" *with his Son* (I Cor 1:2).[1]

In this paper we shall attempt to show how, according to St. Paul, "communion" *(koinōnia)* in the sacramental Body of Christ promotes unity within the Christian "partnership" *(koinōnia)*. To accomplish our purpose we must first understand the nature of the union which exists between the Christian and Christ. Then we shall consider how the faithful, as a social body, are united among themselves.

---

[1] F. Hauck, "Koinōnos," *ThWNT* (Stuttgart, 1957) 3.804.

Finally, we shall point out how the Eucharist effects and strengthens the unity of the Christian "partnership."

I. Union with Christ

To show that Christians are vitally one with Christ and therefore vitally one with each other, Paul most frequently[2] employs the expression, "Body of Christ."[3] It is an expression which must be taken in the Hebraic sense, however, if we are to interpret correctly Paul's teaching on the Church as the Body of Christ. By "body" Paul means not simply the physical part of man as opposed to his soul but the whole reality of man as an animated and personalized body, living a fully human life. Man is a "spirited-body," a "body-person." In Paul's usage "body" is practically equivalent to what we call "personality."[4] For example, he has the whole person in mind when he writes: "your body is the temple of the the Holy Spirit; so glorify God in your body" (1 Cor 6:19-20). Again, when he tells the Romans to present their "bodies as a living sacrifice" (1:21), he means that they should offer *themselves* as a sacrifice to God. Hence, when referring to the "Body of Christ," he means himself. Admittedly, Paul makes a transition from the Body of the incarnate Lord to the idea of the faithful as Christ's Body which no other N.T. writer has made and which we find difficult to understand. What was it, therefore, that prompted Paul to identify so closely the faithful with the Body of the risen Christ?

It has been maintained by some that Paul, in his Major Epistles (1 Cor 12:12-30; Rom 12:4-5), adapted to his own purposes the Greek apologue which compared the state to a gigantic *body* of which the

---

[2] Paul also employs the image of an olive tree and its branches (Rom. 11:16-24), a spouse (Eph. 5:25-31), and a temple (1 Cor. 3:16; Eph. 2:21).

[3] In his earlier Epistles (1 Cor. 6:15, 17; 10:17; 12:12-13, 27; Rom. 12:4-5) the theme, "Body of Christ," is the emergent of a given situation. In his Captivity Epistles (Col. 1:24; Eph. 1:23; 5:23; 4:23, 5, 30) it occupies a more prominent position and the theme is further developed as *sōma* is related to *ekklēsia* and *kephalē*. He thus makes a clearer distinction between the personal Christ and the faithful. Also, as Paul relates *sōma* to *plērōma*, he gives his theme a cosmic dimension.

[4] J. A. T. Robinson, *The Body: A Study in Pauline Theology* (Naperville, 1957) 26-28.

citizens were members[5] and that, in his Captivity Epistles (Col, Eph), he made use of the Gnostic Myth of the Anthropos-Savior.[6] The myth in its Gnostic form,[7] however, appears to be later than the time of Paul and therefore could not have been used by the apostle. In any case, the origin and homogeneous development of Paul's doctrine can be accounted for by his own Christian experience and his O.T. background without having recourse to Greek sources.[8] Therefore, we should be wary of ascribing to Paul Greek "mystical" systems. In all probability, Paul never thought of any union other than a physical (sacramental) union between the faithful and the individual Christ who lived, died, and resurrected.[9]

The truth that Christians are intimately united to Christ to the point of some mysterious identification came to Paul, at least in embryo, on the road to Damascus. This is clear from the words, "Why do you persecute *me?* I am Jesus, whom you are persecuting" (Acts 9:4-5). As Paul came in contact with the Christian community and as he gained deeper insights into the mystery of the Incarnation

---

[5] For texts see J. Dupont, *Gnosis. La connaissance religieuse dans les épîtres de saint Paul* (Louvain, 1949) 435-38.

[6] H. Schlier, *Christus und die Kirche im Epheserbrief* (Tübingen, 1930) 37-48. Against Schlier, E. Kasemann, *Leib und Leib Christi* (Tübingen, 1933) maintains that the theme "Body of Christ," as expounded in Col. and Eph. is already found in 1 Cor. and Rom. But he concludes that in the earlier Epistles Paul is already dependent on the Gnostic myth. The Catholic, A. Wilkenhauser, *Die Kirche als der mystisce Leib nach dem Apostel Paulus* (Münster, 1937) 432-440 also is inclined to think that Paul's doctrine has been influenced by the Gnostic myth.

[7] Just what this myth taught must be reconstructed from vague and scattered fragments. It seems that when Primordial Man fell from his spiritual state by immersion into matter, his spiritual body disintegrated and was dispersed throughout the universe in the form of separate human souls inhabiting material bodies. Subsequently, the Savior came as an envoy from the spiritual world to gather these spirit-fragments to himself and so to restore Primordial Man to the spirit-world to which he originally belonged. What Paul did, it is claimed, was to draw on this myth in order to picture the Christians as members of Christ the Savior, spiritually united to him through grace. See C. Kearns, "The Church, the Body of Christ according to St. Paul," *IER* 90 (1958) 9-10.

[8] P. Benoit, "Corps, Tête et Plérôme dans les épîtres de la captivité," *Exégèse et Théologie* (Paris, 1961) 2:121-28.

[9] Benoit, "Corps," 109.

he was able to elaborate his own doctrine of the resurrection Body of Christ, under all its forms.

One principle in particular, that of "corporate personality,"[10] seems to have guided Paul in his teaching on the Church as the Body of Christ. Our modern mind, bent upon strong individualism, may fail to grasp the full impact of this ancient concept. There are approximations to it in our conception of the nation or the Church as an institution; but these realities, as a rule, are not given the accepted realism of the ancient conception of "corporate personality."

According to this conception, a family, clan, or nation could be treated as a unity which, originally, was conceived as based upon the blood-tie traced back to a common ancestor. In early law, the individual could be punished for the faults of the group, or the group for those of the individual. Thus, Israel had one uniting bond which knit it tightly together: the Covenant by which Yahweh became its God and Israel became his "family." As a people, the Israelites were all in the same covenant relationship; consequently, one person's violation of the Covenant was paid for by all. Later, in the days of Jeremia and Ezechiel, the principle of individual responsibility received emphasis but the lively interplay between the individual and the community was never overlooked. Psychic community meant, above all, a common will and hence a common responsibility.

The whole group was able to function through, or be seen in, any of its members. Sometimes the group coalesced into a single representative individual, a dominant personality, through whom the community achieved its self-identity and purpose. At other times, the group was viewed as the extension of a prominent individual and became, as it were, the area over which the operation of his personality was widened. In this way the community and its representative individual were able to be viewed as forming one single reality, a "corporate personality."

In the history of the Israelites we see that the welfare of the

---

[10] See H. W. Robinson, *Redemption and Revelation* (London, 1944)
[11] See W. D. Davies, *Paul and Rabbinic Judaism* (London, 1958) 36-58. 258-60; also, J. de Fraine, "Adam and Christ as Corporate Personalities," *TD* 10 (1962) 99-102, an article summary of the author's work, *Adam et son Lignage: Études sur la notion de "personalité corporative"* dans la Bible (Brussels, 1959).

nation was closely linked to that of its king. He was the channel through which God's blessings came to the people (Ps 72:17); but, as in the case of the sin of Saul or David, he also was able to bring down punishment on all Israel. In Isaia 40-55 it is the Servant of Yahweh who appears as a corporate personality in that he embraces the "remnant" through which God's plan is effected. The Servant of the first two songs (42:1-4; 49:1-6) seems to be a personification of Israel which was called not for its own salvation alone, but for a prophetic mission to the world. The third song (50:4-9) appears to be a chant of an individual who probably is not to be identified with the Servant. In 52:13-53:12, however, the Servant appears as a definite individual personality who is able to fulfill the mission of his people because they are represented by him and share in his work. Again, in the vision of Daniel, the Son of Man who is enthroned and who is given "dominion and glory and kingdom, that all peoples, nations, and languages should serve him" (7:14) is identified with the "saints of the Most High" whose "kingdom shall be an everlasting kingdom, and all dominions shall serve and obey them" (7:27). The Son of Man of Dn. 7:14 is thus identified with the community of the elect which he gathers together in himself in order that they may reign with him.

As we move into the N.T. the bearing of Jesus upon the concept of "corporate personality" becomes obvious. In his historical mission Christ gathered up the issues of a long past and through his death and resurrection he became the living center of a new community. There had been a moment when the true Israel, the messianic "remnant," had been reduced to one single individual, Jesus. He offered representatively, the final response to the Word of God. When he prayed, "Not my will but yours be done," he made the response on behalf of all men, in advance, when there was no one else to make it. At a later stage he, the "remnant," returned from the exile of death. All who are now gathered to him in the New Israel, participate in his redemptive death and resurrection and inherit the promises (Gal 3:16). Therefore, the New Israel is "in Christ" as the Jews were "in Abraham."

What is said of Israel and its representative as continuing a "corporate personality" is broadened by St. Paul to embrace the solidarity of the human race in Adam and in Christ (Rom 5:12-21;

1 Cor 15:22, 45-49). The concept of solidarity in Adam of all mankind enables Paul to say that "many died through one man's trespass"
(Rom 5:15) and have become alienated from God. Equally, the gift
of "life" is bestowed on all who are "in Christ," as mankind is
brought back to God.

The word "adam," outside the creation story, is generally used in
the Bible not as a proper name but in a collective sense to designate
men in general, the human species, the race of men, or all men. To be
a "son of adam" means simply to belong to human society. But,
since the unity of a group presupposes a leading personality and
because Paul found the word already used as a proper name, he
views Adam as an individual person (Rom 5:12-21). At the same
time, however, he treats Adam as a corporate personality in that
the whole human race, represented by him, is affected by his sin
and is alienated from God.

The return of mankind to God is accomplished first of all in Christ
himself. The incarnation involved the complete self-identification
of the Son of God, who was without sin, with the body of flesh in
its fallen state (2 Cor 5:21). In perfect obedience he accepted the
"end" of sin, which is death, and stripped off the body of sin (Rom
8:3), through which death and its forces have control over human
nature. The Father then resurrected him, the "first-fruits of those
who have fallen asleep" (1 Cor 15:20), and gave him a spiritualized
body, endowed with a new life forever incorruptible.

The resurrection, however, is not limited to Christ as a single
historical individual. His resurrected Body, in which the Spirit has
taken complete possession of matter, is the first cell of the new
cosmos and the eschatological era. Christ, like Adam, is the inclusive
representative of redeemed humanity and Christians constitute with
him a corporate personality, as real as the one formed by un-
regenerated humanity in Adam, its inclusive representative. However, whereas the first Adam, made from the dust of the earth and
animated by the principle of natural life *(nephesh, psyche)* could
communicate only a natural life to his descendants, Christ, the
last Adam, who is animated by the Spirit *(pneuma)* has become, in
virtue of his resurrection, a "life-giving spirit," in that he gives
life (Jn 6:63) through the Spirit whom he bestows on the faithful
(Jn 20:2). Therefore, by coming into contact with Christ, their

representative, men undergo the same change that has taken place in Christ.

The "psychic" and "pneumatic" Body of Christ thus represent the two states of the mystery of sinful man saved by the *agapē* of God, the *terminus a quo* and *ad quem* of God's salvific power. This is nothing other than the drama of "salvation-history": the passage from the world of flesh to the world of God; from the old world marked by the law of sin and death to the new world dominated by the Spirit of sanctification and life; from the world of disobedience to the world of total surrender to the designs of God; from a world separated from God to a world which participates in the very life of God.[12]

It must be stressed, moreover, that we are not dealing here with a mysticism which involves the Greek dualistic antithesis between a material body which is of transient worth and a spiritual principle (soul) which seeks to be eventually liberated from its bodily prison and immersed in divinity. For Paul, as for the O.T. writers, the psychosomatic unity of the human personality is the fundamental conception of man. Sin brought death not only to the soul of man but also to his body; therefore, man's eschatological renewal must include a return to life of the whole man, the human body-person.[13] This renewal is begun in the sacramental rite of Baptism when the whole man is incorporated into Christ and becomes animated by the same Spirit that vivifies Christ. The fact that the sacrament is received on the basis of "faith" goes without saying. However, because man is a body-person, with an ambit of activity which includes a psychial and sensible aspect, faith in Christ must involve the concomitant resolution to join one's whole self *(sōma)* to the whole self *(sōma)* of Christ in the physical rite of Baptism.[14]

In his description of the sacrament of Baptism, especially in Rom 6:1-11, Paul describes the Christian's union with Christ in very realistic terms. The point which Paul wishes to make is that, if it is true for Christ that "the death he died he died to sin, once

---

[12] For a description of Christ's "pneumatic" Body see P. Benoit, "L'Ascension," *Exégèse et Théologie* (Paris, 1961) 2:363-411.

[13] Benoit, "Corps," 110-14.

[14] B. Ahern, "The Christian's Union with the Body of Christ in Cor., Gal., and Rom.," *CBQ* 23 (1961) 204.

for all" (6:10), it is also true for the baptized Christian that he "died to sin" (6:2) and can no longer have traffic with sin. Paul bases his argument on the intimacy of the union between the believer and Christ which is effected in the sacrament. He asks: "Do you not know that all of us who have been baptized into Christ Jesus were baptized into his death?" (6:3). Christians are baptized not merely "in reference" to Christ but they are plunged into the very death of Christ, "so that as Christ was raised from the dead," they too might walk "in newness of life" (Rom 6:4). In Baptism, therefore, the body-person of the individual Christian is united to the body-person of the risen Christ. He becomes a part of Christ's Body so literally that all that happened to Christ, down to the resurrection of his Body, has happened and will happen to the Christian.

We may say, then, that Christ as the representative of the new Israel and of mankind, is in us in that he communicates to the baptized the fruits of his redemption, liberation from death and the bestowal of eternal life to the body-person of each individual. On the other hand, to use a formula very dear to St. Paul, we are "in Christ" in that, through Baptism we have entered, in a very real sense, into the salvific act of Christ, into his death and resurrection; and that we now lead the glorious life of our Savior, as we await our final resurrection.[15]

II. The Church as the Body of Christ

The most characteristic work of the Holy Spirit, on whom the whole Christian life depends, is the creation of a new fellowship *(koinōnia)*. The Christian life, therefore, is not only a life lived in union with Christ; it is also life within a "social" solidarity. Caution is necessary, however, when we speak of the Church as a "social" body.

When Paul, for the first time in his Epistles, explicitly states that the faithful are "the body of Christ," and individually members of it (1 Cor 12:27), we may think that he has only a "moral" or "social" union in mind. The use of the word "body" to mean an

---

[15] L. Cerfaux, *Christ in the Theology of St. Paul*, tr. G. Webb and A. Walker (New York, 1959) 215-222.

organized group, held together in unity by common interests or by one authority, is so familiar to us that we may look upon the Church merely as a "social" body, "morally" united in Christ. This usage of the word, "body," however, was quite unfamiliar, if not entirely unknown to the people to whom Paul wrote.[16] The Apostle himself never speaks of a "body of Christians" *(to sōma tou Christianŏn)* but always of the "Body of Christ" *(to sōma tou Christou)*, the organism of a particular person. Christians do not form a "social" body which is *like* a body; they *are* the "Body of Christ." They belong to the real organism of the incarnate-risen Savior. Paul has pressed the expression as far as it will go.

Faced with the problem of the charismatic gifts at Corinth, Paul points out that diversity, far from impairing unity, is necessary to the whole. All these gifts alike come from one Spirit and they all alike are conferred by God for one purpose, namely, the good of the whole community (1 Cor 12:4-12). To illustrate the principle of unity in diversity, Paul presents the image of the human body which, though being one, has need of many members. The human body has many members, different from one another because each is intended for a different function; nevertheless, they all belong to and derive their life from the same body. Each member with its particular function is necessary for the body; and without a multiplicity of members, there could be no body (13-21). Because each member shows concern for the others, there is no principle of division among the members of the body (21-27). Paul concludes that a similar case obtains with the "Body of Christ" (27).

It has often been noted that the imaginary discussion between the members of the body in Cor. 12:15-21 resembles a fable depicting a quarrel for supremacy between the parts of the body. As put by Livy (II:32.9-12) in the mouth of the consul Meneius Agrippa (503 B.C.), it shows the other members of the body in revolt against the belly, as an idle and useless member. Then follows a defence of the belly, as sustaining all, though it seems to do nothing but take in. This same argument is applied by Dionysius of Halicarnassus (*Ant. Rom.* III, 11.5) to the function of the senate within the commonwealth.[17]

---

[16] Robinson, *The Body*, 49.
[17] For the text see Robinson, *The Body*, 59 n. 1.

The fable, which illustrated so aptly the principle that the constituent parts of a given society should serve the common good, was a particular favorite of the Stoics. Though Paul was familiar with the expressions of the Stoa, it cannot be said that he borrowed his doctrine from the Stoics. The *literary figure* of the body expresses admirably the duties which Christians have toward one another as members of Christ and Paul may have followed the language of the Stoa when he described the diversity at length. But, before ever having used the figure, he was already in secure possession of his *doctrine* that Christians were vitally conjoined to Christ in such a way as to form a mere "moral" or "social" body.[18] This is clear from the earlier eucharistic passage in 1 Cor 10.17 where, as we shall see later, the sacramental Body of Christ draws Christians into a unity of a bodily kind. Consequently, if Paul borrowed the profane apologue, he already had the materials on hand to transfigure it and enrich it with his own Christian doctrine. Christians, therefore, are conjoined to Christ's risen body, drawing from it the selfsame life that vivifies him and them.

In carrying through his analogy of the human body, we would logically expect Paul to say, "So it is with the *Church.*" Instead, he says: "Just as the body is one and has many members, and all the members of the body, though many, are one body, *so it is with Christ*" (1 Cor 12:12). "Christ" here does not signify a "Mystical Christ," the Church,[19] but the personal, "physical" Christ. Christians do not form a "Mystical Christ" but rather are mystically identified with the physical Body of Christ.[20] Paul's purpose throughout this

---

[18] L. Cerfaux, *The Church in the Theology of St. Paul,* tr. G. Webb and A. Walker (New York, 1959) 267.

[19] The expression, "Mystical Body," had been applied originally to the Eucharist. However, it has been sanctioned by tradition and the Encyclical *Mystici Corporis* of Pope Pius XII as a designation for the Church. The term is useful because it helps us to avoid the one extreme of viewing the Church as the "physical" Body of Christ, and the other, of considering it simply as a "moral" body in Christ. Caution is needed, however, lest we get the impression that there are two Christs; the historical Christ and a spiritual, "mystical" Christ. Some authors prefer to speak of the Church as "ecclesial" Body of Christ because the term "mystical" evokes the idea of religious phenomena of another order. See Benoit, "Corps," 113-14.

[20] Cerfaux, *The Church,* 268-69 n. 13.

chapter is to show that Christ's personal Body can be articulated in diversity without ceasing to be a unity.[21] The sense of verse 12 is, therefore, just as the human body, which is one, gathers together into unity all its members, so Christ gathers all Christians into the unity of his glorified Body. United in this manner to the living Christ as members of his Body, the faithful should express in their conduct their sense of this transcendent unity.

Paul then proceeds to show how Christ has become the principle of unity for the members of his Body. "By one Spirit we were all baptized into one body—and all were made to drink of one Spirit" (12:13). The "one body" into which Christians are baptized is the incarnate-risen Body of Christ. The sacrament is administered not simply for the purpose of giving entry into the Church, a social body, but, as indicated in Rom 6:3-5, Christians are "baptized into Christ," the death of Christ in order to live the life of Christ within the unity of his resurrected Body. This unity is achieved and is maintained by the "one Spirit" that vivifies the risen Savior and, through him, all Christians who are joined to him as members of his glorified Body. Further, when Paul says that Christians "were made to drink of one Spirit," he may still have on mind Baptism. However, the idea of drinking evokes the Eucharist, the other sacrament which is concerned with the incorporation of the faithful into the Body of Christ. Earlier he viewed Israel's passage through the Red Sea and the gift of the manna as prefigurations of Baptism and the Eucharist (1 Cor 10:1-5). It is very probable, therefore, that the present context contains an allusion to both sacraments.[22]

Earlier in the same Epistle, where the theme, "Body of Christ," is implicit, Paul has more than a moral union in mind. The physical realism with which he describes this union is striking. Paul opposes the sin of fornication, into which the Christians of Corinth have fallen, by appealing to another bond which the Christian had already contracted. He asks: "Do you not know that your bodies are members of Christ?" (1 Cor 6:15). The intimacy of this union is indicated when he adds, "he who joins himself to a prostitute becomes one body with her" and the "two become one flesh" (1 Cor 6:16). Christ is opposed to a harlot and therefore Paul cannot be thinking

---

[21] Robinson, *The Body*, 60.
[22] Benoit, "Corps," 119; Cerfaux, *The Church*, 270.

of Christ as a moral collectivity. Further, as the one who is joined to a harlot in carnal intercourse is fused with her so to form "one body with her," so he who cleaves to the Lord is "one spirit with him" (6:17). We may have expected Paul to say that the Christian becomes "one body with Christ." Nevertheless, the realism of Paul's description of this union is maintained because, in Pauline usage, "spirit" is not opposed to "body" but to "flesh."[23] Here the "pneumatic" Body of the risen Lord is opposed to a body of "flesh." Thus, because the Christian is united to the "pneumatic" Body of Christ, he becomes "one spirit" with the Lord.

In Paul's Captivity Epistles (Col, Eph) the theme, "Body of Christ," occupies a more prominent position and, as it is related to the "Head" of the Body, a clearer distinction is drawn between the personal Christ and the faithful who, nevertheless, live the very life of the risen Lord. Here, the double sense of the word "head" is to be noted. In the Semitic sense "head" signifies "authority." In this sense Christ is the "Chief"; his authority is supreme not only over men, but over the whole created universe, including all angelic beings (Col. 1:16-17; 2:10). But Christ is also the Head of the Body, the Church, in the Greek, psychological sense (Col 1:18), and thus carries on the vital functions of the Church.[24] By combining the Semitic and Greek meanings of "head," Paul achieves a happy result. The Semitic sense of "Chief" stresses the separation that exists between Christ and the faithful; the Greek sense indicates the vital union that exists between the Head and the Body.

As in the earlier Epistles of Paul, the idea which underlies the theme "Body of Christ" is the physical, sacramental union of all Christians with the resurrected Body of Christ. To bear this out we need only glance at the synthesis of his doctrine in Eph 5.22-32. The faithful "are members of his body" (5:30). The Church is

---

[23] "Flesh" is not a part of man; it is the whole man, body, soul, and mind, in his weakness and morality, in his distance from God, and in his solidarity with a sinful and corrupt creation. "Spirit" is man under the influence and activity of the Holy Spirit. The two active principles of "flesh" and "spirit" struggle constantly for dominion over the "body" of man, which can be identified with the "flesh" in man's sin and corruption and which can also be the bearer of the resurrection. See Robinson, *The Body*, 17-26.

[24] Benoit, "Corps," 131-34.

cleansed in the baptismal rite (26) and is saved by Christ who is the Head of the Body (23). To point out the intimate union which exists between Christ and his Church, Paul turns to the O.T. for the figure of a "spouse." Christ is not only one in authority who must be obeyed; he is a person who is intimately associated with his spouse and "who loves her as his own flesh" (25-29). Paul would have us understand that the union between Christ and his Church is no less real than that between a husband and his wife. To justify the boldness of his comparison he cites Gn 2:24 and concludes: "This is a great mystery—I mean in reference to Christ and to the Church" (31-32). The "mystery" in question is the union of two persons in one flesh, which is perfectly and fully realized only in the union of Christ with his Church. Human marriage is but a shadow and an allegory of the intimacy of this union. Thus, we are driven back to a very real, physical (sacramental) union in which the individual Christian, joined to Christ, is vitally united with his fellow Christians in Christ's resurrected Body.

III. The Sacramental Body of Christ

The physical realism with which St. Paul describes the Christian's union with Christ and the Church, which is his Body, spontaneously evokes the idea of Christ's "Sacramental" Body, the Eucharist. By his applying the term "Body of Christ" both to the sacrament and to the Church we are immediately led to believe that this "sacramental" Body of Christ must surely be connected in some important way with the apostle's teaching on Christian unity.[25] However, the

---

[25] There are good reasons to hold that the very origins of Paul's teaching that Christians together constitute the "Body of Christ" are, in effect, sacramental. The words of institution, "This is my body," which are certainly pre-Pauline, already assign a quasi-theological meaning to the word "body." In relating the narrative of the Last Supper to the Corinthians, Paul insists that what he says is something which he *has received* (1 Cor. 11.23-24) from the apostolic tradition. Therefore, since the term was already in use, it was able to serve Paul as a convenient vehicle for the expression of his doctrine.

In addition, we may point out that the eucharistic celebration of the early Christian community, which so aptly expressed Christian unity, is looked upon by Paul as the very foundation of Christian unity (1 Cor. 10:17). See A. E. J. Rawlinson, "Corpus Christi," *Mysterium* Christi (New York, 1930), 225-44.

relationship between Sacrament and Church is not merely one of terminology. The Eucharist is, as will be pointed out, the very cause of the unity of the Church in that, by drawing the faithful even more intimately into Christ's sacrifice, it transforms them into his risen Body and thus unites them as a community.

a. *Unity in the "Sacramental" Body of Christ.*

In the Acts of the Apostles we see that the Christian "partnership" *(koinōnia)*, of which Paul became a member, found its special embodiment from the very beginning in the Lord's Supper, traditionally known as "the breaking of bread." We are told by Luke that the early Christians "devoted themselves to the apostle's teaching and fellowship *(koinōnia)*, to the breaking of bread and the prayers," and that they "sold their possessions and goods and distributed them to all, as any had need" (Acts 2:42-47). It was quite natural that the unity of the faithful became linked with the unity of the loaf of bread, broken that it was for sharing in common, since the loaf which is broken remains ideally one.[26] The association of these ideas is also had in the early sub-apostolic document known as the *Didache:* "As this broken bread was scattered over the hills and then, when gathered, became one mass, so may Thy Church be gathered from the ends of the earth into Thy Kingdom" (9:4).[27]

Similarly, Paul sees in the "breaking of bread" the expression of Christian unity. But he goes beyond the symbolism involved in the rite. He grounds the unity of the Church in the sacramental loaf which he has expressly declared to be the Body of Christ. He asks the Corinthians, "The bread which we break, it is not a participation in the body of Christ?" Then he replies, "Because there is one loaf, we who are many, are one body, for we all partake of the same loaf" (1 Cor 10:16-17).

Paul then proceeds to show how Christians are drawn into this unity by the eucharistic rite. In receiving the eucharistic Body of Christ the faithful are transformed into Christ in such a way that they *become* what they receive, the very Body of Christ. Paul conveys this truth when he says, "we who are many are one body" (1 Cor 10:17). It must be emphasized that Paul does not mean to

---

[26] L. Cerfaux, *The Church*, 263.

[27] *Ancient Christian Writers*, tr. J. Kleist (Westminster, 1948).

say here that the faithful who partake of the sacramental Body of Christ are welded into a "social" body, united by a "moral" bond to the Lord's personal Body. Certainly, Paul has in mind the unity of the Christian community but this unity is achieved in reference to the very Body of Christ which is received in the Eucharist. In both verses (10:16, 17) "body" refers to the Body of the incarnate Savior with whom Christians become concorporeal, thus forming one living organism.[28] Then, because they are concorporeally one with Christ, they possess the very same unity which is proper to the organism of Christ's risen Body. Therefore, it is the communion in the Body of the risen Christ, made sacramentally present that unites the community of the faithful.

The faithful are then encouraged by the Apostle to manifest in their daily lives the unity which they really possess because of their sacramental union with Christ. He reminds the Corinthians that, because of their common communion in the "old loaf," (1 Cor 10:17) they should be careful lest they make the weaker brethren "to stumble" over such things as the vexed question of eating food offered to idols. The heathen idols, he goes on to say, are non-entities and the food offered to them does not differ from any other common food. Yet, if Christians who partake of this food are to cause scandal, they should refrain from doing so (1 Cor 10:22-30). In the same letter Paul reprimands the Corinthians for the factions they created and the consequent unbrotherly conduct which was in evidence at their eucharistic gatherings. Some of them, not waiting for those whose duties kept them late, drank to intoxication, while others went away hungry from the Lord's table. In Paul's opinion this lack of charity is especially offensive in the celebration of the Eucharist which, by its very nature, is intended to express and foster the unity of the Church (1 Cor 11:23-32).

b. *Communion in Sacrifice*

We are given a further insight into the nature of the union of the faithful with Christ when Paul stresses the sacrificial aspect of the Eucharist. In fact, Paul would have us understand that it is precisely this sacrificial aspect of the Last Supper as well as the Church's

---

[28] Benoit, "Corps," 117.

eucharistic rite that explains how the union between the faithful and the immolated and glorified Christ is effected.[29]

The point of departure for Paul's statement on the Eucharist, as the source of unity, was the danger of syncretism which had arisen from sharing in the sacrificial banquets of pagan worship. He cautions the Corinthians that they cannot belong to two lords, to a demon and to Christ. They who have a "sharing" (koinōnia) in the blood of Christ," and a "sharing (koinōnia) in the body of the Lord" (1 Cor 10:16) must be wary lest, by partaking of food offered to idols, they "become associates (koinōnous) of devils" (1 Cor 10:20). The complex of ideas expressed here by Paul is not peculiar to him for it underlies the sacred meals at the altar both of pagans and Jews. Food offered to a deity was looked upon as the property of the god and it bore the imprint of his divine presence. As the worshippers partook of the food which had been offered to their god, they thereby became united with him.

A similar case obtains at the Lord's Table. Before the Eucharist can become spiritual food for the faithful, the offering of the faithful must be sacrificed and accepted by God. Then, having been accepted by God and drawn into the realm of divinity, it is able to draw the faithful who receive it into union with God. Thus, sacrifice, far from being simply an appendage to the eucharistic rite, really pertains to the very essence of the communion service. It also helps us understand how the Eucharist, uniting us with Christ, brings us into the realm of divinity.

Nor is this sacrificial aspect of the Eucharist an innovation introduced by Paul into the early fellowship-medal which was eaten with joy as the Christians awaited the return of their Lord.[30] The sacrificial aspect of the Lord's Supper was recognized from the beginning. Paul makes this clear when, in presenting the narrative of the Last Supper, he carefully states that what he is reporting has been derived from the tradition in which he had been instructed. He writes: "I *received* from the Lord what I also delivered to you, that the Lord Jesus on the night when he was betrayed took bread,

---

[29] F. Durwell, *The Resurrection*, tr. R. Sheed (New York, 1960) 324-26.

[30] G. Sloyan, " 'Primitive' and 'Pauline' Concept of the Eucharist," *CBQ* 23 (1961) 1-13.

and when he had given thanks, he broke it, and said, 'This is my body which shall be given up for you' " (1 Cor 11:23-24). This tradition which Paul passed on to his converts goes back to our Lord himself who, at the Last Supper performed a prophetic action which pointed to his death on Calvary. But Christ's action did more than merely represent his sacrifice and death. Like the prophetic acts in the past which effectively achieved what they symbolized, Christ's action at the Last Supper not only foretold but already contained his sacrifice. Then, too, Christ's words, "This cup is the new covenant in my blood" (1 Cor 11:25) recall Jeremia's prophecy on the New Covenant (31:31). They also recall the words of Moses and the blood of the animal victims with which he sprinkled the people as he said: "Behold the blood of the covenant, which the Lord has made with you" (Ex 24:8). Thus, at the Last Supper Christ interpreted his death as the sacrificial act by which Yahweh was making a convenant with a New People and that thereby he was replacing the old, broken covenant of Sinai. Hence, we repeat, there is no question of Paul's having read the doctrine of sacrifice into the Last Supper. In fact, the opposite is true. The sacrificial meaning of Christ's death on Calvary and the consequent Pauline doctrine of atonement were derived from Christ's interpretation given at the Last Supper.[31]

That the eucharistic rite by which the Church commemorates Christ's sacrifice on Calvary is of the same sacrificial nature as the Last Supper is clear from Christ's command to "Do this in remembrance of me" (1 Cor 11:24). At first sight it may seem to indicate nothing more than the fact that our Lord wanted his deed on Calvary to be remembered by succeeding generations and that the eucharistic rite itself is nothing more than a vivid way of bringing Christ's sacrifice to mind. Certainly, to our modern mind "remembrance" might mean no more than a pale recollection of a thing or person of the past, no longer present. The Bible, however, takes a more realistic view of "remembrance," The Greek *anamnēsis* and the Hebrew *zekher* have the meaning of "re-calling" and at the same time, making present a thing of the past in order to make it once more operative in our lives. Thus, in the O.T., a man who is dead lives on in his sons or wherever his "name" is remembered. When his name is remembered no more, then he is dead indeed. As a

---

[31] Rawlinson, "Corpus Christi," 241.

matter of fact, the horror of Sheol lay precisely in this that it was the land of forgetfulness and that the dead were no more remembered.

Through their various rites the Israelites relived the wonders of the past, but not merely as a simple memorial. Rather, they actually entered into a here-and-now participation in the saving events. The Mishna instructed each generation to actually feel that it was undergoing these experiences personally. Thus, the Paschal meal, which was the basis of Christ's institution of the Eucharist, was looked upon as a commemoration which actually made present and operative the past deliverance from Egypt.

On the other hand, the Jewish Paschal meal also pointed to a future salvation which was to come in the day of the Messiah. As the people recalled God's redemptive act of the past, their faith in Yahweh's fidelity became strengthened and their hope for the future was thereby nourished. This element of hope was especially noticeable in later Judaism when the Jews looked forward to being led back by Yahweh into the Promised Land (Is 41:18-20).[32]

Now, the same is true of the Lord's Supper which is an *anamnēsis* of Christ's sacrifice. The Church, in her liturgical sacrifice, does not offer God a new sacrifice. Christ suffered "once for all at the end of the age to put away sin by the sacrifice of himself" (Heb 9:26). And yet, by the very command of Christ the Church must "do this in remembrance" of its Lord, so that the redemptive past may become the redemptive present. Here it is precisely that the Church's "remembrance" releases the life-giving stream of Christ's passion and death in order to make his salvific work operative here-and-now in the faithful. Christ, thereby, must touch each individual as he touched the sick and the sinners in Palestine. The whole man, body and soul, must be drawn into Christ's sacrifice so that what was accomplished on Calvary may be effected in each Christian.[33]

The Eucharistic sacrifice which the Church offers, adds nothing to the sacrifice on Calvary which was perfect in its historical realization. Yet, without detracting from the sacrifice which Christ offered once, we may say that something is added to his redemptive work.

---

[32] J. Tillard, "L'Eucharistie, sacrament de l'espérance, ecclésiale," NRT 83 (1961) 567-69.

[33] N. Clark, *An Approach to the Theology of the Sacraments* (Chicago, 1956) 62-68.

The Church, corporately through the minister, and individually through the offering of each member, offers itself to God at the offertory under the forms of bread and wine, as Christ offered himself, a pledged victim, to the Father at the Last Supper. The prayers of the faithful and their own sacrifices, sinners as they are, add nothing to the efficacy of the Cross. And yet, because the oblation of Christ himself is ever accepted by his Father, the sacrifice of the Church, which is his Body, is also certain of being blessed, ratified, and accepted.[34]

The words of St. Paul (2 Cor 4:10-11), which describe the lot of the apostles, are instructive in this regard: "For while we live we are always being given up *(paradidometha)* to death for Jesus' sake, so that the life of Jesus may be manifested in our mortal flesh" (2 Cor. 4:11). The Greek word for "to be given up" is used in the N.T. in reference to our Lord's betrayal and the "giving of himself" to death for us (Mk. 9:31; 10. 33; Eph. 5:25). It is true that Paul here is not explicitly speaking of the Eucharist. However, because for him as well as for his fellow-Christians the Eucharist is the representative act in which the whole Christian life finds its continuance and its supreme manifestation, Paul undoubtedly has the Eucharist in mind.[35] In the "proclaiming" of the Lord's death (I Cor. 11:26) by eating and drinking of the Eucharist, Christians are "always carrying in the body the death of Jesus, so that the life of Jesus may also be manifested in our bodies" (2 Cor. 4:10). Here, the word "body" may stand just as well for the Church as for the individual Christian because the very concept, "communion" *(koinō-nia)*, points to a "communal" participation in Christ's sacrifice and a communal contribution of human suffering to Christ's redemptive work.

We might say, then, that the Last Supper, the Cross, and the Eucharist are linked together because at the heart of each lies the enduring presence and action of the one Christ and the one Body of Christ. Because this is so, each eucharistic rite which the Church enacts, brings the fullness of Christ's sacrifice into his earthly Body, the Church, in which the sacrifice is still not complete. As the faithful offer themselves in sacrifice and are nourished by the Body of

---

[34] P. Benoit, "The Holy Eucharist," *Cross Currents* 8 (1958) 312-13.
[35] G. Dix, *The Shape of the Liturgy* (Westminster, 1946) 254.

Christ, they are drawn toward the fullness of Christ's sacrifice in order to become in truth the Body of the dead and risen Savior.

IV. Resurrection and Parousia

Paul's statement that Christians who partake of the Eucharist, "proclaim the Lord's death until he comes" (1 Cor 11:26), also points out the eschatological significance of the eucharistic rite. The "proclaiming" of the Lord's death is by its very nature a dramatic setting forth and rendering present of Christ's death with an eye to his second coming.[36]

Christians live in the mystery and agony of the "having" and the "not having." They have been baptized and, because they have "put on Christ" (Gal. 3:26-27) they have become "sons of God:" they have been "made alive" for they were raised with him (Col. 2:12-13); they have been "brought from death to life" (Rom. 6:13). Yet, the partial character of this life in the new age is never forgotten. The transformation begun in the faithful at baptism is not yet completed; the body of sin and death, crucified in principle, remains a present though a dying reality. Within their mortal members the powers of this age and of the age to come fight for mastery. Dying with Christ and risen with him, the faithful are not yet glorified; they await the redemption of the body. "When Christ who is our life appears, then you also will appear with him in glory" (Col. 3:4), writes St. Paul. Hence, Paul's words, "until he comes," are not intended as a simple affirmation of time. They contain an element of finality,[37] as if to say that Christians are to proclaim the Lord's death for the purpose of attaining Christ's coming. The Church, the Body of Christ, still encumbered with "the body of this death" (Rom. 7:24), hears the summons of its Lord: become what you are. In obedience to the Lord's command, "Do this in remembrance of me," the Church offers itself to the Father in union with its Lord in every eucharistic rite. Receiving again and again the Lord's Body, charged with life-giving power, it becomes in truth the Body of its risen Savior. In eager longing and confident hope the Church thus looks forward to Christ's coming and its own final glorification. *Maranatha!* "Come, Lord," is the Church's cry.

---

[36] F. Durwell, *The Resurrection*, 326-29.
[37] J. Tillard, "L'Eucharistie," 571.

Conclusion

St. Paul's doctrine of the "Body of Christ," which points out the nature of Christian unity, is presented by the apostle with striking realism. Notwithstanding the fact that we may distinguish between the "natural," "sacramental," and "mystical" Body of Christ, ultimately there is only one Body of Christ. Even though this Body may have several aspects, it never ceases to be the Body that walked this earth, that suffered on the cross, and that gloriously arose from the grave. As the representative of the New Israel, redeemed in his Blood, and the new Adam who embraces all mankind within himself by virtue of his incarnation and resurrection, Christ gathers all men to himself in the unity of his Body.

It is true that Christians are made members of Christ's Body through faith in their Savior. But the physical realism of Paul's language also points and quite persistently, to the Sacraments of Baptism and the Eucharist through which the body-person of the individual Christian is incorporated into the Body-Person of the risen Christ.

In Baptism the Christian receives the Holy Spirit that vivifies the Body of the risen Savior and, as a member of Christ's Body, he begins to live the very life of his risen Lord. This diffusion of Christ's life in the members of his Body is what constitutes the Church. The Church, therefore, is not a social body of believers who are joined to Christ by a "moral" union. The faithful are the Body of Christ, in a very literal sense, because they share the "one Spirit" that unites them in the unity of Christ's glorious Body.

The Body of the risen Savior, of which Christians are members (1 Cor. 12:27), is made present in the Eucharist to unite them ever more closely to itself and to unite them among themselves. As the baptized are joined to Christ in his sacrifice and as they partake of his "pneumatic" Body, charged with vivifying power, they become concorporeal with Christ and become in truth transformed into the Body of Christ. Then, united to Christ in Holy Communion, they also become united with all the members of Christ's Body. Thus, in a very real sense, the Eucharist is the bond of Christian unity.

THE EUCHARIST, BOND OF UNITY, BEFORE
THE COUNCIL OF TRENT

BERARD L. MARTHALER, O.F.M.Conv.

My object in this paper is to contribute to the discussions of this symposium on the Holy Eucharist by providing a rapid survey of eucharistic thought and practise in the millenium between the Apostolic Fathers and the Council of Trent. Through it run two themes. The first, the topic of the conference, is a consideration of the Eucharist as a bond of Christian unity. The second, developed only in passing, is to cite devotional and liturgical practises giving concrete expression to this unity.

Christians of all walks, the faithful as well as the clergy, Protestant as well as Catholics, agree that the eucharist is the sacrament par excellence. Theologians describe the Eucharist in the words of St. Dionysius as the *finis et consummatio omnium sacramentorum*,[1] and historians of dogma recognize it as the center of every development in sacramental theology. The notion of sacrament as an efficacious sign of grace, implicit in St. Paul's references to baptism (Rom. 6, 4-13) and marriage (Eph. 5, 22-23) is first elaborated in connection with the eucharist. It is the starting point for all later theories in sacramental symbolism.

I. Early Church

In his first epistles to the Corinthians when St. Paul, trying to bring peace and unity to that dissension-ridden community, asks rhetorically:

> The Cup of blessing that we bless, is it not the sharing of the blood of Christ? And the bread that we break, is it not the partaking of the body of the Lord? Because the bread is one, we though many, are one body, all of us partake of the one bread (10:16-17).[2]

---

[1] *De eccles. hier.* c. 3, P.G. 3, 424. Cf. St. Thomas, III, q. 63, a. 6.

[2] Cf. F. Puzo, S.J., "La unidad de la Iglesia en función de la Eucharistia (Estudio de Teología Biblica)," *Gregorianum* 34 (1953) 148-159.

The *Didache,* the oldest non-canonical Christian writing we have, gives us the prescriptions regulating "the First Communion of the newly baptized on Easter eve."[3] It embellishes St. Paul's plea for unity with a metaphor which becomes classic in Christian literature.

> As this broken bread was scattered over the hills and then, when gathered, became one mass, so may Thy Church be gathered from the ends of the earth into Thy kingdom (*Ancient Christian Writers,* 9, 4).

Saint Ignatius of Antioch like Saint Paul had to fight divisions in the Christian community. In the face of dissension and schism caused by the Docetists in the churches of Asia, Ignatius urges the faithful to remain in union with their bishops.[4] He proposes the eucharist as the embodiment and motive of that unity which ought to exist between Christians and their pastors. He continues:

> Take care then to partake of one eucharist; for one is the flesh of our Lord Jesus Christ, and one the cup to unite us with His Blood, and one altar, just as there is one bishop assisted by the presbytery and deacons ... (*ACW,* Philad. 4).

The bishop of Antioch seems to say that participation in the one eucharist is the cause of unity, an idea to be made explicit by latter theologians.

Although a layman, and writing for a very different audience from Ignatius, Saint Justin's emphasis on the corporate nature of worship is eloquent testimony that the eucharist was regarded as a bond of unity, not merely by theological writers and mystics, but by

---

[3] J. Quasten, *Patrology,* Vol. 1, p. 33. In noting the close association of this rite with baptism Quasten says, "The opinion advanced more than once, that we have here no specific Eucharistic prayers but simply table prayers, is untenable" (p. 32). Nonetheless, Geo. W. Dollar who recently published a highly tendentious survey of the Eucharist in the early Church holds that Didache 9-10 refers to the agape, cf. *Bibliotheca Sacra* 117 (1960) p. 146.

[4] Saint Ignatius promises to write another letter to the community at Ephesus "... if the Lord should reveal to me that you—the entire community of you—are in the habit ... of meeting in common, animated by one faith and in union with Jesus Christ ... to show obedience with undivided mind to the bishop and the presbytery, and to break the same Bread, which is the medicine of immortality, the antidote against death, and everlasting life in Jesus Christ" (ACW 20, 2).

Christians as a whole. On the day called Sunday, he writes, "all who live in cities or in the country gather together to one place" to per- form the eucharist. Justin also makes a point of mentioning that even the absent brethren participate in the community service when the deacons distribute the eucharist to them.[5]

In the third century it is St. Cyprian who provides the best state- ment on sacramental symbolism, specifically in regard to the eucha- rist. Faced with a crisis brought on by schism he, like St. Paul and Ignatius, points to the eucharist as the ideal manifestation of Church unity.

> For because Christ bore us all, in that He also bore our sins,
> we see in the water is understood the people, but in the wine is
> shown the blood of Christ. But when the water is mingled in
> the cup with wine, the people is made one with Christ, and
> the assembly of believers is associated and conjoined with Him
> in whom it believes; which association and conjunction of
> water and wine is so mingled in the Lord's cup, that that mix-
> ture cannot any more be separated. Whence, moreover, nothing
> can separate the Church ... from Christ. ... Thus indeed the
> cup of the Lord is not indeed water alone, nor wine alone; un-
> less each be mingled with the other, just as on the other hand,
> the body of the Lord cannot be flour alone or water alone, unless
> both should be united and joined together and compacted in the
> mass of one bread; in which every sacrament our people are
> shown to be made one, so that in like manner as many grains,
> collected, and ground, and mixed together into one mass, make
> one bread, so in Christ, who is the heavenly bread, we may
> know there is one body, with which our number is joined and
> united.[6]

The eucharist represents then both the oneness of the people with Christ as seen in the mixing of water with wine; and the unity of the people among themselves as seen in the forming of the "one bread" from many grains. Cyprian's explanation of the ritual mixing of water and wine will appear again and again in later writings.

II. Greek Fathers

Saint Cyprian is a half-century later than Clement of Alexandria

---

[5] I Apol. 65, 66-67. Cf. Jos. A. Jungmann, *The Mass of the Roman Rite: Its Origins and Development* (New York, 1951) I, pp. 22-23.

[6] Ep. 62 (63), 13. P.L. 4, 395-396.

who makes reference to the water-wine mixture. Clement, always the moralist, mentions it in a passage about moderation in drink. Although he sees the ritual as representing union with the divine, his emphasis is very different from that of the Bishop of Carthage who, writing as a pastor of souls, had both eyes fixed on the crises of the times. Clement says in part:

> To drink the blood of Jesus is to participate in His incorruption. Yet, the Spirit is the strength of the Word in the same way that blood is of The body. Similarly, wine is mixed with water and the Spirit is joined to man; the first, the mixture, provides feasting that faith may be increased; the other, the Spirit, leads us on to incorruption. The union of both, that is, of the potion and the Word, is called the eucharist, a gift worthy of praise and surpassingly fair; those who partake of it are sanctified in body and soul, for it is the will of the Father that man, a composite made by God, be united to the Spirit and to the Word. In fact, the Spirit is closely joined to the soul depending on Him, and the flesh to the Word, because it was for it that "the Word was made flesh."[7]

Clement was the first writer to attempt an explanation of the mystery. Camelot says that in portraying the eucharist as a "quasi-incarnation," Clement had used a sound approach.[8] On the other hand, while he recognized the sanctifying effect of the eucharist it remains a symbol of unprecise meaning.

Clement's famous pupil, Origen, says the eucharist "is the typical and symbolical body of Christ,"[9] a phrase ambiguous enough to make the great Alexandrian a favorite of the 'symbolist' opposed to the Real Presence. It may be, as Pourrat charges, that Origen did not sufficiently distinguish the efficacious symbolism in the eucharist from that in baptism, but he did closely associate communion in the sacraments with communion in the Church.[10]

Origen insists that, unless one is pure of conscience he should not attempt to *accedere ad eucharistiam* for *accedere ad tanta et tam*

---

[7] *Paedagogus*, lib. II, c. ii, 19-20. P.G. 8, 410-411.

[8] T. Camelot, O.P., "L'eucharistie dans l'ecole d'Alexandrie," *Divinitas* 1 (1957) p. 82.

[9] In Matt. XI, 14. P.G. 13, 952.

[10] P. Pourrat, *Theology of the Sacraments: A Study in Positive Theology*, 4th ed. (St. Louis, 1930) p. 6. J. Danielou, *Origen* (trans. by W. Mitchell), (New York, 1955) pp. 61-68.

eximia sacramenta, communicare corpus Christi.[11] In the same context the great Alexandrian says *communicare Ecclesiae.* Though he used the phrase only in passing, it is of the utmost importance. For him to communicate with the body of Christ *in mysterio*, is to communicate with the Church: the eucharist and the Church, the same body of Christ, his mystical body as it comes to be called. Thus the union in the Church is a union with—a 'communion'—Christ in the sacrament of the eucharist. Therefore we must not be wanting in charity towards our brethren with whom we approach *ad eamdem mensam corporis Christi, et ad eamdem potum sanquinis eius.*[12]

In the writings of Saint Cyril of Alexandria, two centuries later, we find, not unexpectedly, that his eucharistic theology is colored by his adamant anti-Nestorianism.[13] Nonetheless Cyril points out that one effect of partaking of the eucharist is the physical union (physikēn henotēta) it produces among the faithful, notwithstanding that we differ one from another in body and soul.

> For if all of us partake of one bread, we are all made one body. It is impossible to divide Christ, and therefore neither the body of Christ, called the Church; for according to the teaching of Paul, we are his own members.[14]

The eucharist as a symbol of Church unity—unity of the members with Christ and among ourselves—is not a poetical figure of speech. In the ontological order it is a cause of this unity: it epitomizes the sign which at once effects what it symbolizes and symbolizes that which it effects.

Saint John Chrysostom, the *doctor eucharisticus*, urges us to be commingled with Christ's body "in order that we may become of His body, not in desire only, but also in very fact,"[15] He also uses the figure of the grains to show the unity of the body of Christ; a union "which takes place by means of the food which he gave us."[16]

In this question of the eucharist as in so many other questions, it

---

[11] In Psalm. 37, hom. 2, 6. P.G. 12, 1386.
[12] In Matt. ser. 82. P.G. 13, 1732. Cf. Camelot, *loc. cit.*, p.81.
[13] J. Mahe, "L'eucharistie d'après saint Cyrille d'Alexandrie," *Rev. d'histoire ecclesiastique* 8 (1907) 677-696.
[14] In Joa. xi. P.G. 74, 559.
[15] Hom. 46 in Joa. P.G. 59, 260.
[16] Hom. in I Cor. x, 17. P.G. 61, 200-201.

is Saint John of Damascus who gives us a synopsis of early Greek thought. In communion, he says, 'we partake of one bread and we all become one body of Christ." Since we are united to those with whom we share the sacrament "let us beware lest we receive communion from or grant it to heretics" (Mt. 7, 6). Sharing the sacrament, however, is not merely an expression of unity; it is also its cause "for we are all one body because we partake of one bread." The Damascene warns on the one hand against partaking of the Lord unworthily, and says, on the other, "when we are purified by it, we become one with the body of Christ." The eucharist purges the members of the Church and unites them into a body as pure as the flesh born of the Virgin.[17]

III. Saint Augustine and the West

The thought, if not the spirit, of the Greek Fathers was not unknown in the West during the Middle Ages. Saint John Damascene's teaching on the purity of the Church's members, for example, was frequently cited by the Schoolmen from the twelfth century onwards.[18] It is Saint Augustine, however, who plotted the route that eucharistic theology was to follow in the West for more than four centuries.

In his *De Doctrina Christina* (cf. lib. II) and his *De Magistro* Augustine elaborates the divisions and nature of signs. Though he distinguishes the sacramental sign from its effects he is not always precise about the latter. In his cathechetical sermons, however, there is no question that the eucharist is pictured as the sacramental of Church unity. Augustine returns again and again to the same theme. He wants the newly baptized to see the eucharist as the "mysterium unitatis," the "sacramentum unitatis," the "concordia unitatis" and the "vinculum unitatis." For him unity is the eucharist's *effectus*, its *res*, its *virtus*. The eucharist represents "Christus plenus," "Christus totus," "Christi caput et corpus"; His "corpus totum," "universali," "in plentitudine" and "difinitivum."[19]

---

[17] De fid. orthod. lib. iv, 13; lib. iii, 2. P.G. 94, 1151-53; 985.

[18] Cf. H. de Lubac, S.J., *Corpus Mysticum: L'eucharistie et eqlise au maoyen age*, 2 me éd. (Paris, 1949) p. 191, n. 9.

[19] Taken passim from Augustines' works as quoted in *Florilegium Patristicum XXXV: S. Aurelei Augustini. Textus eucharistici selecti.* Hugo Lang, O.S.B., ed. (Bonn, 1933). Cf. H. Lang, "Eucharistic Teach-

Sermon 227, like Augustine's other eucharistic sermons, was preached on Easter, and was directed primarily to those who had just been baptized. After telling them that the bread is the body of Christ and the chalice contains His blood, Augustine continues, "if you have received worthily you are what you received." In pointing out how the bread instructs them in unity, he embellishes the classic metaphor of the grain, even to the point of suggesting that confirmation is ordered to the eucharist:

> That bread . . . is the body of Christ. That chalice . . . is the blood of Christ. . . . If you have received worthily you are what you received, for the Apostle says: "The bread is one; we though many, are one body." So, by bread you are instructed as to how you ought to cherish unity. Was that bread made of one grain of wheat? Were there not rather, many grains? However, before they became bread, these grains were separate; they were joined together in water after a certain amount of crushing. For unless the grain is ground and moistened with water, it cannot arrive at that form which is called bread. So, too, you were previously ground, as it were by humiliation and fasting and by the sacrament of exorcism. Then came the baptism of water; you were moistened, as it were, so as to arrive at the form of bread. But without fire, bread does not exist. What then does the fire signify? The chrism. For the sacrament of the Holy Spirit is the oil of our fire. . . . Attend, then and see that the Holy Spirit will come on Pentecost. And thus He will come . . . in tongues of fire. . . . Therefore, the fire, that is the Holy Spirit, comes after the water; then it truly becomes bread, that is, the body of Christ. Hence in a certain manner, unity is signified.[20]

We have already seen that Ignatius and Cyprian who made Church unity the key to the doctrine of the eucharistic faced the reality of schism. Pere de Lubac likewise sees St. Augustine's emphatic eucharistic-ecclesiology as a counter thrust against the Donatist movement of his time.[21]

But it was not only eloquent words from pulpits which reminded the faithful that the eucharist represented the unity of the Whole

---

ings of St. Augustine" in *Pro Mundi Vita: Festschrift zum eucharistischen Weltkongress 1960*. Herausgegeben von der Theologischen Fakultät der Ludvig-Maximilian Universität Munchen (München, 1960) p. 45.

[20] Florileguim pp. 12-15. P.L. 38, 1099-1101.

[21] *Corpus Mysticum*, p. 23.

Christ. Liturgical usage told the same story. Two practises in particular made this quite clear. 1) The primitive and original form of the Mass with the bishop surrounded by his clergy in the presence of the congregation gave rise to the principle of concelebration.[22] 2) When distance demanded that outlying churches be established the *fermentum* was the visible link binding the neighborhood church to the bishop. A particle of the *sacramentum unitatis,* consecrated by the bishop, was sent to the priests of the area as an expression of Church unity. Their accepting the *fermentum* was an open acknowledgement of membership in the same *communio.* It was a practice that lasted in Rome into the 10th century.[23]

IV. Early Medieval Controversies

No doubt Saint Augustine's insistence upon an eucharist-oriented ecclesiology accounts for its acceptance in the West. Later writers of the 7th, 8th and 9th centuries, though with ever slackening emphasis, not only borrow his ideas, but they incessantly repeat his formulas as well.[24] During this period, as H. de Lubac has shown, the term *corpus mysticum* referred to the real body of Christ in the sacrament. The medieval writers of this period used the word "mystical" in much the same way that moderns use "sacramental." Next there occurred the first of the famous medieval controversies about the eucharist. With it theologians began to change the focus of heir attention from eucharist's wholly religious aspect to the peripheral, though important, questions of metaphysics and cosmology.

---

[22] J. Jungmann, *op. cit.,* I, pp. 195-199. St. Francis' well-known injunction urging his friars to be satisfied with one Mass daily in each convent is cited by Jungmann (p. 199) as evidence that this was the general practice in religious houses. That such an admonition was necessary seems to me to indicate a tendency to depart from the older usage. Unfortunately, Philip Melanchthon used the text to bolster his own position against private Masses and it has become a point of honor to refute him. I cannot accept, however, Paschal Robinson's statement, "There is nothing in this letter or elsewhere to show that St. Francis reprehended such Masses in any way." Nor does it seem that Jungmann would accept it. P. Robinson O.F.M., *The Writings of St. Francis of Assisi* (Philadelphia, 1906) p. 115, n. 3.

[23] J. Jungmann, *op. cit.,* II, pp. 312 ff.

[24] H. de Lubac, *op. cit.,* p. 23.

In the 9th century—the Carolingian period—much of the literature dealt with usage and practise: communion, ritual, etc. It marks the beginning of the long series of *Ordines Romani* so characteristic of late medieval liturgy. Even the "speculative" questions were of a "practical" nature: the body and blood of Christ, complete and entire in heaven, is also complete and entire in the host and in each of the particles; in communion He is received whole and entire but He lives on intact. Problems such as these gave rise to a discussion about the properties of the eucharistic body of Christ. It is material or spiritual? Is it the same body which was born of Mary, which suffered and died, and is now received daily by the faithful?

The controversy began when Paschasius Radbertus published his views in a treatice *De corpore et sanquine Christi.*[25] He insisted on the identity of the historic and eucharistic body of Christ; otherwise, he said, the latter would be only a shadow, an empty figure. Ratramnus of Corbie answered in a work of the same title saying that the two are different for (among other reasons) "the eucharistic body represents the Church while the historical body did not."[26] It is worthwhile to quote a passage from Ratramnus to show how the two figures to which we have given special attention were subordinated to the needs of polemics:

> We must consider too that the bread is a figure, both of the body of Christ and the faithful themselves. It is composed of many kernels of wheat to permit this symbolism. Just as the bread is only spiritually and not corporeally the body of the faithful, so to it is only spiritually Christ's body. If the wine upon the altar were corporeally converted into Christ's blood, the water mingled with it would necessarily be converted in a corporeal way into the blood of the faithful.[27]

The contest between Paschasius and Ratramnus, carried on in the 10th century by their partisans and intellectual descendants, was only a preliminary to the more important Berengarian conroversy of the 11th century. Berengarius of Tours found himself opposed by three

---

[25] Besides the standard reference works, a recent doctoral dissertation gives a good summary of the controversy with an up-to-date bibliography: J. F. Fahey, *The Eucharistic Teaching of Ratramn of Corbie* (Mundelein, III., 1954).

[26] Cf. Fahey, pp. 47; 67.

[27] P.L. 121, 159-160.

of the best theologians of the time, Lanfranc of Bec, Guitmond of Aversa and Alger of Liege. Berengarius' denial of substantial change in the eucharist was just one of the issues of the dispute, perhaps not even the most important from the standpoint of theological development.[28] The question of substantial change and the dispute about the Real Presence, however, led to an argument over the "sacramental" aspect of the eucharist.

Berengarius, tenacious of the notion that the sacrament was a sign,[29] taunted his opponents with the charge that they suppressed the symbolic aspect in favor of the real. He found it difficult to admit that the eucharist could at once contain the substantial presence of Christ's body and at the same time be a sign of it. To answer him, therefore, Alger of Liege had recourse to the distinction "res significata et significans" or "res et sacramentum"; and a "res significans tantum" or "res tantum." Although neither Alger nor Lanfranc nor Guitmond seems to have grasped the full implication of the notion of *sacramentum-et-res*, all three asserted that in some way the body of Christ is itself a sacrament and a sign.[30]

V. Scholastics

When the smoke of controversy lifted from the last of these disputes it was evident—at least from our vantage point—that the battleground for future skirmishing in sacramental theology would no longer be the same. The terrain had been altered in two principle aspects: 1) The term *corpus mysticum*, as de Lubac has shown, until

---

[28] C. E. Sheedy, *The Eucharistic Controversy of the Eleventh Century Against the Background of Pre-scholastic Theology* (Washington, 1947). Sheedy says that Berengarius' errors "lay at a deeper level than any aspect of Eucharistic theology which was involved." p. 33. Cf. F. Shaughnessy, *The Eucharistic Doctrine of Guitmond of Aversa* (Rome, 1939).

[29] Ironically, the definition of sacrament which has widest acceptance among 11th and 12th century writers seems to have originated with Berengarius, though he attributes it to St. Augustine. "Est enim sacramentum praescribente beato Augustino invisibilis gratiae visibilis forma." *De sacra coena*, p. 114; quoted by Sheedy *op. cit.*, p. 100. Cf. J. DeGhellinck, "Une chapitre dans l'historie de la definition des sacramentus au xii siecle," *Melanqes Mandonnet, Bibliotheque Thomiste* 14 (1930) p. 87.

[30] Lanfranc, P.L. 150, 424; Guitmond, P.L. 149, 1458; Alger, P.L. 180, 792, Cf. Sheedy, *op. cit.*, p. 115-118.

the 9th century always designated the real body of Christ in the sacrament; whereas in the 12th century it begins to refer to the Church, a use introduced by the obscure but influential "Master Simon."[31] And 2) emphasis on the sacramental sign of the Church *in rei veritatem* was superseded by attention to, what we call, the *praesentia realis;* consequently there was a slackening of interest in the sacramentality of the eucharist in favor of detailed metaphysical discussion about matter and form and causality.

Although the fourth book of Peter Lombard's *Sentences* reflects these changes, he passes on the Augustinian heritage to his successors. He clearly distinguishes a "gemina res" in the eucharist: 1) Res contenta et significata est caro Christi, quam de virgine traxit, et sanguinis, quem pro vobis fudit. 2) Res autem significata et non contenta est unitas Ecclesiae in praedestinatis, vocatis, justificatis et glorificatis." The Lombard says the former is the *sacramentum et res*, while the latter is the *res et non sacramentum*, Christ's "mystica caro."[32] The just alone receive the twofold *res*. Those who receive the eucharist unworthily have already cut themselves off from Christ and, therefore, are deprived of the grace of union with the whole Christ.[33]

The 13th century theologians, commenting on this passage of Peter Lombard, explain very carefully that "the effect of this sacrament is not the mystical body of Christ, but rather the *unity* of the mystical body."[34] There is, however, a subtle shifting of emphasis. Saint Bonaventure, for example, says it is through the sacramental grace of the eucharist that "partakers are more intimately incorporated into Christ and thus, as a consequence, more closely united to each

---

[31] *Corpus mysticum*, pp. 116-135. A. M. Roguet, commenting on the evolution of this term, says "This should make us realize, in spite or, perhaps, because of the change in meaning that has occured the close bond we should maintain between the two meanings. The bishop is the one who 'makes the Body of Christ' in both senses of the word." *In Christ in His Sacraments*, edited by A. M. Henry (Chicago, 1958) p. 39.

[32] IV Sent. Dist. viii, 7. P.L. 192, 857.

[33] IV Sent. Dist. ix, 1. P.L. 192.

[34] Albertus Mag. In IV Sent., Dist. 8. art 12, ad 3. Cf. A Piolanti, *II corpe mystico e le sue realzione con l'eucaristia in S. Alberto Magno* (Rome, 1939).

other. This he concludes is the "effectus et res huius sacramenti."[35] In a passage echoing St. John Damascene's insistence on the purity of the communicant, Saint Thomas says "whoever, therefore, receives this sacrament, by that very act shows that he is united to Christ and incorporated among his members, quod quidem fit per fidem formatam quem nullus habet cum peccato mortali."[36]

The words of these great doctors betray an almost imperceptible change in attitudes toward the eucharist. In the patristic period, as we have seen, everyone regarded the eucharist as the *sacramentum unitatis* because it united all the faithful to the bishop, to each other, and thus in the Church which is Christ. The emphasis was on corporate unity in which the Christian was united to Christ. On the other hand, the scholastics focused their attention on the union of the faithful soul with Christ and only consequently on the unity of the Head and members in the Church. A subtle change, perhaps but it developed concomitantly with the spread of the *devotio moderna*. The classic expression of this new piety," the *Imitation of Christ*, is silent about the social significance of the eucharist, it neither refers to I Cor. X 17, nor makes use of the metaphor of the grains of wheat. It seems to make comfort and solace, rather than unity, the *virtus* and *effectus* of the sacrament.[37]

VI. Late Medieval Devotions and Conciliar Decrees

Although the theologians continued to use the metaphor of the grains and the one bread, medieval devotions centered about exposition of the Blessed Sacrament in transparent ostensoria and eucharistic procession.[38] These practices grew out of a desire to prolong the elevation of the Host and the Chalice which had replaced the Communion as the focal point of the Mass.[39] And Communion itself, as the *Imitation* bears witness, was not so much a sacramental manifestation of corporate unity with Christ as it was of a possessive,

---

[35] IV Sent., dist. 8, art. 2, qu. 1 ad 5-6. Cf. S. Simonis O.F.M., "De causalitate eucharistiae in corpus mysticum doctrina S. Bonaventurae," *Antonianum* 8 (1933) 193-228; *praesertim* pp. 209 et seq.

[36] III, q. 80, a. 4, c.

[37] Book IV *passim; praesertim*, c. 10.

[38] P. Pourrat, *Christian Spirituality In the Middle Ages* (Westminister, Md., 1953) Vol. II, pp. 322-323.

[39] Jungmann, *op. cit.*, I, p. 113.

private, physical union with Him. Whereas Saint Augustine preached daily Communion, the Fourth Lateran Council had found it necessary to urge it be received yearly.

Church synods and councils from the time of Berengarin controversy onwards made occasional mention of the eucharist in their decrees. Directed as they were, against specific errors, these pronouncements, even when patched together, give but a two demensional sketch of eucharistic theology.[40] The Fourth Lateran, for example, merely uses the phrase 'mysterium unitatis" (D. 430) without explanation or emphasis. The Council of Florence issued its famous *Decretum pro Armenis* in which the mingling of water and wine is once more a question:

> The chalice of the Lord must, according to the precept of the canons, be offered mixed with wine and water because we see that in water the people are understood, and the blood of Christ is shown in the wine. Therefore, when wine and water are mixed in the chalice, the people are made one with Christ, and the multitude of the faithful is joined and connected with Him in whom they believe (D. 698).

The wording was borrowed from a 4th century decree of Pope Julius. In the intervening thousand years, however, the words had become mere cliches for, as Hugo Lang has pointed out, the *Decretum pro Armenis* does not consider the eucharist one of the "social" sacraments. In ennumerating the seven sacraments the Decree says two of them, orders and matrimony, are orderd "ad totius Ecclesiae regimem mutiplicationemque." The other five are ordered, according to the Decree, "ad spiritualem uniuscuiusque hominis *in seipso* perfectionem."[41]

Although the Council of Trent gave a more complete statement of eucharistic theology than any of the medieval councils, it was the

---

[40] The most important, according to E. Grescher in *Lexikon für Theologie und Kirche s.v.* "Eucharistie" are: Berengarius" oath before the Roman synod of 1079 (D. 355); the anti-Waldensian statement drawn up by Innocent III (D. 424); the declaration of IV Lateran against the Albigensians in 1215 (D. 430); the profession of faith made by Michael Paleogolus at II Lyons in 1274 (D. 465); the decrees of Constance condemning the errors of Wyclif and Huss (D. 581, 626, 666ff); the *Decretum pro Armenis* drawn up at Florence in 1439 (D. 698).

[41] D. 695. Lang in *Pro mundi vita*, pp. 47-48.

spirit of the *Decretum pro Armenis,* via the Roman Catechism, which permeated pastoral theology until our own day. In describing the Institution of the Holy Eucharist, Trent says Christ wanted it to be

> "... a pledge of our future glory and our everlasting happiness; and thus be a symbol of that one *body* of which He is the *head;* and to which He wishes us to be united as members, by the closest bonds of faith, hope, and charity, that we might all speak the same thing and that there be no schisms among us (I Cor. 1, 10).[42]

Trent's statement has the ring of patristic teaching, but it had little impact on catechetics. The self-imposed needs of practical apologetics centered on the metaphysics of transubstantiation and causality. Mystery was sacrificed to popular explanations. The *Imitation Christi* usurped the place of the *Missale Romanum* in the hands of the faithful. The *sacramentum unitatis* was, at best, partially understood; and the *Corpus mysticum* appeared as little more than an aggregate of individuals.

Conclusion

Although this survey of eucharistic ecclesiology covers more than a thousand years, its conclusion can be summarized in a simple equation: the greater the emphasis on the corporate significance of the eucharist, the greater the emphasis on the church unity. To confirm this axiom it is necessary only to look at today's renewed attention to the eucharist as the bond of unity. It corresponds to the vital thrust, within and without the Roman obedience, to heal schism and separation.

---

[42] D. 875.

SOCIAL ASPECT OF THE EUCHARIST:
AID TO UNITY

AIDAN MULLANEY, T.O.R.

Why should Franciscans be concerned with the social significance
of the Eucharist as an aid to unity in Christ's Church? It seems the
best possible answer to this question should be another question:
"Why not?" Saint Francis, we know, was enflamed with a love for
his fellow-men because he saw in them the image of the Crucified.
He loved each and every human being because he saw in them a
relationship with Christ, he saw them as members of the Body of
Christ. The purpose that Francis had in founding his three Orders
was a social purpose as well as an individual one. The Voice from
the Crucifix in the Chapel of San Damiano did not say: "Francis,
come save your soul," but rather, "Francis, go build up my Church
for you can see that it is falling into ruin." Saint Francis built
his entire system of spirituality around the Eucharistic Sacrifice
and the Divine Office. "The dominant position of all that is implied
in the devotion to the humanity of Christ in Franciscan spirituality
is reflected in the importance given the sacrament of the Altar as
a sure instrument for advancement in perfection."[1] And in the
Eucharist Francis beheld the primary and indispensable source of
that relationship—that social significance that bond together the
members of the Body of Christ.

It is the purpose of this paper to report to you some aspects of
the current theological thinking in the Church with regard to this
social significance of the Eucharist. This report will endeavor to
show that a great realization of this social significance of the Eucharist is an aid to unity in the Mystical Body of Christ, the Church.
Not only is this true, it shall be shown, amongst the members of
the Church in fact, but also amongst those Christians separated from

---

[1] Aidan Carr, O.F.M. Conv., *Franciscan Educational Conference*, v. 29,
1948, p. 15.

actual membership in the Church of Christ, yet still possessing the equivalent of the three-fold bond of membership in the minimal degree. It is hoped that this report will promote discussion here on the possible ways we as sons of Francis can promote an ever greater realization of this social aspect of the Eucharist as an aid to the greater unity of charity in the Church and the reunion of all Christians.

History gives abundant evidence that the Christians of the early Church possessed a sense of solidarity—a social consciousness which today's members seek to make more perfectly their own.[2] How did it come about that this social aspect became somewhat dimmed, somewhat lost to view with the passage of time?

Some authors have seen the decline in charity in the Church as beginning with the progress in the external manifestations of the Eucharistic cult that arose in the late Middle Ages: the triumphal processions of Corpus Christi, the prolonged expositions of the Blessed Sacrament, the profusion of flowers, flags and lights: in short, an excessive concentration on the external pomp and circumstance that took away attention from that interior Eucharistic piety that was the hallmark of the early Christians.[3]

In the Eucharistic life of the Church through the ages the attention of members of the Church has been attracted to this or to that aspect of the fecund treasure of the mysteries of Faith. There is always the danger, certainly, that one aspect of the Eucharistic life may be developed at the expense of due and harmonious proportion of these aspects.

The sixteenth century brought into the life of the Mystical Body of Christ the second great defection. This break occurred within the family, so to speak, of the Western Patriarchate. From this

---

[2] cf. Phillip Weller, "The Banquet of the Sacrifice," *North American Liturgical Week, 1947*, The Liturgical Conference, Boston, Mass., 1948, p. 89: "In our day we have so little regard for fellowship in the Eucharist, because the idea of fellowship has so largely disappeared in ordinary human experience."

[3] cf. A Gratieux, "L'Aspect Sociale de L'Eucharist," *La Vie Spirituel*, v. 94 (May, 1956) p. 454, and Fr. Louis Bouyer in his work *Liturgical Piety*, (University of Notre Dame Press, 1954) where he says: "...the medieval period prepared for the abandonment of the liturgy by Protestantism." (p. 15).

sad event onward the attention of the Catholic theologians was centered in the expression of the loyalty of the members of the Mystical Body of Christ to that divine authority given by Christ to enable His Church to endure throughout all ages.[4] In other words, the theologians of the Church, in general, began to think of the Church more as an organization than an organism; more in terms of her external union than in terms of that internal communion common to the life of each member of the Mystical Body of Christ. This, of course, was an understandable reaction to the Protestant revolt against that divinely given authority.

The growing realization of the social significance of the Eucharist, characteristic of our time, has always been closely associated with the revival of interest in the proper celebration of the Liturgy. The remote modern beginnings of this current liturgical revival are to be found in the refoundation of the Benedictine Abbey of Solesmes in 1832 by Dom Prosper Gueranger whose pioneer work laid the foundations for the Liturgical renewal in our own century. In this liturgical renewal three phases may be noted: first, the scholarly investigations that were made into the nature, history, social significance and authority of the Christian liturgy. The second phase was the transmitting of the results of these investigations to the clergy and lay leaders of the Church. The final phase involved the practical application of the true liturgical spirit to the life of the faithful.[5]

Modern liturgical history records that Pope Saint Pius X inaugurated the first phase by the publication of his Motu Proprio on Sacred Music, November 22, 1903. This document specifically directed that Gregorian chant, as restored by the Benedictines of Solesmes, was to become the norm for sacred music in the Church and the frequent reception of Holy Communion was encouraged as a most fruitful means of participation in the sacrifice of the Mass.

A decisive turning point for the modern liturgical movement[6] marks the beginning of the second phase at the Catholic Congress of Malines in 1909. At this Congress Dom Lambert Beauduin, monk of the Abbey of Mont César, was inspired by the guiding principles outlined by St. Pope Pius X in the Motu Proprio of 1903, and

---

[4] cf. Fr. William Busch, "The Sacrifice-Banquet," *Worship*, 3:13, p. 407.
[5] cf. Bouyer, *op. cit.*, p. 58.
[6] ibid.

proposed a principle that was to become a central principle of the modern liturgical movement by defining the liturgy as "the traditional and collective glorification of God, bringing before Him the whole individual man in the whole Christian community."[7]

In historical sequence there followed a series of liturgical firsts: the First Liturgical Week was held at Mont César in August of 1911 under the patronage of Cardinal Mercier and the first international Liturgical Congress took place at Antwerp in 1930.

In Germany, the Benedictines of the Abbey of Maria Laach, under the leadership of Abbot Idlefons Herwegen (-1946), began to publish the first liturgical periodicals. *Ecclesia Orans* made its appearance about 1918 and was soon followed by two scholarly reviews, the *Liturgiegeschtliche Quellen und Forschungen* and the *Jahrbuch für Liturgiewissenschaft* whose editor was the famous Dom Odo Casel.

In the United States the Benedictines of St. John's Abbey in Collegeville, Minnesota, led the way in 1925 with the liturgical review *Oratre Fratres,* which since 1951 is known as *Worship.* The quarterly periodical of the Liturgical Arts Society, *Liturgical Arts,* made its appearance simultaneously with the foundation of the society in 1931. From 1940 on the North American Liturgical Week became an annual gathering of liturgical scholars.

This brief history could not end without mention of the noted Centre de Pastorale Liturgique, established in France in 1943 by the Benedictines, the Dominicans and the Jesuits. This center produces the review *La Maison-Dieu,* which is devoted to all phases of the liturgical apostolate and *L'Art Sacre* a bi-monthly dedicated to liturgical art.

It is chiefly from these liturgical centers and their various publications that the following exposition of the social significance of the Eucharist as an aid to unity is derived.

The Eucharistic Sacrifice: Its Social Significance

Theologically speaking, the Holy Eucharist reduces Itself to three aspects: the Sacrifice, the Sacrament and the Real Presence. To these three aspects correspond the external and liturgical acts of Mass, Holy Communion and the Cult of the Eucharist; or more simply, the Altar

---

[7] ibid.

of Sacrifice, the Table of the Lord, and the Tabernacle of His Presence.

The redemptive work of the God-man on Calvary's height not only atoned for the sin of man, but effected a reconciliation between God and all the human race. Christ the Priest and Victim included in Himself all human kind and in Him and in His Sacrifice on Calvary all humanity participates, having regained through Baptism that union with the Creator which was once lost by the first Adam. "Through the Sacerdotal ministry of Christ in the Mass, the whole Church unites herself intimately and efficaciously, both as offerer and victim, with Christ's sacrifice of adoration, thanksgiving, petition and propitiation."[8] Such participation brings about a conformity on the part of the participants in the Sacrifice that is akin to the interior Sacrifice of Christ the Priest.

Not only the hierarchical ministers of the Eucharistic Sacrifice, but all the faithful are signed with the royal priesthood[9] and have their real part in the Eucharistic Sacrifice that is offered at the altar. This conformity to the interior sacrifice of Christ and this participation in the Sacrifice is realized in a diverse manner according to the measure of the character impressed on the soul in Baptism, Confirmation and in the sacrament of Holy Orders.[10]

> The sacerdotal ministry of the Church makes the sacrificial act of Christ become in a fitting manner the sacrificial act of the Church, while, surrounding the Consecration, and especially the Canon, she explains before the eyes of the people, to obtain their active participation, the sacrificial acts of Christ, namely, adoration (including praise and wonder), thanksgiving (especially recalling the economy of salvation), petition and propitiation (for the living and the dead). Therefore, when the faithful, both internally and externally, as is obvious, in the Mass unite themselves with Christ, as He acts and speaks through the ministry of the priest, in adoration, thanksgiving, petition and satisfaction, they are truly sacrificing in Christ.[11]

The Eucharistic Sacrifice, therefore, is not the offering of our-

---

[8] H. Schmidt, S.J., "The Structure of the Mass," *Studies in Pastoral Liturgy*, Dom Placid Murray, O.S.B., ed. Furrow Trust, 1961.

[9] 1 Peter 1:29.

[10] cf. Archbishop Pietro Parente, in *Eucharistia*, Desclee & Ci., Roma, 1957, p. 626; and Fr. Charles Miller, C.M., "Lay Participation in the Mass: Theological Basis," *Worship*, 33:5 (April, 1959).

[11] H. Schmidt, S.J., *op. cit.*, p. 28.

selves as individuals. The Eucharistic Sacrifice is the offering of the entire Body of Christ. "It is the supernatural act that Christ, the priests, and the faithful perform together."[12] It is the sacrificial act of the Mystical Body of Christ, the Church; Head and members. As a Sacrifice, therefore, the Eucharist signifies and causes the unity of the Mystical Body. This thought has perhaps never been more cogently expressed than by Pope Pius XII in *Mediator Dei*:

> Through the Eucharistic Sacrifice Christ our Lord wished to give special evidence to the faithful of our union among ourselves and with our divine Head, marvelous as it is beyond all praise. For here the sacred ministers act in the person not only of our Saviour but of the whole Mystical Body and of every one of the faithful in this act of sacrifice through the hands of the priest, whose word alone has brought the Immaculate Lamb to be present on the altar, the faithful themselves with one desire and one prayer offer it to the Eternal Father,—the most acceptable victim of praise and propitiation for the Church's universal needs. And just as the divine Redeemer dying on the Cross offered Himself as Head of the whole human race to the Eternal Father, so "in this pure oblation" He offers not only Himself as Head of the Church to the heavenly Father, but in Himself His mystical members as well. He embraces them all, even the weak and ailing ones, in the tenderest love of His Heart.[13]

It is *socially significant* that, in this offering of the Holy Sacrifice, the offering that is made be as complete as possible. This striving for union, basic to the very idea of sacrifice, is the means by which the Eucharist produces that which It signifies. For this union, present and operating in the Sacrificing Act of the Mystical Body, is the one sure cure for division and discrimination, for prejudice, enmity or any exclusiveness amongst the members of that Mystical Body. The Eucharist as a Sacrifice is an aid to unity.

The Eucharist as Sacrament: Social Significance

It is not only as a sacrifice that the Eucharist signifies and effects the unity of the Mystical Body. "By the sacerdotal ministry of Christ

---

[12] Fr. Emilio Sauras, O.P., "The Christian Community and the Eucharist," *Theology Digest*, Spring, 1961, p. 97.

[13] Pope Pius XII, *Mediator Dei*, (NCWC trans.) par. 93.

in the Mass, God accepts the Sacrifice of Christ, Head and members, and communicates Himself to those who offer it."[14] While Holy Communion pertains to the integrity of the Eucharistic Sacrifice, this partaking is obligatory only for the priest who says the Mass.[15] It is something earnestly recommended to the faithful.

The Eucharist as Sacrifice is offered in the context of a social banquet. The social significance of the Eucharist as a sacrament is had in this that it is the sign of and the cause of that complete union of mind and heart that brings about the union of all the members of Christ in the true and universal Church.[16]

A. *Sign of Supernatural Charity*

> The social and fraternal union in charity, suggested by a meal is part of the symbolism of the sacrament. Even when partaken alone the Eucharist does not merely nourish but it radiates that good will in Christ which deepens fraternal bonds of Christian understanding, love and peace—supernatural effects analogous to the social fruits of a meal among friends.[17]

The members of Christ, whatever may be their external differences in the social or economic order, in the communion of the Eucharist receive a supreme lesson in charity: "Every time the Body of the Lord is eaten, he who eats It bears witness visibly, concretely, and publicly pledges more emphatically than by oath, his love and loyalty unto death for his God and for his brethren."[18]

The realization that the partaking of the Body and Blood of the Lord by the members of the Mystical Body is a sign—that is, that this partaking proclaims their identity with the Lord and with each of His members prompts the following question: Can hatreds and enmities possibly exist, in all honesty, amongst those who have born witness by this sign? The unavoidable answer, of course, is

---

[14] H. Schmidt, S.J., *op. cit.*, 26.

[15] Pope Pius XII, *Mediator Dei*, par. 115.

[16] cf. Bernard Leeming, S.J., *Principles of Sacramental Theology*, Newman, Westminster, Md., 1956, p. 376.

[17] Fr. David Regan, S.S.Sp., "Worship Which is Whole," *The Irish Ecclesiastical Record*, 97:2 (Feb. 1962), p. 76.

[18] Maur Burbach, O.S.B., "The Eucharist as the Sacrament of Unity," *The Liturgy and Unity in Christ. North American Liturgical Week, 1960* Washington, D.C., p. 46.

that "in all honesty" one member cannot be loved and the other
despised:

> We cannot serve Him in those who have influences and neglect
> Him in those who are poor or a burden to us. We cannot love
> Him in the white man and be indifferent to His needs in the
> colored person. We cannot reverence Him in our superiors and
> take Him for granted in our equals or despise Him in subjects
> or employees.[19]

B. *Cause of Supernatural Charity*

The Eucharist as Sacrament, represents and signifies, and at the
same time It produces that which It represents and signifies.[20] The
Eucharist is the cause of the unity of the Church. It is the efficient,
final and exemplary cause of that permanent social relationship that
must exist among the members of the Mystical Body of Christ. The
Seraphic Doctor points out the result of the Eucharist on the Mystical Body of Christ:

> What especially inflames us to mutual love, what most ef-
> fectively unites the members is unity with the Head, from
> which through the diffusive, unifying, transforming power of
> love—mutual affection flows to us.[21]

This union with Christ necessarily, then, carries with it union among
ourselves in accordance with the axiom that two things which are
mutually united to a Third are through It united with each other.
It is the spirit of charity, which according to St. Thomas, is the certain participation of the Holy Spirit[22] and which, properly understood, is the cause of the solidarity of the Church. Pope Leo XIII
went so far as to call the Eucharist, properly understood, the soul
of the Church:

> This sacrament is, as it were, the soul of the Church and to

---

[19] Mother M. Jerome, O.S.B., "We Eat Together," *North American
Liturgical Week, 1947*, The Liturgical Conference, Boston, Mass., 1948,
p. 96.

[20] cf. St. Thomas, IV Sent. d. 45, q. 2, a. 3, sol. 1 in c.: "Ad caritatem
autem sacramentum Eucharistiae praecipue pertinet, cum sit sacramentum ecclesiasticae unionis ... Unde Eucharistia est quasi quaedam
caritatis origo seu vinculum."

[21] St. Bonaventure, *Breviloquium*, VI, ix, 3.

[22] St. Thomas, II-II, q. 23, a. 3, ad 3.

It the grace of the priesthood is ordered and directed in all its fullness and in each of its successive grades.[23]

This mutual charity of the members of the Mystical Body should, in the Pontiff's words, be directed "in each of its successive grades." "This mutual interdependence ... is not simply a means of greater order, but a mode of development in depth in the life which is proper to the Mystical Body."[24]

Thus the Eucharist is the final cause, for each member of the body of Christ is nourished, not only that it may become a more perfect member in that Mystical Body, but that this very nourishing, according to the will of the God-man, increases in that member, authentic fraternal charity:

> In the Holy Eucharist the faithful are nourished and grow strong at the same table, and in a divine and ineffable way are brought into union with each other and with the divine Head of the whole Body.[25]

The Eucharist is the exemplary cause of this social relationship established amongst the members and the divine Head. In the God-man there is the most profound union between the human and the Divine Nature in the Person of the Word. The Eucharist as a Sacrament has for this definitive purpose union with God in creature measure akin to the union that is in Christ. In us, however, this union can be only inchoative in the present life, to be perfected in the next.[26] And yet the beginnings of this union must be made visible in the Church today if union amongst the actual members of the Mystical Body is to be made more perfect and if those Christians, who, through no fault of their own, are not actual members are to be drawn to the fullness of the life of the Mystical Body. "Verba docent, exempla trahunt."[27]

---

[23] Pope Leo XIII, *Great Encyclical Letters of Leo XIII*, N.Y., 1903, p. 531.

[24] R. W. Gleason, S.J., *To Live is Christ*, Sheed & Ward, N.Y., 1960, p. 20.

[25] Pope Pius XII, Mystici Corporis (NCWC trans.), par. 20.

[26] cf. Parente, *op. cit.*, p. 626.

[27] cf. Murray, *op. cit.*, 192.

Eucharistic Cult: Social Significance

The late Pope Pius XII in *Mediator Dei* expressly reprobated those who would abolish "newer" forms of Eucharistic devotion in order to return to the ancient, and possible "more pure" liturgical practices of Patristic times. On the contrary, the same Holy Father approves and recommends daily visits to the Tabernacle, Benediction of the Blessed Sacrament, solemn processions, especially at the time of Eucharistic Congresses:

> The Church not merely approves of these pious practices which in the course of centuries have spread everywhere throughout the world, but makes them her own, as it were, and by her authority commends them. They spring from the inspiration of the Liturgy. ... and are undoubtedly of the very greatest assistance in living the life of the Liturgy.[28]

The social significance of the Eucharist as Sacrifice, Sacrament, and Real Presence have received perhaps the most harmonious expression during our modern Eucharistic Congresses. Beginning in the year 1881 International Eucharistic Congresses have been held regularly in the various nations of Christendom. National Eucharistic Congresses are too numerous to mention. This coming together of the clergy and the laity of one nation, or indeed of all the nations of the earth, does not have for its purpose the show of ecclesiastical power. Nor is the Eucharistic Congress a mere external manifestation of faith. More and more the Eucharistic Congress is becoming understood as a gathering of the members of the Msytical Body to celebrate the Eucharist as a Sacrifice, to receive It as a Sacrament and to admire It as Emmanuel, God with us. Father Jungmann, S.J., has interpreted the International Eucharistic Congress as a "Statio Orbis" after the manner of the Roman Stational celebration of the Eucharist by the Bishop of Rome and his clergy and people.[29] Indeed since 1912 the Holy Father has sent to the International Congresses a Legate to act in his name. This concept of the Eucharistic Congress as the "Statio Orbis" was adopted by the German Bishops at their annual meeting at Fulda in 1959.[30]

---

[28] Pope Pius XII, *Mediator Dei*, par. 133.

[29] Josef A. Jungmann, S.J., "The Eucharist and Pastoral Practice," *Worship*, Jan. 1961, p. 377.

[30] cf. Collective pastoral letter of the German Bishops, dated September

The Social Significance of the Eucharist
Amongst Separated Christians

The Eucharist as a Sacrament is a sign and a cause of that complete union of mind and heart that effects the union of all the members of Christ in the true and universal Church. Where unity of mind is lacking, even though there may be the minimal degree of good will that effects a certain kind of relationship to the Mystical Body, there is lacking that complete unity which the Eucharist symbolizes and causes. "Those who are disunited in faith cannot rightly, therefore, communicate at the same altar."[31] In spite of this truth, perhaps because of it, our own generation has witnessed a growing interest, a sincere earnestness, a nostalgic yearning for the

---

30, 1959, translation in the *Grail Review*, first quarter, 1960. "The Eucharistic World Congress is meant to be a Statio orbis, i.e., a meeting, a gathering of Catholics coming from all parts of the globe in order to do the most essential thing on earth: to celebrate the holy Eucharist, to thank our Father in heaven through the Memorial of the sacrifice of His Son, our Redeemer. In Rome it used to be the custom on ordinary Sundays and on minor holy days to offer the holy Sacrifice in different churches. On certain big feast days, however, bishops, priests and faithful gathered around the Holy Father for the Statio Orbis, the communal celebration of the holy Sacrifice by the whole city.

Today the word of the prophet Malachy has been fulfilled: the holy Sacrifice is being celebrated over the whole earth, from the rising of the sun to its going down. Thus a Eucharistic World Congress becomes a Statio Orbis ... It will become for us one great universal Corpus Christi day.

We come together in order to pray with Christ, in the unity of faith and of love. We do not want a religious mass manifestation. As Christians we have become distrustful of mass manifestations, because we know how soon they can become subject to demonical powers.

In the same way, the great World Corpus Christi Day 1960 will not be a demonstration. It is not meant to be a manifestation of ecclesiastical power. For this, so we hope, the Congress will be too simple and too spiritual. Neither is it meant to be only a public confession of our faith. It is meant to be an act of religion, the great Thanksgiving, in which we "proclaim the death of the Lord until He comes." Thus a Congress will not be directed against anybody, neither against a political adversary nor against our fellow men with religious convictions different from our own. It will be a meeting of prayer and sacrifice for all, for the life of the world."

[31] cf. Leeming, *op. cit.*, p. 376.

one altar of Christ and for His one Church amongst those Christians
not in communion with the See of Peter.

For St. Thomas the formal cause of schism is the lack of charity.[32]
Whatever the scholars may determine led to a loss of the true
appreciation of the Mass in the late Middle Ages, most assuredly the
loss of the Eucharist amongst the first Protestants led to the loss
of the sense of the unity of the Church of Christ.

> The so-called reformers imagined that a return to the primitive
> liturgy meant taking the low Mass as the norm, suppressing
> everything in the Canon except the actual words of institution
> of the Eucharist; enlarging upon the penitential features of
> the Low Mass, such as the Confiteor, and in general, not only
> centering everything on the memory of the Passion, but reducing
> everything to it.[33]

Fortunately for the ecumenical hopes of Christendom, mutual
recriminations are no longer the order of the day. Pope John XXIII,
after this announcement of the coming Ecumenical Council, noted
that recriminations and quarrels have led us further and further
apart. New beginnings are being made both in and outside the
Church:

> Protestant as well as Catholic scholars have pointed out the
> deep theological roots of the reformer's antagonism to the Mass.
> The difference of insight into the meaning of the Eucharist
> takes us ... to the heart of the Reformation conflict.[34]

Encouraging signs are to be noted amongst some Anglican and
Lutheran theologians who do not consider themselves at all bound
to the radical principles of the Protestant revolt. Although these
signs *are* encouraging, it would be a mistake to think that a surging
tide is about to sweep the Anglicans and the Lutherans into that
unity that Christ wills for His Church. In fact, outside the Anglican
and Lutheran persuasions there are only scattered indications of an
awakening to the social aspect of the Eucharist.

This section of the paper will attempt to show some of the signs

---

[32] II-II, q. 39, a. 1: "Peccatum schismatis proprie est speciale peccatum ex eo quod intendit se ab unitate separare quam caritas facit.
Schisma autem per se opponitur unitati ecclesiasticae caritatis."

[33] Louis Bouyer, *op. cit.*, p. 42.

[34] Francis Clark, S.J., *op. cit.*, p. 510.

of a growing realization amongst the separated Christians that "the highest function of Christ's priestly Church is to perform His Eucharistic Sacrifice."[35]

a. *Anglican Interest in the Social Aspect of the Eucharist*

In the Anglican community there exists an active leaven—an inherent Catholic tendency that is at work in the different parts of the Anglican system—"hardly perceptible or still weak in some and more active in others: more intense in certain groups, in certain churches, and seminaries, and most especially in the number of monasteries and convents."[36]

The beginnings of Anglican liturgical interest may be discerned in the nineteenth century which saw the rise of Romanticism and the Oxford movement in England. Keble, Pusey, Newman, Church and others searched into the sources of Christian tradition and rediscovered the sacramental heritage of the Church. The second phase of the Anglican liturgical revival corresponds with the period of the revision of the *Book of Common Praper* from 1890 until 1930. The third Anglican phase, the extension of the liturgical interest to the educational and pastoral level has produced some outstanding liturgists.[37]

In recent years since the second world war Anglican theologians, priding themselves in the "glorious comprehensiveness" of the Anglican system, have tried to work out a statement about the Eucharist which would be acceptable to the "Catholic" and Protestant elements of their body. The High Churchmen have, on the one hand, adhered to the Catholic doctrine that the Eucharist is a sacrifice. As understood by one eminent Anglican theologican, the Eucharist is the eternal act of the sacrifice of Christ:

There is an inescapable continuity, even an identity, between

---

[35] *ibid.*, p. 523.

[36] Charles Bouyer, S.J., "The Movement Within Anglicanism Towards Rome," *Unitas*, XIII, 1 (Spring, 1961), p. 11.

[37] During this epoch, the extension of scholarship of the liturgical revival to the pastoral and educational life of the Anglican body, such scholars as A. G. Herbert, Gregory Dix *(The Shape of the Liturgy)*, (*produced such) etc., cf. "The History of the Liturgical Renewal" by Massey Hamilton Shepherd in the *Liturgical Renewal of the Church*, (Oxford University Press, N.Y., 1960), p. 48.

Calvary and the Church, and the Christians within the Church; and the Eucharist is the vessel and the means of that identity, the act which establishes the bridge between Eternity and Time, and makes "identity" the right word.[38]

Of interest, too, is the recently formulated ritual for the Church of South India which strongly affirms the sacrificial nature of the Mass as "the oblation of the Body and Blood of Jesus Christ our Lord."[39] The Standing Liturgical Commission of the Protestant Episcopal Church in the United States recently commented: "Cranmer would have excommunicated them."[40]

On the other hand, the Protestant element of Anglicanism is willing to admit that the Eucharist may be understood as a sacrifice, but in a certain sense—a sacrifice of praise, not the sacrifice of Christ on Calvary.

It is impossible to pretend that these two views are ultimately reconcilable as different emphasis within a common understanding. They do depend on very deep differences in belief as to the nature of God and of His action in the world. There is, therefore, a real tension in the Anglican Communion, and nothing is to be gained by hiding it or pretending that it does not exist.[41]

A Catholic theologian (Father Francis Clark, S.J.) remarks that the High Anglicans have the satisfaction of seeing their fellow churchmen make increasing use of the language of Eucharistic sacrifice, but they are not at all sure that they are talking about the same thing. "The roots of the disagreement are revealed in the different answers still given to the question: Who or what is offered in the Eucharistic sacrifice? The answer of Catholic theology is, first and above all, Christ Himself."[42] The Low Church answer is that we ourselves are offered. Within Anglicanism today there is a new

---

[38] *Bishop Stephen Fielding Bayne, *The Eucharist and the Church*, p. 17.

[39] *Joseph W. Starmann, "The Anglican Liturgical Revival," *Worship*, 29:7 (July, 1955), p. 381.

[40] *ibid.*

[41] *Bishop Stephen Neill, "The Holy Communion in the Anglican Church," in *The Holy Communion*, ed. by H. Martin, London, 1947, pp. 65-66.

[42] Francis Clark, S.J., *op. cit.*, p. 516.

earnestness of search, an openness of mind concerning the sacrificial character of the Eucharist. The same Catholic theologian (Father Clark) wonders in print whether or not the theological storm of the sixteenth century may not be resolved:

> The solution to the problem of the Eucharistic sacrifice is sought in the doctrine of the mystical body of Christ. (by some Anglican theologians). To say that we are offered, as the Evangelicals are prepared to say, and that Christ is offered, as Catholics insist, needs involve no contradiction, since what is offered is both Christ and Christians, who are united by virtue of the mystical union that exists between the Head and the members of the Church.... Does (this argument) offer at long last a solution which was beyond the grasp of the sixteenth century theologians? Is it the synthesis that transcends the Catholic thesis and the Protestant antithesis? Already the new approach has led some Evangelicals to abandon their traditional reluctance to speak of any offering of Christ in the Eucharist.[43]

However much the Anglican theologians may be split on the interpretation of sacrifice, they leave no doubt as to their position on Transubstantiation. For the Anglicans, Christ is present in the sacrament as a whole rather than in the elements:

> We have to do ... not with a transubstantiation of physical *substance* into hyperphysical *substance*, but with the transubstantiation of an *event*, (namely, the breaking of bread) into another *event* (namely, the event of Golgotha.)[44]

b. *The Lutherans and the Eucharist*

In Germany in the last few years Lutheran theologians have been holding discussions on the nature of the Eucharist.[45] These discus-

---

[43] *ibid.*

[44] *Rudolf Otto, "The Lord's Supper as a Numinous Fact," in *Religious Essays*, Oxford University Press, 1937, p. 52.

[45] Recent Lutheran interest in the Eucharistic owes its origin to the Lutheran Liturgical Revival movement of the last century. See especially William Loehe, *Agende für christliche Gemeinde*, 1844; Rudolf Otto, *Idea of the Holy*, and Archbishop Yngve Brilioth, *Eucharistic Faith and Practice, Evangelical and Practice, Evangelical and Catholic*, (translated by A. G. Herbert, S.P.C.K., London, 1930). Fr. Louis Bouyer follows Brilioth in his treatment of the historical analysis of the history of the Eucharist. For the recent history of Lutheran interest in the Eucharist

270   THE HOLY EUCHARIST AND CHRISTIAN UNITY

sions have been based on the "Arnoldshain Theses" which were first
published in 1957 by the Lutheran Commission on the Last Supper,
established by the association of Evangelical Churches in Germany.
In short, these theses insist on the reality of the real presence of
Christ in the Eucharist. The following is representative of orthodox
Lutheran position:

> In the sacrament of the Eucharist we believe, we teach and we
> confess a true, real and substantial presence, exhibition, man-
> ducation and drinking of the body and blood of Christ.[46]

While Lutheran theologians are, for the most part, willing to
affirm their belief in the real presence, their doctrine on eucharistic
sacrifice remains a delicate point for future theological exposition.

c. Evangelicals and the Eucharist

In the Methodist Church today many clergymen are affirming the
historic tie of Methodism with the Church of England in order to
promote a liturgical revival that is closely related and extensively
dependent on the Anglican *Book of Common Prayer*.[47]

Baptist theologian Neville Clark, affirms that the Last Supper and
thus the eucharist is through and through sacrificial in implication
and significance:

> ... if the Last Supper, cross and eucharist are to be linked
> together by grounding the one sacrifice at the heart of each
> and all, there must be established the reality not only of the
> enduring presence and action of the one Christ throughout,
> but also the further and common factor of the one body ...
> Christians are not individuals in a society, not members of
> the body or association which serves and worships Christ, but
> members, joints, ligaments, organs in the body of Christ.[48]

Clark's theological terminology, it appears, is strongly dependent
on Anglican Liturgist Dix.

---

see Fr. George Tavard, "The Eucharist in Protestantism," *Worship*, 35:3
(February, 1962).

[46] cf. Tavard, *op. cit.*, p. 184 of Johan Gerhard (17th century representative exponent of Lutheran orthodoxy, used by Max Lackmann in
Credo Ecclesiam Catholicam, Graz, 1960).

[47] Methodists William Sloan and R. P. Marshall founded the Order
of St. Luke in 1946. Their rule stresses that the Eucharist is the sacrament of redemption by Christ's death.

Congregationalist minister, Elmer S. Freeman, has written a work advocating in the eucharist an evangelical sense of sacrifice "in that the people in the sacrament offer to God material gifts, spiritual in meaning, and offer also themselves in His service."[49] The same minister rejects the doctrines of a special priesthood, transubstantiation, a sacrificial renewal of Calvary, and the real presence as understood by Catholics: "in the celebration of the Lord's Last supper there may be—indeed ought to be—to the worshipper, conditioned only by the degree of his faith and his spirit of devotion, a "real presence" of the Lord in the sacrament as a whole. . . ."[50]

Calvinist Churches in the United States and Europe have been engaged in a liturgical revival and have consequently been making an effort to recover notions on the Eucharist.

> Under carefully guarded Calvinist formulas, one may discern an understanding of the Eucharist which is open to a theology of the sacrifice of Christ, and although it explicitly rejects transubstantiation, it is prepared to accept a "real spiritual" presence in the sacrament.[51]

The Eucharist is

> the commemoration of Christ's offering of Himself upon the cross once for all, and an oblation of all possible praise to God for the same; and the reception and feeding upon Christ crucified, His Body and Blood, followed by thanksgiving . . . The presence of Christ is not physical but spiritual, that is to say, it is by the agency of the Holy Spirit . . . the Body and Blood are really present because spirituality is present.[52]

A representative of the French-Calvinist monastery at Taize-les-Cluny has published a recent work, although not treating of a Calvinistic "real spiritual" presence, does affirm that the eucharist is for him the efficient sign:

48 *Nevile Clark, *An Approach to the Theology of the Sacraments* Allenson Inc., Chicago, 1956; and *Call to Worship*, SMC, 1960.

49 Elmer S. Freeman, *The Lord's Supper in Protestantism*, Macmillan Co., N.Y., 1945, p. 87.

50 *ibid.*, p. 79.

51 Fr. G. Tavard, "The Eucharist in Protestantism," *Worship*, 35:3, p. 187.

52 H. J. Wotherspoon and J. M. Kirkpatrick, *Manual of Church Doctrine According to the Church of Scotland*, Oxford, 1960, pp. 39, 44.

...of the real presence of the body and blood of Christ. ...the memorial of the Lord, the representation, the presentation of the unique and perfect sacrifice of Christ in thanksgiving and intercession, the proclamation of the death of the Lord until He come...The Eucharist is a sacrifice, insofar as it is the presence of the sacrifice of the Cross, and its liturgical *presentation* to the Father,—the Church's *participation* in the Son's intercession,—*the oblation* of the Church by herself in union with the sacrifice of Christ.[53]

At the conclusion of his work the same author (Thurian) states that the Catholic doctrine of transubstantiation intends to be a "protection of the truth of the real presence. It was not a matter of explaining the mystery, but of categorically asserting the reality of the presence of Christ."[54]

Conclusion

Amongst some Protestant theologians, it is clear, there is a growing interest in the doctrine of the Eucharist as a sacrifice. It does seem that it is the responsibility of these sincere Protestant theologians to develop the fullness of their rediscoveries. For example, the whole efficacy of the true Eucharistic Sacrifice depends on the fact that it is Christ Himself who is the Principle Priest of the Mass. These Protestant theologians have not wrestled with the problem of the authority of the instrumental cause of the Eucharistic Sacrifice, the president of the Christian *synaxis*. Now the Protestants have two possible solutions from which to choose. *It is their idea that the sacrament is valid whenever it is performed as Christ performed it, whoever the man may be who carries it out.* Now the first choice: this ceremony is an empty ceremony with no significant social meaning. Modern Protestants are not willing to advocate any more that the eucharistic rite is an empty ceremony. The only other solution left is that the eucharistic rite performed according to the above principle, is valid because of the magic of the words used. As one Catholic theologian points out:

---

[53] Max Thurian, L'Eucharistie: *Memorial du Seigneur, Sacrifice d'Action de grace et d'intercession*, Delachaux et Niestlé, (Neuchatel-Paris, 1959), p. 219. Translation in Fr. Tavard's review above cited.
[54] *ibid.*

Although Protestants do not recognize this fact, theirs is a prejudice borrowed from the degraded nominalist theologians of the Middle Ages. Some of these have already been led to believe that the sacred words "This is My Body" said by anybody, priest or layman, over any piece of bread would consecrate that bread just as surely as does the priest in carrying out the sacred liturgy. But such an idea was certainly a purely magical notion, and completely foreign to Christian tradition.[55]

When sincere searchers acknowledge that the commission given by ordination to perform the Eucharistic rite is, by Christ's own Word, transmitted in the way He prescribed then it will be seen that "the Word of God retains its divine power only when it remains God's own Word, personally spoken in Christ for mankind through the character of the sacrament of Orders."[56]

Finally, there is also a clear Catholic responsibility, as Father Tavard points out,[57] to assist the separated Christians in this awakening to the sacramental life, and specifically the social sacrificial aspect of the Last Supper. How can this be done in practice? I hope we can have some discussion of that point. One way, certainly, will be the growth of our own awareness of the social aspect of the Eucharist and the reemphasizing in our sermons and instructions the Eucharist as a cause and a sign of "social" charity.

---

[55] Louis Bouyer, *op. cit.*, p. 148.

[56] *ibid.*

[57] Fr. George Tavard, *Protestant Hopes and Catholic Responsibilities*, Notre Dame, Indiana, 1960, p. 48.

VERNACULAR IN THE MASS: A BRIDGE TO UNITY AMONG CHRISTIANS

Matthew Herron, T.O.R.

First, can the question of the vernacular be discussed in full view of the statement contained in *Veterum Sapientia?*[1] Yes, that papal Pronouncement simply demands an end to the grave deterioration of the study of Latin among the clergy. There is another conclusion easily drawn from that document, namely: the vernacular concession granted for the sake of the faithful will not excuse the clergy from a thorough knowledge for the purpose of sacred studies and Papal communications.

Since the publication of *Veterum Sapientia,* Cardinal Larraona, Secretary of the Pontifical Liturgical Commission preparing for the Council stated that a majority of the bishops at the Council will favor the use of modern languages in those parts of the Mass whose purpose is instructional such as the Mass of the Catechumens and that permission for such use may be granted. The final result, His Eminence thought, might make the Mass about half Vernacular, half Latin.[2]

Furthermore, Cardinal Koenig of Vienna after attending a meeting of the central commission in Rome stated that *Veterum Sapientia* had been wrongly interpreted. That it in no way intended to forbid discussion about the place of the vernacular in the Liturgy. He said, "this question will be thoroughly examined by the Council."[3]

Then too privileges given to the Polish bishops, South American

---

[1] The Apostolic Constitution, dated Feb. 22, 1962, was published in the AAS 54: 339-68 (May, 1962). An English translation appeared in the Davenport *Catholic Messenger*, March 1, 1962; a summary in the *Clergy Review* 47 (1962) 498-500.

[2] The press conference at which Card. Larraona expressed these views was held in Chicago, May 28, 1962. Cf. "Editor's Notes and Quotes," *Worship* 36 (1962) 486-487.

[3] Cf. *Worship*, 36 (1962) 487; Davenport *Catholic Messenger*, July 26, 1962: "Latin 'Icecap' Seen Breaking Up," (p. 3).

bishops and 1954 privileges conceded to the Germans have been renewed and extended to missions under German supervision. These concessions indicate Rome's attitude toward the Vernacular is sympathetic.[4]

It was the Church of Rome that in the third Century realistically adopted herself to changed conditions and adopted Latin because it was the language of her people. Rome set the precedent, the East followed her example to use the living language; this is the true and most ancient tradition of Rome. Failure to continue this tradition in Carolingian times was due to political and cultural, not religious motivations; the chief argument from tradition favors the Vernacular.

We all must acknowledge—must realize—that if the Reformers had not linked a movement towards the Vernacular with a denial of both the Real Presence and the Real Sacrifice, the use of the Vernacular in the Mass would have enjoyed a natural growth proportionate to the culture expansion of modern European languages. There was a lot of sentiment in favor of the Vernacular at Trent, only the danger of a concession to heresy prevented the adoption of native tongues in the Liturgy.

In the ninth century, Pope John VII publically denied that any language has a monopoly on sacredness:

"... Nor indeed is there anything against the doctrine of faith to chant Mass in the Slavonic tongue, or to read the Holy Gospel or the sacred lessons of the New and Old Testament (in the Slavonic tongue), provided they are well translated and interpreted. (Nor is there any objection) to chanting all the other Canonical Hours, because He who made the three principal tongues, namely, Hebrew, Greek and Latin, likewise created all other tongues for His praise and glory. We command, nevertheless, that in all the churches of your territory, the Gospel be read in Latin, because of the greater honor, and then afterwards, to use a Slavonic translation for the benefit of the people who do not understand the Latin, as seems to be done in certain churches."[5]

---

[4] For particulars, cf. *Worship* 36 (1962) 488-489.

[5] Cf. J. M. Hanssens, S.J., in *Enciclopedia Cattolica*, s.v. "Lingua Liturgica" (col. 1379). The editors of *Worship* [27 (1953) 391] write that, in their opinion, the article by Fr. Hanssens is "the best summary of the question in print."

The whole history of the question in China shows Rome's willingness to go along with any reasonable effort to serve the needs of people.[6]

The other great objection is the problem of correct translation. I find no great difficulty for this simple reason; the Church has authorized official translations of the Scripture which is a more important area than the Liturgy. But the Church does not want the people denied the value of the sacred and inspired word; then why deny them the tremendous spiritual riches of the Holy Liturgy?

The objection is made that we would betray Latin culture. The Church of Christ was not founded nor does it exist to spread and preserve Latin culture; rather, she exists to spread the good tidings, supernaturalize cultures and save souls. One bishop I know objects, "How is this possible? I have sixty-seven different national parish groups in my diocese." It is no problem really. The Bishop could authorize the pastor to say Mass in the language he uses in preaching on Sunday.

Most countries of the world have dialects which the ordinary people use in their common speech. Again I see no problem. The vernacular, if permitted, could be restricted to the official language of the country.

In underdeveloped countries there is a problem, but the Mass could remain in Latin until their civilization has developed to a point where they have a well-developed language of real cultural value.

At Trent, the Fathers were faced with a *hic et nunc* problem which demanded the utmost prudence. They could not approve of the use of the vernacular in the face of the following Protestant dogmatic errors which they condemned.

1. The *very nature* of the Mass demands the use of the vernacular
2. Since the words must be heard, they cannot be said in a low voice
3. The mixture of wine and water was not instituted by Christ but by a foreign elément. Therefore it must be supressed.

---

[6] J. M. Hanssens, *loc. cit.* As late as 1949 the use of Mandarin was permitted in China, even in the Mass, the canon excepted. (col. 1380-1381).

[7] Sess. XXII, cap. 8 and 9; Cf. H.A.P. Schmidt, *Liturgie et langue vulgaire. Le probléme de la lanque liturgique chez les premiers Reformateurs et au Concile de Trente*, (Rome, 1950).

The Reformers in general taught that the Mass was mainly a prayer, not a sacrifice, therefore, it had to be audible. Certainly, if the coming council approves of the use of the vernacular in the Mass, no one will associate that permission with the sixteenth century dogmatic errors concerning the nature of the Mass. That danger has passed.

The arguments based on the Music regulation concerning the use of Gregorian Chant are not as overwhelming as they seem at first sight. Every well-developed language can be adapted to Music if the composers have a mastery of both Gregorian Chant and their own language, and of course, they must be allowed a little freedom which writers of sacred music use right now anyway.[8]

I am in high hope that the work of the various liturgical conferences will bear fruit. Typical of their sentiments is the statement Cardinal Lercaro made at Lugano in 1953:

> "It would seem, therefore, that the widespread hope of our times that the Scripture lessons of the Mass be read by the priest or ministers in the mother tongue, fits harmoniously into the framework of the reforms realized or desired by the Blessed Pontiff ... This ardent hope of all who are lovingly concerned to foster active participation of the faithful in the Sacred Mysteries, today can base itself above all on "Mediator Dei" which recognizes as a matter of principle the usefulness of the mother tongue, although of course it restricts permission for it to the Holy See...."[9]

Would the Christianization of the Roman Empire ever have been accomplished if the Church had not, from the very beginning and with an astonishing firmness, adapted the Hellenistic culture and the languages that predominated throughout the Roman world and in its worship?

The condition of our world today, principally in the great Eastern cultures, resembles the conditions of the ancient world where the Church found herself already in a developed culture and therefore made adaptations. In the Middle Ages the missionary effort of the Church required the creation of a culture, and she exported the Latin

---

[8] Cf. *Worship*, 28 (1954) 165-167.
[9] *Worship*, 28 (1954) 128.

culture. We cannot do that today, but must return to more ancient methods of making converts.

The request for greater freedom in the use of the vernacular is made for the sake of worship itself. The very nature of the Mass and the request of Pius XII in Mediator Dei demands the close union of the people and the priest in the homage paid to God. This can be done to full extent only with the use of a living language which is understood. Reflection on the nature of Christian liturgy is bound to give rise to the desire that some place be found for the living speech of the people.

There is no need for such an important means of the soul's ascent to God, as the Liturgy to remain behind hidden in an unknown tongue. The sacred action performed through prayer and song are perceived as so many strange sounds to the ear. Perhaps in other ages that was necessary to safeguard doctrine, to ward off attacks, but that seems unnecessary today. We now need the same guidance, the same help. The Liturgy provided for the early Christians who took their full and proper part in the Liturgy. They knew what they were doing and why.

According to St. Pius X, the primary and indispensable source of the true Christian spirit is active participation in the solemn and public worship of the church. But as long as the public and solemn worship of the Church remains in its present form, people will not be able to drink or eat in full from the primary source of their spiritual life. The Mass, according to Pius XII, is truly a form of social worship in which all members of the Mystical Body both ministers and people should have their part. The present method of saying Mass makes this practically an impossibility. The people become spectators of one sort or another. But if the family of God in its liturgical assemblies could hear the word of God in its own mother tongue directly and immediately... the active participation of the community so much desired by the saintly Pontiff would seem to be more complete.[10]

As far as a safeguard against doctrine is concerned, Latin could remain a safeguard as long as the official dogmatic statements remain

---

[10] James Card. Lercaro, "Active Participation: The Basic Principle of the Pastoral Liturgical Reforms of Pius X," *Worship*, 28 (1945) 120-128.

in Latin, as long as the official communications are in Latin. A change in language of the liturgy would no more corrupt doctrine than a Bible in the vernacular does, no more than a catechism does, no more than an English Missal does.

The phrase in Mediator Dei "Latin is an imposing sign of unity. Latin is a safeguard against the corruption of true doctrine" is often quoted but applied beyond the meaning of the word. The Pope did not say Latin is a cause of unity. He did not say the whole of the Holy Sacrifice of the Mass in Latin is necessary to hold the Church together. Latin would remain an imposing sign of unity if only the words of the Consecration in the Mass were in Latin.

If an individual has the opportunity to follow the Mass with his intellect as well as with his ears and eyes, the Holy Sacrifice would play a greater role in his spiritual life than now possible. Frankly, I believe that many of our people are bored to death at Mass. They attend only to avoid mortal sin. They understand neither the nature of the sacred action nor the meaning of the beautiful prayers. No one says the use of the vernacular would be a cure-all, but it would certainly improve the present situation.

If the people would understand the Mass and be able to explain it to the people they bring to church, to those outside the Church, to their friends, another barrier to conversions would disappear.

If the vernacular were in use, it would help destroy the idea that the Church is merely an Italian sect that caught the popular fancy during the breakup of the Roman Empire. The use of the native tongue in an identical rite all over the world would help propagate the truth. It would help in demonstrating that the Church is truly Catholic, truly universal. It would help prove membership in the Mystical Body is for all men of every language, every color, and every race. That is more important than keeping a tradition that no longer serves the best interest of the Church and her mission. The argument from mystery is really weak. The Church herself is a mystery, but she is charged with the responsibility of making the mysteries, including the Mass, known to be faithful. As far as possible, the argument seems based on the fallacy that we can have reverence only for the unknown. A full appreciation of the importance of a reality can also be a tremendous factor in the creation of reverence and awe.

We give instructions, sermons, retreats; write books about every phase of the Mass to make our people more conscious of what it is, what place it has in our lives. Why not let the Mass speak for itself? Why not let the Divine Drama manifest its glorious reality to the full man? Let us not exclude total intellectual joy and appreciation; not only for the Catholic, but let the Mass be a channel by which we will reach the intellects of our Separated Brethren as well, a Divine Bridge for Unity.

THE KERYGMATIC APPROACH TO THE EUCHARIST

Isidore McCarron, O.S.F.

I would imagine that as Pastors of Souls and as educators a certain unrest has been detected concerning peoples' attitudes towards God and Religion in general.

Our current periodicals offer methods which are often considered by the unlettered as a panacea. The sophisticated on the other hand often portray a spirit of over-skepticism. In this paper we shall attempt to take a middle of the road approach.

Our aim will be an investigation of a presentation of the Eucharist through a Kerygmatic approach with the notion of Unity in mind.

Having stated the problem, we shall proceed to delimit our topic as well as to define specific terms and concepts as they will be used in this presentation.

Since this is an Educational Meeting, we shall attempt to structure a setting which will appeal to all: Pastors, Curates, Teachers and Catechists.

The group to whom we would like to envision this Religion Lesson being presented is a high school group of students anywhere in the U.S.A. This is a specific, as well as an ideal group, chosen though in view of the over-all "Spirit of Ecumenism." This statement shall be justified as we proceed.

They are to be pupils who have attended a Catholic Elementary School for eight years. Now, because of a shortage of seats in Catholic Secondary Schools, their normal school day is spent in a Public High School, pluralism at its height. Our Religion class finds them in either a Released Time Class, an evening class, a Saturday or Sunday morning class, or during a Vacation Summer School. This class is being taught by a lay man or woman under the competent leadership of a trained Priest, Brother or Sister.

Before proceeding, it is perhaps necessary to explain and maybe even justify the concept that this is the "ideal group" in light of the "Spirit of Ecumenism." First, why this group. We are all sadly aware of the fact that for the most part there is no longer a seat for every Catholic student in a Catholic High School. Are these students, though, no longer members of the Mystical Body of Christ? Could it not be a truism that as Charity begins at home, so also should Ecumenism begin at home. The instruction of these youngsters is so often neglected or poorly given, resulting in a waste of potential Apostolic activity. Thus, a well orgainzed Religion Program with a presentation of the Eucharist included would be an ideal step in the right direction.

Secondly, this group is also ideal from the setting in which they operate. As previously stated, they are operating in a pluralistic society at its height. One into which we, for the most part, have no enterage per se. That is except through the "image" of our students who are already operating in this pluralistic society. They are in an ideal position to take God into a Godless society, provided we have both properly trained and motivated them. They can be the strong link in this chain for unity.

Concerning the Eucharist itself, it would often seem that too frequently we present it merely as a Sacrament. We present it out of its proper context, namely the Mass. In our structuring we shall attempt to present the Eucharist as a unifying force for Eucmenism when seen in its proper perspective of the Mass.

The approach suggested is that of the Kerygma. Much of our current catechetical literature leaves the reader with a feeling that this might be the panacea for all our ills. True, a proper handling of Scripture and Liturgy should be a motivational factor in the lives of our students. The key word, though, is a "proper handling." How many teachers of Religion today in this setting are capable of a proper handling of either Scripture or Liturgy?

To the Franciscan, the Kerygma is not new. The "Mirror of Christ" taught us this lesson many centuries ago with the added concept of "student centered."

Taking Francis as our example, we realize the need to go out to people. In terms of Twentieth Century Concepts, this can be considered as a "student centered approach." Too frequently our teaching of Religion has been involved in a "method" or centered around a "Text book." If the needs of the student are taken into consideration, a more effective approach will result. Considering the groups we have proposed, one realizes that a "Spiritual Orientated Approach" is foreign to them, and consequently fails. It is of greater advantage to use a "Materialistic Approach," that which they are most familiar with.

With these concepts in mind, I would like to partially structure a lesson which could be presented to such a group in order to accomplish the end result desired. The class is that of Junior Year.

Gentlemen, you have probably noticed that the Catholic Press have been giving wide coverage to the Ecumenical Council and the Scandal of our separated Brethren. Sometimes articles such as this fail to leave their impact on us or they fail to motivate us to action. I believe that this springs from the attitude by which we just accept our Religion, we sort of take our faith for granted. This seems especially true with the notion of *Mass*. You ask the majority of people why they go to Mass on Sunday and the responses will be revealing. Answers will vary, but usually along lines such as this: "Because we have to—or the Church says we have to—it's a mortal sin if we don't." I will not argue with your answers, but I do hope that at the end of this lesson we might have some better answers.

It often appears that we fail to apply the fruits of the Mass and the Eucharist during our daily activities. Proposing the theory that this lack of appreciation flows from a lack of historical signification of the symbolisms employed, we shall proceed to investigate the background of the Mass. I am sure that if we truly appreciated the Mass, then the articles previously mentioned would have greater meaning. You would have inquired by this time as to how you could cooperate in this program.

Before we proceed to investigate the historical significance, I would like to leave a few thoughts with you. Let's turn to the cover of Hi-Time.

In many homes today an important function of the family is eating as a unit. The table becomes a uniting bond. The joys and trials of the day are brought together. It is not an act of isolation, it is a communal act in which all participate according to their individual abilities. From time to time we invite to our table friends in order to have them break bread with us. During this visit our efforts are to make this person feel at home, feel part of the Commune.

Does Mass leave this same feeling? What is the answer to all of this?

We mentioned the meaningless symbols. How often the medieval Cathedrals appear to us as rather confusing structures.

But at the time of construction they presented a clear cut pattern.

Also, the importance of the earlier few altars has diminished because of recent numbers and ornateness. Our Roman Liturgy has also undergone a complicated development. This history extends over twenty centuries.

The chief elements in the Christian worship were taken over by the Church. She built on Jewish worship as well as from the customs of the Hellenistic environment.

There were two Liturgical services at the start. On Sunday morning a "service of work" consisting of readings, sermons, and prayer. Then on Sunday evening would be held the ritual repast. This consisted of the celebration of the Eucharist. It was either preceded by or joined with a community meal. In the second century we find this Eucharistic Sacrifice transferred to the morning. It was joined to the service of prayer and instruction.

It is well known that in the ancient Christian basilicas the arrangement of the altar was such that the celebrant faced toward the people. This is still the case in some of the Churches in Rome.

The altar bore only the altar cloths, the sacred vessels, the Paten and the Mass book.

We know that the position of the Priest with his back to the people became the general rule outside of Rome about 1000, the placing of the altar against the rear wall and the addition of the retable followed soon after, but candles were not placed upon the altar until after 1100, and the crucifix probably in the Thirteenth Century when special devotion to the passion of our Lord began its increase.

We may conclude, therefore, these changes came about approximately at the time when the Holy Sacrifice itself had come to be regarded as more or less the exclusive action of the Priest. Perhaps in a sense here is the crux of all our problems.

If we are to be true Apostles then a return to the Mass and the Eucharist as a Corporate act is an essential shift. Our next move will be to develop this concept of a corporate act and then to apply it relative to your area of activity.

Sunday Mass can be likened to a banquet feast. We attend and form a bond of union. This bond should be a lasting one. It is well to keep in mind that this bond is not only a unifying force amongst the laity but also between the celebrant and the laity.

When approaching the Eucharistic Table we are not performing an isolated act. It would also seem that we would be guilty of selfishness if we merely look on this as a receptor of grace and fail to recognize the responsibility incurred. A responsibility to the fellow members of the Mystical Body of Christ.

This responsibility is best exercised in terms of your own environment. On Sunday you attended Mass and partook of the Eucharist in your parish. It should not end there. This should become the uniting bond during the week as you attend classes at school. The members of your school who belong to other parishes, even though Communicating at different Banquet Feasts, have the same uniting bond. The Mass and the Eucharist, the service to unite all Catholics in the one institution. But we should not be contented to let it all stop there. There are others in your classes who are not as fortunate as you are. They do not have the true faith. If Mass has meant anything to us then we will realize our responsibility as an Apostle. You may ask: "What can I do in a setting such as this?" While it is true you may not be in a position or it may not even be a prudent thing to become an activist, at least a negative approach is possible. By this we would suggest a teaching by example. Many are kept from the true faith because of the bad example of Catholics.

Thus, the next time you go to Mass and receive, if you attempt to comprehend I'm sure that you will see your role in terms of Unity.

In conclusion it might be well to point out that this demonstration lesson has been structured in terms of an introduction. Because of a need for creating an attitude in our students an introduction such as this becomes an aid of the Kerygmatic Approach is to be eventually used. We fully realize though that even after this attitude has been established certain difficulties still remain. Probably the greatest weakness is the lack of Scriptural and Liturgical foundations in the lives of our teachers.

With patience and ingenuity a solution will be found.

DISCUSSIONS AND COMMENTS*

FR. JUNIPER CUMMINGS: Father Eldarov in his *Outline of Eucharistic Ecclesiology in Present Day Orthodoxy* has given us evidence of truly catholic learning. His knowledge of both Latin and Oriental theology is obvious. His bibliography is up to date. His scholarship is enhanced by clarity and charity and he has used a sound principle of true Catholic ecumenism. The Church, in the past, has adopted wholesome elements from the Semitic, Greek and Roman cultures so we are not compromising the truth when we look to and learn from the dissidents.

Certainly the theological position of the local church has not been spelled out to date in Catholic teaching. Fr. George has studiously illustrated certain guide lines from the orientals while frankly pointing out their weaknesses as well as their strength.

Earlier we discussed the Protestant emphasis on the societal aspect of the Lord's Supper. When I asked Fr. George if the orthodox faithful had an active realization of this in their Liturgy, he replied that it seemed that their theologians would like to think so, but that in reality most of their faithful did not.

One last comment I would make is that I concur wholeheartedly and wholeheadedly with Fr. George when he mentioned in passing that there is no extra-sacramental grace. Some text books, nonetheless, still refer to it. But all grace comes from the sacraments *in re* or *in voto*. It seems to me that this is true not only of sanctifying grace but also of actual grace. Trent hints at this when saying it is through the Mass that our daily sins are forgiven.

* * * * *

FR. COLMAN MAJCHZAK: Fr. Sylvester's paper, *The Eucharist: Bond of Unity, in St. Paul* is remarkable especially for its well-planned development and use of contemporary scholarship, both Catholic and non-Catholic. To mention some of the outstanding Scripture scholars:

---

* We publish only those comments which have been submitted in writing by the discussion leaders or by the author of the remarks.—Ed. note

286

Ahern, Benoit, and Cerfaux among the Catholics; Clark and Robinson among the non-Catholic.

Another important aspect of Fr. Sylvester's paper was the emphasis on physical realism: our union with Christ is much more than merely moral or social. Though this notion was found in the Fathers, it is being rediscovered and revaluated in present-day Scripture studies.

Thirdly, it makes me happy to hear Fr. Sylvester make of St. Paul a patron of "liberalism" and an opponent of ultra-conservatism. This is surely obvious from even a cursory reading of the many "innovations" of St. Paul in his epistles.

For the sake of this discussion I should like to present but a few questions. The first question is directed to Fr. Sylvester: Do you thing that contemporary non-Catholic biblical scholarship, especially on the Eucharist and the Sacraments, can be effective in influencing ecumenism and a spirit of union, and why? This question arises from considering the works, e.g., of C. Neville Clark, *A Christian Approach to a Theology of the Sacraments,* and J. A. T. Robinson's *The Body.*

FR. SYLVESTER MAKAREWICZ: There is no question of this possibility, even perhaps probability. I think, however, that it is much more important to consider this: that all Christians become increasingly conscious of the value and necessity of the Sacraments; that they learn charity through the Sacraments; that they enjoy the life of the body of Christ. Surely the spirit of ecumenism is the spirit of brotherliness and charity; there is no better approach to breaking down antagonism and building up agape.

FR. COLMAN: The second point of discussion refers to St. Paul. In dealing with St. Paul, we are dealing with a rather odd situation: Paul, a Hebrew steeped in Old Testament tradition, also knew Greek thought. As a matter of fact, he expresses Semitic thought in the terminology of Western thought, dynamic thought-patterns in essentialistic terms. Many moderns are scandalized, not being able to reconcile existentialism with essentialism because they do not pass beyond particulars or beyond universals and abstractions. Thus they do injustice to both existentialist and essentialist thought. Seminary training in both philosophy and theology is often confused and confusing unless these two approaches are legitimately married off and unified. To Fr. Virgil Cordano, then, I direct this question: What do you think of the problem of relating the teaching of Sacred Scripture and Dogmatic Theology?

FR. VIRGIL: Briefly, something certainly must be done in order to clarify the common ground between the two areas. Teachers of Dogma must try to understand what teachers of Scripture are trying to do; they must take another hard look at their "proofs from Scripture" in order to ferret out illegitimate accommodations. I might also suggest that the teaching of Dogmatic Theology should become less "systematic," using the word "systematic" in the sense of "artificial." Correct use of Scripture can make Dogma vital, dynamic, interesting, personal and demanding personal involvement.

FR. COLMAN: A third point of discussion was suggested to me by Gerald Bonner's article, "The Greek East and the Latin West," (*THE EASTERN CHURCHES QUARTERLY,* 13 (1959) 144-153) in which Mr. Bonner maintains that basically what separates the Greeks and Latins is a lack of charity on both sides. This is what he writes:

> If the Latins had shown greater consideration for the Greeks and had not, after 1204, embarked upon that disastrous and most unchristian, attempt to impose Latin prelates and practices upon the Byzantines; if the Greeks, while firmly maintaining the traditional doctrine of the procession of the Holy Spirit, had shown something of the understanding of Theophylact of Bulgaria; and if both sides had determined to maintain (by the grace of God), the union, it may be that the tragic divisions which now afflict us might never have arisen.

I am now soliciting comments from the floor, and especially from Fr. Berard Marthaler, O.F.M.Conv., who's had experience in the Near East.

FR. BERARD: There is no doubt that a lack of charity was and is an element separating the Eastern and Western churches, but other considerations, must also be remembered. In his excellent work, *After 900 Years,* Yves Congar, O.P., discusses the complex issues under the headings of Political factors, Cultural factors, and Ecclesiological factors. The first and the last are generally well treated in the better church history texts, while the cultural factors have not always been given due importance. Two cultural factors, in particular, seem to have been of lasting importance: the development of separate rites which imply a basic difference in outlook rather than mere differences of liturgical usage; and the influence of scholasticism on Western theology. Father Eldarow has summarized the Orthodox attitude to scholasticism in his excellent, "Ellenismo Cristiano e scholasticismo in prospettiva unionistica," [*Miscellanea Fran.* 61 (1961) 3-14]. Finally to mention from personal observation, another divisive influence, the Millet system of the Ottoman Turks. They successfully and deliberately played one national-religious element against another. This policy left deep scars which one can sense in the Near East even today.

BISHOP GRAZIANO (Honduras, C.A.): First, I should like to congratulate Fr. Sylvester on his masterful treatment of an important and practical subject. Second, I would like to add my comments to this last point of discussion, charity and union or reunion. I have had some personal experience in this regard. An Orthodox bishop had occasion to come within the diocese for a short stay, but was unable to find adequate lodging and hence was finally directed to my house. We had a wonderful few days together, much of it in informal conversation. Before he left he expressed the sentiment that such informal, unpressurized, charitable exchanges of opinion could do much to reunite the Eastern and Western churches. And I agree that what often separates us are not intellectual or doctrinal issues, but rather purely human and perhaps prejudicial approaches to the understanding of both our position and their position. We priests, who center our lives and activities around the Eucharist, have many opportunities for bearing the charity of Christ into the lives of others by the sympathatic and understanding sharing of ourselves.

* * * * *

FR. JUNIPER CUMMINGS: In his paper on the *Social Aspect of the Eucharist,* Fr. Aidan asked for ways and means whereby we as Franciscans can bring out the social aspect of the Eucharist. Fr. Matthias Pastore, O.F.M. has given us examples of what young Catholic Action groups are doing. But what about that "old" group—us? Are we having participation in our own Franciscan schools, seminaries, and parishes? Fr. Berard, in his historical survey, quoted Jungman who says St. Francis preferred that only one Mass be offered in each convent. All the friars, even the priests, were to attend that one. It has been suggested that if the Holy See would permit concelebration in monasteries (with stipends for all), then the idea of participation might be realized.

FRANCISCAN
EDUCATIONAL CONFERENCE

FIRST SESSION
Monday, August 6, 8:00 P.M., 1962

The Forty-Third Meeting of the Franciscan Educational Conference was held at St. Pius X Seminary, Graymoor, Garrison, N.Y. About seventy friars participated in the various sessions.

After the opening prayer by the President, Fr. Ernest Latko, O.F.M., Fr. Bonaventure Koelzer, S.A., the Superior General, warmly welcomed all the participants and explained the appropriateness of the theme of this Conference, *The Holy Eucharist and Christian Unity.* The first paper, *The Ecumenical Movement in General,* was read by Fr. Roger Mazerath, S.A. Fr. Ralph Thomas, S.A., led the discussion.

SECOND SESSION
Tuesday, August 7, 9:00 A.M., 1962

Beginning with the second session, the Conference was honored by the very cordial attendance of His Excellency, Bishop Lawrence Graziano, O.F.M., auxiliary bishop of Santa Ana in El Salvador. Fr. Sabbas Kilian, O.F.M., began the morning session with the summary of his extensive and profound paper, *The Dogmatic Foundations of the Unity of the Church.* The discussant, Fr. Maurice Grajewski, O.F.M., offered a number of comments on the paper.

After a brief intermission, the President announced the appointment of the Publicity and Resolutions Committees. Fr. Edward Hanahoe, S.A., spoke on *Ecclesiology and Ecumenism,* illustrating the historical background and the nature of the movement. This was followed by a discussion on the part of Fr. Thaddeus McVicar, O.F.M. Cap.

THIRD SESSION
Tuesday, August 7, 2:00 P.M., 1962

The attendance at the third session was increased by the presence of some twenty Franciscan clerics from Wappingers Falls, N.Y. *Union in the Body of Christ* formed the topic of the paper by Fr. Sylvester Makarewicz, O.F.M. It was further commented on by Fr. Colman Majchrzak, O.F.M. Fr. Berard Marthaler, O.F.M.Conv., followed with a paper on *The Eucharist in the Tradition of the Church up to the Council of Trent.* The discussion was led by Fr. Ernest Latko, O.F.M.

The President announced that a slight change would be made in the program to enable the Conference to close on Wednesday evening. The fourth session would be held Tuesday evening at 7:15. The afternoon session closed about 4:30, after which a photographer took pictures of various small groups of friars. The Executive Board met thereafter.

FOURTH SESSION
Tuesday, August 7, 7:15 P.M., 1962

The evening session was limited to one paper, *The Franciscan Contribution to Christian Unity*, which Fr. Titus Cranny, S.A., graciously consented to read at this session instead of the session originally scheduled for Thursday morning. Fr. Donald Bilinski, O.F.M., commended Fr. Titus for the excellent presentation. The session adjourned at 8:15. Thereafter the following special groups met: The Library Section, the Prefects of Studies, and the Commission for Franciscan Doctrinal Synthesis.

FIFTH SESSION
Wednesday, August 8, 9:30 A.M., 1962

The President opened the fifth session with several announcements. The Friars at Wappingers Falls, N.Y., invited the delegates to their friary for an Italian-style dinner with all the trimmings; the President asked for a show of hands by those members who wished to accept the invitation. He also announced that a tour of West Point after the noon meal would be arranged for the benefit of those delegates who by a show of hands indicated their desire to take part in the tour. He then informed those present that the afternoon session would begin at 3 o'clock instead of at 2 o'clock as scheduled. It was further announced that the group picture of the members of the Conference would be taken near the front entrance of the Seminary building about 11:30 after the close of the business meeting. The business meeting would follow the intermission in the morning session. Since two amendments to the proposed revision of the Constitution were presented for adoption, these were now read: Art. IX. SECTIONS. Section 1. The Executive Board shall be empowered to establish various sections and to approve their by-laws." "Article XI. BY-LAWS. By-Laws may be added to this Constitution by a majority vote in any general session."

Since the speaker who was originally scheduled to prepare the paper for this session was unable to do so, Fr. Aidan Mulaney, T.O.R., generously substituted for him and read a paper of his own on *The Social Aspects of the Eucharist, an Aid to Unity.* Fr. Matthias Pastore, O.F.M., led the discussion.

Before declaring the intermission, the President read a communication from Fr. Sebastian Miklas, O.F.M.Cap., the Secretary of the Conference and Editor of the Report. Fr. Sebastian was unable to attend the present meeting. He informed the members that the Report of the Forty-First Meeting, held in 1960, would soon be distributed, and that the printing of the Report of the Forty-Second Meeting, held in 1961, had now reached the galley-proof stage. At 10:15, the chairman declared an intermission for half an hour.

At 10:45 the members assembled for the business meeting. The President announced that the Executive Board approved a policy that each author of a paper be given several offprints of his paper when the Report is printed. The President next gave a second reading of the two amendments to the proposed revision of the Constitution, namely, Art. IX on Sections, and Art. XI on By-Laws. Fr. Aidan Mulaney, T.O.R., then moved that the revised Constitution of the Franciscan Education Conference be officially adopted. The motion was seconded and carried by unanimous vote. The Resolutions of the 1962 FEC Meeting were read by Fr. Leo Ferreira, T.O.R., and they were accepted as read. The President now announced that the authorities of the Catholic University of America intend to prepare a commemorative volume of the Seventh Century of the birth of Duns Scotus and that they are asking for written contributions on philosophy and the history of philosophy; the friars are invited to cooperate in the project.

The treasurer, Fr. Irenaeus Herscher, O.F.M., read the annual financial report:

August 9, 1962

Receipts

Credit balance in First National Bank, Allegany, N.Y.,
    as of July 25, 1961 _____$3,456.50
Receipts from sale of FEC Reports (as of 8-8-61) _____   345.30
Contributions received from Very Rev. Fathers
    Provincial and Commissaries Provincial _____ 1,871.00
Interest on Deposit (Nov. $52.87; & May '62: $23.14)   76.01

        Total Receipts _____$5,748.81

Expenses

Printing of the 40th FEC Report (1959) _____$2,460.93
Printing of the Program for the 43rd FEC------   75.19
Postage and Stationery (the Secretary: $35; the
    Treasurer: $5.) _____   40.00

        Total Expenses _____$2,576.12
        Balance in Bank as of Aug. 9, 1962 _____$3,172.69

Reports from the various special sections were read to the members. Fr. Maurice Grajewski, O.F.M., reported on the meeting of the Prefects of Studies who discussed the new decree on Latin and Biblical Greek, the Fifth Year of Theology, and the quinquennial examinations after the completion of the theological course. Fr. Donald Wiest, O.F.M.Cap., presented the report on the Library Section. Fr. Ernest Latko, O.F.M., reported on the meeting of the Commission for Fransiccan Doctrinal Synthesis; he remarked that only four members remain of the original group, and he asked for more volunteers to take part in the work.

The next item of business was the election of officers in accordance with the revised Constitution which was adopted earlier in this session. The President read the pertinent numbers of the Constitution. The President and the Vice-President are to be elected for a term of three years; the Secretary and the Treasurer are to be elected for a term of six years. At least two candidates must be nominated for each office. The officers shall be elected separately by secret ballot, an absolute majority deciding the successful candidate. If after two ballots, no election has been effected, the two candidates having the greatest number of votes, shall be the exclusive candidates in the third ballot. In case two candidates shall receive an equal number of votes, the senior member in age shall have the preference. Passive voice shall be enjoyed by one who has attended at least one previous meeting of the Conference. Of the officers elected no more than two shall be elected from the same Franciscan Family.

The elections resulted as follows: *President* for the term 1962-1965: Fr. Ernest Latko, O.F.M.; *Vice-President* for the term 1962-1965: Fr. Juniper Cummings, O.F.M.Conv.; *Treasurer* for the term 1962-1968: Fr. Irenaeus Herscher, O.F.M.; *Secretary* for the term 1962-1968: Fr. Donald Wiest, O.F.M.Cap.

After the announcement that Fr. Matthew Herron, T.O.R., would represent the F.E.C. at the meeting of the Catholic Social Action in Pittsburgh on August 25th, the President adjourned the business session.

SIXTH SESSION
Wednesday, August 8, 3:30 P.M., 1962

The final session of the Conference began at 3:30 P.M. Fr. George Eldarov, O.F.M.Conv., presented a very enlightening paper on *Orthodox Churches and the Eucharist*. The discussant, Fr. Juniper Cummings O.F.M.Conv., praised the speaker's presentation for its clarity, charity and timeliness. In the second paper, Br. Isidore McCarron, O.S.F., spoke of *The Kerygmatic Approach to the Eucharist* on the part of teachers of religion. Br. Robert Smith, O.S.F., commented on the need of training religion teachers in the kerygmatic approach. Lastly, Fr. Matthew Herron, T.O.R., discussed with animation the question of *The Vernacular in the Mass as a Bridge to Unity among Christians*. The discussant, Fr. Gervaise Cain, T.O.R., and some other members disagreed in part with a few of Fr. Matthew's observations.

When the discussion ended, the President announced that the Forty-Fourth Meeting, in 1963, would probably be held at Immaculate Conception Seminary, Troy, N.Y., and that the topic of the Conference would be *The Elements of Franciscan Formation.* An additional Resolution was presented and adopted that the Conference express its prayerful thanks to His Excellency Bishop Lawrence Graziano, O.F.M., for his fraternal charity and paternal inspiration at the Forty-Third Annual Meeting.

The President asked for a motion to adjourn. The motion having been made, seconded and carried, the President closed the 1962 FEC Meeting with prayer.

RESOLUTIONS OF THE FRANCISCAN EDUCATIONAL CONFERENCE

The Committee on Resolutions of the Forty-Third Annual Meeting of the Franciscan Educational Conference respectfully submits the following resolutions:

1. *Whereas* the Franciscan Educational Conference of 1962 is meeting on the eve of the Second Vatican Council, *be it resolved,* that the members pledge their wholehearted loyalty to His Holiness, Pope John XXIII and their filial obedience to the decisions of the Council.

2. *Whereas* the Conference is unanimous in its recognition of the genuine Franciscan hospitality offered to the delegates at St. Pius X Seminary, *be it resolved,* that we cast a vote of thanks to the Very Rev. Bonaventure Koelzer, S.A., Father General of the Friars of the Atonement; to the Rev. Samuel Cummings, S.A., Guardian of the Friary; and to all the Friars of the local community.

3. *Whereas* this Conference has benefited by the more than two decades of exceptional and dedicated services of Father Sebastian F. Miklas, O.F.M.Cap. as its Secretary, *be it resolved,* that the President express the deep appreciation of the membership.

4. *Whereas* the Conference has had as its theme—"The Holy Eucharist and Christian Unity," *be it resolved,* that this Conference shall call the attention of our Provincial Superiors to the timeliness and necessity of lectures and seminars in our seminaries, clericates and colleges as an effective means of fostering the Catholic Ecumenical Spirit.

5. *Be it resolved,* that the Franciscan Educational Conference give a hearty vote of prayerful thanks to His Excellency Bishop Lawrence Graziano, O.F.M., for his fraternal charity and paternal inspiration at the Forty-Third Annual Meeting.

Report of the Library Section
1961-1962

During the Thanksgiving-Day week-end, the Franciscan Teaching Sisters meet at Lourdes High School in Chicago, on Nov. 24-25th.

Under the energetic leadership of Sister Petronia, C.S.S.F., librarian at Madonna College, Livonia, Mich., the Franciscan Sister librarians held a special sectional meeting during the afternoon on Friday, Nov. 24th. Fr. Jovian Lang, O.F.M., librarian at Quincy College, Quincy, Ill., gave an informative talk on *Administration and Budgeting in College and School Libraries.* Sister Mary Chrysantha, C.S.S.F., followed with a discussion of *Some Books for a Franciscan Spiritual Library.* Fr. Donald Bilinski, O.F.M., gave a description and a demonstration on *Low Cost Library Card Duplicators.* The meeting proved most interesting, and though the group agreed to stay way beyond the scheduled time, the time ran out before all the planned material could be covered.

In connection with the convention of the Catholic Library Association at Pittsburgh during Easter Week, 1962, the Franciscan Friar and Sister Librarians held an informal joint meeting on Thursday afternoon from 4:30 to 6:00. The meeting was well attended with some 30 librarians being present. Sister Mary Eone, O.S.F., past-president of the C.L.A., spoke on *Franciscan Libraries, Roots of Freedom.* In his paper on *Franciscan Publishers and Publishing in the U.S.* Fr. Anselm Hardy, O.F.M., assistant librarian at St. Bonaventure University, touched upon the history and activities of twelve Franciscan publishers. Three door prizes consisting of Franciscan books were raffled off before the close of the meeting.

The Friar librarians held the regular meeting of the Library Section of the F.E.C. during the 43rd annual meeting of the F.E.C. at Graymoor, Garrison, N.Y. After the brief general session Tuesday evening, August 7, 1962, six Friar librarians assembled in the Seminary Library room. Fr. Conrad Leake, S.A., the seminary librarian, reported on his study of the contribution of Franciscan writers to the ecumenical movement, the general theme of the current F.E.C. meeting. He said that his researches unearthed only a very small number of published works by Friars on the subject, though many Friars were actively engaged in the work. The meeting then turned to an informal discussion of the projected list of Franciscan Subject Headings. A tentative list had been drawn up in 1953. It was suggested that corrections be forwarded to Fr. Donald Bilinski, O.F.M., the Secretary, and he will print the present list in the Franciscan Librarian Contact. Fr. Donald Wiest, O.F.M.Cap., the chairman, reported that the project of preparing an index to the *Franciscan*

Studies after it became a periodical, begun by the Capuchin clerics of St. Joseph Province, had to be discontinued; he wondered whether the editors of *Franciscan Studies* would be interested in receiving the work done so far, in order to have the project completed by some one else. Two further projects were suggested at the meeting: a union list of Franciscan series with location of holdings; and a compilation, to be printed in one volume, of the papers given in the various meetings of the Franciscan librarians. To obtain better attendance of Franciscan librarians at the meeting of the Library Section, it was urged that the Very Reverend Fathers Provincial be asked kindly to permit more librarians to come to the meetings of the F.E.C.

FR. DONALD WIEST, O.F.M.Cap
Chairman

SUMMARY OF THE ELEVENTH NATIONAL MEETING OF FRANCISCAN TEACHING SISTERHOODS AT MARIAN COLLEGE, INDIANAPOLIS NOVEMBER 23-24, 1962

The eleventh national meeting of the Franciscan Teaching Sisterhoods which convened at Marian College, Indianapolis, November 23-24, 1962, was attended by 330 Sisters representing 27 general or provincial motherhouses located in 11 states-California, Colorado, Illinois, Indiana, Iowa, Michigan New York, New Jersey, Ohio, Pennsylvania, and Wisconsin.

Officiating at the altar, filling the roles of speakers and discussants, and directing publicity were 15 Franciscan Friars.

The theme of the meeting, "The Holy Eucharist and Christian Unity" was developed in the general and sectional meetings and given concrete expression in the daily Solemn High Mass and the final Benediction of the Most Blessed Sacrament, with congregational singing at each service.

Celebrants at the respective High Masses were: Father Ernest Latko O.F.M., president of the Franciscan Educational Conference, and Father Juniper Cummings, O.F.M.Conv., vice-president. In a homily at the second day's Mass Father Juniper emphasized the sacramental character of the Offertory and the need for each participant's oblation of himself to God. "Only *you*", he told the delegates, "can make the symbolic act a reality."

With the greeting of St. Francis, *Pax et bonum*, Father Ernest opened the first general session, at which he presided as chairman. Mother Marie, O.S.F., mother general of the Sisters of St. Francis, Oldenburg, in a brief address of welcome, voiced the hope that the meeting bear fruit in daily increasing love for Christ in the Eucharist, on the part of those in attendance and their charges in the apostolate of teaching.

At this session Father Roger Matzerath, S.A., professor of theology at the Atonement Seminary, Washington, D.C., presented a paper on *The Ecumenical Movement in General,* in which he traced the history of the movement, discussed the theology of the World Council of

Churches, and indicated what should be the Catholic response to this movement. The present Ecumenical Movement, which has as its aim the unity of all Christians in one Church, is the result of three general organizations, the International Conference of Missionary Societies, the Faith and Order Conference, and Life and Work Movement. The latter two merged in 1948 to form the World Council of Churches; in 1961 the Council came to its full state of ecumenical mobilization when the International Missionary Council became a part of the World Council.

The theology of this Council includes the beliefs that the Church of Christ is one and that Christians have unity by their adherence to Christ. However, in the theological interpretation of the Gospel teaching, some disunity still remains. The Catholic response to the Ecumenical Movement, Father pointed out, should involve a deepening of devotion to the personality of Christ; an attempt at clearer understanding of Christ, the Church, and Christianity; prayer for unity; and the elimination of prejudice and ignorance.

Discussion leaders for this paper were: Sister Mary Philip, O.S.F., and Sister Catherine Frederic, O.S.F., both of Peekskill, New York. In the discussion the point was made that the major historic breaks with the Church involved deep lying sociological, national, and cultural causes as well as theological differences. It was further noted that such undertakings as dialogues between Catholic and Protestant theologians and biblical studies by Protestant and Catholic scholars alike augur well for the future. The exercise of charity to non-Catholics was cited as of paramount importance in helping them recognize the Roman Catholic Church as the Church of Christ.

The following session dealt with *The Kerygmatic Approach to the Eucharist.* In a paper on this subject Brother Isidore McCarron, O.S.F., professor of theology at Saint Francis College, Brooklyn, pointed out the obstacle which inadequate training in scripture and liturgy presents to the effective use of the Kerygmatic approach by lay catechists. Brother noted the further need for creating a receptive attitude in the minds of students whose materialistic environment ill prepares them for a spiritually orientated approach to religious instruction. In a demonstration lesson structured for a class of high school boys attending public school and receiving religious education in evening, Saturday or release-time classes, Brother illustrated a materialistic approach intended as an introduction to the study of the Eucharist. The lesson employed concepts familiar to the students—the family meal with its accompanying spirit of fellowship and cooperation—to convey meanings, which have been obscured by changes in the ritual and ceremony of the Mass over the centuries.

The discussion which followed this paper was carried on in separate sections for college, secondary, and elementary levels of instruction.

In the college section, with Sister Margaret Ann, O.S.F.., and Sister Mary Karen, O.S.F., both of Oldenburg, as discussion leaders, the first concern was with the meanings of *kerygma* (the publicly announced message of salvation) and *kerygmatic approach* and the relation of this approach to salvation history, to scripture, to liturgy. The group discussed the advantages of this manner of presenting religious truths, as approximating most closely the manner employed by God in His dealing with His people, when He revealed Himself first through action, and then through the interpretation of this action; as illustrating the unity of the Christian message by centering it on the person of Christ; as emphasizing the need for personal commitment in the Christian's response to the action of God on man.

A way of applying this approach to teaching the Holy Eucharist was suggested: beginning with the scriptural account of the institution of the Eucharist; clarifying the significance of the context of the institution by examining Old Testament types of the Eucharist—as meal, as sacrifice, as covenant; and considering the presentation of the Eucharist in the liturgy, where the action of God is rendered present through symbols instituted by God, and whereby the encounter between God and man in Jesus Christ at the present time may be effectd.

Discussion in the high school section, led by Sister M. Augustine, O.S.F., and Sister Marina, O.S.F. both of Oldenburg, focused on clarifying the concept of the kerygma and on the advantages and difficulties in the use of the kerygmatic approach. The group was in general agreement that this approach was good, that it seemed to follow rather naturally from our commitments as religious. Sectional problems, however, such as large numbers of public school students being taught by CCD leaders without adequate training in scripture and liturgy, or living in areas where the liturgy is not stressed, it was pointed out, would make this approach difficult and at times even a source of confusion.

It also became clear that the kerygmatic approach is intimately concerned with the material taught; it is not a method, but the order of topics differs from that in the "traditional cathechism." For the usual sequence of creed, commandments, sacraments, there is substituted an integrated presentation of God's action in salvation history (biblical), the truth of faith (dogmatic), and the Christian's response (moral).

The elementary education section, under the leadership of Sister M. Jerome, O.S.F., and Sister Rose Carmel, O.S.F., both of Oldenburg, in addition to explaining the kerygmatic approach and its objective, "to restore Christ as the center of religious instruction", made practical applications to teaching the Mass and the Holy Eucharist.

Aims cited in preparing children for First Holy Communion included: inculcating great reverence and sound piety, and fostering ardent desire and joy in prayer and well doing, rather than instilling much knowledge. The importance of Bible stories and examples from the lives of the saints was indicated.

Key ideas proposed in teaching the Mass were: its presentation as the meal of sacrifice, the gift of our Heavenly Father in response to our Eucharistic offering, and the need for uniting ourselves wholly to the intentions of the Father and the Son. Reverence in posture and gestures, as an external expression of internal devotion, and attentive listening to the reading of the epistle and gospel were considered basic elements to incorporate, in training for well-developed participation.

To assist pupils to grow in the divine life, the section concluded, is the teacher's essential task and his high privilege.

Union in the Body of Christ was the subject presented by Father Sylvester Makarewicz, O.F.M., professor of scripture and Greek at Christ the King Seminary, West Chicago.

Through his paper and in the course of the discussion period, Father Sylvester gave an illuminating exposition of one of the most significant as well as sublime doctrines of our Faith, as found in St. Paul's epistles: the doctrine of our union with God and with one another in Christ by the Holy Spirit.

Father explained that the term "Body of Christ," as applied to the Church by St. Paul, admirably expresses the mystical union between the faithful and Christ, effected by Baptism and nourished by the Holy Eucharist. He emphasized the fact that Paul never uses the term "body" in a purely metaphorical sense, e.g., a body of Christians; but always as referring to the organism—in Christ's own glorified body risen from the dead are all of us who have risen to newness of life in Him. In this connection, in answering a question raised during the discussion, Father made clear and emphatic the fact that the union of the members of the Church with Christ is a *physical* union, a real and effective union with the Risen Christ, as body-person to body-person (*soma* to *soma*) through faith and the sacraments of Baptism and the Eucharist. We are *not in Christ* as in some kind of substance, as in a fluid, for example, but mysteriously in His body as members are contained in our organic body. Moreover, the unity of Christian fellowship is directly grounded on the sacramental bread, itself already declared to be the Body of Christ. "Because the bread is one, we though many, are one body, all of us who partake of the one bread" (1 Cor. 10:17).

The term "mystical" does not occur in the writings of St. Paul, but was used by Pope Pius XII in the Encyclical, *Mystici Corporis*, to show that the Church, described as "the Body of Christ," is something more than merely a moral body, that it is something supernatural, the spiritualized, glorified Body of the Risen Christ in whom all the members of the Church are as in their head. An expression that should *not* be used at all, according to Father, is "the Mystical Christ," He is also strongly against the expression "the social Body of Christ," in referring to the Church, because it is misleading, suggesting merely a moral body.

Asked to explain the roles of Christ as Head of Christ's Body and of the Holy Spirit called the "Soul" of Christ's Body, Father explained that we receive the Holy Spirit when we become members, when we are incorporated into Christ's Body. For the Holy Spirit is the Spirit of Jesus, the Advocate, the other Paraclete He promised to His Church, and who was poured out at the beginning of the Messianic era, Pentecost. It is because of this Spirit that we can call God "*Abba*" (Father). By Him we are "in Christ" and therefore God's children and heirs with Christ.

Father also showed how we must try to understand the biblical writer's meaning when we read the Sacred Scriptures, otherwise we will miss what he is telling us. The authors of the Bible, and our

Lord too, were Semites, and they addressed themselves to unsophisticated people in concrete and picturesque language. We must understand their psychology and modes of speaking, and then translate them in terms of our own culture for our students.

Discussion leader for this session was Sister Rose Agnes, O.S.F., Joliet, Illinois, who also compiled and distributed a bibliography of readings on St. Paul, the Mystical Body, the Liturgy and Life of the Church, and the Bible.

In a special session for librarians Father Titus Cranny, S.A., assistant director of the Chair of Unity Apostolate of Graymoor, presented an account of Franciscan contributions to Christian unity.

History points to the fact that for centuries St. Francis was the leader and model of the entire enterprise for unity, and that nearly all his great sons and daughters have espoused this apostolate in some way. St. Anthony of Padua, St. Bonaventure, St. James of the Marches, St. Bernardine of Siena, and St. Lawrence of Brindisi were outstanding promotors of unity.

Today when there is an unparalleled longing for Christian unity among our separated brethren, Catholic Ecumenism can do much to promote Christian unity by manifesting its sincere fraternal affection for them.

Father also stressed that the spiritual regeneration of millions of souls is at stake in our Franciscan apostolate for unity. To achieve this we must turn for direction, inspiration, and motivation to Our Lady of Unity and to our Seraphic Father who will lead us to Jesus through Mary.

Chairman of the library session was Sister M. Petronia, C.S.S.F.; and discussion leader, Sister M. Bernetta, C.S.S.F., both of Livonia, Michigan.

An exhibit of doctoral dissertations by Franciscans was arranged and a bibliography of master's theses by Franciscans compiled by the library staff of St. Bonaventure University, New York, under the direction of Father Irenaeus Herscher, O.F.M., made available.

A list of books on Ecumenism written by Franciscans since 1929 and compiled by Father Conrad Leake, S.A., of Cardinal Spellman Library, Graymoor, was distributed as a reprint from "The Franciscan Librarian Contact." The scarcity of such writings was commented on by the compiler. A comprehensive bibliography of works on Franciscan spirituality was also displayed by the Library Section.

The topic, *Dogmatic Foundations of the Unity of the Church,* was presented by Father Sabbas J. Kilian, O.F.M., professor of theology at Fordham University.

Using excerpts from a comprehensive study, Father showed that the Catholic Church is not a mere juridical organization but an organism—the living *Body of Christ.* It is in this capacity that she has always been understood and appreciated in Catholic theology. It is in this capacity that she can fulfill her two-fold mission, namely to prolong Christ's life and presence in the community of His disciples and to communicate divine sonship to her individual members. This objective sacred element of the Church has been proved through revelation in general and through the words of Our Lord in particular. The same sources prove that the supernatural, mystical element is realized in her as a visible organized establishment.

The activities of the members are produced in many ways but the Church herself remains the same due to her vivifying principle, the Holy Spirit.

In his paper Father demonstrated that the truth of the unity of the Church is implanted within the whole system of truths and that the doctrinal principles of her being were transmitted to us by Christ and are continuously protected and guaranteed by the Holy Spirit. And so, to understand her nature as well as her unity we must contemplate her with Christ's eyes in virtue of His timeless words: "I am with you all days, even unto the consummation of the world."

The basic dogmatic relationships of the Church to each of the three Divine Persons were set forth in detail, with full support from scripture and the teaching of the Fathers of the Church. The ontological possibility of the Church is rooted in the Eternal Idea of the Father, and in both thought-content and becoming the Church is consecrated to the mission of the Son. Involved in this relationship are three articles of Faith: "God is one; mankind is one; Christ is the one final cause of mankind."

The Church depends on Christ not only in her existence, but also in her nature. Since He is her head and principle, His mediation must be carried on by her alone and exclusively. The first two relationships reach their fulfillment in that to the Holy Spirit, the efficacious principle of permanence in the Church. Everything that the Church

has in virtue of her nature is realized here and now by the Holy
Spirit through His gifts and actual graces.

The discussion which followed investigated the relevance of the
dogmatic foundation of unity to the present time with special reference
to the Ecumenical movement and the interest of Protestants in the
search for unity. Representative questions concerned: (1) the existence of a nostalgic longing for the visible Church, in the heart of
Protestantism; (2) the effect of the Holy See's effort to make union
less difficult by emphasiszing points of similarity between the Church
and non-Catholic sects; (3) the hope of appealing to the Oriental
Churches through the Council's presentation of the Church as the
Mystical Body of Christ.

Chairman of this session was Sister Florence Marie, O.S.F.; and
discussion leader, Sister Marie Anne, O.S.F. both of Allegany, New
York.

Addressing the final group-session, Father Berard Marthaler,
O.F.M.Conv., assistant professor of theology at Bellarmine College,
gave *A Survey of the Eucharist as the Bond of Unity Before the
Council of Trent.* This brief history traced the development of
Eucharistic thought and practice during the thousand years between
the Apostolic Fathers and the Council of Trent. Four conclusions
emerged: (1) The corporate significance of the Eucharist received
greater stress, both in the East and in the West, than during medieval times. (2) The Medievalists focused their attention on the union
of the faithful soul with Christ, and as a result there developed a
personal, possessive, private devotion to the Eucharist which has
continued to our own times. (3) The greater the emphasis on the
corporate significance of the Eucharist, the greater the emphasis on
Church unity. (4) The emphasis on the Eucharist as a bond of
unity at the present time is responsible for the attempt on the part
of both Romans and non-Romans to heal schism and separation.

In the discussion following the paper, special interest was shown
in the practice of the *fermentum* as a mark of unity in the early
Church. This practice arose when the establishment of outlying
churches and the need of ministering the distant communities of
the faithful put an end to the concelebration of the Mass by the
priests with their bishop. It consisted in the bishop's sending to
the priests of the area a particle of the *sacramentum unitatis,* which

he had consecrated. Acceptance of the *fermentum* was an open acknowledgment of membership in the same *communio*.

The concluding thought that developed was that today's Catholics could well emulate the early Christians by emphasizing the corporate significance of the Eucharist. This emphasis would elaborate its social aspect to include a wider fellowship with non-Catholics and lead eventually to the fulfillment of Christ's will in full Christian unity.

Chairman of this session was Sister M. Annunciette, O.S.F., Dubuque, Iowa; discussion leaders were Sister Mary Cortona, O.S.F., and Sister Mary Rupert, O.S.F., both of Clinton, Iowa.

At a meeting of the excutive board of the Franciscan Educational Conference, held during the Sisters' conference, it was announced that Father Berard, the last named speaker, is the new editor of the annual *Report* published by the FEC, and that Father Donald Wiest, O.F.M.Cap., of Marathon, Wisconsin, is the new secretary. In his office Father Berard succeeds Father Sebastian Miklas, O.F.M.Cap., who has completed 20 years of distinguished service.

It was further announced at the executive board meeting that the next annual meeting of the FEC will be at Immaculate Conception Seminary, Troy, New York, in August, and that its theme will be: "Elements of Franciscan Friar Formation."

During the conference the Mothers General and Mothers Provincial also met for the purpose of establishing a standing committee of Sisters to plan and arrange future annual meetings. A committee of seven Sisters was chosen under the temporary chairmanship of Sister Mary Carol, O.S.F., Oldenburg, who was general chairman of the present meeting.

At the final general session a summary of the papers and the related discussions was presented by Sister Margaret Ann, O.S.F., Oldenburg. Representing the Resolutions Committee, Sister Mary Aniceta, S.S.J., South Bend, Indiana, proposed a set of resolutions, which were unanimously adopted. Most significant of these was the following: "That each Sister attending the Franciscan Educational Conference, as a faithful daughter of Mother Church, renew her pledge of loyalty to His Holiness, Pope John XXIII, by continuing to pray earnestly for the success of the Ecumenical Council."

INDEX

Adam of Faversham, 6
Adam, Karl, 120, 156, 159 ff., 177, 180, 205
Afanasseu, N., 210 ff.
Albania, 41
Alber, Erasmus, 22
Ambrose, St., 189
Anglicans, 96, 114, 204, 206 ff.
Aniceta, Sister M., 307
Annunciette, Sister M., 307
Anthony of Padua, St., 1
Armenians, 11, 13 ff.
Athenagoras, Patriarch of Constantinople, 219
Augustine, St., 112, 120, 186, 196, 201, 246-247, 301

Badius, Conrad, 22
Baglione, Luca, 25-26
Balkans, 39 ff.
Bartoloneo de Pisa, 22
Basil, St., 195
Baum, Gregory, 59
Bea, Augustine Cardinal, 117
Beaudin, Don Lambert, 257
Benedictines, 257 ff.
Berengarius of Tours, 218, 249 ff.
Bernadine of Siena, 2, 13, 25
Bernetta, Sister M., 304
Bonaventure, St., 1, 7 ff., 251
Brent, Charles H., 63
Bulgakov, S., 209, 213

Calvanism, 31, 271
Canon Law, 119, 142, 144
Catherine Frederic, Sister, 300
Christocentrism, 126
Clare, St., 2
Clement VII, 27
Clement of Alexandria, 183, 185, 193, 194, 243-244

Clement of Rome, 185, 188, 192
Collette of Corbie, St., 2, 20-21
Constantinople, 6, 33 ff., 39 ff., 48, 50, 219
Copts, 11, 18
Cordano, Virgil, 288
Cortona, Sister M., 307
Councils
  Florence, 7, 13 ff., 253
  Lateran IV, 3-4, 253
  Lyons I, 6, 17
  Lyons II, 7
  Trent, 24, 253, 276
  Vatican I, 6, 10, 87, 205
Couturier, Abbé Paul, 94
Cranny, Titus, 1 ff., 304
Credibility, 205 ff.
Cyprian, St., 192-193, 198-199, 201, 243
Cyril of Alexandria, 195, 245
Cyril of Jerusalem, 190
Cummings, Juniper, 286, 289, 299

De Lubac, H., 217, 247 ff.
D' Espine, H., 59, 71, 78, 79
Didache, 233, 242
Dieckmann, H., 130, 134, 158, 161
Dionysius, St., 241
Dogmatic Foundations of the Unity of the Church, 117, 208

Ecclesia discens, ecc. docens, 143, 174 ff., 179, 188, 191, 194
Ecclesiology and Ecumenism, 82 ff.
Ecumenical Movement: General Conspectus, 55 ff.
Eldarov, George, 209 ff.
England (Reformation in) 27 ff.
Epiphanius, St., 183-184, 195
Eramus, 25
Eucharist: Bond of Unity Before

308